ROME
ACCESS®

KT-222-269

Orientation

Tradition holds that Romulus founded Rome on 21 April 753 BC. Every year modern Romans honor that date, usually with earnest speeches about how to deal with the city's pollution, traffic, and inadequate transportation system. But when the celebration turns serious, it is performed in a truly Roman fashion, worthy of the city that was once the center of the known world. Toward dusk a special brigade of firefighters with torches spreads out along the rooftops of **Capitoline Hill** and lights hundreds of Roman dish candles. Gradually the outlines of the buildings on the Capitoline and **Michelangelo**'s grand staircase leading up to the **Campidoglio** shimmer in flickering flames. And near midnight throngs swarm the bridges over the **Tiber** and watch fireworks burst in the sky.

Around the time of Romulus, the area just north of Capitoline Hill was the site of the advanced Etruscan city-states that dominated central Italy. Inland to the east were tough Sabine and Latin shepherding tribes; to the south were sophisticated Greek colonial towns like Naples and Paestum. It was the fusion of their energies—before they all variously went to war with and against each other—that caused Rome to develop from a tiny trading post on the Tiber to a populous city. Eventually it became an empire that extended from Armenia in the east to Spain in the west, from Egypt in the south to Scotland in the north. With the growth of commerce, progressively bigger and grander markets and meeting places were needed: The **Foro Romano** (Roman Forum) had its beginnings in the seventh century BC and led (geographically and historically) to the last and largest—the **Foro di Traiano** (Trajan's Forum) with its more than 150 shops, fountains, and covered walkways.

The next few centuries were tempestuous times, marked by the remarkable expansion of the Roman Empire and the increasing power and wealth of its emperors who built their sumptuous homes atop **Palatine Hill** (the word "palace" derives from the name of this hill). During this era, the **Pantheon** was erected; it is the most perfectly preserved of Rome's ancient structures, and the sight of its floodlit columns at night is unforgettable. These early centuries were also a time of religious conflict between those who remained faithful to the traditional gods and the followers of the new Christian religion. In spite of their persecution, these converts not only triumphed but made Rome their capital. The history of Christianity can be traced here from the humble catacombs of the **Appian Way** to the power and glory of **Vatican City**.

Almost five centuries after the birth of Christ, the Roman Empire, a victim of its own success (and excess), collapsed into unattended rubble, danger, and disease. The once grand forums reverted to pasture land, the **Colosseo** (Colosseum) became a wool factory, and the triumphal arches and columns of the emperors were ground into marble dust. The city's population dropped drastically. Rome slumbered until about the 14th century when the papacy returned here from its exile in Avignon. Then, as the city awoke, defensive walls were reinforced and aqueducts restored. The more than 200 towers that were constructed during this period testified to the presence of soldiers ready and able to defend Rome (when not feuding with each other) from outsiders.

Rome's full flowering occurred in the Renaissance of the 15th and 16th centuries. Ancient racetracks were transformed into piazzas—**Piazza San Pietro** (St. Peter's Square) and **Piazza Navona**, for example—as **Michelangelo** and later **Bernini**, under the patronage of the popes, redesigned the city's public spaces and ancient buildings to create new masterpieces. Such painters and sculptors as Raphael and Caravaggio became the interior decorators for cardinals and princes. Today, much of Western civilization's rich heritage of art and architecture can be found in Rome's museums, churches, and excavations.

A walk through Rome's **Centro Storico** is a splendid journey through the ages. When strolling through the center you'll pass effortlessly from classical ruins to early Christian churches; past medieval brickwork and Renaissance villas into splendid Baroque piazzas and Art Nouveau quarters. One of the greatest charms of Rome is to stumble upon a piece of Roman wall incorporated into a Renaissance palace or a Baroque fountain in the courtyard of a very modern hotel. Such juxtapositions have made travelers through the ages feel as if they have stepped into a time warp.

On most days in Rome, you can shop for artichokes in the outdoor market at **Campo dei Fiori** or buy designer clothes in chic emporiums on **Via dei Condotti**; people watch for the price of an espresso at the outdoor cafes in **Piazza del Popolo** or go for broke at an elegant rooftop restaurant overlooking the Roman Forum; walk hand-in-hand around the Colosseum in the moonlight, or dance the night away in a New Wave disco on **Via Veneto**. All of this is possible because Rome has ensured her survival by transforming herself with each new epoch—without ever giving up her past. This, more than anything, has earned her the title "The Eternal City."

How To Read This Guide

ACCESS®ROME is arranged by neighborhood so you can see at a glance where you are and what is around you. The numbers next to the entries in the following chapters correspond to the numbers on the maps. The text is color-coded according to the kind of place described:

Restaurants/Clubs: Red   **Hotels:** Blue
Shops/ Outdoors: Green   **Sights/Culture:** Black
♿ **Wheelchair accessible**

Rating the Restaurants and Hotels

The restaurant star rating takes into account the quality of the food, service, atmosphere, and uniqueness of the restaurant. An expensive restaurant doesn't necessarily ensure an enjoyable evening, while a small, relatively unknown spot could have good food, professional service, and a characteristic atmosphere. Therefore, on a purely subjective basis, stars are used to judge the overall dining value (see star ratings at right). Keep in mind that chefs and owners change often, which can drastically affect the quality of a restaurant, for better or worse. The ratings in this guidebook are based on information available at press time.

The price ratings, as categorized at right, apply to restaurants and hotels. These figures describe general price-range relationships among other restaurants and hotels in the area. The restaurant price ratings are based on the average cost of a three-course meal for one person, excluding tax and tip. Hotel price ratings reflect the base price of a standard room for two people for one night during the peak season.

Restaurants

★	Good
★★	Very Good
★★★	Excellent
★★★★	An Extraordinary Experience
$	The Price Is Right (less than $40)
$$	Reasonable ($40-$65)
$$$	Expensive ($65-$90)
$$$$	Big Bucks ($90 and up)

Hotels

$	The Price Is Right (less than $100)
$$	Reasonable ($100-$210)
$$$	Expensive ($210-$320)
$$$$	Big Bucks ($320 and up)

At press time, the exchange rate was about 1,600 lire to $1 US.

Map Key

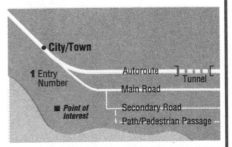

City/Town
1 Entry Number
■ *Point of Interest*
Autoroute
Tunnel
Main Road
Secondary Road
Path/Pedestrian Passage

To call Rome from the US, dial 011-39-06, followed by the local number. When calling from inside Italy (including within the city of Rome), dial 06 and the local number.

Getting to Rome

Airports

Aeroporto Leonardo da Vinci (FCO)

Serving domestic and international carriers, **Aeroporto Leonardo da Vinci** (65951)—Europe's sixth largest—is in the southwest suburb of **Fiumicino.** The 29-kilometer (18-mile) trip to downtown takes a minimum of 45 minutes by car, an hour by bus, and a half-hour by express train.

Airport Services

Airport Emergencies	65953133
Business Service Center	65952607
Currency Exchange	65953438
Customs	65954882, 65954343
Flight Information	65954455
Foreigners Reception Service	65953772
Immigration	65953593
Lost Baggage	65954252
Lost and Found	65953343
Police	65953595

Airlines

Air France	4718
Alitalia	65631, 65641 (domestic), 65642 (international)
American	42741240
British Airways	65011513, 1478/812266
Canadian	65011462
Delta	1678/64114 toll free in Italy
Iberia	65010688, 1478/31055
Lufthansa	46601
Olympic Airways	47867334
Sabena	4873377, 65011481
Swissair	8470534, 8470555
TWA	65954941, 47211
United	48904140
USAirways	4746954, 4888161

Getting to and from Aeroporto Leonardo da Vinci

By Bus Bus service is offered *only* at night when the train (see below) doesn't run. Buses leave the airport at 1:15AM, 2:15AM, 3:30AM, and 5AM for **Stazione Tiburtina.** They depart **Tiburtina** for the airport at 12:30AM, 1:15AM, 2:30AM, and 3:45AM. The trip takes about 45 minutes. Tickets are purchased on the bus. The bus—marked "Roma"—leaves from a parking lot in front of the Arrivals building.

By Car From the airport follow the signs to the Autostrada **(A12).** Take it heading east to the *Roma Centro* exit. To get to the airport from downtown Rome, take A12 west, following the *Aeroporto* signs. Get off at Exit 30.

Rental Cars The following rental car companies have counters (open until midnight) at **Aeroporto Leonardo da Vinci:**

Avis	65011579, 1678/63063 toll free in Rome
Europcar	65010879
Hertz	1678/68016 toll free in Rome
Thrifty	65010347, 4820966

By Taxi There's a cab stand outside the Arrivals terminal at the airport. The fare from the airport to downtown is about $45; the price rises with each piece of luggage, and there are above-the-meter charges for late-night, holiday, and Sunday service. Use only licensed yellow or white (the official EC color) cabs. Another alternative is to use one of the licensed chauffeur-driven cars advertised in the Arrivals area. They have a fixed price of about $50, regardless of the destination.

By Train Both express and local train service runs between the airport and the center of Rome. Follow the bilingual (Italian/English) signs in the Arrivals area marked "Stazione" and "Railroad Station." There are two ways to reach it: elevator and overpass or escalator and underpass. An express train leaves the airport railroad station every hour from 7:30AM to 10PM. It goes nonstop to **Stazione Termini.** The trip takes 30 minutes. Trains depart **Track 22** at **Termini** hourly from 6:50AM to 9:20PM.

The local train leaves the airport railroad station every 20 minutes from 6:25AM to 11:25PM and makes several stops, including **Ostiense** (where there's a connection to the subway), and **Stazione Trastevere** and **Stazione Tiburtina** (buses and cabs abound at both these stations). This train *does not* go to **Termini.** Local service departs **Tiburtina** every 20 minutes from 5AM until 10:30PM. It's about a 30-minute ride. Tickets for both express and local trains going to Rome are for sale at the ticket office or from vending machines at the entrance to the tracks. At **Termini,** tickets can be purchased from the ticket office at **Track 22** or at any newspaper stand in the station.

Aeroporto Ciampino (CIA)

Ciampino (794941) is used primarily for commercial charter flights—there are only minimal services for travelers. The airport is 16 kilometers (10 miles) southeast of downtown Rome.

Getting to and from Aeroporto Ciampino

By Bus A **COTRAL** bus links the airport with **Stazione Anagnina,** the terminus of *Line A* on the **Metropolitana** (subway), a trip of about 15 minutes.

The subway ride will get you to the center of Rome also in about 15 minutes. The bus departs every 30 minutes between 7AM and 11PM.

By Car The **Via Appia Nuova** is a straight shot from the airport directly into the center of town; if you are going to the north or west sections of the city, take Exit 23 to connect with the **GRA**, the ring road encircling the city. To get to **Ciampino** from Rome, reverse the above directions and take Via Appia Nuova south; the airport exits are clearly marked.

Rental Cars

The following rental car companies have counters (open until 8PM) at **Ciampino:**

Avis ....79340195, 1678/63063 toll free in Rome

Europcar 79340387

Hertz 79340616, 79340095

Thrifty 79340137

By Taxi Cabs for hire line up outside the Arrivals terminal. A trip to downtown takes about 20 minutes, and the basic fare is about $30; expect surcharges for luggage and for night, Sunday, and holiday service.

Bus Station (Long-Distance)

COTRAL bus company (167431784) serves the **Lazio** region. Buses depart from various points throughout the city.

Train Station (Long-Distance)

Italy has recently switched to a single railway information number (1478/88088) accessible throughout Italy as a local call. Another useful option is the Italian railway's Internet site (www.fs-on-line.com), which allows users to print out a detailed train schedule simply by typing in their departure and arrival points.

Rome has two main rail stations: the centrally located **Stazione Termini** (Piazza dei Cinquecento, between Via Marsala and Via Giovanni Giolitti), the arrival point for most international and national trains; and the smaller **Stazione Tiburtina** (Piazzale della Stazione Tiburtina and Circonvallazione Nomentana), on the eastern edge of the city. **Tiburtina** has good bus connections, but taxis are sometimes in short supply; avoid arriving at this station at night if possible.

Both the **Stazione Termini** and the **Stazione Tiburtina** connect to the subway and are hubs for numerous commuter and long-distance trains. Porters are scarce, but there are luggage carts at both stations. **Termini** offers more visitor-related services, such as money exchange, *Il Drugstore*, a 24-hour convenience store in the basement, and a clean, spacious self-service restaurant. At press time, the tourist information desk (48906300) was temporarily located near the Piazza dei Cinquecento entrance, while the **Termini** station was undergoing renovations.

Getting Around Rome

Bicycles and Mopeds Rome's hills, unforgiving traffic, and cobblestone streets make cycling a less-than-desirable way to get around the city—except perhaps in the parks and on Sunday. *Motorini* (mopeds) are the fastest way to get around if you know how to handle one and aren't intimidated by kamikaze drivers.

It's easy to find a bicycle to rent by the hour or day—just look on the street for a gathering of yellow two-wheelers. The bike-rental entrepreneurs often move their "offices" but can usually be found near such tourist spots as **Piazza del Popolo, Trastevere,** and **Villa Borghese.** A nine-mile bike path traces the Tiber on the **Vatican** side, beginning north of **Ponte Cavour.**

Motorini can be rented (by the hour, day, or week) from **Scooters for Rent** (Via della Purificazione 84, at Piazza Barberini, 4885485) and **Happy Rent** (Via Farini 3, between Via Gioberti and Via Cavour, 4818185), where English is spoken. **Happy Rent** also has a Help Line from 9AM to 7PM, in case of mechanical problems. **Motorent** (3225240) in **Section 3** of the parking lot under the **Villa Borghese** is open seven days a week and accepts credit cards. All operators require an ID (e.g., passport).

Buses and Trams Rome's buses are comparatively inexpensive but are also unpredictable and extremely crowded. Buy a bus map at the green **ATAC** information booth (167431784) at the bus depot

outside **Stazione Termini** or from a newspaper kiosk. There are no transfers, but tickets are good for unlimited use on any bus, tram, or subway line for a 75-minute period. There are also daily, weekly, and monthly passes that permit unlimited travel on these lines. Besides saving money, passes allow you to get on at the front of the bus, which is convenient during rush hours; otherwise, buses are boarded from the rear and exited from the middle doors. Tickets and passes must be purchased before boarding, and are available at green bus stop ticket booths, bars, tobacconists, and newsstands that display the **ATAC** sign outside, or from vending machines at some stops.

Tickets are validated by a machine at the rear of the bus that stamps them with the time, date, and bus number. Failure to display a correctly stamped ticket or a pass (which doesn't need to be stamped) to the controllers, who can board at any time and place, could result in a hefty fine—payable in any currency. (The many people who don't stamp tickets aren't necessarily skirting the law—they may have passes.)

Two key routes for tourists are the *No. 64,* which goes from **Stazione Termini** to the **Vatican** (pick it up at, among other points, **Piazza Venezia** in the center of town); and the small electric-powered *No. 119,* which runs Monday through Friday from **Piazza del Popolo,** past **Piazza Navona,** to **Piazza di Spagna.** *Tram 30*'s route offers an excellent introduction to the city. It passes most of the major monuments and takes about an hour. With a 75-minute ticket, you can get on and off as often as you want, as long as you stamp in your last ride before the time limit is up.

Each *fermata* (bus or tram stop) has a yellow-and-black sign that lists the buses that stop there and key streets on their routes. Arrows indicate the direction in which the buses are heading. Most buses run from 5AM until midnight, although some stop at 9PM; this is indicated at the bottom of each route listing. Popular routes have a night service listed under the *servizio notturno* column. This is often different from the daytime, so check the route carefully. Conductors on night buses sell tickets.

Whatever means of public transport you use, do not underestimate the skill and ingenuity of pickpockets. They are extremely enterprising with their hands, razor blades, and other means of getting into your pockets or purses. Make photocopies of your documents for easy replacement, and leave the originals and any other valuables in your hotel safe.

Driving In the film *Ben Hur,* the wheels of the chariots that raced around the **Circus Maximus** were outfitted with blades. Not much has changed: The kill-or-be-killed spirit still prevails. Driving around Rome today still requires the courage of a gladiator—and the patience of Job. Lanes are for the ingenuous and red lights an opinion. Motor scooters swarm around cars like wasps, convinced that their greater maneuverability absolves them from all laws. Cars zoom the wrong way down one-way streets that can change directions with the seasons. Most important, large sections of central Rome are closed to vehicles without special permits. Simply crossing the street should be enough to satisfy any craving for living on the edge, but if you feel truly lost without wheels, make the arrangements to rent a car in the US and avoid paying VAT, the European value-added tax.

Parking If anything is worse than driving in Rome, it's parking. Some streets (mostly along the Tiber) have parking meters for which you must purchase a ticket from a machine and leave it on the car. There are very few public garages; the best is under the **Villa Borghese**—enter at the top of Via Veneto. Street parking is rarely permitted downtown, and even when it is, good luck finding a space.

Subways Rome's subway system—the **Metropolitana**—has only two lines *(A* and *B),* which are grossly inadequate for the city's size and population. New lines are always being inaugurated, but the digging is soon held up, either by bureaucracy or by the discovery of major artifacts that must be investigated and cataloged.

Line A runs from the northwest **(Stazione Ottaviano)** near the **Vatican** to the southeastern edge of the city **(Stazione Anagnina).** *Line B* runs northeast **(Stazione Rebibbia)** to southwest **(Stazione Laurentina).** The lines intersect at **Stazione Termini.**

The subway operates daily from 5:30AM to 11:30PM. Tickets are sold at newsstands, tobacco shops, bars,

and from vending machines at most stations. Street entrances to the subway are marked with a big red "M." (See "Buses," above, for further ticket information.)

Taxis Rome is a taxi-poor city: Cabs are infrequent, rarely air-conditioned, and usually cannot be hailed. They are also the most expensive in Europe. There are taxi stands in the most populated areas frequented by tourists. Authorized cabs are yellow or white and have plainly visible meters; avoid unlicensed cabs, especially at the airports and train stations. Taxis are also available by calling 3570, 4994, 4157, or 88177. There are surcharges for late-night (after 10PM), Sunday, and holiday service, for any luggage that goes in the trunk, and for travel time to a pickup point (a restaurant, for example) if you call for a taxi.

Tours

By Boat For a leisurely look at the city and its outskirts, take a cruise down the Tiber to the ruins at **Ostia Antica** aboard the *Tourvisa* (4463481). Boats operate Tuesday through Sunday from May through October. The company also offers motorboat tours along the Tiber. They depart daily at 11:30AM and 5:30PM from **Ponte Umberto,** which is between **Piazza Navona** and **Castel Sant'Angelo.**

By Bus An **ATAC** blue tourist bus *(No. 110)* gives tours of the city daily at 2, 3, 5, and 6PM. The three-hour excursion costs about $9 and covers all the major sights. There is no guide, but passengers are given a leaflet in English that describes the sights the bus passes. Tickets are available at the green **ATAC** information booth at the bus depot outside **Stazione Termini** (46952252); the bus departs from here.

Rome's largest and oldest touring company, **CIT Viaggi** (Piazza della Repubblica 68 and 12 other locations, 47211, 47941, 472172), offers the widest variety of bus tours (in different languages) around the city. **Appian Line** (Piazza dell'Esquilino 6, 4878861; fax 4742214) also runs different guided bus trips—some in English—including a popular nighttime excursion. **Appian Line** gives a 20-percent discount to children under 12. For about $18, **Ciao Roma Shuttle Tour** (Via Cavour 113, 4743795; fax 483403) offers ticket holders an audio guide and the option of getting on (or off) the bus at any of 11 historic spots throughout the city.

By Carriage *Carrozzelle* (horse-drawn carriages) can be hired at most major tourist attractions, ranging from a half-hour (about $30) excursion to a full-day drive. A carriage can accommodate up to five passengers. Be sure to agree on the fee before setting out—there should be a card posted in the coach listing charges. The driver is required by law to issue a receipt.

By Foot Scala Reale (Via Varese 46, between Via del Castro Pretorio and Via Vicenza, 44700898, mobile phone 0348/3307181; fax 44700898) gives personalized walking tours for individuals or groups by informed bilingual (Italian/English) architects and art historians. Choose either a half-day excursion of

Roman sites, a full-day trip to places outside Rome, or a bike or *motorini* tour.

Secret Walks (Viale delle Medaglie d'Oro 127, northwest of Piazzale degli Eroi, 39728728, mobile phone 0330/290783) offers English-language walking tours led by actors, artists, musicians, and scholars; specialty tours include wines and wine shops. There's also a guided tour for wheelchair-bound travelers on the first Saturday of every month.

By Plane For a total look at the Eternal City from the sky, contact **Umbria Fly** (88641441; fax 8123137). The trip lasts 20 minutes and costs about $75 a person.

Walking This is the best way to explore the city, but be sure to keep alert and be careful of speeding cars, especially in downtown Rome. This city was built before the automobile age, so often there are no sidewalks. Remember that local drivers believe that stopping at red lights is more of an opinion than a requirement. Cross at the white stripes; even then, be careful because cars don't always slow down at the sight of a pedestrian, and motor scooters almost never do. But unless death seems a real possibility, try not to be intimidated. Maintain your pace, make eye contact with the driver, look determined, and head purposefully for the opposite curb.

FYI

Accommodations In addition to hotels, Rome offers a variety of alternative accommodations. *Pensioni* are the Italian version of bed-and-breakfast inns; religious houses, usually convents or rectories, are very economical but may have some restrictions on noise or reentry hours; residences are apartment-type hotels available only by the week or month.

To make reservations at any type of hotel, call 6991000 daily, from 7AM to 10PM. The service, sponsored by over 200 hotelkeepers, is free and multilingual.

Climate Rome's weather is almost as dramatic as its history and architecture. Between January and March there are many days of bright sunshine (often four or five at a time), and temperatures rarely drop below freezing. Rainy days are almost as common, though, and occasionally a few snowflakes may drift down (the most you can expect is a brief snowfall in January or early February). By April and May, Rome experiences traditional spring weather of sunshine interspersed with showers and nights that can be surprisingly damp and chilly. Temperatures soar in June, when nights are brilliant and cloudless, and rain is a rarity. Expect plenty of hot sun and high humidity in the summer, especially in July, with dramatic thunderstorms possible from mid-August to October. In late September, storms can last as long as three days, with vertical curtains of water that give way to clear skies and sunshine. October is the month of the *Ottobratta* (Indian Summer) when the oblique rays of the sun produce a special diffuse light, and the days become shorter and cooler. But mild days linger even during November and December—for those last alfresco lunches of the year—except when it rains (which it may do for several days in a row); the rain can make it extremely chilly, even indoors. On those days, it's best to dress in layers—warm sweaters, coats, and waterproof shoes.

Average Temperatures (°F)

Month	High	Low
January-March	50	40
April-June	75	52
July-September	95	80
October-December	70	55

Consulates and Embassies

American Consulate Via Vittorio Veneto 121 (at Via Buoncompagni)..................................46741

American Embassy Via Vittorio Veneto 119/A (at Via Leonida Bissolati).............................46741

Australian Embassy Via Alessandria 215 (at Corso Trieste) 852721

British Consulate and Embassy Via XX Settembre 80/A (at Piazzale Porta Pia) 4825441

Canadian Consulate Via Zara 30 (between Via Nomentana and Corso Trieste) ..445981, 8415341

Canadian Embassy Via Giovanni Battista 27 (at Via Antonio Nibby) 445981

Drinking Wine plays a key role in the life of most Romans. There is no minimum age limit in Italy, so even the very young drink wine—sometimes mixed with water—at family meals and celebrations. Perhaps because everyone is expected to have at least a taste of wine at the table, Romans seldom overindulge in alcohol, and very little drunkenness is seen in public or in private. The water from public fountains, like all of the water in Rome, is potable and has a high calcium content. Most Romans, however, prefer the taste of *acqua minerale* (bottled mineral water), either *gassata* (carbonated) or *non gassata* (noncarbonated).

English-language Bookstores The following shops either stock books in English exclusively or have a good selection.

Ancora Bookshop Via della Conciliazione 63 (at Via Padre Pancrazio Pfeiffer).........................6868820

Anglo-American Book Company Via della Vite 102 (at Via Mario de' Fiori) 6795222

Corner Bookshop Via del Moro 48 (between Via della Pelliccia and Vicolo del Cinque)...............5836942

Economy Book and Video Center Via Torino 136 (between Piazza dell'Esquilino and Via Nazionale) 4746877

Holidays Banks and stores are closed, and public transport is reduced on the religious and state holidays listed below. And except for a few restaurants, everything (including public transportation) shuts down on Labor Day (1 May). In addition, a three-day bridge holiday often occurs when a holiday falls on the weekend. Expect massive delays, if not complete lack of services, on:

Capo d'Anno (New Year's), 1 January

Befana (Epiphany), 6 January

Pasqua (Easter), 4 April 1999, 23 April 2000

Pasquetta (Easter Monday), 5 April 1999, 24 April 2000

Liberazione (Liberation Day), 25 April

Festa del Lavoro (Labor Day), 1 May

Festa della Repubblica (Republic Day), 2 June

Festa di San Pietro e Paolo (Feast of Sts. Peter and Paul), 29 June

Ferragosto (Feast of the Assumption), 15 August

Tutti Santi (All Saints' Day), 1 November

Victoria (Victory Day), 4 November

Festa della Madonna Immacolata (Feast of the Immaculate Conception), 8 December

Natale (Christmas), 25 December

Santo Stefano (Second Christmas), 26 December

Hours In winter (September through May), most retail stores are open Monday from 4 to 7:30PM, Tuesday through Saturday from 10AM to 1PM and 3:30 to 7:30PM. In high season (June through August), they extend their evening hours until 8PM, and may either open Monday morning or Saturday afternoon (sometimes both). Food stores follow nearly the same schedule, but also close Thursday afternoon. Generally, it's worth calling ahead, as more and more shops are staying open on Saturday afternoon, during the midday break, and sometimes even on Sunday.

Throughout this guide, opening and closing times are listed only by day(s) if "normal" operating hours apply (see above); in all other cases, specific hours are given (e.g., 6AM-2PM, daily 24 hours, noon-5PM). "No midday closing" means that an establishment stays open throughout the day.

Medical Emergencies If there's an emergency, go to the *Pronto Soccorso* (emergency room) of any hospital. Three of the most centrally located emergency rooms are at **Ospedale San Giacomo** (Via Antonio Canova 29, between Via del Corso and Via di Ripetta, 36266362), **Fatebenefratelli** (6837299) hospital on Tiber Island, and the university hospital, **Policlinico Umberto I** (Viale del Policlinico, between and Piazza Giorlamo Fabrizio, 4462341).

In nonemergency situations, ask your hotel concierge or contact the consular section of your embassy (see page 9) for help in finding a doctor or dentist. Two hospitals with English-speaking staff are the private **Salvator Mundi International Hospital** just west of Trastevere (Viale delle Mura Gianicolensi 67, between Largo Giovanni Berchet and Via Giovanni Livraghi,

588961) and the **Rome American Hospital** (Via Emilio Longoni 69, 22551) on the eastern edge of Rome near the Prenestina interchange of the **Grande Raccordo Anulare (GRA)** ring road.

Money The basic unit of Italian currency is the lira. There are few bills: The largest is 100,000 lire, diminishing to 50,000, 10,000, and 1,000. Everything else is a coin. Be forewarned: Annoyingly minuscule 50- and 100-lire coins are now in circulation, and the two coins are equal in size, so look before you pay. *Gettoni* (phone slugs) have been almost totally replaced by phone cards, so avoid getting them as change.

Banks are open Monday through Friday from 8:30AM to 1:30PM and 2:45 to 3:45PM (although afternoon hours may vary with individual banks). One convenient central bank is **Banca Nazionale del Lavoro** (Via Vittorio Veneto 11, between Piazza Barberini and Via Molise, 47031); it's open for money exchange Monday through Wednesday, and Friday from 8:30AM to 1:30PM and 2:45 to 4PM; and on Thursday from 8:30AM to 6PM.

You can also change money at either of two banks at **Stazione Termini: San Paolo di Torino** (platform 11, 6902639) Monday through Saturday from 8:30AM to 7:30PM; or **Banca di Roma** (4873706) Monday through Friday from 8:25AM to 1:35PM, and Saturday from 8:30AM to 11:30AM. The central post office in **Piazza San Silvestro** exchanges foreign currency Monday through Friday from 8:25AM to 5:30PM, and Saturday from 8:25 to 11:50AM. **American Express** (Piazza di Spagna 38, 67641) is open Monday through Friday from 9AM to 5:30PM, and Saturday from 9AM until 12:30PM.

Another way to get lire is by using a Visa or MasterCard (with a PIN number) or your bank card at ATM machines that show a Cirrus network symbol. The exchange rate is the same as at the bank, and there is no commission or service charge; but check with your bank before leaving home, as some charge a hefty fee for using overseas ATMs.

Avoid machines that change dollars into lire because they are often broken and do not return money.

Personal Safety Violence is rare in Rome, but petty crime is not. Never carry more than you can afford to lose. Keep your money in a waist or neck pouch and don't carry bags or camera cases. Leave your passport, plane tickets, and larger amounts of cash in the hotel safe and make sure that luggage and valuables are not visible in a rented car. Be alert in **Stazione Termini** and the surrounding area. As in the transit hubs of most cities, criminal activity is higher here.

It is safe to walk the streets of Rome at night and stroll in the parks during the day, although a woman alone should stick to well-lighted populous areas and never jog at night in **Villa Borghese.** Women should wear their purses across the chest bandolier-style to thwart bag snatchers on motorbikes. If your purse is grabbed, let go of it—the bag snatchers won't, and you may incur more injury than the bag and its contents are worth. Report the loss to the police and the embassy, since very often, the bag and documents, minus the money, will turn up in a post box or a backyard. Men should carry their wallets in a front pocket or waist pouch. Be especially alert for pickpockets on buses. Be direct and forceful with Gypsy children. Do not let them get close to your bags or pockets and be alert to their orchestrated distractions.

Unsolicited attention on crowded buses is referred to as *la mano morta* (the dead hand), the removal of which sometimes requires a sharp elbow jab or a well-placed heel kick. Latin gropers are best ignored, but if they persist, throw your right hand out in front of you in a gesture of scorn and say what Italian women say: *Crepa!*, which is the equivalent of "Drop dead!"

Pharmacies Most drugstores are open Monday through Saturday, with a midday break from 1 to 4PM. The *farmacia* in **Stazione Termini** is open daily from 7AM until 11:30PM with no midday closing. There are two 24-hour pharmacies: **Internazionale** (Piazza Barberini 49, 4825456), and **Spinedi** (Via Arenula 73, 68803278).

Postal Service The main post office in **Piazza San Silvestro** is open from 8AM until 8PM. Other branches close at 1:30PM. The Vatican post office on St. Peter's Square is open Monday through Friday from 8AM to 7PM, Saturday until 6PM. In summer special post office vans are stationed in **St. Peter's Square,** and the post office in the **Vatican Museums** has the same schedule as the museums. Mail sent through the Vatican beats the Italian post by at least two or three days.

Publications For news in English, the daily *International Herald Tribune* is available at most newsstands and includes an English insert on Italian news. To find out about what's happening around the city, buy *Roma C'è* at most newsstands on Thursday. It has an English-language section and lists movies (in English and Italian), concerts, art exhibitions, museum schedules, etc.

Wanted In Rome is another good source for what's on where; it's published biweekly and is available at downtown newsstands. *Carnet,* an English-language monthly listing of events, is available at tourist offices (for locations, see "Visitors' Information Office" on page 12). Three Italian daily newspapers—*Corriere della Sera, La Repubblica,* and the local *Il Messaggero*—also carry entertainment listings.

Rome's telephone directory's supplement, *TuttaCittà,* has detailed maps of the city and invaluable information on bus routes, taxi stands, postal codes, etc. Bars and cafes normally have it on hand.

Restaurants Dating from the time when restaurants were primarily run by families, Italian law states that all such establishments must observe one closing day per week (hotel restaurants are exempt from this regulation). Closing days are posted on a sign outside. Although most dining is à la carte, some restaurants offer a fixed-price *menù turistico,* a "one from column A, one from column B" affair of two or three courses. Always make restaurant reservations if possible, especially on weekends. Lunch is usually served between 1PM and 3PM; dinner between 8PM and 10:30PM (sometimes around midnight in summer). For more information about a typical Roman meal, see "Buon Appetito!" on page 184).

Shopping Rome is a window-shopper's paradise. Haute couture boutiques of the world's most famous fashion designers are mingled with jean stores and junk shops. To increase the lure, many of Rome's shopping streets are (more or less) traffic-free pedestrian zones. The best buys are found during two sale periods—in January and mid-July to September—when savings can be considerable.

The heart of Rome's shopping district is **Piazza di Spagna.** The streets leading out of the square—Via dei Condotti, **Via Borgognona, Via delle Carrozze,** and **Via Frattina**—are all lined with chic designer boutiques. Running north from the piazza (and connecting to **Piazza del Popolo)** is **Via del Babuino,** filled with antiques shops and fashionable clothing boutiques; slightly west is **Via del Corso,** which caters to a sporty, younger clientele. **Via Margutta,** parallel to Via del Babuino, is another good hunting ground for antiques. Across the river from **Piazza del Popolo** are two streets—**Via Cola di Rienzo** and **Via Ottaviano**—where stock tends to be less pricey than on the other side of the Tiber. Some of Rome's best food emporiums with take-out departments can also be found here.

Most neighborhoods have outdoor markets. For food, flowers, inexpensive clothing, or "antiques," try the **Via Sannio Flea Market** near the **Basilica San Giovanni in Laterano** or **Campo dei Fiori.** They are open Monday through Saturday from early morning until 1:30PM. You can also join the fray on Sunday morning at the huge **Porta Portese Flea Market** in Trastevere, which has everything from Senegalese wood carvings to fake Etruscan pottery. Romans will tell you that the only people who make any money here are the pickpockets and that if your watch is stolen on the way in, you can buy it back on the way out.

Smoking Smoking is still popular in Rome, although it is prohibited on buses, the subway, domestic air flights, and in public offices. On first-class train cars, tickets for nonsmoking sections disappear first, so be sure to plan ahead.

Street Plan If Rome's street numbers seem topsy-turvy, it's because they are. Some streets have even numbers on one side and odd on the other; on other streets, the numbers follow consecutively down one side of the street and up the other. And sometimes the numbering begins as if at random in the middle of the street.

Taxes There is a hefty 19 percent IVA (Value-added, or VAT) tax tacked on to restaurant and hotel bills. A sales tax of 14 to 19 percent is also included in the price of most goods. This money is refundable to visitors with non–European Community passports, but only if they ask for it, and the purchase is at least 300,000 lire. Look for the "Tax-Free for Tourists" signs in store windows.

Some stores will credit VAT refunds directly to credit card accounts. This is the best way; otherwise, the store will issue you a voucher for the refund that can be redeemed for cash at a service desk at the airport. You will have to show the goods to a customs official who will then validate the voucher. It can be redeemed at the refund stand in the duty-free shop, or you can mail back a tax-exemption form to Italy when you get home (within 90 days of the purchase) in the envelope the shop should provide with the receipt. Needless to say, they do not make this easy, in the hope that you will forget about it or run out of time.

Telephones Phone numbers in Rome have as few as four digits or as many as eight and all numbers are subject to change without notice, which can be alarming as well as annoying. In addition, the increasing demand for new phone numbers has recently led to a change in dialing throughout Italy: Every call must be preceded by the area's two-digit code. In Rome, you must prefix each call with 06. Directory assistance can be reached by dialing 12.

Public telephones in Rome are most commonly found in *caffès* and restaurants and occasionally on the street. To use them, you'll need 100- or 200-lire coins or a telephone card—sold in 5,000- or 10,000-lire quantities at tobacco shops and phone company counters at train stations and airports.

Direct-dial calls to the US from Italy can be made by dialing 001, followed by the US area code and the phone number; be advised that direct-dial calls made from hotel rooms often are billed at higher rates. To avoid these extra charges, calling card and collect calls to the US also can be made via the AT&T operator (1721011) or the MCI operator (1721022). When using a calling card in a public place, check that no one is eavesdropping in order to copy your number.

To reach a long-distance operator for a call within Italy, dial 1795; for an international call, dial 170.

Tipping Restaurant gratuities can be a knotty problem, but tipping is generally optional. If service is included in the bill, as it often is, it's not necessary to leave anything. If the waiter was especially helpful or if service is not included, it's polite to leave about 1,000 lire per person or about 10 percent above the check.

Tip porters, hotel maids, and concierges according to the quality of service, and round out taxi fares. Some

theater and cinema ushers expect a 1,000-lire tip for showing you to your seat; self-appointed parking lot attendants ask 2,000 to 3,000 lire.

Toilets Rome lacks sufficient public lavatories. You either have to walk confidently past the concierge in the nearest hotel or go to a cafe and "buy" bathroom privileges for the price of a drink. Toilet paper is not always available in a *bagno* or *toiletta,* so carry a packet of paper tissues.

Viewing Art Bring along opera glasses or binoculars for seeing fine details on domes and high ceilings; a pocket mirror can help you examine the fully restored **Sistine Chapel** frescoes without getting a stiff neck. A pocket flashlight is also useful, especially for visits to the catacombs and other enclosed sites. Carry a pocketful of 500-lire coins to keep the lights turned on in churches.

Visitors' Information Office The **Azienda Promozione Turistica di Roma (APT,** Provincial Tourist Office) is behind the **Grand Hotel** near the **Termini** train station (Via Parigi 5, between Via Pastrengo and Via Vittorio Emanuele Orlando, 48899253, 48899255). It's open Monday through Friday from 8:15AM to 7:15PM, Saturday from 9AM until 1:30PM. **APT** branches are open daily from 8AM to 7PM at **Termini** (4871270), and in the customs area at **Leonardo da Vinci** airport (65954471). In addition, there are tourist information kiosks in **Largo Carlo Goldoni** and Via del Corso, **Piazza delle Cinque Lune** (just northeast of Piazza Navona), **Piazza Sidney Sonnino** (just south of Ponte Garibaldi in Trastevere), and on **Via Nazionale** near the **Palazzo delle Esposizioni.** All are open Tuesday through Saturday, and Sunday morning.

The information offices distribute free maps, hotel listings, and *Carnet* (see "Publications" above). The **Ufficio Informazioni** (Vatican Tourist Information Office) is on the south side of **St. Peter's Square** (69884866). It's open daily, except on major Catholic holidays.

Enjoy Rome (Via Varese 39, between Via del Castro Pretorio and Via Vicenza, 4451843; fax 4450734; info@enjoyrome.com) is a friendly independent information office near **Stazione Termini.** The staff here books hotels and gives guided walking and bike tours. Other services include a message board and free baggage deposit. The office is open Monday through Friday from 8:30AM to 2PM and 3:30 to 6:30PM, and Saturday mornings. Telephone service is available Monday through Friday until 10PM.

Phone Book

Emergencies

Police Emergency..113

Fire..115

Ambulance...5510

Dentist
  Dr. Peter Althoff, Via Salaria 280
 8554069

Emergency Rooms (Pronto Soccorso):
  Ospedale San Giacomo (Via Antonio Canova 29)
 36266362
  Fatebenefratelli (Tiber Island)...................6837299
English-speaking Doctors:
  Dr. Ettore Lollini 86211170
  Dr. Frank Silvestri......................................485706

Hospitals:

International Medical Center
(Via Giovanni Amendola 7) 4882371

Rome American Hospital
(Via Emilio Longoni 69)................................22551

Salvator Mundi Clinic
(Viale delle Mura Gianicolensi 67) 588961

Poison Control 490663

Visitors' Information

Bus...167431784

Museum Hours 110

Postal Information 160

Taxi......................................3570, 4994, 6645, 4775

Time...161

Youth Hostel 4871152

Festive Festas

January
Haute couture fashion shows, major hotels.

La Befana Toy Fair, Piazza Navona.

Winter sales (8 January)—clothes, shoes, and linens.

February
Carnevale (Mardi Gras), **Piazza Navona,** Via Cola di Rienzo, Via Nazionale.

March
Visiting Day (16 March), **Chapel of Palazzo Massimo alle Colonne.**

San Giuseppe Feast Day (19 March).

April
Rome's birthday (21 April) celebration, **Campidoglio;** fireworks over the **Tiber.**

Spring Azalea Festival, Spanish Steps.

May
Antiques Fair, Via dei Coronari and Via dell'Orso.

Art Fair, Via Margutta.

Industrial Exhibition, Via Cristoforo Colombo.

International Horse Show, Villa Borghese (Piazza di Siena).

International Rose Competition, Rose Garden just to the south of the **Circus Maximus,** on **Aventine Hill.**

International Tennis Annual, Foro Italico.

June
San Giovanni Feast Day (23 June).

July
Expo Tevere—exposition of Italian regional products, along the Tiber quays between **Ponte Margherita** and **Ponte Sant'Angelo.**

Noantri Festival Street Fair (last two weeks in July), along Viale di Trastevere.

Outdoor theater in nearby **Ostia Antica.**

Summer sales—clothes, handbags, shoes.

August
Summer closings—most shops, restaurants, cafes, and even some museums close for at least two weeks.

Miracle of snow outside **Santa Maria Maggiore** (5 August).

Opera in the park held at **Villa Borghese** or **Parco del Celio,** near the **Baths of Caracalla** (check *Roma C'è*).

September
Fall Art Fair (repeat of May fair).

Second part of **Expo Tevere.**

October
Fall Antiques Fair (repeat of May fair).

Sagra dell'Uva—Grape Harvest Wine Festival (First Sunday of October), southeast of Rome in the **Castelli Romani** village of **Marino;** free wine flows from fountains.

November
All Souls' Day (2 November)

Rome opera season opens.

December
Feast of the Immaculate Conception (8 December). The Pope goes to **Piazza di Spagna.**

Christmas concerts and *presepi* (nativity scenes) in various churches.

Christmas Eve Midnight Mass, St. Peter's Basilica.

Christmas Day Mass, Chiesa di Sant'Ignazio.

Vatican City and The Borgo

When you stand on the right spot in **Piazza San Pietro** (St. Peter's Square)—a disc in the pavement to the right of the obelisk—it's not only the columns of the surrounding portico that line up, but also two thousand years of history. In ancient times the ground underneath the portico was part of a popular racetrack (the Emperor Caligula's hippodrome). Later, following the collapse of the empire, the racetrack was abandoned, and the area eventually became a necropolis. Both ancient Romans and early Christians are buried under the piazza, and although no definitive proof exists, it is believed that the Apostle Peter is among them.

Constantine, the first Christian Roman emperor, built the original **Basilica di San Pietro** (St. Peter's Basilica) in AD 315 to honor this site. Completed in 50 years, it was almost as large as today's cathedral. By the 16th century the Catholic Church could no longer handle the crowds of pilgrims, and a new St. Peter's was commissioned. It took 200 years to construct this basilica, first according to a design by **Bramante**, and later by **Michelangelo**, who added the towering dome that symbolizes the basilica. Finally, in the second half of the 17th century, **Bernini** completed the complex with a sweeping colonnaded piazza.

Perhaps the world's greatest collection of Renaissance art is located inside **St. Peter's** and in the nearby **Gallerie e Musei Vaticani** (Vatican Galleries and Museums). The basilica and the museums are the only buildings within Vatican City that are open to the public; otherwise, entrance is by permission only. Before embarking on a visit, consider the following: The museums are always jammed, but are less crowded in the early hours and at lunchtime; allow at least two hours for the most basic visit and two days if you want to

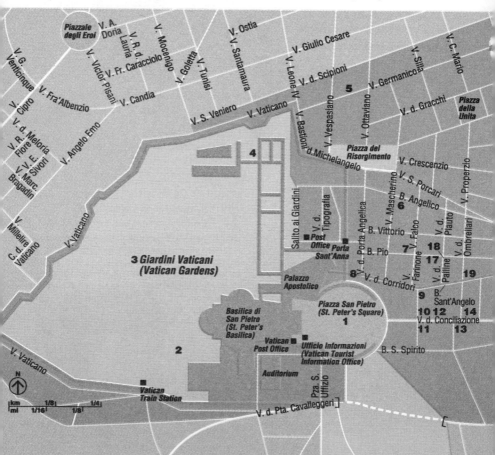

walk all 4.5 miles of galleries. Head to the museums first; they close earlier than the basilica—which is open without interruption until 6PM in winter and 7PM in summer. Also remember the dress code inside the basilica: no miniskirts, shorts, or bare shoulders.

Close to Vatican City is The Borgo, a small neighborhood on the route that medieval pilgrims took to reach St. Peter's. For centuries, these travelers made their way across the **Tiber** and through what was then a warren of narrow streets to burst suddenly into the vast open space of **St. Peter's Square**. But in 1936 Mussolini's architects, **Marcello Piacentini** and **Attilio Spaccarelli** (whose name appropriately translates as Attila, The Little Chopper), slashed a new approach to the Vatican through the old medieval quarter. Old buildings were torn down to make way for the broad, impersonal **Via della Conciliazione**. Wedged between **St. Peter's Square** and **Castel Sant'Angelo**, today's Borgo nevertheless remains a fascinating neighborhood full of shops and restaurants.

Hadrian started to build his mausoleum here along the Tiber in AD 135 (it was completed in AD 139, one year after his death). Through the centuries, this monument (now the **Castel Sant'Angelo**) was slowly transformed into a fortress. It eventually became so strong that in 1377, when the papacy returned to Rome from exile in Avignon, the pontiff and his court claimed it as their personal citadel—it was connected to the Vatican by an enclosed passageway—and site of the papal prisons. For centuries, the adjacent bridge, **Ponte Sant'Angelo**, bore the heavy traffic of religious pilgrims making their way to **St. Peter's Basilica**.

Vatican City

A line of white travertine stones that runs across **St. Peter's Square** between the two arms of **Gian**

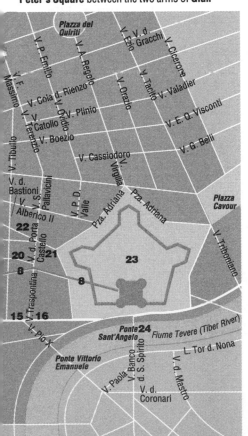

Lorenzo Bernini's colonnade forms the border between Vatican City and the City of Rome (illustrated on page 16). Vatican City has two private entrances: One is just to the left of the basilica; the other is located outside the square through the **Porta Sant'Anna** (St. Anne's Gate). Swiss guards are on sentry duty at both points, dressed in the orange, yellow, and blue uniforms reportedly designed by Michelangelo. The guard changes every two hours, but don't bother to wait—unlike almost everything else in Vatican City, no ritual is involved.

Until 1870, the popes ruled Rome and most of central Italy. When Garibaldi's nationalist patriots united Italy for the first time since the Caesars, the Romans, who thought they were overtaxed by the popes, welcomed the new rule. The outraged and humiliated pope, who considered the nationalists usurpers, declared himself a prisoner in the Vatican. On 11 February 1929 Benito Mussolini ended this enmity by signing the Lateran Pact, which created the independent state of Vatican City, and returning some of the papal treasures that were seized in 1870.

Vatican City is the youngest and one of the smallest European states, covering about 108 acres and boasting a population of under a thousand. Despite its small size, the entity has a supermarket, drugstore, post office, and train station. It is governed by one sovereign ruler—the pope, who is also the religious leader of the world's 900 million Catholics. Most Rome-based cardinals and bishops live outside the papal city but have Vatican passports and license plates; about half the lay employees also live on the other side of the Vatican's walls. The Vatican publishes its own daily newspaper, L'Osservatore Romano (written in Italian but with weekly digests in various languages) and has a radio station that broadcasts in 26 languages.

1 Piazza San Pietro (St. Peter's Square)

The great dome of **St. Peter's Basilica** dominates the skyline as you enter **St. Peter's Square.** Whether draped in sunlight or floodlit at night, it hovers above the church like a gigantic air balloon about to take off. Next, your eyes descend to **Gian Lorenzo Bernini**'s majestic colonnade, with its two "arms" reaching out in an architectural embrace formed by four rows of 284 Doric columns each 64 feet high. On top are 140 statues of Christ and various saints (illustrated on page 17). Built a century after the basilica (1656-67), **St. Peter's Square** is actually an ellipse. At its center is an 83-foot-high obelisk that was shipped from Heliopolis, Egypt, by Caligula in AD 37 to decorate the center of his racetrack. It stood next to the sacristy inside the private grounds of Vatican City until 1586, when Pope Sixtus V, on the advice of the architect **Domenico Fontana,** had it moved to the center of the square. It took six days for the obelisk's 312 tons to be winched to the ground and rolled along on logs, and it took over a hundred men and a pulley drawn by 14 oxen to hoist it into place. For centuries the folklore was that the golden ball crowning the obelisk contained the ashes of Julius Caesar, but during the move it was opened and found empty. The ball was subsequently replaced with the present iron cross, in which—says another legend—there is a splinter of the crucifixion cross. On either side of the obelisk are twin fountains (pictured below). The one on the left was designed by **Bernini;** the other (which dates from 1614 and is attributed to **Carlo Maderno**) was moved to its present position by **Bernini** to balance the design. In the pavement between each fountain and the columns closest to it is a flat stone disc. Stand on either one to see the set of four rows of columns suddenly line up, one behind the other. They disappear into a single sight line, attesting to the precise engineering skill of their creator.

The large building to the right of the basilica is the **Palazzo Apostolico,** where the pope lives and works. Every Sunday when he's in Rome, the pope addresses the crowd from a top-floor window. A long red-and-gold drapery is hung from this window shortly before noon to announce his appearance.

On St. Peter's Square:

Ufficio Informazioni (Vatican Tourist Information Office) To the left of the basilica on the south side of the square are orange signs pointing to this information center. There's also a first-aid station, a book and gift store, and rest rooms here. Shuttle-bus service to the **Vatican Museums** (a 20-minute walk away) leaves from here every 20 minutes from 9AM until 12:30PM. Purchase tickets inside the office. ♦ M-Sa. 69884866

Vatican Post Office This is one of the post office's three locations. Another is near the newsstands to the right of the basilica, and a third inside the museums before the ticket windows. All three carry **Vatican City** stamps—some of them philatelic—and accept letters, postcards, and small packages. Note: The stamps are not valid outside the papal city. ♦ M-Sa. 69882

Basilica di San Pietro (St. Peter's Basilica) The basilica is many things: a celebration of Roman Catholicism, a treasure house of some of the world's greatest art, a triumph of architecture, and an occasion for meditation on the vicissitudes of history. This building is the second basilica to stand on this site. The first, built by Emperor Constantine in the fourth century, was nearly as large and as handsomely decorated. But by the 16th century, more than a thousand years of wear and tear—and its siting on a slope of the Vatican Hill—had taken a toll. By the late Renaissance, the Catholic Church was newly prosperous—its economy revived by the discovery and exploitation of the New World—and Pope Julius II commissioned the brilliant architect **Donato Bramante** to replace the crumbling basilica with a new church that would surpass the old. **Bramante**'s plan, unveiled in 1506, called for a radical change: The former basilica's Romanesque blueprint was abandoned in favor of a more

*Piazza San Pietro
(Saint Peter's Square)*

MARJORIE J. VOGEL/RHODE ISLAND ORIGINALS

*Basilica di San Pietro
(St. Peter's Basilica)*

MARJORIE J. VOGEL/RHODE ISLAND ORIGINALS

symmetrical Greek-cross design. Both Pope Julius II and **Bramante** died within a decade of the start of rebuilding, and with them this plan also died. Over the next 30 years the job of completing the basilica passed to six other Renaissance artist/architects, including **Raphael,** before it was finally taken up by **Michelangelo.** Before his death in 1564, **Michelangelo**'s giant, 137-foot diameter cupola had soared to 230 feet—more than half its eventual 448-foot height. In 1614 **Carlo Maderno** completed some much-disputed modifications, elongating **Michelangelo**'s floor plan, and adding his own facade, including the central balcony from which the pope issues Christmas and Easter blessings. The election of a new pope is also announced from here.

The interior of the cathedral is deceptive—its harmonious proportions and carefully wrought perspective artfully conceal its true dimensions. Look closely, and you'll see column bases that are much taller than people and pillars almost as large as houses. The walls are 26 feet thick, and the interior is 610 feet long (about two yards longer than St. Paul's Cathedral in London). Within the five-gated portico, most of the bronze doors are from the first basilica, although one panel of the first door on the left is modern. The work of Giacomo Manzù (1963), it portrays Pope John XXIII welcoming delegates to the Ecumenical Council of 1962, including the first black

African cardinal. The last door on the right is open only during Holy Years, which occur every quarter-century. In a tradition dating from 1300, the pope uses a silver hammer to break the door's seal, and those who come to Rome during these years receive a special blessing. The year 2000 is a Holy Year.

Within St. Peter's Basilica:

Red Porphyry Disc Taken from a pagan basilica and set in the pavement in front of the center doors of the entrance, this disc of porphyry—a rare purple-colored marble—marks the spot where more than 20 emperors—including Charlemagne and Frederick II—knelt to be crowned by the pope.

Prior to World War II, on major feast days, the colonnades of St. Peter's Square and the basilica were illuminated by hundreds of Roman dish candles. The ramps, stairs, and tops of buildings were revealed by these gently flickering lights, lending a magical effect. At dusk, two runners would stand poised at either end of the colonnades with a flaming brand in one hand. At the firing of a pistol they would start to run, dipping their torches at every step to light the candles as they passed. It was a race to see who would arrive first at the very top of the dome of St. Peter's. By the end of the race, the church and the square were bathed in glowing light.

Papal Audience

The pope holds a general (public) audience every Wednesday when he is in the city. In good weather it is held in **St. Peter's Square,** which holds 24,000 seats; in winter or inclement weather, the audience takes place in the **Vatican**'s 9,000-seat auditorium (designed by engineer Pier Luigi Nervi in 1971) or in **St. Peter's Basilica.** The starting hour varies with the season, and tickets are essential for the winter or indoor audiences. A general audience lasts about two hours. Standing room in the square is usually plentiful but distant from the papal throne.

To obtain a ticket, plan ahead. Catholics should ask their bishop's chancery to write to Rome at least two months in advance, or they may write directly to the **Prefettura della Casa Pontificia** (Citta del Vaticano, 00120 Roma). If you have Jesuit connections, write to the **Jesuit Curia** (Borgo Santo Spirito, 00193 Roma). If you are in Rome already, ask for help from the local American Catholic church—**Chiesa di Santa Susanna** (Via XX Settembre and Largo di Santa Susanna, 4882748). If all else fails, the best bet for last-minute audience requests is the office of the **North American College** (Via dell'Umiltà 30, at Via dell'Archetto, 6789184). The pope also appears at noon, sharp, at his library window to bless the crowd in the square below each Sunday when he is in Rome, or at **Castel Gandolfo** in the **Castelli Romani** when he is on summer holiday.

MARJORIE J. VOGEL/RHODE ISLAND ORIGINALS

Pietà In the first chapel on the right is the marble statue of the Virgin Mary holding the dead body of Jesus. Carved by Michelangelo when he was only 25 years old, it is the only piece he ever signed (his name appears on a band across Mary's breast). The statue has been behind protective glass since 1972 when a deranged man struck it in 15 places with a hammer and broke off the tip of the Virgin's nose. The restorations are hardly noticeable.

Monument to Queen Christina of Sweden
Christina, an orphan queen from the age of six, was educated as if she were a prince and became one of 17th-century Europe's most learned women. (She studied philosophy under Descartes.) A skilled politician, she helped bring the Thirty Years' War to an end and then stunned Europe by abdicating her throne to become a Roman Catholic. She moved to the papal court and eventually died in Rome in 1689 in **Palazzo Corsini** in Trastevere. Christina's second baptism in Innsbruck is depicted on this bas-relief. In the chapel next door are monuments to two 20th-century popes: Pius XI (1922-32) and Pius XII (1939-58).

Bronze Statue of a Seated St. Peter
No one knows who carved this statue or when. Some believe it is the work of the 13th-century sculptor Arnolfo di Cambio; others say it is paleo-Christian—a difference of a thousand years. The right foot has been polished to soaplike smoothness since 1857 when Pope Pius IX granted an indulgence to anyone who kisses it. On St. Peter's feast day (29 June), this statue is dressed in gold brocaded robes.

MARJORIE J. VOGEL/RHODE ISLAND ORIGINALS

Bernini's Baldacchino Although St. Peter's body was never recovered after the Barbarian invasions, this 1633 canopy (illustrated above) enshrines the spot where Catholics believe the first pope was buried. It stands as tall as a five-story building and was commissioned by Pope Urban VIII. Its twisted

ST. PETER'S BASILICA

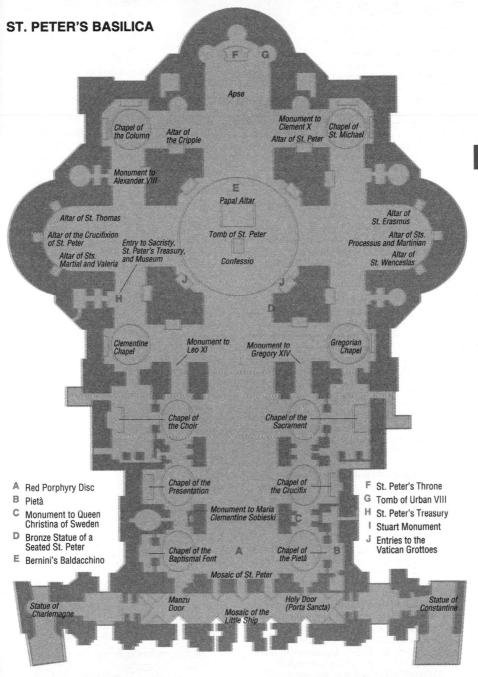

Apse

Chapel of the Column

Altar of the Cripple

Monument to Clement X

Altar of St. Peter

Chapel of St. Michael

Monument to Alexander VIII

E

Papal Altar

Altar of St. Thomas

Altar of St. Erasmus

Altar of the Crucifixion of St. Peter

Tomb of St. Peter

Altar of Sts. Processus and Martinian

Entry to Sacristy, St. Peter's Treasury, and Museum

Altar of Sts. Martial and Valeria

Altar of St. Wenceslas

Confessio

J

J

H

D

Clementine Chapel

Monument to Leo XI

Monument to Gregory XIV

Gregorian Chapel

Chapel of the Choir

Chapel of the Sacrament

A Red Porphyry Disc

B Pietà

C Monument to Queen Christina of Sweden

D Bronze Statue of a Seated St. Peter

E Bernini's Baldacchino

Chapel of the Presentation

Chapel of the Crucifix

F St. Peter's Throne

G Tomb of Urban VIII

H St. Peter's Treasury

I Stuart Monument

J Entries to the Vatican Grottoes

Monument to Maria Clementine Sobieski

C

Chapel of the Baptismal Font

A

Chapel of the Pietà

B

Mosaic of St. Peter

Statue of Charlemagne

Manzu Door

Mosaic of the Little Ship

Holy Door (Porta Sancta)

Statue of Constantine

columns recall the medieval canopy in the original St. Peter's basilica. The columns are decorated with bees, the heraldic symbol of Urban's family—the Barberini of Florence. The bronze of the four 95-foot columns once covered the crossbeams in the portico of the **Pantheon,** which the Barberini pope did not hesitate to recycle for his own use. This led to one of Rome's most famous antipapal

lampoons: "Quod non facerunt barbari, fecerunt Barberini" (What the barbarians didn't do [to the **Pantheon**], the Barberini did).

St. Peter's Throne Bernini's wizardry continues behind the 1665 bronze altar where a full nursery school of cherubs surrounds a sunburst with a dove—the symbol of the Holy Spirit—in the center. The altar encases an ancient wooden chair that legend says St. Peter sat in while preaching to the Romans. Its ivory-carved panels can be seen better in the replica in the **Treasury** (see below).

Tomb of Urban VIII More than 15 years before his death in 1644, Pope Urban VIII commissioned **Bernini** to design this tomb. When unveiled in 1647, it was immediately recognized as a masterpiece and inspired imitations all over Europe. Note the bronze skeleton registering the death of the pontiff in the Book of the Dead. On the left is Charity holding a baby and on the right, Justice.

St. Peter's Treasury Through the years the **Treasury** was systematically raided—by Vandals in 455, Saracens in 846, Normans in 1084, the Spanish in 1527, and finally by Napoleon's troops in 1798. Many dazzling items, however, remain in the nine small rooms, including gifts given to the popes over the centuries by emperors, kings, and other heads-of-state. Most are religious objects in silver or gold, beautifully worked and encrusted with jewels. There are also drawings showing the first basilica. The immense, vigorously realistic bronze tomb of Pope Sixtus IV (1493) inside was made for the earlier basilica by **Antonio Pollaiuolo.** The tomb is decorated with representations of the Liberal Arts (which you can see from an elevated platform) because Sixtus IV was a patron of education and the arts. More recent gifts include Lyndon B. Johnson's bust of himself—presented to a somewhat surprised Pope Paul VI—which has not yet found its permanent niche.

Stuart Monument In 1817 Antonio Canova, one-time honorary president of Philadelphia's Academy of Fine Arts, created this elegant monument to the last of the Stuarts—the Old Pretender, James Edward (who died in 1766)—and his sons—Charles Edward (better known as the Young Pretender or Bonnie Prince Charlie) and Cardinal Henry Stuart, the Duke of York. The Stuarts lived in Rome after fleeing England with the English royal seal. When Cardinal Henry Stuart returned it to King George IV in the 1820s, the British monarch graciously paid for this tomb. Facing it is the monument to James's wife, Mary Clementine Sobieski, where the inscription "Queen of England, France and Ireland" obviously confuses her with her predecessor, Mary Queen of Scots.

In May 1938 Hitler and 500 aides arrived in Rome to visit Mussolini. He also planned to see the city's magnificent works of art and announced that he would begin by visiting the Vatican Museums the following day. He was unable to do so, however, when Pope Pius XI shut down the museums and announced that he was leaving that day for his summer residence at Castel Gandolfo.

Vatican Grottoes Pillars of the earlier church are visible here, as are the tombs of many popes: Pius II, Pius XII, John XXIII, Paul VI, John Paul I, and the only English pope, Nicholas Breakspear, who took the name Hadrian IV in 1154. Bas-reliefs depict scenes from the Old and New Testaments, and one of the most precious treasures in the entire **Vatican** is here: an angel that is the sole remnant of Giotto's original mosaic from the first basilica. The entrance to the grottoes is reached by either of two narrow staircases near the main altar—one behind Bernini's statue of *St. Andrew,* who holds an X-shaped cross for his martyrdom, and another opposite the statue of the Roman centurion *St. Longinus,* who pierced Christ's side with a lance and was later converted.

Excavations Beneath St. Peter's In 1939 workers preparing a place in the grottoes for the tomb of Pius XI came upon elements of the first basilica. Beneath that, they also found a patch of wall of Nero's circus with a section of the ancient necropolis beside it. An archaeologist dated the tombs—some were of early Christians and others, decorated and vividly painted, were of patrician Romans of the second and third centuries. There were also numerous graffiti, including one in Greek deciphered as reading "Peter is here," which was found more or less in the place traditionally believed to be his grave. ♦ Guided tours only (90 minutes, in English); reserve at the Information Office in St. Peter's Square

MARJORIE J. VOGEL/RHODE ISLAND ORIGINALS

Entrance to the Dome Take the elevator or hike up the interminable narrow, sloping staircase to a walkway that goes around the base of the interior of the dome. From here, look down on the antlike people encircling the altar 160 feet below. Outside is the roof of the basilica where there are toilets and a gift shop. The wise, the weak of heart, and those who suffer vertigo will stop here and content themselves with the view. The indomitable will continue the climb up the one-way staircase between the inner and outer shells of the dome (332 steps) to the base of the lantern on top of the world's tallest brick dome. ♦ Admission. Enter from the exterior to the right of the Holy Door

2 Studio del Mosaico (Vatican Mosaic Studio) There are no paintings in **St. Peter's**, instead there are delicate micromosaics. For centuries the **Vatican** has had its own workshop where mosaics and micromosaics are repaired and cut and new works assembled, including copies of works by Van Gogh, Goya, and Picasso. ♦ M-F, by permission only; apply at the Information Office in St. Peter's Square. 6984466, 6984866

3 Giardini Vaticani (Vatican Gardens) The only way to see the inside of **Vatican City** is to take a bus tour of the gardens. The two-hour excursion includes two formal floral gardens that change with the seasons, exotic trees that were gifts to the Vatican, a well-tended rose garden, and the beehives that produce the pope's honey. The bus makes several stops

for camera buffs. ♦ M-Tu, Th-Sa 10AM March-Nov; Sa 10AM Dec-Feb. Reserve at the Information Office in St. Peter's Square. 6984466, 6984866

4 Gallerie e Musei Vaticani (Vatican Galleries and Museums) The best months to see the **Vatican Museums** are November and February; the best time of day is at lunch time or just before closing. Any other time the wait in line can be an hour or more—as the museums average as many as 25,000 visitors daily during peak season. The main entrance for all the **Vatican Museums** is on Viale Vaticano, a brisk 15-minute walk from **St. Peter's Square** down Via di Porta Angelica (also not far from the **Ottaviano** stop on the *A Line* of the subway or the terminus of the *No. 64* bus line). There is also a shuttle bus (fee charged) that goes between **St. Peter's Square** and the museums via the **Vatican Gardens**. It is usually crowded and fills up quickly, but it lets you off at a convenient side entrance where there is no line. The shuttle leaves the square every 20 minutes from in front of the **Information Office**. If you come in

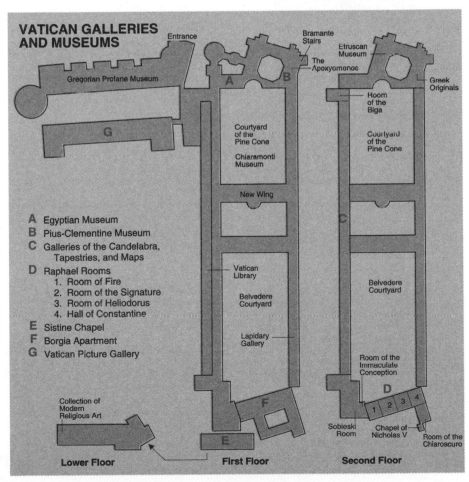

VATICAN GALLERIES AND MUSEUMS

A Egyptian Museum
B Pius-Clementine Museum
C Galleries of the Candelabra, Tapestries, and Maps
D Raphael Rooms
  1. Room of Fire
  2. Room of the Signature
  3. Room of Heliodorus
  4. Hall of Constantine
E Sistine Chapel
F Borgia Apartment
G Vatican Picture Gallery

the main entrance (see floor plan on page 21), take the elevator to the ticket offices. (After visiting the museums, everyone descends the much-imitated grand spiral staircase with its twin stairways that permit two streams of visitors to move simultaneously up or down without passing each other.) The itinerary below does not cover all of the more than 100 galleries in the museums but highlights their most famous items. (Note: The numbers in parentheses in the entries below that follow the names of key works refer to catalog numbers in the **Vatican**'s official guide to the museums.) There are book and souvenir shops throughout the museums and two snack bars. ♦ Admission; free the last Sunday of the month, unless it is a holiday. M-F 8:45AM to 3:45PM, Sa 8:45AM to 1:45PM mid-Mar through Oct; M-Sa 8:45AM to 12:45PM Nov to mid-Mar. There are English-language cassette guides for rental; a special itinerary is available for visitors with disabilities. Viale Vaticano (west of Viale Bastioni di Michelangelo). 69883333

Within the Vatican Galleries and Museums:

Egyptian Museum This museum has something for everybody. Several pieces document the love affair of Julius Caesar and Cleopatra when their two great civilizations influenced each other's art and culture. One room is dedicated to the Emperor Hadrian's young male lover Antinous, another relationship where age did not matter. When Antinous drowned in the Nile, the grieving ruler made him a god and had hundreds of statues of him placed throughout the empire. In one room is the colossal white marble statue that shows Antinous dressed as the Egyptian god Osiris, who also died in the Nile. Pope Gregory XVI, who founded this section of the museum more than 150 years ago, took these sculptures from **Hadrian's Villa** at Tivoli (see the "Day Trips" chapter). Another room houses a granite throne belonging to Rameses II (2100 BC). His mother, Queen Tuia, is portrayed in an enormous basalt statue. And don't miss the mummy.

Pius-Clementine Museum Immediately to the left of the far end of the **Egyptian Museum** is this museum of Greco-Roman sculpture. Pass through a square hallway to a round vestibule and into a small apartment. Pope Leo X lent these foyers to Leonardo da Vinci so he could carry out experiments in alchemy, but da Vinci knew better than to waste time on dreams of turning base metal into gold. Instead he studied anatomy for his drawings. The pope finally evicted Leonardo when he heard rumors that the artist had received women of easy virtue in the rooms in order to examine them for gynecological sketches. In the center of the first vestibule stands a Roman copy in marble of an original fourth-

century BC bronze by Lysippus called *The Apoxyomenos,* or *The Cleanser,* from the Greek word "to wipe off." It shows a young athlete wiping the oil from his skin with a scraper—now lost—after winning a wrestling match. Visible from the second room of the apartment is the so-called "pope's elevator," a circular ramp designed by **Bramante** that allowed the pontiff to ride to the upper floors on the back of a mule.

When the sun is shining, the **Octagonal Courtyard** is a good place to pause because the niches around this outdoor court display some of the Vatican's major sculptural works. The famous *Laocoön,* carved by Hagesandrus of Rhodes, is a moving composition from the second century BC. It depicts a dramatic scene from Virgil's *Aeneid* in which the Trojan priest, Laocoön, and his two sons struggle for their lives against two enormous sea serpents. This was how Athena punished Laocoön for voicing the opinion that something was fishy about the Trojan Horse and that maybe the Trojans shouldn't let it into the city. At some point in antiquity, the sculpture was broken up. In 1506 scattered pieces of the dismembered group were found, and it was reassembled. But in 1905 archaeologist Ludwig Pollak saw what he claimed was the still-missing raised arm of Laocoön in a Roman shop. A second restoration of the sculpture was undertaken in 1957, but later contested.

In another niche of the courtyard stands the sublime *Apollo Belvedere.* Like many of the statues in the museum it is a Roman copy of a Greek bronze from the fourth century BC. Nearby is the *Venus Felix,* a copy of the Aphrodite of Cnidos by Praxiteles, which stirred up prudery when it was first displayed. Also on view are three works sculpted by Antonio Canova around 1800: *Perseus,* holding the severed head of the Medusa (inspired by the *Apollo Belvedere*), and two statues of boxers. The room off the **Octagonal Courtyard** opposite *The Apoxyomenos* is dedicated to animal sculpture. Kind of a marble zoo, here demure Egyptian felines cavort with wild boars and bunny rabbits. The mosaics on the wall and floor were made from tiny chips of marble in the early centuries of the Christian era. To the right, in the **Statue Gallery,** are two celebrated ancient sculptures: the *Sleeping Ariadne* (museum catalog no. 11) and the *Satyr at Rest* (22). Just ahead in the center of the **Room of the Muses** is one of the most influential sculptures of the ancient world— the *Belvedere Torso,* which bears the inscription "Made by Apollonius, Athenian, son of Nestor." The youthful Michelangelo often sketched this first-century Greek statue. Its influence is evident in much of his later work, from the nudes he painted on the

Sistine Chapel ceiling to the slave torsos he left unfinished.

The **Round Room** has a third-century mosaic floor depicting sea gods and a large porphyry basin found near the Senate building in the Forum. The towering gilded *Hercules* (8) dates from the first century BC and was found in the **Teatro di Pompeo** (Theater of Pompey) near Largo Argentina where Julius Caesar was assassinated. Another statue (4) commissioned by Hadrian shows his young favorite, Antinous, this time in the guise of the Greek god *Dionysus.* On one side of the giant *Hercules* is yet another likeness of *Antinous* (6) and on the other is the bearded, forlorn *Hadrian* himself.

Next door in the **Greek Cross Room** are pieces of very rare marble. Two extraordinary peach-colored telamons (architectural supports) flank the doorway, two pink-and-gray granite sphinxes sit next to the exit, and two gigantic coffins made of porphyry sit on the right and left sides of the room. The one resting on panthers was the tomb of Constance, the murderous daughter of Emperor Constantine; the other, originally made for the emperor himself, was used as the tomb of his mother, St. Helen, because Constantine died and was buried in Constantinople. There is also a statue that is believed to be a likeness of *Cleopatra* (21), Caesar's mistress and Antony's wife.

Galleries of the Candelabra, Tapestries, and Maps

A staircase leads to this gallery located in a long corridor lined with windows, originally an open walkway between two papal palaces. The first section of the gallery is named for the monumental marble candlesticks under the arches that were beautifully sculpted almost 2,000 years ago.

The length of the gallery contains a series of heroic Roman nudes, some with fig leaves plastered on, some with them ripped off, depending on the prudery or innocence of the age. In the process many fine sculptures were disfigured; heads, too, sometimes rolled, whereupon another statue's head would be stuck onto a headless body in a mix-and-match fashion. To get some idea of the food served at ancient Roman banquets, be sure to look for the second-century mosaics (12) in this gallery. Using the Vermicelli style, the artist used very small pieces of colored glass sliced off from thin glass tubes. This art form and the pasta of the same name share a picturesque linguistic origin: "little worms."

On the left wall of the central gallery are tapestries made 1524-31 in the Brussels workshop of Pieter van Aeist from designs of Raphael and his students. The one portraying the nativity has accurately drawn animals—

the popes at this time had a private zoo that included many exotic species and a famous baby elephant that Bernini used as the model for his statue in **Piazza Minerva.** There's also a tapestry showing the *Supper at Emmaus,* which depicts the risen Christ appearing to two of his disciples; the perspective lines are so perfect that Christ's eyes follow you as you pass. Notice the carefully drawn bottle and glasses in the wine cooler on the ground.

The final section of this triple gallery contains 40 frescoed maps by cosmographer Ignazio Danti (1580-83). They show intriguing early conceptions of papal lands and other regions of Italy, notably 16th-century Venice, as well as boisterous sea battles. The windows on the right provide a good view of the **Vatican Gardens** with their rolling lawns, pavilions, and spreading trees. Those on the left look down on the **Courtyard of the Pine Cone,** named after a large marble pine cone that stands there, and the **Belvedere Courtyard.**

Raphael Rooms

When Pope Julius II refused to live downstairs in the Borgia apartments created by his detested predecessor Alexander VI, he moved into these new apartments and commissioned the then-25-year-old Raphael to redecorate the walls.

Within the Raphael Rooms:

Room of the Fire (1514-17)

Except for the masterly *Fire in The Borgo,* the frescoes in this room were done by Raphael's helpers based on the master's drawings. The ceiling, however, is by Perugino. The subject of the room's decorations is a great fire that engulfed **St. Peter's Square** in 847. Pope Leo IV extinguished the fire by making the sign of the cross. You can see the first **St. Peter's** in the background. Over the doors is a fresco showing the *Coronation of Charlemagne* in **St. Peter's.**

Room of the Signature (1508-11)

Ceremonial signings of papal bulls or ordinances took place in this room. It is also the location of Raphael's first major fresco, *The Dispute Over the Sacrament;* it was painted when his own style was starting to crystallize. Opposite is the famous *School of Athens,* one of the greatest paintings in the world, renowned for its balance between composition and theme. Raphael painted the ancient Greek philosopher-heroes, whom Renaissance intellectuals were rediscovering, along with some contemporary heroes of his own. In the center, at the top of the steps, is Plato (in fact, a portrait of Leonardo da Vinci) discoursing with Aristotle; note the symbolism of Plato pointing up to the spiritual world while Aristotle points down to earth. The solitary seated figure—with drooping stockings—is officially the philosopher

Heraclitus, but the head is that of Michelangelo. Raphael added him after the painting was finished (and after he had seen the **Sistine Chapel**) as a tribute to his rival. The bent-over bald man on the right holding a compass is Euclid, but it is also a portrait of the architect **Bramante.** In the foreground on the far right, their heads level with the blue-and-white columns, are Il Sodoma (the Sodomist—the nickname of the openly homosexual painter Giovanni Antonio Bazzi of Siena) and, peeking timidly from behind him, Raphael himself in profile. Uncovered during the restoration was a statue of Athena and three handprints on the fresco's veneer—one possibly belonging to Raphael. On the window wall is *Parnassus,* with Apollo playing a lyre, encircled by his muses. Later, unsolicited additions to this room include some early graffiti, among which are some words of praise for Martin Luther dating from the 1527 Sack of Rome and some more recent "scratches" such as the one made by Dubois in 1829. (These later graffiti are in the window embrasure behind the round marble tables that were used for seats in the Renaissance.) Look up and down before leaving this room: It has a gilded ceiling with elegant painted sibyls and a remarkable marble mosaic floor.

Room of Heliodorus (1512-14) There are four important frescoes here by Raphael and his assistants: One documents the *Miracle of Lake Bolsena,* in which a previously skeptical priest sees the host dripping blood onto the altar cloth; another is of Pope Leo I driving Attila the Hun away from Rome in 452. Attila, on a black horse, looks understandably alarmed by the appearance in the sky of the armed Sts. Peter and Paul. The central figure in this painting has had a number of face-lifts: Pope Leo was first modeled on Julius II, the pope who commissioned the work; then, when Julius died, his image was painted over with the likeness of Giovanni de' Medici, the new pope. As it happened, Raphael seemed to have spotted the rising star in the de' Medici court, for he had already painted Giovanni—with a red hat in the left foreground—standing behind the pope. This may be the only great painting where the same figure appears twice. On the opposite wall, in the *Expulsion of Heliodorus,* Raphael's impressive portrait of Pope Julius remains intact, sitting on a portable throne (Raphael painted himself among the throne bearers). The fourth major fresco in this room, the *Deliverance of St. Peter from Prison,* is worth noting for the ethereal light emanating from the angel about to rescue the sleeping St. Peter from prison.

Hall of Constantine (1517-24) After his death, Raphael's assistants decorated this room with frescoes from his sketches. The paintings depict the life of Emperor Constantine, including his conversion to Christianity and his victory over Maxentius in the Battle of Saxa Rubra, a mile north of the still-standing ancient Roman bridge, Ponte Milvio. From the corner of the adjoining **Room of the Chiaroscuro,** a door leads to the extraordinary **Chapel of Nicholas V** with frescoes (1447-51) by the Dominican monk Fra Angelico—the first in a stream of great Renaissance masters lured by the popes from Florence. This tiny jewel of a chapel is exactly as Pope Nicholas left it five centuries ago. The pastel-colored frescoes with gold highlights depict scenes from the lives of two early martyrs, Sts. Stephen and Lawrence. Notice how perfectly drawn the trompe l'oeil brocade is on the lower walls.

Sistine Chapel Built toward the end of the 15th century, the chapel's lower walls were decorated by the finest artists of the Renaissance, including Botticelli, Perugino, Ghirlandaio, Pinturicchio, and Signorelli. Michelangelo later painted the end wall and ceiling (see diagram on page 25).

Since medieval times, the Catholic Church has divided history into three periods: the world before Moses received the law from God; the period that followed the law; and the period after the birth of Christ. Michelangelo's ceiling describes the first era, beginning with the *Creation.* The frescoes on the side walls—painted by the other artists—depict the remaining two periods.

The 10,000 square feet of splendidly restored ceiling was painted by Michelangelo in his mid-thirties. He had first declined the papal commission to repaint the original star-spangled blue ceiling—he considered painting a minor art, not in the same league as architecture or sculpture—and accepted the commission only after the pope threatened war against his native Florence. Mostly working alone, he painted more than 300 figures in just over four years. The theme, the story of humanity before the coming of Christ, is articulated in nine main panels, each set in an architectural framework supported by figures of the prophets, the sibyls, and 20 classical nude youths. In the lunettes (the spaces between the windows) below are portraits of the ancestors of Christ. The center panels depict events from the Book of Genesis, including *The Fall of Man, Noah's Sacrifice, The Flood,* and *Noah's Drunkenness.* In the central panel, *The Creation of Adam,* there is an almost palpable dramatic tension in the space between the fingers of Adam and the hand of God.

Unfortunately, the chapel walls oozed humidity, and within a century of its creation, restorers made some ill-advised attempts (including using wine and olive oil) to protect Michelangelo's work. More recently (1985-92), the ceiling was completely refurbished.

THE SISTINE CHAPEL

Walls

A **The Baptism of Christ**
Perugino, Ghirlandaio, Fra Diamante

B **The Temptation of Christ**
Botticelli, Fra Diamante

C **The Calling of the First Apostles**
Ghirlandaio

D **The Sermon on the Mount**
Rosselli, Unknown

E **The Handing Over of the Keys**
Perugino, Unknown, Botticelli

F **The Last Supper**
Rosselli, Botticelli, Ghirlandaio

G **The Resurrection of Christ**
Paludano (replaces Ghirlandaio),
Botticelli, Ghirlandaio

H **The Disputation Over the Body of Moses**
de Lecce (replaces lost Signorelli),
Ghirlandaio, Unknown

I **The Testament of Moses**
Signorelli, Botticelli, Rosselli

J **The Punishment of Korah, Datan, and Abiron**
Rosselli, Fra Diamante

K **Moses Receives the Tablets of the Law**
Rosselli, Fra Diamante

L **The Crossing of the Red Sea**
Rosselli, Fra Diamante

M **Events from the Life of Moses**
Botticelli, Unknown, Ghirlandaio

N **The Journey of Moses**
Perugino, Ghirlandaio, Botticelli

O **The Last Judgment**
Michelangelo

Michelangelo's Ceiling

1 The Division of Day from Night
2 The Creation of the Heavens
3 The Division of the Land from the Waters
4 The Creation of Adam
5 The Creation of Eve
6 The Fall of Man
7 Noah's Sacrifice
8 The Flood
9 Noah's Drunkenness
10 Zacharia
11 Judith and Holofernes
12 David and Goliath
13 The Punishment of Haman
14 Jonah
15 The Brazen Serpent

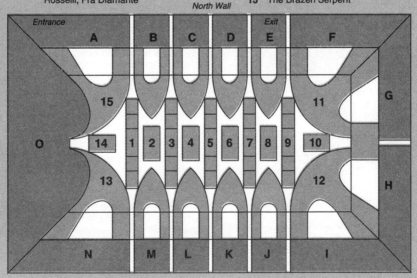

The previous restorers' additions, plus centuries of accumulated grime caused by the smoke from the altar candles and torches, had to be removed. The project was financed by Japan's Nippon Television Network, which gave the refurbishers $18 million over 15 years in exchange for exclusive rights to all forms of photography of the restoration work and the restored frescoes. Among the restorers' discoveries was that Michelangelo used paper cartoons that were transferred by pin dots (still visible) for the broad outlines. He then painted swiftly and directly onto the wet plaster with no further sketching. The cleaning also revealed that the ceiling is brilliantly colored and that Michelangelo may

have been more influenced than previously thought by the bright colors of the Venetian masters who were his contemporaries. Although most scholarly opinion about the restoration has been solidly positive, a few wonder if the ceiling isn't too clean now and whether some of the previous uniformity and modeling may have gone down the drain with the dirt.

Three decades after painting the ceiling, Michelangelo was commissioned by the Medici pope Clement VII to paint the wall behind the chapel's altar. Then in his sixties, Michelangelo devoted almost seven years to *The Last Judgment* and in the end painted his drooping face onto the shorn skin of

St. Bartholomew. To create a sense of sky—and as if to obliterate the wall itself—he ground semiprecious lapis lazuli into a fine powder and applied it to the wall to form a glowing, celestial blue background in which figures of the saved and damned rise and fall.The nakedness of many of the figures shocked some of the pious after Michelangelo finished the masterpiece. They were further agitated at seeing Christ without a beard. Biagio da Cesena (the papal chapel's master of ceremonies) called the nudes "indecent" and said they were "better suited to a bath-house or roadside wine shop than to the pope's chapel."

Michelangelo's reply was to paint Biagio's head onto the figure with an ass's ears in the lower right-hand corner of the *Inferno.* Twenty-three years later, another pope, Pius IV, ordered Daniel da Voltera to paint loincloths on all of the nudes. He need not have bothered; bad glues and candle smut eventually made this fresco nearly invisible. When it was cleaned in 1994, 15 of the loincloths were removed, but the others, some of which could not be taken off without damaging the fresco, were left intact over the no longer offensive parts.

The **Sistine Chapel** is now used only when the College of Cardinals meets to elect a new pope. To protect the chapel, a high-tech climate control system was installed in 1993. Before that, the windows were opened, and pigeons from the square often flew in to see what all the fuss was about. Bring binoculars or hand mirrors for viewing the ceiling. No photographs are permitted. The best time for serious viewing, unless you like neck strain and elbow-to-elbow crowds, is just before closing time or when the pope has a public audience or is giving his blessing in St. Peter's Square.

Borgia Apartment These papal quarters were built in 1492 by Alexander VI, the Borgia pope. He and his successors lived here until they were replaced a century later by today's papal apartments. Note the scratches on the window seats for a board game popular at the time in **Room VI.** The walls were frescoed by Pinturicchio, and if they could speak, what tales they would tell. Alexander Borgia, whose family crest was appropriately a bull, was a tough, unscrupulous, and violent man. He fathered several children out of wedlock, one of whom, the well-known Lucrezia Borgia, was ironically the model for a portrait of *St. Catherine* in **Room V, The Room of the Saints.** In **Room VII** Pope Alexander is shown kneeling piously before the Risen Christ, and the young soldier standing nearby is thought to be his son Cesare, while the young Roman (not in uniform) is Cesare's brother, whom he murdered along with one of Lucrezia's

husbands. The apartments and nearby rooms house the **Collection of Modern Religious Art** opened in 1973 by Pope Paul VI. It includes paintings and sculpture by contemporary masters from August Rodin to Ben Shahn.

Vatican Picture Gallery (Pinacoteca)

Some of the world's most famous masterpieces fill the 18 rooms of this picture gallery. Paintings are numbered in chronological order starting with the 11th century. Some highlights are: **Room II,** Bernardo Daddi's *Madonna del Magnificat,* a masterpiece of early Italian Renaissance art, and Giotto's *Stefaneschi Triptych* in the center of the room; **Room IV,** Melozzo da Forlì's heavenly choir of angelic musicians; **Room VIII,** works by Raphael, including his luminous *Transfiguration* and eight tapestries in silk and wool with silver thread highlights intended for the lower walls of the **Sistine Chapel; Room IX,** Leonardo da Vinci's ghostly unfinished portrait of *St. Jerome;* **Room XII,** Bellini's *Entombment* and Caravaggio's darkly real *Deposition,* or *Descent from the Cross,* which Napoleon admired so much he had it carried off to the Louvre. Finally, in **Room XII** is a rare painting of a youth by the man who designed **St. Peter's Square**—Gian Lorenzo Bernini, better known for architecture and sculpture than painting.On the way out of the museums, don't miss the fresco of Michelangelo's original plan for **St. Peter's.** It's over the doorway just before the **Vatican Library.** If you compare it to the present plan, you'll see how right he was—his is much more dynamic.

The Borgo

The blocks in this medieval neighborhood are called **Borgo Pio, Borgo Santo Spirito, Borgo Sant'Angelo,** and other names developed from the German word "burg" (town). From the Middle Ages on, generations of Saxon innkeepers ran hostels and taverns here, with names like The Sun, The Helmet, and The Maiden. This custom survives today in the dozens of eateries and shops catering to 20th-century pilgrims.

5 **Girarrosto Dal Toscano** ★★$$ Even if you think that your feet won't carry you another inch, force them to totter the three short blocks almost straight down from the **Vatican Museums** to this pleasant dining spot specializing in Tuscan cuisine. Pasta dishes include *bombolotti Giulio Cesare* (elbow-shaped pasta in a sausage-and-cream sauce), *fettuccine ai funghi porcini* (with wild mushrooms), and *pici alla toscana* (home-made spaghetti with a spicy game sauce). Such typical Tuscan favorites as *fagioli al fiasco* (white beans slowly steamed in a pot then dressed in olive oil and garlic) and grilled T-bone steak are also on the menu. Finish the meal with a cream-filled cake that has hot chocolate poured on at the last moment or a

double chocolate mousse. Both indoor and outdoor tables are available. ♦ Tu-Su lunch and dinner; closed in August. Reservations recommended. Via Germanico 56 (between Via Ottaviano and Via Vespasiano). 39725717

6 Paoline Multimedia Nuns run this well-stocked shop, which sells books, tapes, and films in four languages, including English. Most are about Christianity and the city of Rome. ♦ M afternoon; Tu-F; Sa morning. Via Mascherino 94 (at Borgo Angelico). 6872354; fax 68308093

HOTEL S. ANNA

7 Hotel Sant'Anna $$ Built in the 16th century, this small hotel now has 20 air-conditioned rooms with private baths and telephones, a breakfast buffet room (included in the rate), and courtyard for the aperitif hour. Two rooms on the ground floor are designed for people with disabilities. ♦ Borgo Pio 133 (at Via Falco). 68801602; fax 68308717

8 Leonine Wall After the Saracens raided the Vatican treasury in AD 849, Pope Leo IV built this defensive wall to contain the area from the hill behind **St. Peter's** to the river. Part of it includes an enclosed passageway running along the top of the wall that the popes used to escape from the Vatican to the fortified **Castel Sant'Angelo.** ♦ Along Borgo Sant'Angelo and Via Corridori

Alfredo a S. Pietro

9 Alfredo a San Pietro ★★$$ Homemade fettuccine is the bill of fare at this long-established trattoria. Top it with one of the traditional sauces, *al sugo* (tomato and basil), *ai frutti di mare* (seafood), or the rarer *al limone* (lemon, parmesan cheese, and butter). ♦ M-Th, Sa-Su lunch and dinner. Via Corridori 60 (at Via Rusticucci). 6869554

10 Caffè San Pietro $ This coffee shop is also a luncheon cafeteria, which makes it a good place for a quick sandwich. In the

category of dubious honors: The young Turk who tried to assassinate Pope John Paul II had his coffee here before entering **St. Peter's Square.** ♦ Daily. Via della Conciliazione 40 (at Via Rusticucci). 6864927

11 Ancora Among other stock, this English-language bookstore carries all of the Vatican's videocassettes and audio tapes. ♦ M-F; Sa morning. Via della Conciliazione 63 (at Via Padre Pancrazio Pfeiffer). 6868820

12 Palazzo dei Convertendi (Converts' Building) Raphael died in this building designed by **Donato Bramante** in 1510. Once located in another part of Rome, it was dismantled block by block and reassembled here in the late 1930s. It is not open to the public. ♦ Via della Conciliazione 34 (between Via dell'Erba and Via Rusticucci)

13 Palazzo dei Penitenzieri (Penitents' Building) Built in 1480 by Cardinal Domenico della Rovere—according to plans by **Baccio Pontelli**—as an institute for the priests hearing confessions at the basilica, this palace's facade recalls that of Palazzo Venezia. The Vatican Secretary of State uses the hotel today (see below) as an unofficial guest house. ♦ Via della Conciliazione 33 (at Via dei Cavalieri del Santo Sepolcro)

Within the Palazzo dei Penitenzieri:

Hotel Columbus $$ This hotel has a handsome ornate dining room, frescoed public rooms, and an attractive courtyard. Some of the 100 guest rooms are spartan, but all have private baths. Amenities include breakfast, air-conditioning, and parking facilities. Best of all, it's a stone's throw from **St. Peter's.** ♦ 6865435; fax 6864874

Within the Hotel Columbus:

In the summer 1,600 people tour the Sistine Chapel hourly. July sees an excess of 200,000 visitors, and the total for the year is more than 2 million.

The census of 1526 lists the following businesses practiced in Rome: 236 hoteliers, 134 bakeries, 100 salami shops, 90 spice sellers, 88 butchers, 76 gardeners, and 58 water sellers.

The Jubilee of 2000

The new millennium has caused a flurry of activity the world over. Rome, especially, has been busy gearing up for the year 2000, as it coincides with the Jubilee—a profound religious celebration with roots reaching back to biblical times.

The Law of Moses decreed a sabbatical year every seven years, when debts were forgiven, slaves were freed, and land was allowed to rest. Every "seven times seven years" (rounded up to 50), a particularly important year of pardon and penitence occurred. Traditionally this special event was announced by the *Jobel,* an ancient Hebrew horn, and thus the name, Jubilee. Pope Boniface VIII revived the practice in 1300, inviting Christians to visit the Eternal City on a ritual journey of redemption. That year, one million pilgrims heeded the call. Ever since, the Catholic Church has begun each century with a Holy Year, encouraging Christians to do penance and to visit Rome. To date, 26 major and 120 special Jubilees have taken place.

With more than 25 million visitors expected in 2000 (almost double that of a typical year), modern-day Rome has spent nearly a decade and $1.5 billion primping and building. Jubilee-related improvement projects include expanded roadways, increased parking capacity, and new pedestrian zones. At the **Roman Forum,** long-unused sewage tunnels were converted to walkways, so tourists can walk undisturbed from one part of the forum to another. The subway system was extended to include a line from the edge of Rome to stations near the **Vatican.** A simultaneous cultural initiative led to the complete overhaul of more than a hundred churches, five major museums, and scores of archaeological sites. The beautiful mosaics of **Santa Maria Maggiore** were restored, toilets were installed on the roof of **St. Peter's,** and the columns of **Bernini's** colonnade around **St. Peter's Square** were scrubbed white. To eliminate the often endless lines at the **Vatican Museums,** an entrance complex—with gift shops, cafes, and waiting areas—was erected.

From Christmas Eve 1999 to early in 2001, an unprecedented number of churches, museums, and monuments will open their doors—and stay open longer, often all day and sometimes even into the evening. Special Jubilee masses, festivals, and concerts will also be in full swing. Throughout the year, several churches, including the **Basilica di Santa Maria Sopra Minerva,** will host more than 200 concerts and 3 dozen operas celebrating women in music. Choral works spanning the centuries—including Verdi's *Requiem,* Schumann's *Scenes from Goethe's Faust,* and Bach's *St. Mark Passion*—will be performed at **Auditorio Pio XII** and **Auditorium di Roma.** A full calendar of art exhibits will showcase secular and religious works, from Borromini and Rubens to ancient, medieval, and Beaux-Arts traditions.

For those visiting Rome during 2000, the greatest challenge may be finding accommodations. Though hotel space is limited, the Italian governmant has enacted new laws that encourage families to convert their homes into bed-and-breakfast inns. However, budget lodging—like nun-run guest houses and special "railway hotels," with couchette-style beds in a series of trains parked in stations around the city—will likely be booked solid by religious pilgrims.

The problem of price-gouging, a seemingly inevitable result of such a huge influx of visitors, is being addressed by a government charter establishing quality services at agreed prices. Businesses that adopt the charter will be able to display a yet-to-be-decided special logo; in theory, the logo's appearance should guarantee fair play.

To help visitors make the most of their visit, specially created Jubilee information centers staffed by English-speaking personnel have been set up around Rome: at the **Museo del Risorgimento** (Tuesday-Saturday, 06/69924664) in **Piazza Venezia;** in the **Mazzoniana** wing of the **Stazione Termini,** on the Via Giovanni Giolitti side; and within the **Auditorio Pio XII,** on Via della Conciliazione. E-mail access (agenzia@romagiubileo.it) and a web site (www.romagiubileo.it) with links to other sites are also available.

La Veranda ★$$$ The Renaissance atmosphere in the frescoed dining room or the pampering under the sun umbrellas in the courtyard just might make up for the standard but reliable continental fare served here. It's very popular for weddings and banquets, so be sure to book ahead. ◆ Daily lunch and dinner. Reservations recommended. 6872973

14 Palazzo Torlonia A smaller version of Andrea Bregno's **Palazzo della Cancelleria,** this handsome edifice was built in 1504 with materials sacked from the **Colosseum.** It was first owned by an Italian cardinal; the next proprietor, the British monarchy, quartered its ambassador here until Henry VIII broke with the Catholic Church. The French Tourlan family (which made its fortune providing victuals to Napoleon's troops during their occupation of Rome) now owns the building, and the current Prince Torlonia (the name has been Italianized) is among the highest ranking laypersons in the Church. The building is not open to the public. ◆ Via della Conciliazione 30 (at Via dell'Erba)

15 Chiesa di Santa Maria in Traspontina (Church of St. Mary's at the Bridge) This Carmelite church was named after an ancient Roman bridge that once stood nearby. Built 1556-87, it boasts a magnificent altarpiece. Before Mussolini constructed his boulevard through the neighborhood, a covered walkway led from the church, past gardens, and toward **St. Peter's Square.** ♦ Via della Conciliazione 14 (at Vicolo del Campanile)

16 Auditorio Pio XII (Pius XII Auditorium)
Owned by the Vatican, this has been the temporary home of Rome's **Santa Cecilia** symphony orchestra; at press time, the new **Auditorium di Roma** (see page 147), designed by **Renzo Piano**, was scheduled to become the orchestra's main stage. Concert hours vary, but most performances are at 5 and 8:30PM. ♦ Via della Conciliazione 4 (at Via Traspontina). Box office 68801044

17 Hostaria Roberto ★★$ The menu here is from central Italy, with its traditional vegetables prepared in myriad ways. Try the *saltimbocca alla Romana* (veal rolls with cheese and sage in a wine sauce)—it will literally "jump-in-the-mouth." A reliable and economical place to lunch on Sunday after the pope's appearance in the square at noon. ♦ M, W-Su lunch and dinner. Borgo Pio 60 (at Vicolo delle Palline). 68803957

18 Dolceborgo Pasticceria This hole-in-the-wall bakery sells fresh pastries, including the Neapolitan *sfogliatella* (a ricotta-filled sweet) and ice cream. Sandwiches are also available. ♦ Tu-Su. No credit cards accepted. Borgo Pio 142 (at Vicolo delle Palline). 68802779

19 Hostaria Orfeo da Cesaretto ★★$$
The meal begins with crunchy fresh bread, dipped in first-pressed olive oil. *Spaghetti alle vongole veraci* (with double-horn clams in their shells), *risotto verde*, and *tagliolini alla spigola* (ribbon pasta with delicate whitefish) are good first courses. Entrées include *piccata al limone* (thin veal slices in lemon sauce), *filetto al Barolo* (steak fillet in red-wine sauce), and fresh fish cooked to order. Pizza baked in a wood-burning oven is available in the evening. For dessert try the homemade crème brûlée. ♦ Tu-Su lunch and dinner. Vicolo d'Orfeo 20 (at Borgo Sant'Angelo). 6879269

20 Hostaria Tre Pupazzi ★$ Plain Roman cooking, like potato gnocchi and *baccalà* (dried codfish), is served here. There are always plenty of fresh vegetables and fresh fruit for dessert. This dining spot is located on the corner of Via dei Tre Pupazzi (Street of the Three Puppets), so named for a fragment of medieval sculpture set in the wall near the

restaurant's side door. ♦ M-Sa lunch and dinner; closed in August. Borgo Pio 183 (at Via dei Tre Pupazzi). 6868371

21 Da Romolo alla Mole Adriana ★$$ This restaurant occupies the site of an ancient dock beside **Castel Sant'Angelo,** where an inn once served river captains and their crews. Today's trattoria has preserved this old-fashioned air, but the boat traffic has been replaced by an endless stream of cars. Don't be put off; this is a culinary island of such traditional Roman cuisine as *spaghetti alla carbonara* (with eggs, cheese, and bacon). Pizza is also served in the evening. ♦ Tu-Su lunch and dinner. Via di Porta Castello 19 (at Borgo Vittorio). 6861603

22 Hotel Atlante Star $$$ Though its lobby is beginning to show wear and tear, this hotel boasts a few frills: Guests with advance reservations are picked up at the airport and whisked to the hotel by limousine; all 61 rooms have phones and private baths, and some have terraces; and the 8 suites have large circular Jacuzzis. The same management also runs the more modest **Atlante Garden,** a short distance away. ♦ Via Giovanni Vitelleschi 34 (between Largo Porta Castello and Via dei Bastioni). 6873233, 1678/62038 toll free in Italy; fax 6872300; atlante.star@atlantehotels.com; www.atlantehotels.com

Within the Hotel Atlante Star:

Les Etoiles ★★★★$$$ The panoramic rooftop terraces of this dining spot are among the best places to count the towers, domes, and campaniles of the Roman skyline—or film **St. Peter's** from close range. Enjoy an aperitif and dinner outdoors or inside where there is live piano music nightly. Despite such offerings as grilled shrimp and sea bass, the menu emphasizes meat dishes: Try the duck breast with wild fruit and balsamic vinegar or the beef carpaccio. ♦ Via dei Bastioni 1. 6893434; fax 6872300.

23 Castel Sant'Angelo The bulk of this structure (illustrated below), one of the most familiar silhouettes of Rome, was commissioned in AD 135 by Hadrian to serve as his mausoleum. The emperor died in 138, and the building was finished in 139 under his successor, Antoninus Pius. Personal grandeur prompted the monument, but so did necessity: There was no space left across the river in the

Mausoleum of Augustus, the older imperial burial chamber. The structure originally looked something like a tiered wedding cake on a square platter: The foundation, about 275 feet on each side, supported a circular tomb of marble-faced brick; a columned portico ran around the outside, and on top of that was a small round temple set in a garden planted with cypresses. Statues adorned the upper parapets, including one of Hadrian as a sun god driving a four-horse chariot.

With the building of the **Aurelian Walls** around the city in the third century, the mausoleum lay within the Roman defenses—this was the beginning of its transformation from monument to fortress. When Goths attacked the city in 410, the Romans fled into the tomb for refuge and hurled Hadrian's statues down on the enemies below. The building acquired its present name in 590. The city was suffering an outbreak of plague, and Pope Gregory the Great ordered all Romans to participate in a procession to the **Vatican** to pray for the city's deliverance. When Gregory saw a vision of the Archangel Michael hovering over Hadrian's tomb, he knew his prayers had been answered. A statue of St. Michael was soon hoisted atop the mausoleum, a chapel built inside, and the name officially became **Castel Sant'Angelo.** The conversion to fortress was completed during the medieval power conflict between the papacy and the noble Roman families. The square base was chipped away to create a protective hollow ring, and four corner towers were added. The popes moved from their traditional Lateran Palace residence into the **Vatican** and constructed a half-milelong fortified passageway connecting it to the safety of the fortress. When the Borgia pope

Alexander VI fled here in 1492, he built sumptuous apartments for himself with frescoed walls and all the creature comforts. But life inside the castle was not comfortable for everybody: It was also the papal prison and the site of numerous executions. Benvenuto Cellini, the 16th-century Florentine goldsmith, did time here, as did the heretical monk Giordano Bruno. In 1870 the Italian government claimed the castle as state property, and 30 years later the composer Giacomo Puccini set the climax of his opera *Tosca* on its parapets. During World War II the fortress came full circle when it served as an air-raid shelter. Today it is one of Rome's most interesting museums, and the gardens surrounding it are a popular park.

Just inside the museum's entrance are three scale models of the building in its ancient, medieval, and Renaissance incarnations. Take a moment to study these before mounting the long, winding ramp that leads up through the structure and through history. The ramp (which has vestiges of the original mosaic pavement) goes over a drawbridge and past the chamber before it emerges in the main courtyard, the **Courtyard of the Cannonballs.** High in the wall next to the sepulchral chamber, which once held Hadrian's remains, is a plaque with his epitaph in Latin written by the emperor himself:

"Vague, wandering soul
Guest and companion of my body
prepare now to descend to places pallid,
    rigid and bare
Your play at last has ended."

Above the courtyard are the papal apartments. In the **Pauline Room** note the painted trompe l'oeil doorway and the mysterious dark figure

Castel Sant'Angelo

MARJORIE J. VOGEL/RHODE ISLAND ORIGINALS

climbing the stairs, who legend claims is the out-of-wedlock son of one of the Orsini popes. Also on this level are three huge 16th-century strongboxes where the papal treasury was kept. Nearby is the elegant papal bathroom frescoed by Raphael's studio with motifs of classical mythology. This bath, engineered in the 16th century, was one of the first private tubs to have hot water since the days of the Roman Empire. Continue all the way to the upper terrace at the foot of the huge bronze statue that gives the castle its name. This is also where the heroine of *Tosca* leaps to her death—supposedly into the Tiber. ♦ Admission. Tu-Sa 9AM-10PM; Su 8AM-8PM. Lungoteveres Castello and Vaticano. 6819111

Within Castel Sant'Angelo:

Michael's Sandwich Bar $ Set on the castle's top level, this charming cafe has outdoor tables with magnificent views of **St. Peter's**, the Tiber, and the rest of Rome.

The bill of fare is limited to salads, sandwiches, and sometimes a pasta dish, but the location and views make a lunch here worthwhile even if you are not interested in the museums. ♦ Tu-Sa; Su morning. 68191167

24 Ponte Sant'Angelo Designed by **Hadrian,** this bridge is the best approach to his mausoleum. The three central arches are original; those at either end were added in the 17th century and rebuilt in 1892. The bridge was the scene of a tragedy during the 1450 Holy Year when tens of thousands of pilgrims, who had gathered to see St. Veronica's veil exhibited, panicked as they returned to the city's center across this bridge. In the ensuing crush, 170 people were killed. This bridge was also where the young Beatrice Cenci, accused of incest and patricide, was beheaded. The poet Shelley immortalized her story in a verse drama, *The Cenci.* The angels carrying the symbols of Christ's passion (1672) come from Bernini's workshop.

Bests

Maureen B. Fant
Author/Editor/Translator/Publisher

A stroll along the Aurelian Walls—It looks like a symbol of the grandeur that was Rome, but it really marks the beginning of the end. When Rome was truly great, there was no need for walls.

Mercato di Piazza Testaccio—Rome has many large public markets, but this is mine, located in the epicenter of traditional Roman food, the **Testaccio** neighborhood near the old slaughterhouse. I gauge the seasons not by the calendar but by what's new at the market. Another reason I'm partial to it is that it is named, in Roman dialect, for a singular archaeological site, **Monte Testaccio,** a large hill of ancient amphora fragments.

The Terme Museum—I love to walk around and read the ancient epitaphs being used as statue bases—the closest link we have with the ordinary people of ancient Rome.

The Colosseum—Our neighborhood monument.

Brian Williams
Illustrator/Author

Secret Treasures: Rome is so rich a city that it can hide, with impunity, sights and monuments that anywhere else would be required seeing. Everyone who has wandered near **Piazza Navona** has been enchanted by **Pietro da Cortona**'s exterior for **Chiesa di Santa Maria della Pace,** filling its tiny square in a knockout play of convex and concave forms. There are no signs, though, to the flanking door that leads you to the cloister, an early masterpiece of **Bramante,** or into the church itself, where, among other curiosities, there are Michelangelesque frescoes by Raphael.

Nearby, in Via dei Coronari, the **Chiesa di San Salvatore in Lauro** hides a few pretty *quattrocento* cloisters and a nicely restored chamber with an elegant mannerist ceiling fresco by Salviati. Ask the gracious young *signora* for permission to look around.

Farther afield, between the **Colosseum** and the **Lateran Palace,** the **Basilica di San Clemente** is justly revered for its treasures on many levels: Medieval and Renaissance in the current church; ancient fading frescoes in the older church below; and farther down still, Roman brick paving, rushing aqueduct, a mossy **Mithraeum.** In the same neighborhood but less well known is the strange convent and **Chiesa di Santi Quattro Coronati.** Fortified from the days when it was surrounded by meadows and bandits, the convent's high dilapidated forecourts lead to the church. Now the tricky part: A tiny medieval cloister can just be seen through a tiny window; if the moment is right you might be let in to wander under the arcades of potted plants and thousand-year-old carvings. Also, in the last courtyard before the church, try buzzing the convent for admission to the small **Oratory of San Silvestro,** whose vivid Byzantine frescoes transport one to the Rome of 1246. The cloistered nuns will accept your offering for the visit through a rotating dumbwaiter and pass you a key.

Getting Around: Do as the Romans do. Buy or rent a cheap little *motorino,* especially in August when traffic is light, and ride and park your scooter anywhere. Traffic cops, increasingly strict about keeping unauthorized autos out of the city center, still don't seem to notice when Vespas drive—or drive the wrong way—down a restricted street. Insurance, helmets, two-on-a-one seater? Who cares?

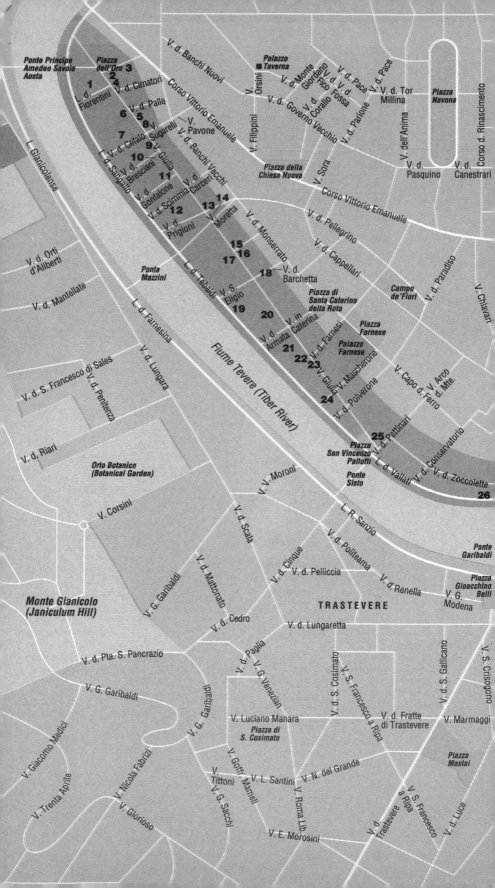

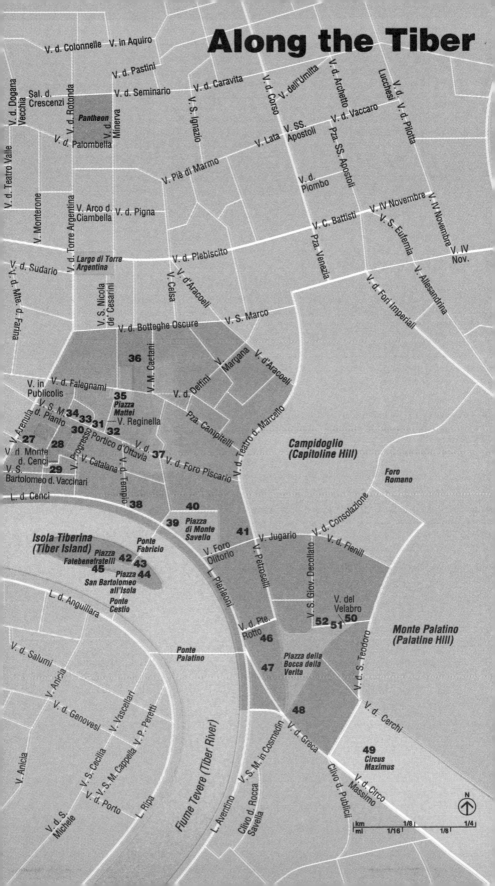

Along the Tiber

V. d. Colonnelle   V. in Aquiro

V. d. Pastini

V. d. Dogana Vecchia

Sal. d. Crescenzi

V. d. Rotonda

V. d. Seminario

V. d. Caravita

V. d. Corso

V. d. Umiltà

V. d. Archetto

Lucchesi

V. d. Pilotta

Pantheon

V. d. Minerva

V. d. Palombella

V. S. Ignazio

V. d. Vaccaro

V. SS. Apostoli

Pza. SS. Apostoli

V. Lata

V. d. Piombo

V. Teatro Valle

V. Monterone

V. Arco d. Ciambella

V. d. Pigna

V. Piè di Marmo

V. C. Battisti

V. IV Novembre

V. S. Eufemia

V. IV Novembre

V. IV Nov.

V. d. Sudario

V. Torre Argentina

V. d. Plebiscito

Pza. Venezia

V. Allesandrina

V. d. Fori Imperiali

V. d. Mte. d. Farina

Largo di Torre Argentina

V. S. Nicola de' Cesarini

V. Celsa

V. d'Aracoeli

V. S. Marco

V. d. Bottegue Oscure

36

V. in Publicolis

V. d. Falegnami

V. M. Caetani

V. Margana

V. d'Aracoeli

35

V. d. Delfini

Piazza Mattei

V. Reginella

Pza. Canipitelli

V. Teatro d. Marcello

Campidoglio (Capitoline Hill)

V. S. M. d. Pianto

34 33 31

30

32

Portico d'Ottavia

V. d. Tempio

V. d. Foro Piscario

Foro Romano

27

V. d. Monte d. Cenci

28

V. Progresso

V. Catalana

37

29

V. S. Bartolomeo d. Vaccinari

V. d. Arenula

L. d. Cenci

38

V. d. Consolazione

V. d. Fienill

40

39

Piazza di Monte Savello

41

V. Jugario

Isola Tiberina (Tiber Island)

Piazza Fatebenefratelli

42 43

Ponte Fabricio

V. Foro Olitorio

V. Petroselli

V. S. Giov. Decollato

V. del Velabro

45

44

Piazza San Bartolomeo all'Isola

Ponte Cestio

V. Pierleoni

52 51 50

Monte Palatino (Palatine Hill)

L. d. Anguillara

V. d. Salumi

Ponte Palatino

V. d. Pte. Rotto

46

V. d. S. Teodoro

V. d. Cerchi

V. Anicia

V. d. Genovesi

V. Vascellari

47

Piazza della Bocca della Verita

V. S. Cecilia

V. S. M. Cappella

V. P. Peretti

48

V. d. Greca

49 Circus Maximus

V. Anicia

V. d. Porto

L. Ripa

Fiume Tevere (Tiber River)

V. S. M. in Cosmedin

V. d. Circo Massimo

V. d. S. Michele

L. Aventino

Clivo d. Rocca Savella

Clivo d. Publici

N

km mi   1/16   1/8   1/8   1/4

Along the Tiber

Rivers were more than bodies of water to the ancient Romans—they were gods. And Rome's main river, the Tiber, has always played an important role in its history. It was the major means of transport for most goods—from marble to wine—that were imported from the far corners of the empire. The city's first marketplace, the **Forum Boarium** (Bovine Market), was at the Tiber's edge. A trading post where animals and hides could be swapped or a goatskin of wine bartered for a clay pot, the market was probably established in the eighth century BC. For centuries docks lined the Tiber's banks, and small and large boats were pulled upriver by oxen treading well-worn tracks along its high banks. The Tiber also contributed to the food supply—its waters once held over 100 varieties of fish, including trout, salmon, and sturgeon. But the river's gifts had a price; it flooded regularly, and its high-water markers can still be spotted on the walls of buildings in the city's oldest quarters.

For the first 16 centuries of Rome's existence, people avoided living in the marshy and malaria-ridden areas bordering the river. But during the Middle Ages, when pilgrims flocked to Rome by the thousands—first to do penance and then to visit the new **St. Peter's Basilica**—regular routes were established along the Tiber leading to the **Vatican**. This area soon became built up with shops, inns, and taverns. For centuries the **Ponte Sant'Angelo** bore most of the traffic, but during the Renaissance, a new street, **Via Giulia**, connecting to the **Vatican Bridge** (now called **Ponte Vittorio Emanuele**), was designed to provide an alternative route. This street soon became one of the most popular addresses for the newly wealthy, who built impressive palazzi along it, with backyards facing the Tiber. Today this milelong street is a pedestrians-only shopping area, and the palazzi have been transformed into antiques shops and restaurants.

The **Aurelian Walls**, which gave protection to the Trastevere district for the first time, were built in AD 271. When that area became popular, the Jews who lived there were forced to move to the other side of the Tiber, to a district that would become a locked ghetto in the 16th century. Today about 2,000 Jewish residents live here in the shadow of Rome's distinctive synagogue.

Just south of this area are the ruins of the **Circus Maximus**, the stadium where the chariot races of ancient times took place. In the river between the **Ghetto** and Trastevere is **Isola Tiberina**, the only island in the Tiber, where the art of healing has been practiced for more than 2,000 years. Ancient Romans brought their sick slaves here; later, plague victims were quarantined on the island; still later, an order of monks built a famous teaching hospital here. Today the island is the site of one of the city's most popular maternity wards.

Until the late 19th century both sides of the Tiber were lined with sloping banks that came down to the river's edge. They were covered with trees and flowers and inhabited by fishermen and farmers and a few scattered country taverns. But after two disastrous floods, one in 1853 and another in 1870, the Minister of Public Works of the newly formed Italian Republic approved a plan to build high stone embankments. The walls now contain the river's devastating floods, but they have also changed its character forever. The only reminders of its past are the fishermen who gather here on Sunday morning, the sycamore trees that stand along the river's banks, and the occasional flock of cormorants that each winter still descend from Northern Europe to join the swarms of gulls that inhabit the Tiber—the river that was once a god.

Via Giulia

In medieval times the only access to **St. Peter's Square** for the swarms of pilgrims from all over Europe was through the narrow streets of **Via del Pellegrino** and **Via dei Banchi Vecchi**. In his autobiography, the 16th-century goldsmith Benvenuto Cellini tells of the gangs of brigands, pickpockets, and unscrupulous curio hawkers who made the narrow pilgrim route unpleasant and hazardous. In an early attempt at urban planning, Via Giulia—named for Pope Julius II (1503-13)—was cut through the mass of medieval hovels as a way to bring more pilgrims into the papal city.

When the street was newly opened, real estate was cheap, and artists rushed to buy property; **Sangallo** the architect, Raphael the painter, and Cellini himself all lived here. Buildings on the west side of the street once had gardens in the back that sloped down to the **Tiber.** Originally, **Bramante** was going to design all the buildings to unify the architectural style. This plan never materialized, but a hundred years later Via Giulia was the most fashionable street in town. Today it is one of Rome's few almost car-free zones.

1 Chiesa di San Giovanni dei Fiorentini In Renaissance times each Italian city-state had its own church in Rome; this was the Florentines' church, dedicated to their patron saint. It should really be called the architects' church, since so many architects worked on it, and **Borromini** is buried inside. At least a dozen architects, including **Raphael, Peruzzi,** and **Michelangelo,** submitted drawings to win the contract to design this church. **Sansovino** won, but had a falling out with the pope, so **Antonio da Sangallo** was chosen to take over the construction. In 1620—a century after the original competition—**Carlo Maderno** added the cupola. The facade, like those of many Florentine churches, was left unfinished, then completed in the 18th century by **Lorenzo Corsini. Borromini**'s tomb is in the floor by the main altar—of necessity simple because he committed suicide. ♦ Via Giulia and Piazza dell'Oro

2 Taverna Giulia ★★$$$ An upscale eating emporium, this place is much beloved by Americans who toured Rome with their parents and now return as retirees. Italian food critics give it fair marks for remaining faithful to the severe principles of Ligurian cooking. Here's where to find out what authentic *pasta al pesto* tastes like, or spaghetti cooked with a few potato slices and green bean slivers, in a sauce of basil, garlic, pine nuts, pure Ligurian olive oil (it has a low acid content), and grated cheese. Anything that has just arrived from Genoa is a good bet. ♦ M-Sa lunch and dinner; closed in August. Reservations recommended. Vicolo dell'Oro 23 (just east of Piazza dell'Oro). 6869768

3 Le Antiquarie Appropriately located just off **Piazza dell'Oro,** this tiny shop sells antique furniture, jewelry, and art objects. The gilded and painted furniture, some old, some not so old, is mostly from the region around Venice, the ceramic dishes are from Faenza, and the costume jewelry is from Hollywood. ♦ M afternoon; Tu-F; Sa morning. Via del Consolato 19 (just west of Corso Vittorio Emanuele). 6896898

4 Via Giulia 82 This charming house was built at the end of the 15th century and is one of the oldest in the area. Pope Julius II gave it to the Confraternity of the Fiorentini. Note the large rustic doorway, the small courtyard, the elegant balcony on the first floor, and the heraldic swirls on the facade—the remains of a form of house decoration called graffiti that was scratched into the fresh cement. ♦ At Via dei Cimatori

5 Raphael's House Legend says this house belonged to the great Renaissance painter and architect. Actually the land was his, but he died before the house, which he designed, was constructed. ♦ Via Giulia 86 (at Vicolo delle Palle)

6 Il Palazzetto (Little Palace) The Florentine **Antonio da Sangallo,** called on to finish the **Chiesa di San Giovanni dei Fiorentini** (see above), had three lots on this street. This house that he had built for himself in 1536 was so admired that when he died, it was quickly bought by a son of Cosimo de' Medici. Today this elegant Renaissance building houses city offices. ♦ Via Giulia 79 (at Vicolo Orbitelli)

7 Palazzo Sacchetti The rear of this palace built in 1542 backs directly onto the river. As a result, it was often flooded—as **Vasari,** who succeeded **Sangallo** as architect, testified in a letter to a friend. Once owned by the Medici, it is a vast structure surrounding a central courtyard. On the river side it has a walled-in formal Italian garden with giant sculpted heads scattered about. On the corner of Via Giulia and Vicolo del Cefalo are the remains of the palazzo's marble fountain—a boy on a dolphin. ♦ Via Giulia 66 (at Vicolo del Cefalo)

8 Via Giulia 102 Through the arched doorway of this building other archways appear to emerge in a trompe l'oeil perspective. Along the back wall of the building's inner courtyard, a delicate pastoral scene reveals a young maiden standing beneath a set of porticoes. The colors of her figure have faded, but the archways are clearly seen and echoed by the design of the building's facade above her. ♦ Between Vicolo Sugarelli and Vicolo delle Palle

9 Chiesa di San Biagio della Pagnotta Built atop a Roman temple, this Eastern Orthodox church is so old that it had already been rebuilt in the 11th century. **G.A. Perletti** added the facade in 1730. A bit of St. Biagio's throat is preserved in a reliquary on the main altar and is considered to have miraculous properties for healing tonsillitis. Pagnotta means "loaf of bread," and on St. Biagio's feast day (2 February) priests hand out small blessed loaves of bread. ♦ Via Giulia (between Via dei Bresciani and Vicolo del Cefalo)

10 Cardinal Hotel $$ Pope Julius II commissioned **Bramante** to design a magnificent municipal building, and giant stones were pillaged from the **Roman Forum** for its construction. Started in the second half of the 15th century, work on the structure was suspended after a few years—both the pope and the artist had died. The unfinished but habitable building served various functions over the years—various cardinals used it as a private mansion, and it even did a turn of duty as the **Hungarian Embassy.** In the late 1970s it was transformed into a hotel and is the only hostelry in this area. All that remains of the original structure are some exterior massive stones on the corner of Via Giulia and Via dei Bresciani. Decor leans heavily toward gilt and red velvet, and the whole place could use a good airing. The 66 rooms, however, are air-conditioned, and some on the fifth floor have balconies with nice views. There's a bar, but no restaurant. ♦ Via Giulia 62 (at Via dei Bresciani); main entrance on Via dei Bresciani. 68802719; fax 6786376

11 Carceri Nuovi (New Prisons) Formerly a prison for minors, only the barred windows of this large structure built in 1827 by **Giuseppe Valadier** face onto Via Giulia. In the old days, when it and the prison next door (hence the plural in the name) were in use, this part of the street was cut off by two heavy chains and wrought-iron palings guarded by sentries. Today it houses the **Museo di Criminologia** (Museum of Criminology), visited mostly by police chiefs and criminologists. ♦ Visits only by special permission from the **Ministry of Justice** (568849). Via del Gonfalone 29 (at Via Giulia). 68300204

12 Oratorio del Gonfalone In medieval times, *gonfalonieri* were flag bearers; the Confraternità dei Gonfalonieri was their guild or protective association. The guild's charitable work provided money for medical assistance, burial costs, and dowries to poor spinsters. However, in the early 16th century a lot of the guild's wealth was diverted into decorating the interior of this oratory designed by **Domenico Castelli.** In 1573 Mannerist painter Federico Zuccari, Europe's best-known painter after the death of Titian, and other artists painted the 12 frescoes of the *Passion of Christ;* be sure to note the figure of Judas, gripping a purse. When Italy was united in 1870, the state confiscated many

unconsecrated Church-owned buildings. The Capitolo di San Pietro, a body of priests who run the **Vatican's** earthly holdings, sued the state over this building and won it back. There are four superb processional candleholders with golden cherubs holding up the lanterns. The two-tone, terra-cotta tile floor (1548) is original. The **Oratorio** is now the site of one of Rome's best chamber-music orchestras—the season runs from November through June. Check *Roma C'è* or daily newspapers for schedules. Tickets are available only by telephone Monday through Friday morning or at the door an hour before the concert. ♦ Vicolo della Scimmia 1B (between Via Giulia and Lungotevere dei Sangallo). 6875952

13 Il Drappo ★★$$ This Sardinian restaurant has only a few, ever-crowded tables (with more in summer in the open-air courtyard). Meals begin with *carta da musica,* the traditional, thin, crunchy Sardinian flat bread. Other specialties include pasta topped with *bottarga,* the poor man's caviar that comes from tuna or mullet roe, *culingiones* (ravioli), and *porceddu* (roasted suckling pig). Desserts include *sebadas,* cheese-filled pastries lightly fried in oil and doused with hot honey, and a delicate prickly pear sorbet. ♦ M-Sa lunch and dinner; closed part of August. Reservations required. Vicolo del Malpasso 9 (between Via dei Banchi Vecchi and Via Giulia). 6877365

14 Chiesa di San Filippo Neri In 1623 Rutilio Brandi from San Gimignano, who suffered from gout, commissioned this now-ruined church as an offering. Today only the facade remains of architect **Filippo Raguzzini's** church. In 1940, Mussolini bulldozed this area for a large road that was supposed to join Ponte Mazzini with the **Chiesa Nuova** on nearby Corso Vittorio Emanuele, but the street never materialized. A tiny fruit-and-vegetable market operates in the little square behind the church Monday through Saturday mornings. ♦ Via Giulia and Via Moretta

L'ARIETE
ASSOCIAZIONE CULTURALE

15 L'Ariete: Artists Cooperative Gallery A high standard of work is on view at this cooperative gallery, where exhibits change monthly. Some figurative painters show their work here, but the majority are abstract artists. No gallery percentage is added to the price of the paintings. Works are reserved during an exhibition and sold directly by the artist afterward. ♦ M-Sa 4-8PM. Via Giulia 140/E (at Via Sant'Aurea). 6875641

R.EG.IV R.VII
PIAZZA
DE' RICCI

16 Palazzo Ricci This nobleman's palace built in 1634 has been converted into elegant private apartments. The facade preserves a rare example of graffiti decoration. Instead of perishable frescoes, many buildings in late Renaissance Rome were decorated in this manner, which required scratching (the meaning of "graffiti") a design into wet plaster. ♦ Via Giulia 146 (at Via Sant'Aurea)

17 Chiesa di Spirito Santo dei Napolitani An ancient church and convent for Dominican sisters stood on this site in the 14th century, and 200 years later it was rebuilt for the Confraternity of the Neapolitans. What is here today is an ornate Neapolitan Baroque church designed by **Carlo Fontana** in 1700. ♦ Via Giulia 20 (between Via San Eligio and Via San Filippo Neri)

18 Via della Barchetta The name of this street means "small boat" because it once ran down to a small ferry slip at the Tiber's edge. Now the part of the street between Via Giulia and Lungotevere dei Tebaldi has been renamed Via San Eligio. This narrow, single-block lane leading to Via di Monserrato is lined with tiny shops and artisan workshops.

On Via della Barchetta:

Hostaria Da Giulio ★★$$ Spilling out into the street in summer is this freshly refurbished small (10 tables) but reliable trattoria. Under its vaulted ceilings, diners can enjoy such well-prepared dishes as fried, mozzarella-stuffed zucchini blossoms and an assortment of veal dishes. ♦ M-Sa lunch and dinner. No. 19. 68806466

19 Chiesa di San Eligio Don't miss this little church down a small side street. Its full name is **Sant'Eligio degli Orefici,** named after the goldsmiths' patron saint. **Raphael** started the building in 1516, but the beautiful dome was added later and changed the style from High Renaissance to Baroque. ♦ Via San Eligio and Lungotevere dei Tebaldi

20 Chiesa di Santa Caterina da Siena This 1526 building comprised the church, oratory, and living quarters for Sienese priests living in Rome. (Note the coat of arms of Siena on the facade.) **Baldassare Peruzzi**'s facade was given a late-Baroque face-lift in 1770 by **Paolo Posi.** ♦ Via Giulia (between Via dell'Armata and Via San Eligio)

20 Palazzo Cisterna The Latin inscription on the facade states that this impressive building (ca. 1560) was designed by the artist **Giacomo della Porta** for his own use. ♦ Via Giulia 163 (between Via dell'Armata and Via San Eligio)

21 Palazzo Falconieri The Oldescalchi princes' coat of arms—an eagle, leopard, and incense burner—appears on the facade of this building, but in 1606 a member of the even more aristocratic Farnese family bought the palace. Three decades later it passed to the Florentine Falconieri family. In 1649 Rome's great Baroque architect, **Francesco Borromini,** added the beautiful, open-arch loggia at the top and the menacing breasted falcons (the Falconieri family symbol) on the facade. The palazzo is not open to the public. ♦ Via Giulia 1 (between Via Mascherone and Via dell'Armata)

22 Chiesa di Santa Maria dell'Orazione e Morte Because the monks who founded this church collected and buried the unclaimed dead, the facade is decorated with skulls and a macabre reminder: "me today, thee tomorrow." It was constructed in 1576 and rebuilt in 1737 by **Ferdinando Fuga.** All but one of the passageways to the nearby river, with large underground halls for storing corpses, were sealed up when the Tiber embankments were built. The walls of the remaining corridor are decorated with human bones. ♦ Via Giulia 261 (between Via Mascherone and Via dell'Armata)

23 Arco di Palazzo Farnese This is Via Giulia's most evocative corner— **Michelangelo**'s vine-draped overhead walkway connects the **Palazzo Farnese** to its outlying buildings on the river's edge (they're now hidden behind the flood embankment and the Lungotevere). Originally this whole wing of the palazzo was to be arcaded and extended to the quay and then to span the river with a new bridge joining the palazzo to its "country" house in Trastevere—the **Villa Farnesina.** The bridge, however, was never built.

Via Giulia was once the widest street in Rome. During the pre-Lenten Carnival season in the 18th century races were run on it, and oxen pulled decorated carts along its cobblestones. Jousts were organized, and an effigy that the horsemen had to pierce with a lance at full gallop was hung from this arch. ♦ Via Giulia and Via dei Farnesi

24 Fontana del Mascherone (Fountain of the Giant Mask) Before **Carlo Rainaldi**'s fountain was built, this was a landing for a ferryboat that crossed the river. Construction began in 1570, but 50 years passed before the fountain was finally joined with water from a new aqueduct, the **Acqua Paola.** During Carnival the fountain was spiked so that the mouth of the mask spewed red wine. ♦ Via Giulia and Via Mascherone

25 Handles As the English name of this unique shop implies, on sale here are tons of door handles in brass, ceramic, and wood. Other brass and copper hardware is also sold, including fireplace equipment and bathroom fixtures. Worldwide shipping is available. ♦ M afternoon; Tu-F; Sa morning. Via dei Pettinari 53 (at Piazza San Vincenzo Pallotti). 68803119

25 Ponte Sisto Hotel $$ At press time, this hotel was scheduled to re-open after extensive renovations. Its central location and larger-than-usual accomodations make it a worthwhile place to stay. It caters primarily to groups, so reserve well in advance. A pleasant outdoor courtyard with trees is a good place to have drinks. ♦ Via dei Pettinari 64 (between Piazza San Vincenzo Pallotti and Via Capo di Ferro). 6868843; fax 68308822

26 Evangelista ★★★$$ Nowhere is the Roman artichoke (bigger and tenderer than others) prepared better than at this wonderful dining spot. Instead of being deep fried, the artichoke is flattened between two bricks and baked in the oven—a method invented by the owner's grandfather. The result is a light, crisp but greaseless, melt-in-your-mouth delicacy. Move on to *fagiano al cognac con polenta di farro* (pheasant cooked in Cognac with spelt). ♦ M-Sa lunch and dinner. Lungotevere dei Vallati 24 (between Via Arenula and Via del Conservatorio); rear entrance on Via delle Zoccolette 11/A (between Via Arenula and Via del Conservatorio). 6875810

27 Pica ★$ This bar-*gelateria* makes some of the best gelato in Rome. In summer there are outdoor tables, and the place stays open until 3AM. Try the *crema di fragoline di bosco* (cream and wild strawberries), *riso* (rice), or one of 60 other flavors. ♦ Daily 8PM-midnight. Via della Seggiola 12 (between Piazza de' Cenci and Via Arenula). 6868405

28 Palazzo Cenci The Cenci family was immensely wealthy when Beatrice, one of Francesco Cenci's 12 children, was born in 1577. Francesco, who was known for his violent temper and brutality toward his family, was tried for sodomy, convicted, and pardoned on payment of 100,000 *scudi*. In 1595 he imprisoned Beatrice and his second wife in a remote castle in the Abruzzo region and continued to torment them. By 1598 they could stand no more and arranged to have

Francesco killed by faking an accident in the castle. The truth came out, and all were arrested. The 24-year-old Beatrice and her stepmother were beheaded. One brother was tortured and killed; the youngest brother was sentenced to life in prison but pardoned after one year. The family's immense property holdings were confiscated by Pope Clement VIII, exciting general suspicion that this may have been the whole point of the pontifical harshness. Guido Reni immortalized Beatrice in a riveting portrait, and Shelley wrote a blank verse tragedy *(The Cenci)* in which Beatrice is portrayed as a heroic figure fighting oppression.

Behind the late–15th-century main entrance to this vast palace, built on a small hill atop the crumbled ruins of the 220 BC **Circus Flaminius,** is a charming Renaissance courtyard with Doric columns on two sides and a loggia of Ionic columns above. Down Via del Monte dei Cenci to the right is another facade of the palace and a little church that contains the (empty) family burial chapel. (Beatrice is buried in Trastevere's **Chiesa di San Pietro in Montorio.**) A mass is celebrated each year in this chapel on 11 September, the date of Beatrice Cenci's execution. The attractive 17th-century entrance from the piazza on the palace's east side begins, unusually, with a flight of stairs to connect with the rest of the palace. ♦ Piazza de' Cenci 56 (at Via dell'Arco de' Cenci)

Within the Palazzo Cenci:

Al Pompiere ★★$$ Dine under the high frescoed ceiling of the Cenci family's 15th-century palace in this Jewish-Roman restaurant. Specialties include a medley of batter-fried vegetables called *fritto vegetariano* and *pennette* (short quill-shaped pasta) cooked *al limone* (in lemon sauce). This is also a good place to sample one of the glories of the Ghetto cuisine—*fiore di zucca ripieno* (battered and fried zucchini blossoms stuffed with tiny pieces of mozzarella cheese and anchovies). Try the white tiramisù with raspberry sauce for dessert. ♦ M-Sa lunch and dinner; closed in August. Reservations recommended. Via di Santa Maria de' Calderari 38 (at Via dell'Arco de' Cenci). 6868377

On 13 April 1986 Pope John Paul II participated in a special service at Rome's central synagogue, marking the first recorded papal visit to a Jewish place of worship. This paved the way for the Vatican to recognize the state of Israel in 1994.

Floored in Rome

During the Middle Ages, the Cosmati—a cooperative or group of families (Cosma, Cosmatus in Latin, is the last name of the oldest and most active of the group)—were stonemasons and sculptors. This enterprising bunch created a dazzling inlaid marble-and-glass technique for decorating everything from cloister columns to candleholders. But it was the Cosmati's floors that were the talk of the medieval world, so much so that from the 12th to the 13th centuries, churches in many parts of what is today Italy rivaled one another in the splendor of their "cosmatesque" floors.

The Cosmati recycled marble fragments from ancient ruins and combined them with cubes of colored glass to produce intricate geometric patterns saturated with the blood red of imperial porphyry, the dusty yellow of antique *giallo,* and the elegance of serpentine green. Their workshops were in the **Campus Martius** near the **Pantheon,** an area not chosen by chance. Scattered about were the raw materials of the

Cosmati's trade: broken columns, fallen friezes, and half-buried cornices that had been spared or overlooked by the barbarian invaders.

Over a dozen churches in Rome have cosmatesque floors. The most impressive are at **Santa Maria in Trastevere, San Clemente, Santa Maria in Aracoeli,** and **Santi Quattro Coronati.** There are other sites, but their floors have been heavily restored and their interiors so altered by later additions that the floors have lost their original intention—an inexpensive substitute for rugs.

The Cosmati based their designs on Byzantine models and ancient Roman mosaics, but they also bear an uncanny resemblance to American patchwork quilting patterns despite the arts being more than 500 years apart. Fairly easy to identify among the Cosmati are waves, stars, and interlocking circles, common in such quilting motifs as Irish chain, bear's paw, star of Bethlehem, wedding ring, and others.

Ghetto

Rome's Ghetto is the oldest continuous community of Jews outside the Middle East: There were Jews in Rome as early as the second century BC; by the second century AD Rome had more than a dozen synagogues and about 40,000 Jewish residents. Today there are about 35,000 Jews in Italy, 14,000 of whom live in Rome.

The **Circus Flaminius** racetrack was built here in 220 BC on a spot of flat land that was then outside the city walls. In the 16th century the abandoned circus became the home of Rome's Jews, who were forced to move across the river from their settlement in Trastevere when that area became gentrified.

Until the 13th century the Jews and the papacy avoided open conflict; in fact, Jews often served the papal courts as advisors, bankers, and physicians. However, during the Renaissance, and especially the Counter-Reformation, the papacy became much less tolerant. In 1555 Pope Paul IV decreed that all Jews must live and work in the Ghetto. He built walls around it, set a curfew, and locked the residents within its gates at night. Frequent river floods and serious overcrowding added to the degradation of the area. Jews were allowed to deal only in used clothing and furniture, and outside the Ghetto women could wear no more than three rings, men only one. So despised was Paul IV that when he died in 1559, he had to be buried in secret for fear of an uprising.

Ghetto rules were eased after Paul IV's death, and the Ghetto's walls started coming down with the 18th-century Enlightenment. But it wasn't until after Italian unification in 1870 that the Ghetto was definitively abolished, and Jews were allowed to own land, hold government office, and enter the professions.

At the start of Mussolini's reign some 50 years later, the dictator (and most of Italy's Catholic population) was tolerant of the Jews. However, under pressure from Nazi Germany in 1938, Il Duce changed his policy and passed oppressive racial laws. Jews lost their jobs, especially as civil servants and teachers; their children were not allowed to attend public schools; and some were deported to concentration camps in Germany. During the 1943 German occupation of Rome, many Jews were murdered by Nazi soldiers; some were hidden by other Roman citizens in private homes and convents.

Like the early Christians, Jews buried their dead in catacombs. Originally six were in use from the first to the fourth centuries; today all but two have disappeared. One is near the main Christian catacombs on the **Appian Way.** The other, ironically, is in the garden of Mussolini's former residence, **Villa Torlonia.** Both catacombs can be visited only with special permission from the **Union of Italian Jewish Communities,** Lungotevere Raffaelo Sanzio 9, 5803670.

29 Piperno ★★$$$ Many claim this perpetually crowded restaurant serves the best and most authentic (though nonkosher) Roman Jewish cuisine in Rome. Its specialty is *carciofi alla giudea,* an artichoke flattened so that it looks like a chrysanthemum and then deep fried in olive oil until it is both crunchy and tender. A hard balance to achieve, the results here are at times hard and greasy. The best of the offerings fried in this manner, however, is *mozzarella in carrozza,* tiny pieces of bread, soaked in broth, dipped in egg, filled with mozzarella, and deep-fried to a golden crisp. For dessert, consider *le palle di nonno* (grandfather's balls), two piping hot cream puffs filled with sweetened ricotta cheese and chocolate bits. ♦ Tu-Sa lunch and dinner; Su lunch; closed in August and from Christmas to New Year's Eve. Reservations required. Via del Monte dei Cenci 9 (between Piazza delle Cinque Scole and Via Beatrice Cenci). 68806629, 6861113

30 Chiesa di Santa Maria del Pianto (Church of St. Mary of the Weeping) This church houses a fresco of the Madonna that was seen shedding tears on 10 January 1546 when it hung outside on the walls of the **Portico d'Ottavia.** At the time, the weeping was considered to be a reaction to a nearby riot, the nature of which is not recorded. However, by the time this church was built in 1612 by **Nicolo Sebregondi** to protect and honor the weeping image—now on the main altar—it was decided that the Virgin was mournful because her fellow Jews had not been converted. ♦ Via Santa Maria del Pianto 1/C (at Via Progresso)

31 Casa di Lorenzo Manilio This is one of several Renaissance dwellings in the Ghetto. Built in 1468, it belonged to Lorenzo Manilio, who renovated it in 1497. Manilio proudly declared this refurbishment in a travertine stone inscription running the length of the house, which says that he put up the legend in the 2,221st year after Rome's founding. He decorated the facade above the doors with antique fragments that he took from the Appian Way: One is a lion attacking a doe; another a dog and a rabbit. These give evidence to the humanistic and archaeological interests that thrived in Rome in the late 15th century. ♦ Via del Portico d'Ottavia 1 (at Piazza Costaguti)

Within Casa di Lorenzo Manilio:

Il Forno On a corner, tucked inside a doorway of the above building is a Jewish pastry shop that is one of Rome's prides. The macaroons are legendary, the nut-and-raisin biscotti will last forever, and the ricotta cheesecake, well. . . ♦ M-F, Su

32 Menorah 85 Here is a bookshop filled with books and information on the Ghetto, the synagogue, and Roman-Jewish cooking. ♦ M afternoon; Tu-Th; F morning. Via del Portico d'Ottavia 1/A (at Via Reginella). 6879297

Fontana delle Tartarughe (Turtle Fountain)

MARJORIE J. VOGEL/RHODE ISLAND ORIGINALS

33 Zi'Fenizia The only kosher pizzeria in the Ghetto, this take-out shop also prepares roasted chickens that are so popular you have to order them a day in advance. ♦ M-Th, Su 7:30AM-9:30PM; F until early evening. Via Santa Maria del Pianto 64 (at Piazza Costaguti)

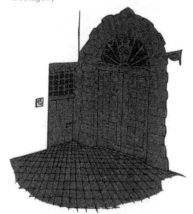

33 Il Sanpietrino ★★★$$ This stylish, friendly osteria, owned by the Di Mauro family, is housed in what was once the stables of the Costaguti family (for whom the piazza is named). The Di Mauros, who are also wine producers, offer an impressive list of wines to accompany their contemporary take on traditional Roman cuisine. Drawing much of its inspiration from the sea, the menu's offerings include *tagiolini con seppie e zucchine* (fresh egg pasta with cuttlefish and zucchini) and *filetto di cernia* (fillet of grouper in a light fish sauce with spinach, pine nuts, and raisins). Pine-nut custard and crème brûlée with candied orange are among the grand finales. ♦ M-F lunch and dinner; Sa dinner. Piazza Costaguti 15 (between Via Santa Maria del Pianto and Via in Publicolis). 68806471; fax 68806479

34 L'Enoteca di Anacleto Bleve ★★★$$ This handsome wine shop has one of the best selections of wines, olive oils, and vinegars in Rome. The eponymous proprietor also created a cozy, rustic dining area that retains its character as the former bottling room. The lunchtime-only menu is rooted in tradition as well—but with a twist of imagination. For example, the *involtini* here are rolls of smoked salmon—instead of the usual beef or veal—filled with crabmeat.

The cheese platter always has a pleasant surprise or two and makes a fine light lunch, unless you follow it up with the tiny babas soaked in *limoncello* (lemon liqueur). ♦ M-Sa lunch; closed three weeks in August. Via Santa Maria del Pianto 9/A (at Via in Publicolis). 6865970, 68300475

35 Fontana delle Tartarughe (Turtle Fountain) The design of this playful Florentine fountain by **Giacomo della Porta**—executed in 1585 by **Tadeo Landini**—in the middle of **Piazza Mattei** is brilliant: Four boys each hold in one hand a pet dolphin, who is happily squirting water, while with the other hand each boy nudges another pet, a turtle, into the fountain basin to drink. Walk around the fountain and watch how the patterns created by the boys' arms and legs keep changing. ♦ Piazza Mattei

36 Palazzo Mattei di Giove The courtyard of this palazzo built in 1598 by **Carlo Maderno** is one of the most ornate in Rome. In it are displayed the owner's—Marchese Asdrubale Mattei—collection of heroic statues, set on pedestals around the rim. Plastered into the walls behind them are fragments of reliefs, epigrams, and inscriptions from Roman and Paleo-Christian tombs. Busts of Roman emperors peer down from niches high above. The first floor houses the **Centro Italiano di Studi Americani** (Center for American Studies, 68801613) which has a research library and periodicals from the United States.

A short detour down the tiny Via Michelangelo Caetani leads to a wall plaque marking the spot where the body of Christian Democratic party chief Aldo Moro, kidnapped and murdered by the Red Brigades, was found in 1978. ♦ Via Michelangelo Caetani 32 (at Via dei Funari)

After gelato, *grattachecca* (shaved ice topped with syrups or fruit juices) is the summer cooler most Romans prefer. This carryover from the turn of the century is still served in little kiosks along the banks of the Tiber throughout summer. *Grattachecca* comes in a variety of flavors, including fresh squeezed lemon, coffee, and mint. Most of the stands are crowded and stay that way well past midnight, especially when the temperature soars. Try one of the following: Sor Mirella (Lungotevere degli Anguillara and Ponte Cestio); Fonte d'Oro (Lungotevere Raffaelo Sanzio and Ponte Garibaldi)—the oldest in Rome (its wrought-iron kiosk dates from 1913); and Chiosco Ara Pacis (Lungotevere in Augusta and Ponte Cavour), which boasts a special tamarind-and-peach topping.

Bridges of the Tiber

1 Ponte Milvio Part of the **Aurelian Walls** fortification, this bridge played a strategic role in ancient times as the northern gateway for all the celebrated roads that led to Rome. The great battle of Saxa Rubra (AD 312)—the decisive victory for Constantine and Christianity—ended when Maxentius was killed on this bridge. Since then it has been rebuilt and refortified often, most recently in 1850 after Garibaldi blew up part of it to stop the French invasion. It has been a pedestrians-only bridge since 1980.

2 Ponte Duca d'Aosta This bridge connects the **Lungotevere Flaminio** to the **Foro Italico,** a sports arena built under Mussolini. Built in 1939 by **Viacenta Fasole** and **Antonio Aureli,** its pompous, fascist-style architecture is classically inspired.

3 Ponte del Risorgimento Connecting **Viale delle Belle Arti** to **Viale Giuseppe Mazzini,** this 1910 bridge is named after Italy's 19th-century *Risorgimento,* a rebirth of national pride that led to the unification of the Italian states in 1870. Many of the Tiber bridges are named after the political leaders of this period, including its three great heroes: Mazzini, Garibaldi, and Cavour.

4 Ponte Matteotti This bridge runs from the **Naval Ministry** to **Piazza delle Cinque Giornate.** Built in 1929, it was named after Giacome Matteotti, a popular Socialist politician assassinated by Mussolini's thugs in 1923. The public outcry that came after Il Duce's action nearly brought down fascism, but Mussolini initiated a crackdown that abolished all remaining semblances of democratic government.

5 Ponte Metropolitana This bridge carries the sub-way to two stations on the **Vatican** side of the Tiber.

6 Ponte Margherita This bridge connects **Piazza del Popolo** to **Via Cola di Rienzo,** a shopping street on the **Vatican** side of the river. It was named for Queen Margherita, who was only 19 when she married Prince Umberto I in 1868. Because her father-in law the king was a widower, Margherita played the queen's role for state occasions. When widowed in 1900, she moved to the **Palazzo Margherita** (now the **American Embassy**).

7 Ponte Cavour Linking the **Ara Pacis** to **Via Vittoria Colonna,** this bridge was built in 1901 and named after Count Camilio Benso Cavour. Influenced by France's July Revolution of 1830, he started *Il Risorgimento,* a newspaper in which he advocated a unified Italy with a constitutional monarchy. By 1848 a general frenzy for constitutional government broke into war in Italy and throughout Europe. Rulers were forced to cede some form of self-government to their subjects. Cavour masterminded the whole Italian unification as the prime minister of Piedmont, but he didn't live to see his dream come wholly true: He died in 1861, almost ten years before Italy was officially unified.

8 Ponte Umberto This 1895 bridge runs from **Via Giuseppe Zanardelli** and the **Museo Napoleonico** to **Palazzo di Giustizia.** Umberto I was the second member from the royal house of Savoy to become King of Italy. He came to power in 1878 when his father Vittorio Emanuele II died, and he reigned until he was assassinated in 1900.

9 Ponte Sant'Angelo Built by Emperor Hadrian in AD 134 to connect the city proper with his mausoleum (now **Castel Sant'Angelo**) and finished in 139, a year after his death, this bridge is notorious as the execution site of Beatrice Cenci. She and her mother and brother were incarcerated in the dreaded **Tor di Nona** prison after she killed her father, a sadistic man who had terrorized his family. At 24 she was beheaded on the corner of this bridge for patricide. Between 1598 and 1660, Bernini and his school carved the 10 angels (Bernini sculpted 2) holding instruments of Christ's passion that line both sides.

10 Ponte Vittorio Emanuele This bridge, built in 1911, stretches from **Corso Vittorio Emanuele** to **Via della Conciliazione**. It is named for Vittorio Emanuele II, who was named king of the new state in 1870. Hitherto ruled by the pope, Rome was by no means ready to welcome the king with open arms: When he arrived on New Year's Eve 1870, the new king headed for **Palazzo del Quirinale,** but the pope, who had left only the day before, had locked the palace and taken the keys with him.

11 Pons Neronianus When it existed, this bridge was named for Nero, who reigned AD 54-68. Nero had his circus just to the left of where **St. Peter's Basilica** now stands, and he needed a bridge to get there. It collapsed in the Middle Ages during a particularly high flood, but the foundations are still visible when the water level is low.

12 Ponte Principe Amedeo Savoia Aosta Named for Prince Amedeo, a member of the Savoy family from Piedmont, this late 19th-century bridge runs from **Via Giulia** to the tunnel and the **Ospedale Santo Spirito** on the **Vatican** side of the river.

13 Ponte Mazzini Running from the **Carceri Nuovi** (New Prisons) on Via Giulia to **Carcere Regina Coeli** (Regina Coeli Jail) in **Trastevere,** this bridge, opened in 1908, is named for the Italian patriot Giuseppe Mazzini (1805-72). Mazzini started his political career by joining the Carbonari, a secret society of patriots, which quickly got him imprisoned. There he became resolute in his decision to liberate Italy from foreign and domestic tyranny. From 1832 on, Mazzini lived a clandestine life, was often in prison, and incited revolutionary movements in Sardinia, Genoa, and Savoia. In 1848, he was one of the triumvirate (with Garibaldi and Cavour) who administered Rome for the brief time that the city was a republic (when the pope fled during Garibaldi's abortive invasion). Two years before his death in 1872, he saw his dream become reality—Italy was a unified country.

14 Ponte Sisto (Pons Aurelius) This much-photographed bridge, with a round opening in the center, is among Rome's oldest; the original was built around AD 200 when Christian martyrs were thrown from it into the Tiber. It was damaged in 772, but Pope Sixtus IV rebuilt it for the Holy Year of 1475, and it was subsequently renamed in his honor.

15 Ponte Garibaldi One of Italy's most celebrated heroes, Giuseppe Garibaldi (1807-82), gave his name to this bridge. After leading his brigade of "Red-shirts" to several victories throughout Italy, the only obstacle to Garibaldi's dream of unification was the conquest of Rome. But his cry, "Roma o morte!" (Rome or death!) did not stir the people in 1861, and it wasn't until 1867 that he began his march on Rome. He was defeated, however, by papal troops aided by the French and was sent into exile to Caprera. In 1870 he fought alongside of the French against the Germans in the Franco-Prussian War. In that same year Rome was finally conquered, and by 31 December, Vittorio Emanuele II of Piedmont had arrived in Rome to rule Italy.

16 Ponte Fabricio Since 62 BC this stone bridge has joined **Tiber Island** to the left bank. It is the only one of the ancient bridges with its original structure still intact. Romans also call it "Ponte Quattro Capi" for the four-faced ancient markers showing the god Janus at the beginning of the bridge. In the Middle Ages it was also known as **Ponte degli Ebrei** because of its proximity to the Jewish **Ghetto.** The present parapet was added in 1679 under Pope Innocent XI. The original balustrade was bronze.

17 Ponte Cestio (Pons Cestius) The architect Cestius built this bridge in 30 BC. It was the first stone bridge from Tiber Island to the right bank (Trastevere). The pedestals had statues depicting Emperors Valens and Gratian, who rebuilt the bridge in AD 369. It was reinforced at various times from the 12th to the 18th centuries. When the embankments were constructed in 1888, part of the bridge was again rebuilt, faithfully copying the old form.

18 Ponte Rotto In the bed of the Tiber remains only a single arch of the **Pons Aemillus,** which today is known as the "Broken Bridge." Though the bridge itself (dating from 179 BC) was made of wood, stone was used to build the piers, making it the first stone bridge over the Tiber.

19 Ponte Palatino This bridge stretches from **Lungotevere dei Pierleoni** to **Lungotevere Ripa** and is opposite the **Temple of Virile Fortune.** The view of Tiber Island from this bridge enables you to see why the ancient Romans described it as the bow of a ship. There's also a good vista from here, down along the water's edge, of the 2,600-year-old **Cloaca Maxima**. In 600 BC the Etruscan king Tarquinius began this great engineering feat: an arched underground drainage canal built to dry up the swampy valley of the first forum and carry off sewage to the river. Today it still keeps the **Roman Forum** dry.

20 Pons Sublicius Built by King Ancus Marcius about 600 BC, the very first bridge to cross the Tiber in Rome helped to develop good relations between the growing settlement of Romans (named after Romulus) on **Palatine Hill** and the Etruscans on the right bank. The original bridge is no longer standing; it was built only of wood so that in the event of an attack it could be quickly destroyed to prevent the enemy from crossing. This bridge is the most historically famous—it was here that Horatius and his two companions held the bridge against the Etruscans.

21 Ponte Aventino Running from **Piazza dell'Emporio** to **Porta Portese,** this bridge is also called "Ponte Sublicio" on modern maps.

37 Portico d'Ottavia **Celius Metellius** built this portico in 146 BC, and Augustus revamped it in 27 BC as an elegant covered passageway dedicated to his sister Octavia. From antiquity to the beginning of the 20th century, Rome's main fish market was located between its columns. Freshwater fish was the most common type sold, but marine fish were brought up the Tiber from Ostia to the nearby port of Ripa Grande. In the eighth century, part of the portico was incorporated into the **Chiesa di Sant'Angelo in Pescheria** (Church of Holy Angel of the Fish Market). On one of the walls of this church is a Latin inscription from the ancient market regulating fish measurements. It states that the head of any fish longer than the diagram had to be given to the magistrates. Since the head was considered a delicacy, especially in soups, this was probably an early kickback. ♦ Piazza Sant'Angelo in Pescheria and Via del Portico d'Ottavia

37 Da Giggetto ★$$ Every kind of battered and deep-fried variety of Roman-Jewish cooking—from salt cod fillets to zucchini blossoms—are distributed here by stolid, humorless waiters. Ignore them and enjoy the food (especially the chickpea soup flavored with rosemary). Book outdoors where the tables are set among the ruined columns of Ottavia's portico. ♦ Tu-Su lunch and dinner; closed in July. Reservations recommended. Via del Portico d'Ottavia 21/A (at Piazza Sant'Angelo in Pescheria). 6861105

37 Limentani Descend into the "catacombs of china," a vast labyrinth of tiny rooms chock-a-block with everything from Venetian glass to rustic pottery, all at reduced prices. Among the brand names hidden away on dusty shelves are Alessi and Richard Ginori.

♦ M-Sa. Via del Portico d'Ottavia 47 (at Piazza Sant'Angelo in Pescheria). 68806686

38 Sinagoga (Main Synagogue) On the Tiber flank of this synagogue, built in Assyrian-Babylonian style in 1904 by **Costa** and **Armanni,** is a plaque commemorating Jews deported by the Germans during World War II. Inside is a small museum documenting the more than 2,000 years of Jewish life in Rome. Contemporary Roman artist Eva Singer designed the stained-glass windows. It is actually two places of worship, since the separate **Sephardic Synagogue** is also here. Guided tours of the synagogue are given in English. ♦ Admission to museum. M-F 9:30AM-2PM, 3-5PM; Su 9:30AM-12:30PM. Lungotevere dei Cenci and Via del Tempio. 6864648

39 Chiesa di Madonna della Divina Pietà This is one of the churches where Jews were obliged to attend sermons on Sunday mornings. It bears an inscription from the Book of Isaiah over the door in Latin and Hebrew: "I spread out my hands all the day unto a rebellious people which walketh in a way that was not good after their own thoughts." ♦ Via del Portico d'Ottavia and Via Monte Savello

40 Teatro di Marcello Construction for this theater started under Julius Caesar in 11 BC and was finished under Augustus, who dedicated it to his nephew, son-in-law, and heir-apparent Marcellus, who died at age 19. It was huge (only half of it remains today) and could hold up to 20,000 spectators. Like many of the Roman ruins in the Middle Ages, it was converted into a family fortress. Three rich papal families (Savelli, Orsini, Caetani) built their palaces on top of or into the theater.

Portico d'Ottavia

MARJORIE J. VOGEL/RHODE ISLAND ORIGINALS

Teatro di Marcello

MARJORIE J. VOGEL/RHODE ISLAND ORIGINALS

Today there are very posh apartments atop the ruins. The visible Doric archways at ground level (what's left of the original 41 arches) were rented out as shops until 1932. During the summer open-air concerts are held amid the ruins. ♦ Check *Roma C'è* for concert schedule. Piazza Monte Savello

41 Chiesa di San Nicola in Carcere (Church of St. Nicholas in Prison)
Built in the 11th century out of the ruins of three Roman temples (parts of them are incorporated into the sides of the building), the name of this church refers to St. Nicholas's incarceration by the anti-Christian emperor Diocletian. He was subsequently released by the convert Constantine. **Giacomo della Porta** restored it in 1599. ♦ Via del Teatro di Marcello (between Via Foro Olitorio and Via del Foro Piscario)

Isola Tiberina (Tiber Island)

Tiber Island has been associated with the art of healing since as far back as the third century BC. After a respite from a plague, the Romans chose it as the site of a temple to the Greek god Aesculapius, the son of Apollo and the god of medicine. First they sent a ship to his temple at Epidaurus, Greece, to fetch a statue of him. As the ship was sailing up the **Tiber,** they dropped a snake, Aesculapius's symbol, overboard, thinking that they would build the temple wherever it stopped. It swam directly to Tiber Island. Aesculapius became the Roman god of medicine, the snake the permanent symbol of physicians (the caduceus), and the temple—traces of which are still visible along the southern quay—became famous for its healing waters. Today the huge **Fatebenefratelli Hospital,** established in 1548 by the Hospitalers of St. John of God, continues this tradition.

42 Chiesa di San Giovanni Calibita Redone in the 18th century, this church, part of the **Fatebenefratelli Hospital,** is worth visiting to see its splendid marble interior and the best painting on the island, Matia Preti's *Flagellation of Christ.* ♦ Via Ponte Quattro Capi 12 (at Via dei Caetani)

43 Palazzo dei Caetani-Pierleoni In the Middle Ages, this was the stronghold of several antipopes, one of whom, Anacletus II, came from the Jewish Pierleoni family, which had converted to Christianity. His eight-year reign ended in 1138 when his rival, Innocent II, was recognized as the legitimate pontiff and Anacletus declared an antipope. His palace became a Franciscan monastery in the 17th century and, after the unification of Italy, a Jewish hospital and home for the aged. It is mostly in ruins today, but still standing is the 11th-century **Torre dei Caetani,** one of the few remaining of some 200 defensive towers that dominated the skyline of medieval Rome. This one guarded the bridge to the island and once contained a toll booth for collecting fees to cross into the city. ♦ Via dei Caetani

"Something quite powerful happened to me yesterday. While I was standing on one of the Tiber bridges, waiting for friends (it was night), I saw the descending staircase that carries one down to water level. I descended quickly and found myself on a patch of mud and sand. It was very dark, but I could make out the arches of the bridge over my head and, along the river's length, I could see the lamps, an infinite number of lamps. I was about twenty meters below the level of the city, and its din came muffled to me as from another world. I really never thought that in the heart of a metropolis it was enough to descend a staircase to enter the most absolute solitude."

Pier Paolo Pasolini, Writer and Film Director

Chiesa di San Bartolomeo

MARJORIE J. VOGEL/RHODE ISLAND ORIGINALS

43 Sora Lella Trattoria ★$$ At the foot of the tower is the only restaurant on the island. Before her death in 1993 it was managed by the formidable octogenarian Sora Lella, a much-loved Roman actress. (*Sora* is Roman dialect for *signora*.) The cuisine, as one might expect, could not be more Roman, as is the service—brusque and slow. But the location is one of Rome's best. ♦ M-Sa lunch and dinner; closed in August. Reservations recommended. No credit cards accepted. Via Ponte Quattro Capi 16 (at Via dei Caetani). 6861601

43 Alfonso's Bar ★$ Stop for good coffee and sandwiches at this coffee bar run by Alfonso, whose sideline is hiring out the white limousines that transport brides to their weddings at the adjacent church. He'll also pack you a picnic lunch to eat along the quay below. ♦ Daily. Via Ponte Quattro Capi and dei Caetani

43 Confraternità de Gesù Facing **Piazza San Bartolomeo all'Isola**, an ornate doorway leads to the oratory of a famous 18th-century marching and burial society. Like all such confraternities, the society existed to do good works (this society's specific mission was to rescue people from the Tiber, a function now handled by the River Police). The members were recognized by their red hoods, and they held processions around the island until about a generation ago, when the tradition died out with the last remaining members. In the basement the bones of deceased members and of drowned bodies recovered from the Tiber are displayed along the walls. Ask at the door for permission to visit. ♦ Piazza San Bartolomeo all'Isola

44 Chiesa di San Bartolomeo A favorite for weddings, this church was built at the end of the 10th century by the Holy Roman Emperor Otto III on the site of the ancient **Temple of Aesculapius.** (A wellhead on the steps to the main altar is the last evidence of the medicinal spring that was always a feature of Aesculapius's temples.) The church has been restored several times, as evidenced by its Baroque front and Romanesque bell tower, and very little remains of the original. Visit the millers' chapel, where frescoes depict the floating water mills that until a hundred years ago were moored around the island. St. Bartholomew, who was flayed to death, is the patron saint of skin disorders. ♦ Piazza San Bartolomeo all'Isola

Adjacent to Chiesa di San Bartolomeo:

Il Monastero di San Bartolomeo (Monastery of St. Bartholomew) An archway leads to the garden of the monastery of the Franciscan fathers who serve the chapel. The garden is decorated with stylized religious sculptures—the work of one of the friars, Father Martini. The River Police have their quarters in what used to be the city morgue at the end of the garden.

45 Steps A flight of stairs leads down from the piazza to the quay. Carved in travertine blocks below the foundation of the monastery garden is the stern (although some say the bow) of a Roman galley with a relief of Aesculapius and his winged, twined serpents, Caduceus. This is all that remains of his boat-shaped temple.
♦ Piazza Fatebenefratelli (west of Piazza San Bartolomeo all'Isola)

Circus Maximus and Environs

The "Great Circus," built in the fourth century BC in a natural valley between the **Palatine** and **Aventine Hills,** was in use through the fourth century. The **Circus Maximus** was the largest stadium in Rome—at the height of its popularity it accommodated 300,000 spectators—and the prototype for all the racecourses of the ancient world. The track was designed to contain teams of two-, three-, and even four-horse chariots. Betting was hugely popular, and Romans wagered fortunes on their favorites. Winners could celebrate, and losers could forget their troubles in the myriad shops and taverns that surrounded the stadium.

Temple of Virile Fortune

MARJORIE J. VOGEL/RHODE ISLAND ORIGINALS

46 Temple of Virile Fortune This second-century BC temple is thought to have been dedicated to Portunus, who in medieval times became Fortunus, a river god. Converted to a church in the ninth century, it later became the official house of worship of the Armenian community. Like the nearby **Temple of Vesta** (see below), it is a rare example of a pre-Imperial Republican temple, strongly influenced by Greek architecture. ♦ Via Petroselli and Piazza della Bocca della Verità

47 Temple of Vesta The oldest (second century BC) standing marble temple in Rome (pictured below) has 20 Corinthian columns and a cylindrical cell inside. It has been misnamed for centuries because its circular

Temple of Vesta

MARJORIE J. VOGEL/RHODE ISLAND ORIGINALS

form resembles the **Temple of Vesta: Goddess of the Hearth** in the **Roman Forum.** An inscription says that it was dedicated to Hercules the Conqueror. ♦ Piazza della Bocca della Verità

48 Chiesa di Santa Maria in Cosmedìn

Constructed in the sixth century on the foundations of temples dedicated to Hercules and Ceres, this church was enlarged in the eighth century by Pope Hadrian I to be the official place of worship for the Greek community. (The street to the right of the church is called Via della Greca.) Uncertainty remains about the Cosmedìn part of the name, because it is Greek for ornament or embellishment and also refers to an area of Constantinople. The 12th-century belfry, seven stories tall, is the highest Romanesque bell tower in Rome. Embedded in the 12th-century portico on the left-hand wall is what may be the most famous stone manhole cover in the world (illustrated at left). It was carved as a giant face to cover a drain, and the water entered through its mouth. Some centuries ago, it was given the name "Bocca della Verità" (The Mouth of Truth), along with the legend that liars who put their hands in its mouth would have them bitten off. Another version has it that hidden behind the stone was a priest with a wooden cane who swatted the hands of suspected liars. Mothers still bring their children here for a playful test that also attracts fiancées and suspicious wives. The image of a nervous Audrey Hepburn standing before this stone in *Roman Holiday* has become an icon of cinema history. The interior is a jewel of medieval church architecture, and the polychrome mosaic floor is one of the glories of the famous Cosmati (a group of families who were stonemasons and sculptors). From the 12th to the 13th centuries the Cosmati decorated churches all over Italy with ancient marble arranged in geometric patterns, many of which bear a remarkable resemblance to traditional American patchwork quilt designs. ♦ Piazza Bocca della Verità (between Via della Greca and Via dei Cerchi)

49 Circus Maximus

The movie wasn't filmed here, but this is where Ben Hur raced his chariots several thousand years ago. At that time this vast tract (two football fields in width and a half-mile long) was ringed with marble bleachers from which spectators screamed their encouragement to the charioteers. The emperor watched from his ornate box on Palatine Hill, and the magistrates, who refereed the

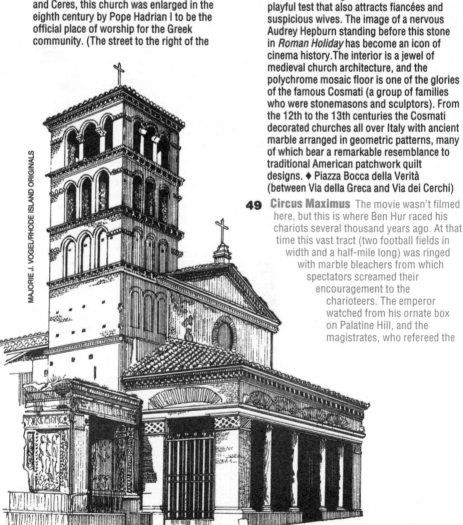

MAJORIE J. VOGEL/RHODE ISLAND ORIGINALS

Chiesa di San Giorgio in Velabro

MARJORIE J. VOGEL/RHODE ISLAND ORIGINALS

Arco di Giano (Arch of Janus)

races, had a special stand at the end nearest the Tiber. Down the center ran the *spina* (spine), with obelisks to mark where the chariots had to wheel around and race in the other direction. Only the outlines remain today, overgrown with grass, along with some ancient benches at the end farthest from the river. ♦ Bounded by Viale Aventino, Piazza di Porta Capena, Via Ara Massima d'Ercole, Via del Circo Massimo, and Via dei Cerchi

50 Chiesa di San Giorgio in Velabro The 13th-century altar of this church—originally built in the 7th century—has mosaic decoration by the Cosmati family of marble workers who were famous for their glass-and-marble mosaic floors. The portico and bell tower were added in the 12th century. A fresco of Christ, the Virgin Mary, and three saints is from the school of Pietro Cavallini (1295). The charm of this carefully restored medieval church (illustrated on page 48) is its simplicity. ♦ Via del Velabro (between Via di San Teodoro and Via San Giovanni Decollato)

50 Arco degli Argentari (Arch of the Money Changers) The guild of the money changers built this arch in AD 204 to honor Emperor Septimius Severus, his wife, Domna, and his two children, Geta and Caracalla—all of whom were depicted here in sculptured relief in the act of making a sacrificial offering. Later, Caracalla killed his sister, so his image was broken off. The arch now leans against the corner of the adjacent church. ♦ Via del Velabro (between Via di San Teodoro and Via San Giovanni Decollato

51 Arco di Giano (Arch of Janus) Janus was the Roman god who protected crossroads. This fourth-century arch (pictured above) was built as a covering to protect travelers at this important junction between the **Forum Boarium** (the ancient cattle market and the oldest of the forums), which occupied the present-day **Piazza della Bocca della Verità,** and the **Forum Olitorio** (a vegetable-and-fruit market in ancient times). ♦ Via del Velabro (between Via di San Teodoro and Via San Giovanni Decollato)

52 Palazzo al Velabro Residence $$ This apartment-hotel was originally a 16th-century palace. Now it has 34 apartments with sitting rooms and kitchenettes; some have terraces overlooking the garden in the back. There's a one-week minimum stay. ♦ Via del Velabro 16 (at Via San Giovanni Decollato). 6792758, 6793450; fax 6793790

Bests

Frances D'Emilio
Author/Correspondent, Associated Press

I never tire of walking my favorite squares, each time trying to discover a new detail, a different effect of the light which transforms the city hour by hour. On 15 August, you can see something most Romans won't—stunning views of the city as it was meant to be—without cars (most natives will be out of town on holiday). All you need is a hat to shade the sun, a good map, comfortable shoes, and a survival pack (Rome's stores, from pharmacies to milk stores, will be shuttered that day).

Best *baccalà* (fried, salted cod): At **Panattoni**—nicknamed the "Morgue" for its marble-topped tables.

Campo de' Fiori

If all of Rome is colorful, the neighborhood surrounding the square called **Campo de' Fiori** (Field of Flowers) is a veritable rainbow. Once a grassy field (hence, a *campo,* not a piazza) where public hangings took place, today it is the site of one of Rome's most theatrical events: a bustling, circuslike outdoor market. The surrounding narrow alleys teem with trattorie, wine bars, used clothing shops (especially on **Via dei Giubbonari** and **Via del Governo Vecchio**), jewelers, and antiques dealers. Here the street names are a record of Rome's retailing history: *Giubbonari* translates as jacket makers or clothiers; **Via dei Cappellari** is where the hat makers worked; the nail makers were on **Vicolo de' Chiodaroli**, the crossbow makers on **Via dei Balestrari**, and tin washbowl makers on **Vicolo de' Catinari**. Unseen beneath this tangled warren of picturesque streets lies history—the substructure of the **Teatro di Pompeo** where Julius Caesar was assassinated on the Ides of March in 44 BC.

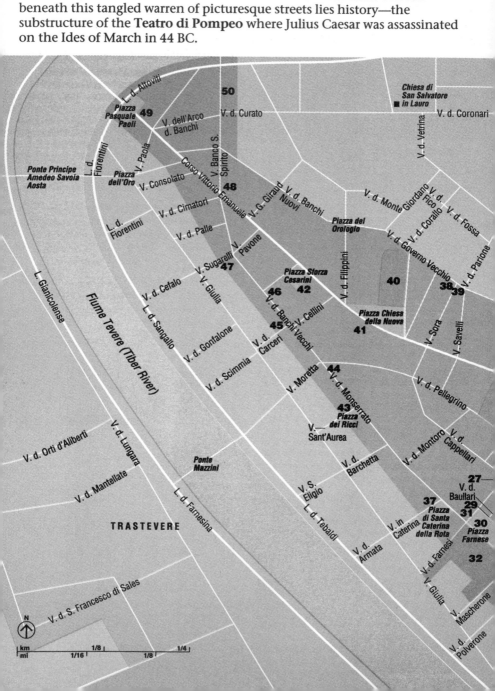

Seeking a large tract of land in about 55 BC to realize his dream of a giant theater-temple complex, military leader and statesman Pompey chose this area by the **Tiber** because periodic flooding had left it almost vacant. The complex began with the entrance to a semicircular auditorium, where **Via del Biscione** is now located; from there, two 100-columned porticoes continued down the present-day **Via del Sudario** and **Via di Sant'Anna**, ending at **Via di Torre Argentina** with the row of (now ruined) temples. Bounded by the theater, porticoes, and temples was a vast public garden. This extraordinary piece of urban planning employed the theories of **Vitruvius**, an ancient Roman architect whose influence revived during the Renaissance. When it was finished, the complex was called **Campo de' Fiori**, which may have referred to Pompey's portico-bounded garden or to a beautiful woman named Flora, with whom Pompey was in love.

For 400 years, **Campo de' Fiori** remained one of the great sights of Rome, but by the fifth century, it had fallen into ruin. During the late Middle Ages, the powerful Orsini family used pieces of Pompey's theater to build a fortress, traces of which are still visible on Via del Biscione. Subsequently, the name **Campo de' Fiori** came to refer to the open-air market, which continues today. By the early 14th century, in place of Pompey's ancient theater-temple complex stood a piazza that was the center of medieval Rome.

Later, during the High Renaissance, Via del Governo Vecchio and **Via dei Banchi Nuovi** became the site of many government and business offices. Today **Campo de' Fiori** teems with locals and visitors alike, remaining popular because it combines Rome's rich past with its vital, everyday present.

1 Piazza Sant'Andrea della Valle Instead of today's steady stream of cars, roaring scooters, and buses, a waterway once flowed in this piazza. In fact, the ancient Roman general Agrippa once dammed up the water to create a small artificial lake. The Roman historian Tacitus describes a notorious picnic hosted by Emperor Nero that took place here on a floating barge decorated with gold and ivory and rowed by slaves. Nero had decorated the shores of the lake as well—one side with beautifully dressed women; the other side with women who were, in a manner of speaking, beautifully undressed. "When night came," Tacitus recorded, "the woods and the houses all around rang with songs and were resplendent with lights." Today this piazza forms a kind of traffic apron in front of the **Chiesa di Sant'Andrea della Valle** and is bordered by some of the least charming buildings in Rome. However, a lovely Renaissance fountain, attributed to Carlo Maderno, stands in the center of the piazza.

2 Chiesa di Sant'Andrea della Valle Carlo **Rainaldi** designed this 1665 church's elegant Baroque facade, set in motion by the thrust and counterthrust of columns and overhangs, and designed to be held together with sculpted angels (instead of scrolls) at either corner. Inside the cavernous interior, the frescoes of Domenichino and his rival Giovanni Lanfranco document the change, as the rigid style of the High Renaissance evolved into the more fluid Baroque. Domenichino's earlier paintings on the vault of the apse (representing the life of St. Andrew, the church's patron) appear static, like paintings made on an easel for a gallery wall. By contrast, the frescoes on **Carlo Maderno**'s soaring dome (the second-highest in Rome after **St. Peter's**) by Lanfranco were done using a trompe l'oeil technique, which took the curved surface into account.

In another burst of inspiration, Lanfranco also incorporated the natural light from the windows as an element of his composition (effects later employed by **Bernini**). Lanfranco's ground-breaking work then spurred Domenichino to new heights as he painted the pendentives (representing the evangelists), which have been compared to figures in Michelangelo's **Sistine Chapel** frescoes. This church is also where the first act of Puccini's only Roman opera, *Tosca,* takes place. Outside, on the left side of the church, look for the Roman statue identified only as a Roman citizen. It's one of the so-called "talking" statues made famous during the 18th-century populist protests, usually assailing the pope. In the course of such a protest, a disparaging placard would be hung about the statue's neck, at the risk of the protester's own. ♦ Piazza Sant'Andrea della Valle (between Piazza Vidoni and Largo dei Chiavari)

3 Palazzo Massimo alle Colonne **Baldassare Peruzzi** built this palazzo in 1536 for the Massimo family (one of the oldest noble Roman families) on the former site of the **Odeon** of Emperor Domitian (next door to **Domitian's Stadium**—now **Piazza Navona**). The **Odeon** was a small semicircular theater, which explains the curved front of the main palazzo, called *alle Colonne* after the portico of Doric columns at the main entrance where, according to an old tradition, anyone without lodging is allowed to sleep. During the late 1970s, a distant relative of the Massimo family, down on his luck, spent many nights in that open loggia. The public is allowed indoors once a year, on 16 March, to commemorate the anniversary of St. Philip Neri's miraculous resuscitation in 1583 of another young member of the Massimo family. ♦ Corso Vittorio Emanuele 141 (at Piazza di San Pantaleo)

4 Souvenir—Cornici e Stampe In addition to postcards and guidebooks written in various languages, this souvenir shop has an above-average collection of prints of views of Rome. ♦ M-Sa Jan-Mar, June, Aug-Nov; M-Sa, Su morning Apr-May, Dec; closed in July. Via della Cuccagna 19 (between Piazza di San Pantaleo and Piazza Navona). 6875822

5 Palazzo Braschi This huge, roughly triangular pile designed by **Cosimo Morelli** is an example of quantity over quality. Constructed by Pius VI of the Braschi family for his nephews in 1792, this palazzo was the last in Rome to be built for the family of a pope. Special exhibitions are occasionally mounted here. The **Museo di Roma** (6875880) is housed in the palazzo. ♦ Piazza di San Pantaleo 10 (between Via della Cuccagna and Via di San Pantaleo)

6 Piazza di Pasquino This piazza is named after the most famous of Rome's many "talking" statues, so-called because they were draped with placards—usually with lampoons or satirical rhymes written on them. The figure here takes its name from a 16th-century tailor, Pasquino, who lived in the area and was renowned for his bitter wit—particularly at the expense of the papacy. The pithy satires hung on the statue (often by students from the nearby **University of Rome**) came to be called *pasquinades*. The statue itself is a Roman copy of a Greek original showing Menelaus holding Patroclus, slain in the Trojan War.

7 L'Insalata Ricca 2 ★$ The name of this chain of seven small restaurants means "rich salad," and you can believe it. They come in large bowls that can be shared or serve as a main course. A favorite here is *insalata alle noci,* with walnuts and feta cheese; another standout has olives, mozzarella balls, and artichoke hearts. Pasta is also featured here, including many vegetarian varieties. There is a slightly more upscale branch at Largo dei Chiavari 85 (at Corso Vittorio Emanuele, 68803656). ♦ Daily lunch and dinner. Piazza di Pasquino 72 (between Via di San Pantaleo and Via dei Leutari). 668307881

7 Cul de Sac ★★$ In this former wine shop, the red lentil and white bean soup served with homemade bread is so good that it attracts a steady stream of diners—come early to avoid waiting on line. Order wine by the glass or the bottle. ♦ M lunch; Tu-Su lunch and dinner.

Piazza di Pasquino 73 (between Via di San Pantaleo and Via dei Leutari). 68801094

8 Piccola Farnesina ai Baullari Despite its name, this small Renaissance palazzo designed by **Antonio da Sangallo the Younger** had nothing to do with the noble Farnese family. It was built in 1546 for Thomas Le Roy, a French emissary to the Holy See. Le Roy, who had been ennobled by François I, had the facade decorated with the fleur-de-lis, which closely resembles the Farnese iris; hence, the confusion. The side facing Corso Vittorio Emanuele, where the entrance is located, is a 19th-century addition. ◆ Corso Vittorio Emanuele 168 (at Vicolo dell'Aquila)

Within the Piccola Farnesina ai Baullari:

Museo Barracco Barone Giovanni Barracco donated his collection of superb classical, Egyptian, and Assyrian artwork to the city in 1902. Housed upstairs in **Room II** of this refurbished museum is the oldest Egyptian statue in Italy—a relief of the court official Nofer (ca. 2750 BC). In the same gallery is a series of very fine Egyptian portraits, including a third-millennium pharaoh. **Room III** on the same floor is often locked; ask a guard to open it to see the late–sixth-century BC Grecian *Head of a Youth.* ◆ Admission. Tu-Sa; Su morning. 68806848

9 Il Fornaio The bread here comes in different colors and shapes, and the take-out pizzas are baked daily. The pastries and tarts often look better than they taste. At Christmas the windows are full of edible manger figures and marzipan villages blanketed by icing snow ◆ Daily (no midday closing). Via dei Baullari 4 (at Corso Vittorio Emanuele). 68803947

RISTORANTE LA POLLAROLA

10 Ristorante La Pollarola ★★$$ The menu at this rustic dining spot is strong in traditional Roman dishes, so the *penne all'arrabbiata* (in a hot spicy garlic-and-tomato sauce) is always up to snuff. Be sure to try the restaurant's creation—*pollo con porchetta* (half a roasted chicken stuffed with herbs, rolled in bacon, and baked in a red wine and wild boar sauce). Sit outside in nice weather or dine inside next to the Roman column that's part of the wall. ◆ M-Sa lunch and dinner; closed in August. Piazza Pollarola (between Piazza del Paradiso and Piazza del Teatro di Pompeo). 68801654

11 Grotte del Teatro di Pompeo ★★$$ The green fettuccine with gorgonzola sauce and the *risotto al radicchio* served at this

traditional restaurant are certainly worth a try. A good price/quality ratio further distinguishes this dining spot near the ruins. ◆ Tu-Su lunch and dinner. Via del Biscione 73 (at Piazza Pollarola). 68803686

12 Teatro di Pompeo $$ This attractive small hotel is built on top of the ruins of the **Teatro di Pompeo,** where Julius Caesar was assassinated on the Ides of March in 44 BC. Breakfast is served either in your room or in the cavernous cellars of the *teatro.* The 13 smallish rooms are tastefully understated: white walls, exposed chestnut-beam ceilings, and terra-cotta floors accented by hand-painted tiles and colorful geometric rugs. Breakfast, central air-conditioning, mini-bar, and color satellite TV are included. ◆ Largo del Pallaro 8 (just west of Via dei Chiavari). 68300170; fax 68805531

12 Der Pallaro ★$ The menu at this long-established Roman trattoria changes every day, but the fixed price for three hearty courses with wine included is hard to beat. Each course features a sampling of different dishes. Eat in the homey dining room or alfresco at the outdoor tables. ◆ Tu-Su lunch and dinner; closed two weeks in August. No credit cards accepted. Largo del Pallaro 15 (at Via dei Chiavari). 68801488

13 Teatro di Pompeo Only underground traces remain of this once-grand theater built in 53 BC, and these survived only because of a ruse. By senatorial decree all previous theaters had been made of wood, but Pompey was able to build his of stone by erecting a temple at the top of the auditorium in such a way that the tiers of seats appeared to be steps leading up to the altar. To complete the illusion, he had the entire structure dedicated to Venus. At the dramatic dedication ceremony, 500 lions and 18 elephants were killed in the 40,000-seat auditorium. To get a feel for its layout, walk down the curved Via di Grotta Pinta, which traces the outline of the ancient theater's semicircular auditorium. Today it's the site of a tiny working theater, the **Teatro dei Satiri** (6871639). Two vast porticoes surrounding public gardens led away from the auditorium down Via del Sudario and Via di Sant'Anna. Spectators assembled here, patronizing the various taverns—precursors of the myriad trattorie enclosed in the former complex's outline. Like the great Roman thermal baths, which also included small theaters, this complex was a versatile public space. When the **Curia** (the building in the **Roman Forum** where the Senate met) was closed for restoration in the spring of 44 BC, the senators moved into one of the 100-column porticoes that Pompey had adorned with fine marble statuary nine years earlier. The Senate's move was not without ironic overtones—later that same year Caesar gutted the Senate and appointed himself consul and dictator for life.

The fates of Pompey and Caesar were interwoven in several ways. Pompey was Caesar's son-in-law, and the two had been close political allies. With Crassus, they had formed the original triumvirate that ruled over the still (technically) republican Rome. Initially, Pompey was the most successful; by the time he built this theater to enhance his popularity with the Roman masses, he was already ruling the greater part of the Roman world, while his father-in-law, Julius, had only the two provinces of Gaul. The third triumvir, Crassus, died the year Pompey built the theater. Pompey's wife, Julia, died the year before that, leaving the two ambitious men with nothing but a geographic buffer between them. Sensing trouble, the Senate (by an overwhelming majority) ordered both Pompey and Caesar to disband their armies. Pompey's refusal to comply gave Caesar the pretext to declare war and march his army down from Gaul into Italy. In 49 BC he made his famous crossing of the Rubicon River at the northern end of the peninsula and headed south. Pompey suffered military losses and fled—to military defeat in Greece and to death a year later in Egypt.

During the next four years, Caesar had free reign, which culminated in his announcement of his own divinity. But on the morning of the Ides of March in 44 BC, when the Senate was to proclaim him King of the Orient, Caesar walked into Pompey's theater, heedless of warnings, and was repeatedly stabbed by a group of senators, including his adopted (some say biological) son Brutus. Ironically, he fell and died at the base of the statue of his old enemy, Pompey.

The ochre-red-orange Rome of visitors' memories and poets' dreams is a relatively recent phenomenon. The true colors of Rome, experts now contend, are much older and much brighter. In the 17th and 18th centuries, they say, Rome was a Rococo confection of sky blues, pearly whites, and dusty pinks, and it was only at the end of the 19th century that the pastel palette was abandoned in favor of the browns, ochres, and vermillions we are used to today.

14 La Tartaruga Cantina ★★★$$ Inviting with its wood-and-tile interior, which is accented by ubiquitous wine bottles, this cozy, family-run cantina is one of Rome's newest additions. Fresh ingredients from the nearby **Campo de' Fiori** market come together in such daily specials as fish soup with broccoli, a memorable *risotto alle erbe* (hearty but subtly flavored rice dish cooked with mountain nettle), and a rich, satisfying beef braised in Barolo wine. The wine list is extensive. ♦ Tu-Su lunch and dinner. Via del Monte della Farina 53 (between Vicolo de' Chiodaroli and Via del Sudario). 6869473

15 Dar Filettaro a Santa Barbara ★$ This hole-in-the-wall Roman institution spreads out in summer to fill a tiny piazza that retains the shape of a section of the **Teatro di Pompeo.** It is always crowded, especially on Friday nights when Romans like to eat *filletto di baccalà* (battered and deep-fried hunks of salt cod), served at paper-covered, communal tables and accompanied by cheap, raw Castelli wine. Once may be enough, but the experience is pure *romana.* ♦ M-Sa dinner from 5:30PM; closed in August. No credit cards accepted. Largo dei Librari 88 (at Via dei Giubbonari). 6864018

16 L'Angolo Divino $ Started as a neighborhood wine and olive oil shop where locals brought their own bottles for refills, this place is now an upscale wine bar, complete with creative snacks and its own sommelier. ♦ Tu-Su. Via dei Balestrari 12 (between Piazza

della Quercia and Via dei Giubbonari).
6864413

17 Ruggeri This is a good place to stock up for a picnic. Choose among several prosciuttos and salamis, and such cheeses as water-buffalo mozzarella or baked ricotta. Add a little bread, a few olives, some wine, and a couple of figs from the *Campo* to make the perfect meal on Tiber Island or in the **Villa Borghese.** ♦ M-Sa. Campo de' Fiori 2 (at Via dei Balestrari). 68801091

17 Il Fiorentino One of the best butcher shops in Rome, this place features beautiful cuts of veal and an interesting selection of ready-to-cook dishes. Try the stuffed peppers, meat loaf, and various kabobs. ♦ M-Sa. Campo de' Fiori 17 (between Via dei Balestrari and Via della Corda). 68801296

18 Campo de' Fiori Rome's oldest produce market, this is a wonderful place to stroll among heaps of burnished eggplants, mounds of long-stemmed, gray-green artichokes, hillocks of blood oranges, and trays of shimmering seafood, including the mighty snout of a whole swordfish (in May). The stalls are shaded by the ubiquitous *ombrelloni* (big, white canvas umbrellas). The array is garden fresh, though imports from Spain and South America also turn up, so don't buy wild strawberries in November or chestnuts in May if you want locally grown produce. A few stalls specialize in "exotic" produce like ginger or sweet potatoes, which here are called *patate americane,* probably because they are most often bought by Americans for Thanksgiving. Appropriate to the square's name, a colorful stretch of flower sellers lines one end. There's also lots of shouting, bargaining, and bustle. It all ends at 1:30PM when the sanitation trucks arrive to sweep up the mess. ♦ M-Sa mornings

19 Cook's Brasserie $ The vast menu offers oodles of pasta dishes and nearly as many main-course salads, plus soups and pizza—and you can sit outside and watch the show in the market. ♦ M-Sa lunch and dinner. Campo de' Fiori 53 (between Via dei Giubbonari and Piazza del Biscione). 6875530; fax 2604836.

19 Pasta all'Uovo Have a look inside this fresh pasta shop, and you'll see such standards as ravioli and cannelloni, but you may not be familiar with others, including *rotolo di ricotta,* a kind of strudel filled with ricotta and spinach. ♦ M-Sa. Campo de Fiori 55 (between Via dei Giubbonari and Piazza del Biscione). 68803524

20 Da Pancrazio ★$$ A descent into the lower cavelike dining room of this popular eatery is a trip back in time—it was part of the stage in Pompey's vast stone theater (note the reconstruction hanging on the wall at the entrance) and the place where the newly deified Julius Caesar gasped his last breath in bitter disappointment more than 2,000 years ago. Don't expect the food to be much in this heavily trafficked tourist mecca—stick to such standards as fettuccine or veal scallopini. ♦ M-Tu, Th-Su lunch and dinner; closed part of August. Piazza del Biscione 92 (just east of Campo de'Fiori). 6861246, 68803956

21 Hotel Campo de' Fiori $ Fewer than half of the 27 rooms in this tiny hotel have a private bath or shower, so advance reservations are a must. There is an agreeable roof garden, but no restaurant and no air-conditioning in summer, when the noise from the *Campo* goes unabated. ♦ Via del Biscione 6 (at Piazza del Biscione). 68806865; fax 6876003

22 Antica Norcineria A good way to recognize this hundred-year-old sausage shop is by the hanks of prosciutto hanging from the ceiling and the mouth-watering aroma coming out the door. Over a dozen kinds of dried and fresh sausage and a host of cured pork products are sold here. Try a slice of *finocchiona,* a garlic-and-fennel salami. ♦ M-W, F-Sa. Campo de' Fiori 43 (between Piazza del Biscione and Via dei Baullari). 68806114

22 Hostaria Romanesca ★★$ As its name indicates, this trattoria serves heaping bowls of traditional Roman home cooking. Given its location and popularity, the food is surprisingly good. It hasn't been upscaled to ridiculous heights or thinned down to accommodate tourists. *Bucatini all'amatriciana* (fat spaghetti in a bacon, onion, and tomato sauce) comes dusted with pecorino cheese. On Sunday, when the market is closed, this is a peaceful place to sit in the sun and have a leisurely lunch. There are only eight tables, so reserve ahead. ♦ Tu-Su lunch and dinner. Reservations recommended. Campo de' Fiori 40 (between Piazza del Biscione and Via dei Baullari). 6864024

23 Grappolo d'Oro ★★$$ Its proximity to the *Campo*'s produce market is an advantage this restaurant takes to heart. It's a good place to try *puntarelle,* a curly-leafed salad green—actually the spikes of the chicory plant—that is found only in Rome. The salad is dressed with oil, garlic, and specks of anchovy. A sliced and caramelized *arancio* (whole orange) makes a showy ending to a good meal. ♦ M-Sa lunch and dinner; closed in August. Piazza della Cancelleria 80 (between Campo de' Fiori and Corso Vittorio Emanuele). 6897080

24 Palazzo della Cancelleria This restored 1513 palazzo is the largest single building of its epoch surviving in Rome. In fact, many art historians praise this as Rome's first monument of the Renaissance. Other art historians decry its very existence because, to build it, tons of marble were plundered from the nearby **Teatro di Pompeo.** In any event, no one knows who was the main architect—maybe **Andrea Bregno** or perhaps his brother. The 1539 facade is the work of **Domenico Fontana.** Inside is one of the best preserved Renaissance courtyards in Rome, the proportions of its elegant double loggia of antique columns so carefully calculated that it appears airy and delicate. Taking a cue from such classical architects as **Vitruvius, Bramante** strove to have every part of it in perfect scale, using mathematical formulas to determine what harmonized. The money to build this vast palace was supposedly won by one papal nephew from another during a night of high-stakes gambling. But the palazzo's builder and first owner, Cardinal Raffaele Riario, was guilty, it seems, of more than just gambling; he supervised a failed attempt to murder Lorenzo de' Medici and did murder Lorenzo's brother, Giuliano. A few centuries later, the palace passed into the hands of Cardinal Henry, Duke of York, and brother of the Catholic pretender to the British throne, Bonnie Prince Charlie. When Napoleon occupied Rome (1809-14), the palazzo housed the law courts, and subsequently it became the papal chancellery—hence its name and the reason it remains part of **Vatican** territory. During the 1950s, the Sacra Rota met here to hear marriage annulment proceedings. Today classical music concerts are held in the *salone,* which was supposedly frescoed from floor to ceiling in a hundred days by Vasari. Check *Roma C'è* for upcoming concerts. ♦ Piazza della Cancelleria (between Via del Pellegrino and Corso Vittorio Emanuele)

Within the Palazzo della Cancelleria:

Wisteria watchers will not want to miss seeing this spectacular purple vine bloom in mid-April. The Orto Botanico in Trastevere has several ancient gnarled wisteria sinensis, including a rare ghostly white vine along the gate of its back entrance on Janiculum Hill. Wisteria can also be found at Villa Sciarra, draping the palazzi along Via Margutta, and running up the banister next to the steps to the Campidoglio.

Chiesa di San Lorenzo in Damaso Built as part of the original palazzo, this 1495 church replaced a fourth-century chapel founded by Pope Damasus I. The door was designed by **Giacomo da Vignola.** Over the high altar is the *Coronation of the Virgin* by Federico Zuccari.

Ditirambo ★★★$$ The homemade fare at this new trattoria offers a delightful respite from heavy Roman cuisine. Everything is made fresh daily, from the scrumptious breads and filled pastas to the tempting desserts. Start with *gnocchi di ricotta,* light-as-air almond-flour dumplings in a light vegetable sauce with zucchini flowers. The second course might include hearty rabbit with sage, a light zucchini flan, or a dish of five Italian cheeses. Be sure to save room for the fresh-baked cookies or berry tart. ♦ M dinner; Tu-Su lunch and dinner. Piazza della Cancelleria 74-75. 6871626

25 MozArt's This shop specializes in lutes, but mandolins, guitars, and harps can also be mended here. In addition, the staff builds violins and collects unusual pianos, like the twin to Beethoven's—shorter than a standard grand and with just six octaves. After leaving the shop, turn left and walk down Via Acetari (Vinegar Lane), a colorful, tiny street. ♦ By appointment only. Via del Pellegrino 10 (at Piazza della Cancelleria). 6875488, 7006109

25 Marco Aurelio Gioelli Marco Aurelio Olivetti designs and sells fine jewelry on the premises. His work features silver or gold with precious stones and gold-plated silver with semiprecious stones. Choose from the many antique-inspired styles in delicate designs or chunky motifs. ♦ Tu-Sa (no midday closing). Via del Pellegrino 48 (at Arco degli Acetari). 6865570

26 Il Forno di Campo de' Fiori Get in the crowd (no lines, no numbers), be aggressive, and shout your order in this bread and pastry shop. Many claim the *pizza bianca* ("white pizza"), hot from the oven with only a brushing of olive oil on top, is the best in Rome. Breads of all kinds (including cornmeal, rye, and whole wheat) are stacked on shelves behind counters with ricotta tarts and apple cakes. ♦ M-Sa. Campo de' Fiori 22 (between Via dei Cappellari and Piazza della Cancelleria). 68806662

26 La Carbonara ★$$ This venerable tourist restaurant, named for the famous Roman dish, has for some strange reason chosen to substitute short pasta for the traditional spaghetti and to ensure that every serving is always the same uniform bright yellow. There are, however, plenty of other good things on the menu, and lunch outdoors at one end of the *Campo* is a memorable event. ♦ M, W-Su lunch and dinner. Reservations recommended. Campo de' Fiori 23 (between Via dei Cappellari and Piazza della Cancelleria). 6864783

26 Hosteria La Barese ★$ In summertime, the outdoor tables at this regional restaurant bump up against those of **La Carbonara,** and patrons of both enjoy the same view of the *Campo*. The cuisine, however, is not the same. The owners here are from Bari, where *orechiette alla barese* (earlobe-shaped pasta with broccoli and hot peppers) is a regional specialty. Main courses include deep-fried seafood and chicken with peppers. ♦ M-Tu, Th-Su lunch and dinner. Campo de' Fiori 28 (between Via dei Cappellari and Piazza della Cancelleria). 6861312

27 Casa di Vanozza Look for the coat-of-arms, for herein lies a fascinating tale. This private residence—built in the 15th century—was once an inn. It was acquired in the 16th century by Vanozza Caetani, mistress of the notorious Spanish pope, Alexander VI (1431-1503). Raised to the papacy in the signal year of 1492, Alexander's corrupt dealings, combined with his neglect of spiritual concerns, contributed greatly to the development of the Protestant Reformation. Vanozza bore him four children, among them the notorious Lucrezia and Cesare Borgia. She had amassed a fortune by the time the pope switched his attentions to another local beauty, Giulia Farnese, and used the money to invest in this building and three hotels. Once Alexander was dead and buried, Vanozza affixed the still-visible shield, which combines the coats of arms of her husband and the Borgias—who made it all possible. ♦ Vicolo del Gallo 13 (at Via dei Cappellari)

Burned for his Beliefs

The statue of Giordano Bruno, brooding darkly under his monk's cowl, is Rome's most dramatically anticlerical monument and a vivid reminder of the love-hate relationship between Rome and the papacy.

Persecuted in Counter-Reformation Italy for his alleged heretical beliefs—including championing Copernicus's theory of the universe—Bruno fled to France and England, where he taught for a while at Oxford. In his book, *The Embassy Affair,* John Bossy claims that Bruno may even have been the infamous Henry Fagot who spied for the British against the French. Bruno was finally summoned back to Italy by the Inquisition. After seven years of imprisonment, he was taken—bound and gagged— to **Campo de' Fiori** and burned at the stake here by order of the Holy Office on 17 February 1600. Ever since then, this spot has been Rome's rallying point for dissenters, radicals, and revolutionaries.

The reliefs on the base of Ettore Ferrari's bronze statue show John Wycliff, Jan Hus, and others who strayed from orthodoxy. The statue was erected in 1870 by a group of reformers who again defied the pope—this time to unite Italy. The inscription "To G. Bruno, The age by him foretold, Here where the pyre burned" was a compromise. The hardline reformers would have preferred his famous last words to his judges: "You tremble more to pronounce this sentence than I to fulfill it."

28 La Vineria ★$ This popular wine shop is a mecca for university students, young professionals, and anyone who shares the outsider spirit of Giordano Bruno standing in the center of the *Campo.* Inside is a long bar and seats along the wall, and there are outdoor tables in the summer. Sandwiches and light snacks are also available. ♦ M-Sa. Campo de' Fiori 15 (between Via della Corda and Vicolo dei Baullari). 68803268

29 Caffè Farnese ★$ This is one of the very few cafes in Rome where you can have a croissant, instead of the horn-shaped Roman *cornetto,* with a morning cappuccino. (These croissants, however, would never pass muster with the largely French clientele from the nearby **French Embassy.**) ♦ Daily. Vicolo dei Baullari 106 (at Piazza Farnese). 68802125

30 Piazza Farnese Typically Roman and wonderfully dramatic is the juxtaposition of this square and **Campo de' Fiori,** only paces away. The *Campo* is medieval and as severe as the brooding statue of Giordano Bruno in the center, while this piazza is Baroque and as delightfully incandescent as its two splashing fountains—bathtubs recycled from the **Baths of Caracalla.**

31 Osteria ar Galletto ★★$$ Everything a visitor to Rome could want is found at this dining spot: good food and a postcard-perfect setting in front of a majestic Renaissance palace. Starters include *alici* (fresh anchovies) marinated in olive oil and lemon juice. The specialities here are game and wild mushrooms (and truffles in season), so be sure to try *galletto alla diavola* (a whole chicken flattened and then baked to crisp perfection). ♦ M-Sa lunch and dinner. Reservations recommended for outside tables. Piazza Farnese 102 (between Via di Monserrato and Vicolo del Gallo). 6861714

31 Casa di Santa Brigida $$ This 14th-century property overlooking **Piazza Farnese** was once home to Saint Bridget. It now serves as a guest house run by nuns. Though the solemn environment may not be for some, others welcome the serenity of TV-less rooms. All 23 guest rooms feature antique furnishings and private baths; some offer views of the handsome piazza below, while others have a bird's-eye view of **Palazzo Farnese** (see below), site of the French consulate. An elevator, spacious library, sunny roof terrace, and complimentary breakfast round out the amenities. ♦ Piazza Farnese 96 (entrance on Via di Monserrato). 68892596, 68892497; fax 68891573, 68219126; brigida@mclink.it; www.brigidine.org

32 Palazzo Farnese In the 15th century, a member of the Tuscan Farnese family married into the powerful Caetani family of Rome and was catapulted into Rome's high society. A century later Cardinal Alessandro Farnese commissioned architect **Antonio da Sangallo** to build him a palazzo in the banking and governing district of that time, which was near **Campo de' Fiori.** Suddenly elected Pope Paul III, Alessandro appealed to **Sangallo** to create a more worthy mansion. **Sangallo** began by tearing down the three large houses standing on the site. After he died in 1546, **Michelangelo** took over and added the crowning touch: a grandiose projecting roof cornice. And how right he was—try to imagine the building without it.

After Pope Paul III died in 1549, the work continued to drag on—for decades—until 1573, when **Giacomo della Porta** finished it. He carried out most of **Michelangelo**'s ideas, including the lovely archway over Via Giulia, as well as the buildings and gardens leading down to the river. One flight up, the great fresco artist Annibale Carracci (with some help from family and friends) painted the ceiling of the salon (now the French ambassador's private dining room) with scenes from classical mythology.

The astronomical building costs made the palace the butt of jokes scrawled on placards and hung about the necks of Rome's sharp-witted "talking" statues. The palazzo was also expensive to maintain, and so Cardinal Odoardo Farnese's heirs deserted it after he died in 1626. In 1635, a deal was struck that gave the building to the French Embassy in exchange for an Italian Embassy building in Paris. Cardinal Richelieu and the Duc d'Estrées held court here, and former Queen Christina of Sweden, who removed all the fig leaves from the nude sculptures, also held court here. Puccini capitalized on its rich historical background when he made the palazzo the setting for the second act of his opera *Tosca.*

Although it is closed to the public, you can arrange a visit by writing several months in advance to the **Cultural Service of the French Embassy,** Piazza Farnese, 00186 Rome.
♦ Piazza Farnese (between Via del Mascherone and Via dei Farnesi). 686011; fax 68601331

33 Farnese This shop is the Tiffany's of tiles, offering antique and modern styles, as well as authentic antiques (priced accordingly). All are gorgeous and sold by the square meter. Under the vaulted ceiling of an ancient Roman building on the lower floor is a display of rare, centuries-old tiles. Purchases will be shipped anywhere to adorn swimming pools, floors, or bathrooms. The store was designed by Tullio Di Donato, who launched the white-on-white tile vogue. ♦ M-Sa. Piazza Farnese 52 (between Vicolo dei Venti and Vicolo del Giglio). 6896109; fax 6874793

34 Restauro Farnese Drop into this first-rate workshop for the repair of porcelains and ceramics and watch these experts at work. They'll attempt anything, but they do not guarantee complete success with glass and crystal. Wood restoring is done next door.
♦ M afternoon; Tu-F; Sa morning. Piazza Farnese 43 (between Via della Corda and Vicolo dei Baullari). 6869294

35 Palazzo Spada Sixteenth-century cardinals were a jealous lot, and they tried to outdo each other in their building projects. This outstanding 16th-century palace was built in 1550 for Cardinal Gerolamo Capo di Ferro by **Caravaggio** and **Giulio Mazzoni.** Cardinal Bernardino Spada acquired it in 1632; his descendants sold it to the government in 1926. Some critics consider the Mannerist-style white stucco decorations on the facade and inner courtyard frivolous. They depict satyrs, centaurs, and tritons amid well-fed cherubs holding up generous festoons of fruits and flowers. The wedding-cake effect, however, is impressive and forms a beautiful contrast with the dark shadows inside the arched portico on the ground level. The most extrordinary feature of this courtyard is the trompe l'oeil tunnel **Francesco Borromini** created in 1652 for Cardinal Spada's brother. On the other side of the library window to the left of the entrance, there appears to be a long pillared gallery leading off majestically to another courtyard with a large heroic statue in the middle. But it's all a trick, a grand optical illusion created by a rising floor, descending ceiling, and gradually diminishing columns. Admission to the cardinal's private collection of paintings upstairs includes a visit to **Borromini**'s masterpiece. First pay the admission fee at the entrance, then go up the steps to the **Galleria Spada:** four sumptuous rooms lined with paintings by Titian, Andrea del Sarto, and Pieter Brueghel, among others. Be sure to see the two huge globes; the sphere of the New World is among its earliest depictions.

The palazzo also houses state rooms, which can only be visited with special permission, generally only given to art scholars (write to **Ufficio Intendenza,** Dr. Cantarelli, Palazzo Spada, Piazza Capo di Ferro 13, 00186 Roma; or fax him at 6827238). Here you'll find a statue of *Pompey,* at the base of which Julius Caesar is said to have been killed. Experts disagree about the statue's authenticity, but most everyone agrees that the palazzo's throne room is of special interest. Visiting popes were entertained in such a salon; therefore, throne rooms are found only in the kind of homes that a pope might visit—the palaces of princes, dukes, and a few marquises. ♦ Admission. Free for architecture and art history students. Galleria Spada Museum: Tu-Sa; Su morning. Piazza Capo di Ferro 13 (at Via Capo di Ferro). 6861158

36 Sergio alle Grotte ★$ Go early or be prepared to stand in line for a table in this small, wood-beamed, rustic trattoria. The specialty here is pizza baked (in full view) on the stones of a wood-burning oven. If pizza with zucchini blossoms isn't on the menu, ask for it. ♦ M-Sa lunch and dinner. Vicolo delle Grotte 27 (at Via Capo di Ferro). 6864293

37 Ristorante Monserrato ★★★$$ This wonderful small restaurant is always a pleasure, either at lunchtime outside under the *ombrelloni* (extra-large canvas umbrellas) or for dinner inside one of two cozy rooms. Try such specials as *spaghetti allo scoglio* (with seafood) or a simple veal fillet perfectly grilled and mouth-wateringly tender. The house dish is *bombolotti all'astice* (short pasta in a garlic-and-tomato sauce and half a Mediterranean lobster)—a meal in itself.
♦ M, W-Sa lunch and dinner; Tu dinner. Via di Monserrato 96 (at Piazza di Santa Caterina della Rota). 68804095

38 Fratelli Paladini This sandwich and pizza shop is easy to find—look for the crowd spilling out into the street. All social classes come here, from shop clerks to police officers to cabinet ministers. The atmosphere at lunch is quick and chaotic, but the pizza bread—hot from a wood-burning oven—that the guys in T-shirts behind the counter slice and stuff with *mortadella, bresaola* (air-dried beef), and *rughetta* (wild arugula), among other fillings, is legendary. Everybody eats standing up or in the street. Down it all with bottles of either mineral water or wine that are set out on the counter. This could be one of the most satisfying meals you have in Rome—and you won't believe the bill. ♦ M-Sa 8AM to 7PM. Via del Governo Vecchio 29 (at Via Sora). 6861237

39 Via del Governo Vecchio 104 On the facade of this 17th-century palazzo, ancient frescoes of the owner, his secretary, and his pet parrot are barely discernible among later bas-reliefs of 19 worthies in festooned frames. The religious Confraternity of the Stigmata were once owners. It's not open to the public. ♦ Between Vicolo Savelli and Via Sora

40 Chiesa Nuova—Santa Maria in Vallicella This "New Church" dates back to the 16th century, when it replaced a smaller medieval Franciscan church and convent. Built by **Matteo di Città di Castello** and **Martino Longhi,** the church and the adjoining **Oratorio** (Oratory) belong to the Congregation of Oratorians founded in 1561 by St. Philip Neri. Neri believed that spartan, unadorned churches and preaching to the masses would help counter the Protestant Reformation, but these views died with Neri, and the interior was given its exuberantly Baroque decoration by Pietro da Cortona. His astonishing ceiling painting depicts Neri's vision of the Virgin Mary holding up part of the old church when it threatened to fall down on the congregation. Surrounding the altar are three early–17th-century paintings on slate (to prevent reflections) by the Flemish master Peter Paul Rubens.In front of the church is a fountain that Romans fondly call **La Zuppiera** (The Soup Tureen). It was built in the mid-16th century for **Campo de' Fiori** and later transferred here. ♦ Piazza della Chiesa Nuova (between Via della Chiesa Nuova and Via de' Filippini)

Adjacent to the Chiesa Nuova:

Oratorio dei Filippini (Oratory)
Borromini was a Baroque artist and architect, and Baroque was theatrical. According to his original plan, the oratory's facade was to be a series of undulating curves like a stage set. However, permission allowing the facade to jut out into the square was denied, and **Borromini** was forced to limit its scope. The greatly flattened facade, nevertheless, looks three-dimensional thanks to **Borromini**'s skillful use of concave and convex elements. Inside, **Borromini**'s banded ribbons run up the walls into the ceiling. In 1670 the Queen of Sweden commissioned a musical text to be performed here from **Bernini**'s son Pietro, who called it an *oratorio.* Since then the **Oratory** has premiered the work of many famed musicians, including Scarlatti, Bach, Handel, and Haydn, and is still being used for musical events, including oratorios (check *Roma C'è*). The building's restored clock tower, visible from **Piazza del Orologio**

around the corner, further illustrates **Borromini**'s genius for convex and concave surfaces, which here undulate in an almost musical fashion.

41 Bella Napoli Among the delicacies offered at this pastry shop are such world-famous Neapolitan cakes and pastries as *pastiera* (a ricotta pie made with whole kernels of wheat and flavored with orange water) and *sfogliatelle* (crispy ricotta-filled turnovers), eaten warm and dusted with powdered sugar. ♦ M-F, Su 7:30AM-9PM. Corso Vittorio Emanuele 246 (between Via Sora and Vicolo Cellini). 6877048

42 Da Luigi ★$$ The menu at this trattoria in the tree-shaded **Piazza Sforza Cesarini** relies heavily on fish—not a strong point of Roman cooking. (Rome is too far from the sea to get absolutely fresh fish. Moreover, never order fish on Monday, because there is no Sunday catch.) Stick to the veal dishes, a strong point of Roman cooking. ♦ Tu-Su lunch and dinner. Piazza Sforza Cesarini 24 (between Corso Vittorio Emanuele and Vicolo Sforza Cesarini). 68805463; fax 6864777

42 Pizzeria Polese ★★$$ Like **Da Luigi,** this trattoria offers reliable food in a charming setting, especially in warm weather, when it's possible to dine alfresco under canvas umbrellas and flickering candles. This is the better of the two restaurants. The menu, which is shaped like a wine carafe, changes daily. Try the *risotto radicchio e gamberi* (with shrimp) or *bresaola, rughetta,* and *parmigiano,* drizzled with lemon juice and olive oil—it's hard to beat. ♦ M, W-Su lunch and dinner; closed in August. Piazza Sforza Cesarini 40 (between Corso Vittorio Emanuele and Vicolo Sforza Cesarini). 6861709

43 Pierluigi ★★★$$ Sit outside in summer and admire the frescoes on **Palazzo Ricci** (see 37) while dining at one of Rome's liveliest and most reliable restaurants. The *spaghetti ai crostacei* (a haul-in of shrimp, mussels, clams, and other shellfish) is always on target. The *straccietti* ("rags," or strips, of beef) with a wreath of raw *rughetta* (wild arugula) on top are reason enough to reserve a table, but you might also be attracted by the homemade chocolate cake topped with whipped cream. ♦ Tu-Su lunch and dinner. Reservations recommended. Piazza de' Ricci 144 (at Via di Monserrato). 6861302

44 Casa di Pietro Paolo della Zecca Eleanor of Portugal lodged in this building in

1462 before her wedding to Emperor Frederick of Austria; a plaque proclaims "Al Austria Spetta Dominare Tutto" (Austria will rule all). The original property was a triangular lot set at an acute angle where Via di Monserrato intersects Via del Pellegrino; in an early example of city planning the apex of the triangle was confiscated by municipal authorities to create **Piazza della Moretta.** ♦ Via di Monserrato and Via del Pellegrino

45 Enoteca Il Goccetto

★$ This cozy neighborhoood wine-store–turned–wine-bar is always full of connoisseurs hunting the rare bottle and locals enjoying a glass of Prosecco and a snack after work. ♦ M-Sa; closed most of August. Via dei Banchi Vecchi 14 (at Via delle Carceri). 6864268

46 Pietro Simonelli—Laboratorio del Maschero
Masks to be used for Carnival, the theater, or wall decoration are offered at this shop/factory. You can watch these artistic face coverings being made out of papier-mâché or plaster. ♦ M afternoon; Tu-F; Sa morning. Via dei Banchi Vecchi 125 (at Vicolo Sforza Cesarini). 6868912

47 Studio dell'Incisore Santucci
For engraved visiting cards or stationery printed with your coat-of-arms, this is the place to come. The engravers work right in front of you. ♦ M afternoon; Tu-F; Sa morning. Via dei Banchi Vecchi 103 (at Vicolo Sugarelli). 68806071

48 Enoteca del Corso

This wine shop has one of the best cellars in Rome and the widest selection of Champagnes. Tasting is encouraged, and light sandwiches accompany it. Browsing will turn up the perfect gift bottle of balsamic vinegar, extra-virgin olive oil, or quince jam. ♦ M-Sa. Corso Vittorio Emanuele 293-95 (between Via Giovanni Giraud and Largo Ottavio Tassoni). 68801594

49 Biancaneve
★$ In this cafe at the end of Corso Vittorio Emanuele, crowds of young people sit nightly on the side facing the illuminated **Castel Sant'Angelo,** and devour *la mela stregata*, the bewitched apple that did in Snow White, after whom the bar is named. In this case the enchanted fruit is a ball of zabaglione ice cream coated with bittersweet chocolate. ♦ M, W-Su 8AM-1AM. Piazza Pasquale Paoli 2 (at Corso Vittorio Emanuele). 68806227

50 Antiquaria Sant'Angelo
Tucked into a corner by Ponte Sant'Angelo beneath an ancient Roman portico, this fascinating print shop welcomes browsers. Besides carefully chosen prints and antique books, including some rare guides to Rome, there is also a collection of letters of the alphabet taken from old prints—the staff will frame any initials you want. ♦ M-Sa. Via Banco di Santo Spirito 61 (between Vicolo del Curato and Piazza Ponte Sant'Angelo). 6865944

Bests

Stephen Clifford Wilson
Lecturer, University of Rome

Strolling and lifting one's eyes to above ground-floor level in almost any downtown street and enjoying the architectural styles, from the Classical and Medieval through Renaissance and Baroque.

In spite of the tourists, highish prices, and slowish service, the incomparable **Caffè Greco** (a national monument), to relax and read my paper over coffee or chat over a preprandial Campari.

The 10AM sung Latin Mass on Sunday in **Santa Maria Maggiore;** the most dramatic and ritualistic of services in the most sumptuous of Roman basilicas.

Looking for traces of the exiled and doomed Stuart kings of England (Bonnie Prince Charlie, his brother Cardinal York, etc.), like Canova's masterpiece of a memorial in **St. Peter's.**

The splendors of the great Roman palaces, like the **Galleria Doria Pamphili** and state rooms.

The bus service, which takes you almost everywhere—but beware of the hordes of very professional pickpockets.

A walk around the **Ghetto,** the world's oldest Jewish community.

Entering **St. Peter's Square** with new visitors from the side rather than full frontal, and watching them gasp.

The **Chiesa di Sant'Agnese Fuori le Mura,** with its catacombs and the tomb of Constantia: three treats in one.

Drinking fresh water from the fountains of Rome.

Standing in the middle of the **Quattro Fontane** crossing (exceedingly dangerous) to see the three obelisks.

Lunch on the terrace of the **Casina Valadier** on a clear day; forget about the food and enjoy the view.

Restaurants/Clubs: Red	Hotels: Blue
Shops/♥ Outdoors: Green	Sights/Culture: Black

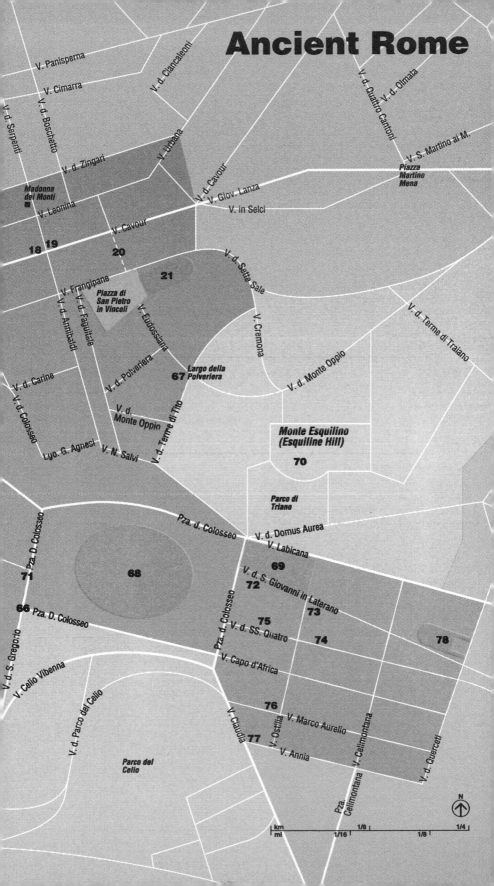

Ancient Rome

V. Panisperna

V. Cimarra

V. d. Boschetto

V. d. Serpenti

V. d. Zingari

V. d. Ciancaleoni

V. Urbana

V. d. Cavour

V. Giov. Lanza

V. in Selci

V. d. Quattro Cantoni

V. d. Olmata

V. S. Martino ai M.

Piazza
Martino
Mena

Madonna
dei Monti

V. Leonina

V. Cavour

18 19

20

V. Frangipane

V. d. Amibaldi

V. d. Faguitale

Piazza di
San Pietro
in Vincoli

21

V. Eudossiana

V. d. Sette Sale

V. Cremona

V. d. Terme di Traiano

V. d. Carine

V. d. Colosseo

V. d. Polveriera

Largo della
Polveriera

67

V. d.
Monte Oppin

V. d. Terme di Tito

V. d. Monte Oppio

Monte Esquilino
(Esquiline Hill)

70

Lgo. G. Agnesi

V. N. Salvi

Parco di
Triano

Pza. d. Colosseo

V. d. Domus Aurea

V. Labicana

69

72

V. d. S. Giovanni in Laterano

73

Pza. D. Colosseo

71

68

Pza. d. Colosseo

75

V. d. SS. Quatro

74

78

66 Pza. D. Colosseo

V. Capo d'Africa

V. d. S. Gregorio

V. d. Celio Vibenna

76

V. Marco Aurelio

V. Celimontana

V. d. Quercett

V. d. Parco del Celio

V. Claudia

77

V. Ostilia

V. Annia

Parco del
Celio

Pza
Celimontana

N

km
mi

1/16

1/8

1/8

1/4

Ancient Rome

Throughout history Romans have always staged spectacular parades for which good roads and broad avenues are a must. Slicing through the heart of Rome is a perfect procession path—the **Via dei Fori Imperiali** (Street of the Imperial Forums). Running in a straight line between the **Colosseum** and **Piazza Venezia**, it is the only broad boulevard in Rome's historic center. Built by dictator Benito Mussolini in 1931-33 to celebrate "the past and present grandeur of Rome," the avenue was a perfect fascist parade ground. To make way for this road, medieval towers and Renaissance churches and palaces were torn down, and the **Imperial Forums,** which had been buried for centuries, were uncovered. These public areas, built by Julius Caesar and the emperors Augustus, Vespasian, Nerva, and Trajan, were extensions of the original ancient **Roman Forum.**

Rising above and surrounding this odd and fascinating mixture of the ancient and the modern are four of Rome's seven hills: **Capitoline**, **Palatine**, **Quirinal**, and **Esquiline.** Legend says that the first Roman residents arrived from the Alban Hills to the east and built huts on these hilltops. The clusters of settlements gradually evolved into villages where daily life centered around forums—an early form of today's piazzas—in the valley below. The forums served both as lively marketplaces where livestock, food, and goods were sold and as public squares lined with administrative buildings and religious temples.

The fledgling city's strategic combination of a navigable river and defensible hilltops spurred commerce and growth hampered by only one major problem—frequent flooding when the **Tiber** overflowed its banks. At the end of the sixth century BC, the ambitious Tarquinius Priscus, fifth king of Rome, drained the valley with a canal system that emptied into the river through a large sewer—the **Cloaca Maxima**—and made the valley into an open piazza, or forum.

After the second-century BC victory over Carthage, the state paved the roads leading through the **Roman Forum** so that triumphant generals returning from abroad could parade down **Via Sacra** (Sacred Road) in chariots—past white marble buildings and towering statues of former leaders and under arches where only emperors or victorious generals were allowed to pass—on their way to the Capitoline Hill. Each leader had a self-promoting triumphal arch erected (three remain—the **Arch of Septimius Severus, Arch of Titus,** and **Arch of Constantine**) on which picture stories in bas-relief promoted the leader's military accomplishments. At the end of Via Sacra stood the **Colosseum**, the center of another kind of spectacle, where life—both animal and human—was treated as trivial.

As Rome grew, and the empire spread throughout the world (and its leaders sought new ways to glorify their accomplishments), new gathering places and public areas became necessary. Julius Caesar was the first to build a new forum in his own honor in 51 BC; Augustus, the first emperor, followed his example 20 years later. The **Foro di Traiano** (Trajan's Forum) was the last and the largest of the imperial forums. Much of the **Mercato di Traiano** (Trajan's Market) is well preserved, but two-thirds of Caesar's and Nerva's forums lie buried below Mussolini's parade road. A plan to unearth them and create a single huge archaeological park in the area is backed by Rome's cultural community but not its bureaucracy and so languishes in the dusty bottom drawers of City Hall.

When the Roman Empire collapsed in the fifth century, the Goths came from the north, conquered, and shifted the capital to Ravenna, abandoning Rome and all its forums. The buildings were no longer maintained, the sewer system became so clogged that the valley reverted to swampland, and frequent earthquakes left a thick layer of rubble everywhere. By the Middle Ages the ground had risen to cover all but the tallest of the ruined buildings, and these were systematically plundered by powerful families who used the marble to build fortresses in and around the old imperial forums.

Capitoline Hill and the Imperial Forums

The smallest but most important of Rome's seven hills, the Capitoline was the citadel for the very early city and the site of the capital of the Western world during the Roman Empire. At its top is **Piazza del Campidoglio,** the first modern square in Rome, and some say the most beautiful. Here ancient worshipers left offerings at the temple to Jupiter and kept their city treasury in the basement of the temple to Juno Moneta (from which the word money is derived). Here Brutus came with bloody hands to speak of the murder of Julius Caesar, Petrarch was crowned with laurel leaves, and Admiral Nelson's troops hoisted the British flag in 1799 in time to keep Napoleon from taking all. At the base of Capitoline Hill are the remnants of the five great **Imperial Forums** that were built over a 165-year period by Julius Caesar and four of the emperors who succeeded him.

1 Piazza Venezia Named for the imposing **Palazzo Venezia** on its western side, this 1911 square is the terminus of the ancient thoroughfare Via del Corso. Today four main thoroughfares disgorge Fiats and Alfa Romeos into the piazza. No traffic light could cope—or match the performance of the white-gloved police officer who elegantly directs traffic, usually while being videotaped by tourists. The fake palace opposite the palazzo was built as its mirror image for a Venice-based insurance company; it is now the **Ministry for the Environment** (appropriate, given the high levels of car exhaust and other pollution in this neighborhood) and bears an authentic 16th-century

Venetian emblem—the Lion of St. Mark—on the facade. A plaque on its wall indicates that this is where demolishers destroyed the house in which Michelangelo died in 1564.

2 Palazzo Bonaparte On the north side of **Piazza Venezia** is this 1660 palazzo where Letizia Bonaparte, Napoleon's mother, lived until her death in 1834. She passed the day sitting on the first-floor balcony watching the carriages rumbling by. On the ground floor is a charming courtyard. The building is not open to the public. ♦ Piazza Venezia 5 (at Via del Corso)

Within the Palazzo Bonaparte:

Caffè Napoleon ★$ Many claim this coffee bar has the freshest and best-tasting *cornetti*—the horn-shaped Roman breakfast roll—in the Centro Storico. The whole-wheat variety, *cornetto integrale,* filled with marmalade, is a welcome novelty. Hot and cold light lunches are served at the upstairs tables. ♦ M-Sa 6:30AM-8:30PM. No phone

3 Palazzo Venezia This palace may have the most famous balcony in history after Juliet's, though for less romantic reasons: It was from here, on the central balcony, that Mussolini declared war on France in 1940 and on the United States in 1941, with thousands cheering below on both occasions. Built in 1467, probably by **Leon Battista Alberti,** the architecture illustrates the transition from a medieval fortress to a building already showing the softer graces of the Renaissance. Pietro Barbo (later Pope Paul II)

Palazzo Venezia

commissioned the building upon being made a cardinal. In 1564 another pope swapped the palace for favors from *La Serenissima* (the Republic of Venice), which used it as an embassy—hence the name of the palace and the piazza. In 1798 Napoleon, after seizing Venice, gave the palace to the Austrians as their embassy.

During World War I, while Italy was fighting against Austria, the building was expropriated by the Italian king. Benito Mussolini later took over its huge—70 feet long by 40 feet wide by two stories high—**Sala del Mappamondo** (Map Room), so-called because it contained a painting of the world as envisioned in 1495. Il Duce's visitors had a long walk to approach him at his desk, and his various mistresses reported that he liked to dally with them on the floor or on the stone steps leading to the windows. When the Allied troops liberated Rome in June 1944, the palace was opened to the public for the first time. Today it is a museum with a splendid collection of tapestries, ancient arms, medieval sculpture, silver and ceramic artworks, and paintings. The palace also hosts temporary exhibitions, advertised by large banners on the facade.
♦ Admission. Tu-Su morning. Piazza Venezia 3 (between Piazza di San Marco and Via del Plebiscito; alternative entrance at Via del Plebiscito 118). 6798865.

4 Monumento a Vittorio Emanuele II/Altare della Patria (Monument to Victor Emmanuel/Altar of the Nation)
Dubbed by detractors as the "wedding cake" or the "white typewriter," this monument was built in 1885-1911 by **Giuseppe Sacconi** to commemorate the unification of Italy in 1870

and Vittorio Emanuele II, the new country's first king. Since it was constructed of Brescian marble and not travertine, like most Roman monuments, it has never lost its blinding luster and remains out of harmony with its surroundings. The king is depicted in a bronze equestrian statue, and two fountains represent the Adriatic and the Tyrrhenian Seas that bathe the Italian peninsula. Two bronze chariots transporting statues of winged victories (1908 works by Carlo Fontana and Paolo Bartolini) top it off. Next to the fountain on the left is a fragment of a first-century BC tomb.

After World War I, the **Altare della Patria**—Italy's Tomb of the Unknown Soldier—was added to the monument. Sentries guard the memorial night and day, and heads of state tie up traffic regularly to place wreaths in front of the tomb, which is flanked by two eternal flames. History buffs may enjoy the **Museo Centrale del Risorgimento** (Central Museum of the Risorgimento) inside the monument. It houses a collection of 3,000 drawings of Italian Army uniforms from 1866 to the present. ♦ Admission. Tu-Su 9AM-1PM. Piazza Venezia (between Piazza di San Marco and Via dei Fori Imperiali). 6793526, 6793598

5 Piazza del Campidoglio From the days of Imperial Rome to the present, this piazza at the top of Capitoline Hill has had the same basic U-shape of three buildings (originally, two temples and an office building) around an empty hollow. For approximately 1,000 years the piazza's edifices faced downward to the busy forums, but by the Renaissance the buildings were abandoned, the hollow overrun by sheep and goats, and the center of Rome had shifted to **St. Peter's Square.**

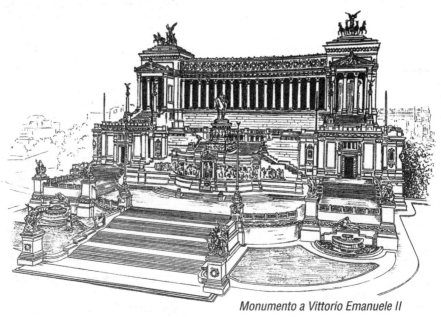

Monumento a Vittorio Emanuele II

Michelangelo's new design in 1538 (which took its final form 110 years later) turned the hilltop buildings around by 180° and made the piazza look upon Renaissance Rome, rather than the ancient city. He rearranged two preexisting buildings and added a third, designing new facades for all three; in the middle he created a piazza and designed a great staircase leading to it to harmonize with a much older adjacent staircase leading to the **Chiesa di Santa Maria in Aracoeli** (see page 68). Climb the stairs looking upward to see the statue of *Marcus Aurelius* emerge against the background of Renaissance facades (the statue is a copy; the original is in the **Palazzo dei Conservatori**, see below). The monumental statues of *Castor* and *Pollux*—the Gemini of the zodiac—stand at the top of the steps; they are all that is left of their temple that once stood in the forum below. On the night of Rome's birthday, 21 April, the staircase and buildings are outlined with hundreds of Roman dish candles. The road at the top of the staircase leads off to the right and through an archway to a park and belvedere with a singular view of the Roman skyline.

6 Palazzo dei Conservatori (Palace of the Conservators) Pope Sixtus IV opened this museum (the first recorded public gallery) on 18 January 1471 so that Romans could admire statues from antiquity. It was a courageous act, as they were considered pagan art works and not worthy of admiration. The building stands on the river side of the piazza, partly on the site of one of ancient Rome's most venerable places of worship—the **Temple to Capitoline Jove**, dedicated in 509 BC to one of Rome's three most important gods. Roman generals, returning from the provinces, rode here in pomp to give thanks for their victories, and consuls came to the temple to take their oaths of office. Although it was built and rebuilt various times, the temple finally crumbled in the sixth century AD.

The original structure of the palazzo dates from the 15th century. It was altered in 1568 by **Giacomo della Porta** according to a design by **Michelangelo** and rebuilt in 1820 when the French returned works that Napoleon had stolen and shipped to Paris. In the courtyard **Michelangelo** placed pieces of a colossal statue of Constantine that once towered 40 feet over the nearby **Basilica di Maxentius.** One of the huge hands with its index finger pointing upward remains from this colossus. A gigantic head and probably the other hand are from a statue of the Emperor's third son, Constantius II, who became emperor in AD 337. (Colossal statues were never meant to be viewed this closely, and only the figure's nude parts were in marble; the clothed parts were made of wood

covered with burnished or painted bronze). The courtyard also has reliefs from **Hadrian's Temple** in **Piazza di Pietra,** representing the foreign provinces under his rule. In a small room on the ground floor is the original of the second-century statue of *Marcus Aurelius* from the **Piazza del Campidoglio,** which managed for centuries to avoid rapacious vandals and popes only because it had been mistakenly identified as representing Constantine, the first Christian emperor. The oldest equestrian bronze work to survive intact from antiquity, the statue was brought indoors (after a decade of restoration was completed in 1990) to protect it from pollution. It had to be restored since legend says that Rome will fall when all the gilding flakes off the statue.

One flight up is the main collection where the museum's most famous statues from antiquity are located, including the *Spinario*— a striking lifelike statue of a messenger boy removing a thorn from his foot (third century BC)—and the *Capitoline She-wolf*—the enduring symbol of Rome by an unknown Etruscan artist. This statue is more than 2,500 years old and therefore older than the legend about a she-wolf and a woodpecker rescuing the infant twins Romulus and Remus who became the cofounders of Rome. The two sucking infants were added in the 16th century, their Renaissance realism in striking contrast with the stylized Etruscan wolf. Baroque works of merit here are Bernini's marble statue of *Pope Urban VII* on his throne (1639) and Alessandro Algardi's bronze of *Pope Alexander X* (1650).

In the top floor **Picture Gallery** are paintings by Titian, Tintoretto, Rubens, Caravaggio, and Velázquez. Veronese's *Rape of Europa* is a copy but by Veronese himself. The largest painting is Guercino's *Burial and Glory of St. Petronilla* (1621), originally painted for **St. Peter's Basilica** (Petronilla is an obscure saint once thought to have been St. Peter's daughter). This gallery's two Caravaggio pictures, one of a pubescent *St. John the Baptist,* the other of *The Palm Reader,* are

Capitoline She-wolf

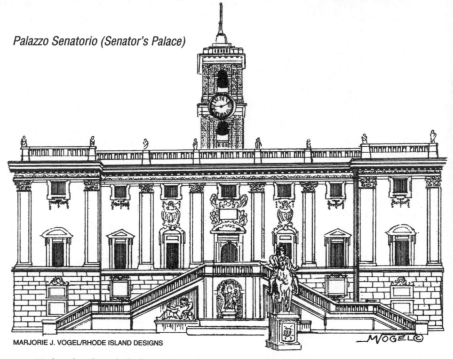

Palazzo Senatorio (Senator's Palace)

MARJORIE J. VOGEL/RHODE ISLAND DESIGNS

not to be missed, nor is the large statue of *Hercules* (probably first century BC and designed to stand in a circular temple), which has still intact almost all of its original gold-leaf covering. This floor also has a major collection of Meissen porcelain. ♦ Admission (includes entrance to the Palazzo Nuovo, see below). Tu-Su 9AM-7PM. Piazza del Campidoglio. 67102071

7 Palazzo Senatorio (Senator's Palace)

Attempts by Romans to have their own civic government were repeatedly thwarted by the popes, and their one-time scheme to elect 11 municipal senators was reduced to one senator—of the pope's choosing. The palazzo has served as the seat of Rome's civic administration since the 12th century. It is another example of Rome's many-layered history—the facade conceals an earlier medieval fortress built on the vaulted walls of the first-century BC **Tabularium** (the office where the *tabulae,* bronze registers of tax duties for all the empire, were kept). The massive stone block foundations of this building are visible from the rear. In 1551 **Michelangelo** was commissioned by Pope Paul III to transform the entire square and remodel the facade of the palace. His plans were carried out by **Giacomo della Porta, Girolamo Rainaldi,** and **Carlo Rainaldi** in 1582-1605. Today the mayor's office and other administrative offices are housed here. Since a 1986 earthquake, the bell tower leans 20 inches to one side. ♦ Piazza del Campidoglio

8 Palazzo Nuovo (New Palace) The **Palazzo dei Conservatori** and this look-alike building —**Michelangelo** designed them as a pair— form the **Musei Capitolini.** If time allows a visit to only one, choose this edifice built by **Girolamo Rainaldi** and **Carlo Rainaldi** in 1654. Housed here are master works of Greco-Roman sculpture, the best of which were donated by Pope Sixtus IV because they were overcrowding the **Lateran Palace.** The best works are one flight up: *The Dying Gaul*—his back visible as you climb the stairs—is the most famous sculpture in the museum; others of renown are two striking bronze centaurs from **Villa Adriana;** a bust of Hadrian's handsome favorite, *Antinous,* crowned with laurels; a fat *Young Hercules* (actually a portrait of the Emperor Caracalla at age five) strangling a serpent; and the curvaceous *Capitoline Venus* (second century) who has a room all to herself. The **Hall of the Emperors** contains 65 busts of the Roman emperors, only a few of which are labeled. Documentation in the **Hall of the Philosophers** is better and the hall has figures of Homer, Socrates, Cicero, Sophocles, and Euripides, and the striking head of Emperor Julian the Apostate. ♦ Admission (includes entrance to the Palazzo dei Conservatori, see page 67). Tu-Su 9AM-7PM. Piazza del Campidoglio. 67102071

Behind Palazzo Nuovo:

Chiesa di Santa Maria in Aracoeli

According to legend, there was a temple here

as early as 614 BC, and the sibyl to whom it was dedicated predicted the impending birth of Christ to the Emperor Augustus. The first Christian church here, **Santa Maria in Capitolo,** was built by the Benedictines in AD 591. When it was taken over by the Franciscans in 1250, they changed the name to **Aracoeli** (Altar of Heaven). In the Middle Ages most of Rome's commercial, social, spiritual, and political life centered around this church. The style is mostly Romanesque, and it is filled with precious marble and finely turned columns salvaged from the ancient temples of the forums in the valley below. Climb the steep staircase that penitents negotiated on their knees in the Middle Ages or opt for the shorter staircase off **Piazza del Campidoglio** behind **Palazzo Nuovo**. This is one of Rome's most popular churches on Christmas Eve: The music is special, the location enchanting, and Gypsies come in their finery. The second chapel of the left nave has a famous manger scene at Christmas, and children the world over write letters to the greatly revered doll-like wooden Christ-child figure called *Bambi Gesù*. (This copy was

crafted after the original was stolen in 1994.)

9 Foro di Traiano (Trajan's Forum)
Partially excavated in the 19th century, this was the last, the largest, and the most ambitious imperial forum to be built. This walled rectangle measured 387 by 292 feet (bigger than four football fields); some 850,000 cubic meters of earth had to be moved and deposited between the Quirinal and Capitoline Hills. The forum was designed by the Syrian architect **Apollodorus of Damascus** in AD 113. **Apollodorus** was also responsible for a colonnaded piazza in front of the domed **Basilica Ulpia** (which housed the judiciary system), the celebratory tall victory column near it—**Trajan's Column** (see page 70)—libraries, a lost equestrian statue of the emperor in the center, and, hovering over it all, a market that backed up to the bedrock of a hill and rose six stories. The magnificent **Basilica Ulpia** with its marble-faced pillars and rich carvings was the first building to go up. Next came the twin libraries, one for Greek manuscripts, the other for Latin. In 312, when Constantine, who was already commander in

Foro de Traiano (Trajan's Forum)

Gaul, entered Rome as conqueror and saw the forum for the first time, he could not contain his amazement. With uncharacteristic modesty he declared, "I will never be able to construct anything like it."

9 Colonna Traiana (Trajan's Column) Erected in AD 113 to commemorate Trajan's military victories in Dacia (part of today's Romania and Transylvania), this column stands 131 feet tall and is made of 19 blocks of marble, each 4 feet high and 11.5 feet in diameter. It originally was topped with a bronze statue of the emperor, replaced in 1587 by a likeness of St. Peter. The sculptor/architect **Apollodorus** designed and decorated this column as a spiralling marble chronicle narrating the major events of Trajan's military exploits in more than 150 episodes and 26,000 characters. There was no soundtrack, of course, to this early form of newsreel, but it was in technicolor since, like many Roman monuments, it originally had brightly painted figures. Scenes show troops fording the Danube River (in their armor!), soldiers preparing for battle by offering sacrifice, and, in every sixth frame, Trajan (taller than the rest) surveying his defeated enemies. The emperor's ashes, which were placed in an urn at the foot of the column's 185-step interior spiral staircase, were stolen during the Middle Ages. This, and the column honoring Marcus Aurelius in **Piazza Colonna,** are the only pillars in the city still standing where they were originally built. ◆ Via dei Fori Imperiali (between Via Alessandrina and Piazza Venezia)

10 Mercato di Traiano (Trajan's Market) A restored merchandise mart, this is the only surviving second-century urban complex. A wall divided this two-story half-circle of buildings abutting the hill from the forum proper; the bedrock of the hillside became the foundation for another six stories. Two larger halls on the forum level seem to have been auditoriums for students or the public; nearby were taverns and tiny shops. On the main floor beneath the arcades and vaulted halls—this was the first use of barrel vaulting—were offices and depositories for oil, wine, and grains. On the top floor were fish ponds—one linked to the aqueduct for fresh water, another that received salt water from Ostia. During the Middle Ages a fortified citadel was constructed on top of the ruined market. ◆ Admission; free last Sunday of the month. Tu-Su 9AM-6:30PM. Enter on Via IV Novembre, between Largo Magnanapoli and Via Magnanapoli

11 Foro di Cesare This 54 BC forum was partially uncovered in 1932, along with the ruins of the **Temple of Venus Genitrix,** which had been built to house Caesar's art collection and to emphasize his claim that he was a descendant of Venus. The bronze statue of

Julius Caesar is a modern copy dating from Mussolini's day, and the pedestal bears the inscription "dictator perpetuus." ◆ Bounded by Via dei Fori Imperiali and Clivo Argentario, and Via del Tulliano and Via di San Pietro in Carcere

12 Foro di Augusto Enclosed in a medieval house are the remains of the forum that the emperor Augustus built in 42 BC to celebrate his military victory at Philippi where, among others, Cassius and Brutus—Caesar's assassins—were slain. The wide flight of steps once led to a temple dedicated to Mars, the god of war. Augustus's complex included a hall containing his seven-times–life-sized statue, the base of which still exists and carries imprints of the colossal feet. ◆ Via Alessandrina (between Via Cavour and Via Magnanapoli)

13 Foro di Nerva Originally called the **Forum Transitorium** because it led into the **Forum of Vespasian** immediately to the southeast, this AD 97 forum was excavated just a few years ago. In the middle of it was a large temple dedicated to Minerva. Two columns and a richly carved frieze are all that remain of the forum. ◆ Via dei Fori Imperiali, Via Cavour, and Via Alessandrina

14 Hotel Forum $$$ As its name suggests, this 76-room hotel has a spectacular view of the **Imperial Forums,** and the ambience reflects its neighbors. Officials of the Food and Agricultural Organization (FAO) of the United Nations keep it full; others like the vista at sunset from its rooftop terrace. Stick to drinks and avoid the mediocre restaurant. Amenities include a buffet breakfast and air-conditioning. ◆ Via Tor de' Conti 25 (at Via Madonna dei Monti). 6792446; fax 6786479

15 Marble Works Giulio Benassati cuts, polishes, sculpts, and sells marble in sizes from large tombstones to tiny earrings. He also produces intarsia tables—large and small, multicolored and black-and-white—with tops of geometric designs in various kinds of marble. ◆ M afternoon; Tu-W, F-Sa; Th morning. Via Tor de' Conti 4/A (at Via Cavour). 82001524

Quartiere Monti (Gladiators' Quarter)

Artisans, escaped slaves, gladiators, thieves, and gamblers once lived in this small, colorful neighborhood that spreads across a hillside between the **Colosseum** and **Santa Maria Maggiore** above the **Imperial Forums.** In the days of the Roman Empire these slopes were a shantytown (for a time the young Julius Caesar lived here to show he was one of the people), and the back alleys were mean streets.

Today it is a bustling, nouveau-chic district of boutiques, curio and wine shops, trattorie, and churches, whose link to antiquity continues in the old street names like **Via dei Serpenti** (Street of the Snakes). The 16th-century **Madonna dei Monti** church on that thoroughfare has a modern mosaic of the Madonna crushing a serpent on its outside wall. Just a block away is the site of the ancient, lost temple to Hygieia, the daughter of Aesculapius, the god of healing. Hygieia symbolized health (hygiene) and is traditionally depicted with a cup of healing potion in one hand and a serpent in the other. The serpent drank the potion from the cup, shed its skin, and emerged to begin a new life. Gladiators, hoping for the same longevity, prayed in her temple before and, if they survived, after combat.

Intersecting Via dei Serpenti is **Via degli Zingari,** the street where Gypsies were required to reside in the 19th century.

16 **Angelino ai Fori** ★$$ Bobby Kennedy gave a birthday party for his wife Ethel here in 1962 and presented her with a Vespa, which she then proceeded to drive through the cozy dining spot. The pasta with fresh tomato and basil is always good here, as is the *spaghetti alle vongole veraci* (double-horn clams served in their shells with garlic, parsley, and olive oil). Seafood, especially scampi, is a specialty, but never on Monday. Sunday lunch is always crowded. ♦ M, W-Su lunch and dinner. Largo Corrado Ricci 40 (at Via Cavour). 6791121

17 **313 Cavour** ★$ With its wood paneling and ceiling fans, this popular wine bar looks like a midwestern American bar, only without the bar. And in place of the jukebox is a giant vintage red Coca-Cola® cooler. The clientele is mostly collegiate, but the conversation these days is more likely to be about Rolex watches and Alfa Romeos than politics or revolution. It's a good place for a glass of wine and a light lunch—the cheeses and pâtés are excellent, as are the salads and savory pies. ♦ M-Sa lunch and dinner; Su dinner; closed in August. Via Cavour 313 (between Via dei Serpenti and Via dell'Agnello). 6785496

18 **Valentino** ★★$ Simple but good food and terrific prices ease the pain of waiting to dine at this popular, smoke-filled eatery. Pasta dishes include *rigatoni alla norcina* (with sausage and cream) and *penne ortolana* (with peas, mushrooms, and prosciutto). Also good are slivers of liver from the grill or *picatina di vitello* (braised veal slices doused with lemon). Mimosa cake or puffy mille-feuille wind up the feast. ♦ M-Th, Sa-Su lunch and

dinner. Via Cavour 293 (at Via dei Serpenti). 4881303

19 **Palatino** $$ This comfortable, bright, 210-room establishment has plenty of conveniences like private baths, air-conditioning, a garage (rare in central Rome), business services, and a bar. The terrific location makes up for an indifferent restaurant. Breakfast is included. Ask for a room away from the street. ♦ Via Cavour 213 (at Via dei Serpenti). 4814927; fax 4740726

20 **Via San Francesco di Paola** Not a street but a staircase leading through a tunnel between Via Cavour and **Piazza San Pietro in Vincoli,** this is also known as the **Salita dei Borgia** because the tower in the piazza belonged to the dreaded Borgia family, as did the palazzo under which this tunnel passes. It was in this palace that the beautiful and notorious Vanozza Cattanei, mistress of Pope Alexander VI—and mother of Lucrezia and Cesare Borgia, his out-of-wedlock children— gave a family dinner on the evening of 14 June 1497 that ended with Cesare stabbing to death the Duke of Gandia, his stepbrother.

21 **Chiesa di San Pietro in Vincoli (Church of St. Peter in Chains)** According to legend, this church is on the site where St. Peter was condemned to death. Nearly 400 years later Empress Eudoxia came into possession of the chains Peter wore in prison, and her mother later gave her another set of chains that allegedly had shackled him in Jerusalem. It was Eudoxia who erected this shrine for the relics, which are encased under the main altar. A sarcophagus in a small crypt behind the altar houses the bones of the seven Maccabees brought to Rome from Constantinople in 560. But the reason most people visit this church is to see Michelangelo's fiercely powerful statue of *Moses.* In the early 16th century, the artist was commissioned by his patron, Pope Julius II, to carve his monumental tomb to be placed here. If the lone statue looks out of perspective on its present pedestal, it's because it was intended to be the pinnacle of a funerary monument that was to include 40 statues. But Julius died before the tomb was finished, and his remains were buried in **St. Peter's** beneath a simple stone marker. Moses is depicted at the moment when God first appeared to him in the *Book of Exodus,* and every muscle in his body reveals the tension of that event. A supposed profile of Michelangelo is tucked away in a lock of Moses's flowing beard (beneath his lips). Also noteworthy are a fresco by Antonio Pollaiuolo depicting Rome during the 1476 plague and a beautiful seventh-century mosaic of St. Sebastian in front of the second altar on the left. ♦ Piazza di San Pietro in Vincoli and Via delle Sette Sale

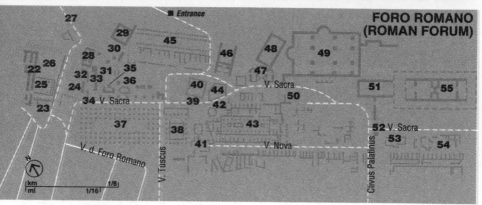

FORO ROMANO (ROMAN FORUM)

Foro Romano (Roman Forum)

The best way to maneuver through this vast grave-yard of time is to keep the huge white monument in nearby **Piazza Venezia** in mind. Most of what once stood in the **Roman Forum** was of the same over-the-top monumentality and, some would say, vulgarity.

In the seventh century BC, however, this site was only an empty clearing at the foot of the **Capitoline Hill.** Villagers gathered here to talk about money, sheep, politics, religion, and sports. Gradually the forum came to be surrounded by buildings of wood, then tufa, and eventually by towering marble law courts and temples. Religious rites, town meetings, banquets for gladiators, orations, festivals, and dancing all took place in what was, in effect, the world's first outdoor mall. ◆ M-Sa (no midday closing); Su morning. Two entrances: Via della Salaria Vecchia (just southwest of Via dei Fori Imperiali), and Piazza del Colosseo and Via Sacra. 6990110

22 Tabularium The majestic arches of this public records office were a true feat of Roman engineering; built in 78 BC, they were constructed to last centuries. The empire's records, stored inside, were written on wooden tablets coated with wax, on parchment, papyrus scrolls, stone, and engraved bronze plates. The historian Suetonius (who worked as a lawyer-turned-writer under Trajan and Hadrian) recounted that 3,000 original records were lost in a fire during a civil war in AD 69; Emperor Vespasian had them recast.

23 Portico degli Dei Consenti (Portico of the Council of the Gods) Statues of 12 of the Roman gods and goddesses—Mars, Mercury, Neptune, Vulcan, Vesta, Juno, Jupiter, Minerva, Apollo, Diana, Vesta, and Venus—stood in pairs in this long, elbow-shaped portico next to the **Temple of Vespasian.** A sacred banquet to honor them was held here annually.

24 Temple of Saturn This temple (illustrated on page 73) was built in the Ionic style where Clivus Capitolinus Road—leading uphill—joined Via Sacra. It was erected in 497 BC (on top of an even earlier altar to Saturn) by Consuls Sempronio Atratinus and Minucius

Foro Romano (Roman Forum)

Temple of Saturn

Augurinus to honor the god of the harvest and prosperity. The city's treasure was kept here, and during the god's festival, the Saturnalia, which was celebrated from the end of December to the beginning of January, his statue was draped and carried in procession through the city. It was one of ancient Rome's most popular festivals, in which one and all abandoned themselves to merrymaking.

25 Temple of Vespasian Built by Vespasian's son Titus, this temple was made to look bigger than it really is by a clever but unknown architect. The shops nearby sold terra-cotta *tanagras* (votive figurines) that people took into the temple to leave as offerings or break against the altar after they had prayed.

26 Temple of Concord This temple was first erected by Camillus in 367 BC to commemorate the political reconciliation between the patricians and ordinary Roman citizens (plebeians); it was later rebuilt. Augustus redecorated the temple with spoils from defeated Germans, and his wife Livia made it into a museum filled with priceless works of art. In the back is the **Basilica Optimio,** a small office building.

27 Clivus Argentarius (Silversmith's Lane) Emperors and generals climbed through this alley up to the Capitoline during their triumphal processions. Often dragging prisoners in chains, they passed the silversmiths, coin dealers, money changers, money lenders, and usurers who worked along this stretch.

28 Arch of Septimius Severus This richly decorated arch (illustrated on page 74)—built in AD 203—was once topped by a bronze chariot pulled by six snorting horses. Dedicated to the emperor and his sons, Caracalla and Geta, it honors Roman victories in Mesopotamia. The figures representing the Tigris and Euphrates Rivers are supine to show defeat.

29 Curia (Senate Building) The fate of the world was decided in this building (which burned to the ground at least five times) during the days of the Roman Empire. Six hundred senators sat here on wooden benches, all on an equal level. At the end of the hall was a low podium for the president.

30 Comitium Ancient Rome's first assembly place and the first incarnation of the forum as a civic center was originally a round, sunken terrace with wooden steps where people sat. Before there was a **Curia** or a basilica courthouse, people of all classes held town meetings here to debate the issues of the day, to elect ministers and religious leaders, and to decide on punishments. According to Pliny, the infamous Cellerus—lover of vestal Cornelia—was flogged to death here; it was also the site of gladiator combats. The **Comitium** existed until 145 BC, when its functions were transferred to the **Temple of Castor and Pollux,** whose high podium let speakers be seen and heard by all. Next to the **Comitium** is the **Lapis Niger,** a black marble slab that marks a burial place of great

Arch of Septimius Severus

MARJORIE J. VOGEL/RHODE ISLAND ORIGINALS

antiquity (supposedly the tomb of Romulus) that had to be shut down in order to build the first paved forum.

31 Forum Magnum This piazza was the center of activity in the **Forum.** At the northwest corner was the **Comitium,** the heart of the forum. Bordering the entire south side was the grandiose **Basilica Giulia.** Nearby was the prison with its death row and rooms for executions, the mint (by the small temple to Jove), the convent where the Vestal priestesses tended the sacred flame, and the **Defense Department** building.

32 Umbilicus Mundus Legend has it that this low, flat cylinder that looks like a giant column base was the true center—literally, the belly button—of Rome; it is also called **Umbilicus Mundus et Urbis,** meaning "we are the city, we are the world." In fact it is a vestige of an ancient sacred votive well where Romans placed offerings and then hauled a heavy stone disc over the wellhead to deter thieves.

33 Rostra This stone speakers' platform is named for the prows of enemy ships captured in battle at Amtoi in 339 BC that were brought home to Rome and affixed here. Words of orators spoken on this platform changed the course of history. When the great orator Cicero was assassinated in AD 43, his head and hands were cut off and put on the **Rostra,** where he had so often addressed Romans.

34 Arch of Tiberius After Germanicus, one of his generals, defeated the Allemani or Germans, Tiberius built this arch in honor of himself. (As did Germanicus, when a great soldier won a battle against a terrible foe, he took the name of the people he conquered).

35 Pillar of Phocas Dating from 608—after the Fall of the Roman Empire—this pillar is topped by a statue of Phocas (later Emperor of Byzantium), who seized Byzantium for the Holy Roman Empire.

36 Lacus Curtius A wellhead enclosed by a railing was a holy spot from the earliest times and is a vestige of a small pond by the old necropolis. In Augustus's day citizens came to pray and throw coins into the well to ensure the Emperor's good health.

37 Basilica Giulia (Julius) Construction of this giant law court bordering one whole side of the **Forum Magnum** was begun by Julius Caesar in 54 BC. Columns ran around the perimeter—about the length of a football field—creating five rectangular aisles. Wooden walls soared two stories high and divided it into four courtrooms where civil cases, especially inheritance suits, were heard. It was a popular pastime for Romans to come here and listen to the judges and lawyers dispute cases. Still visible today are a gameboard scratched on the marble stairs outside and a plaster copy of part of a frieze detailing the story of Aeneas.

38 Temple of Castor and Pollux This temple (illustrated above) was dedicated to another famous set of twins, "the Dioscuri," brothers of Helen of Troy. Riding their winged horses, Castor and Pollux came to Rome's aid in a battle against the Etruscans in 499 BC. They were revered thereafter as patrons of the Republic, and when they returned to the heavens, they became the main stars in the Gemini constellation. Only three of the lofty 41-foot Corinthian columns (sixth century) are still standing.

39 Arch of Augustus This triumphal arch had one large central opening flanked by two smaller ones. Only the bases are still visible.

40 Temple of Julius Caesar Built to honor the first mortal elevated to divinity, this 42 BC temple stands on the spot where Caesar's body was burned after he was assassinated in the **Teatro di Pompeo** and where hysterical people in their grief threw everything they could—chairs, jewelry, and clothes—onto the funeral pyre. At the time of the death of Nero, the last emperor of Caesar's family, there was a great storm, and the heads of the four statues of family members on pedestals in front of the temple were struck by lightning and toppled to the ground.

41 Oratory of the 40 Martyrs The chapel that stood on these foundations was probably built by Hadrian. It honored 40 soldiers who died in a frozen pond in Armenia (part of the empire). Who they were and why they died has been lost in the mists of time.

42 Temple of Vesta: Goddess of the Hearth The round building that once stood here was a copy of a simple original building that had a thatched roof and reed walls. Here burned the sacred fire symbolizing the eternity of the state; it was allowed to go out only once a year, on New Year's Day (1 March) when the *pontifex maximus* (high priest and often emperor) came to relight the flame. The blood from a horse that had been sacrificed to Mars was then sprinkled on the altar.

Although the New Year's ceremony was considered too holy for outsiders, many other festivals were open to the public, including the ceremonial emptying out of the vestal dustbin when burned bones and other sacrificial debris were taken to the **Cloaca Maxima,** the sewer. Other holy days at this temple included Harvest, Vintage, and Lupercalia. When there was a sacrifice at the temple, the vestals wore woolen hoods of white bordered with purple. Behind the temple in the field of Palatine Hill was the **Sacred Grove** where the fruit and sweet-smelling trees grew. Via Nova ran from this grove to the **Arch of Titus.** Besides the sacred fire and grove, there was a traditional fig tree, olive tree, and vines—the symbols of Rome.

42 Scala Annulariae (Ring Makers' Stairs) Precious rings of pearls, rubies, cameos, and scarabs from Egypt were made on this street, as were men's gold thumb rings. An ancient track is all that remains.

43 House of the Vestal Virgins The vestal virgins tended the sacred flame of Rome and were proud that they could light up the night like the day with their oil lamps—the most sophisticated in existence, with hundreds of flames within one lamp—although a gust of wind could cause a dreadful fire. In fact, their first house burned down. This structure had a beautiful atrium with a floor covered with black-and-white mosaics; in the center was a fountain and flower garden. Around the edge were 48 columns of green-and-white marble downstairs and coral upstairs, with statues between each column. On the ground floor was a mill for grinding the salt used for sacred cleansings, rooms for guarding the secret documents, and a marble tank of holy water. The vestals lived upstairs. The walls and floors were heated, and there was a private bath reached by a bridge. The apartment of the high vestal (mother superior), covered with frescoes, was the most luxurious.

Vestals were revered and respected, and the mother superior was powerful. Protocol put them right after the empress, and they enjoyed seats of honor at the **Colosseum,** the theaters, and the circus; simply by passing a criminal in the street, they could stay his execution if they chose. Since no one dared enter their quarters, the emperors' last wills

Temple of Antoninus and Faustina

and the secret documents of the Senate were kept there. Religious law forbade vestals to drink water from the aqueducts—they could imbibe only water from the Egeria Spring far out on the Appian Way, and once a week they all boarded wagons and went to draw water in big jugs. They wore pure-white sleeveless gowns that fell to the ankles with a simple girdle around the waist. Around their heads were six bands of twisted linen, like a coronet.

Originally, the six vestal virgins were expected to serve for seven years, beginning in puberty, then were free to leave and marry at any time. Later a vestal was chosen while still a child of five or six and served for 30 years. On entering the order, her hair was shaved off and hung from a tree. After her hair grew back, it was worn quite long. She was educated during the first 10 years, for the next 10 she learned to perform the rites, and in the last 10 she taught newcomers. After that she could resign and even marry, but woe to a vestal caught with a man during her service— the penalty was burial alive.

44 Regia In ancient times high priests had their offices here, in front of the **Temple of Antoninus and Faustina,** and until one of the Tiber's flash floods washed away this and other buildings, it was here that the priests kept records of annual acts and public events.

(The Tiber flooded the valley almost every year and usually did little harm, but about once every century there was a truly devastating flood.) Here also was the house and porticoed courtyard garden of the *pontifex maximus,* a high priest who was the head of the state clergy. His role was later usurped by the emperors. The pope is often referred to as the Pontiff.

45 Basilica Aemilia This is the second-oldest basilica ever constructed (179 BC)—Cato the Censor built the first in 184 BC—and it was one of four such basilicas in the forum used for business transactions and legal proceedings. Early basilicas did not always have walls and often began as small open halls with pillars holding up a roof so that business could be conducted even in inclement weather; three rows of marble columns divide this one into four aisles. Just behind was a row of stalls for money changers, the **Tabernae Argentariae,** whose roof terraces had a portico from which a crowd could watch the gladiator games that took place in the **Forum.** Later, basilicas like this became the model for the great Christian churches of Rome, including **St. Peter's.**

46 Temple of Antoninus and Faustina Built in AD 160, this temple (illustrated above) has a beautiful flight of stairs. Legend has it that

Faustina was a faithless wife, but the tolerant Antoninus put up with her wanderings and even elevated her to a goddess when she died.

47 Temple of Romulus Here (illustrated above) is a lovely, rare circular building (be sure to look at the beautiful bronze doors), erected by Maxentius to honor his son Romulus (not one of the twin founders), who died young.

48 Temple (Library) of Peace Behind the **Temple of Romulus** was a small, dazzling temple built by Vespasian around AD 80 and dedicated to lasting peace. The **Forum of Peace** was a large complex with a library, survey office, and a treasury where the spoils of the Temple of Jerusalem were kept, including the seven-branched candelabra depicted on the **Arch of Titus.**

Soothsayers predicted that these two sacred temples would become a place of worship for the new Christian religion and that a new church—the **Church of Cosmos and Damiano** —would be built by Pontifex Maximus Felix IV early in the sixth century in the main hall of the **Temple of Peace.** Some of the polychrome-marble pavement of the original temple is still visible behind the church. Its vestibule made use of another temple. The church contains an early (sixth-century) mosaic showing Sts. Peter and Paul against a dazzling background of flowers and palm trees and a famous 17th-century crèche that may be visited all year.

49 Basilica of Maxentius and Constantine Construction on what was to be the largest covered building in the world started in AD 306. Eight giant columns held up a gilded bronze roof, and between them towered white marble statues.

Prisoners, or defendants, stood on a round stone in front of the tribunal, where the judge was seated; railings and the **Altar of Apollo** separated the accused from the judge. Three of the huge coffered vaults that remain, measuring 80 feet by 67 feet by 57 feet, have inspired architects of all generations.

After Constantine defeated the basilica's patron Maxentius, he changed the building by moving the main entrance to the Via Sacra and putting a colossal statue of himself there; thus it is also known as the **"Basilica of Constantine."** The statue was so large that it had to be sculpted on site, and one of the feet was as long as a person's leg.

50 Horrea Margaritaria (Porticus Neronis) These were the arcades of the *margarita* (pearl) dealers, and this whole street on one side of the **House of the Vestal Virgins** was their market. Pearls were the most admired jewels in Rome. Roman matrons wore them as necklaces, as diadems in their hair, or as hanging earrings. Nero is reported to have arranged a "rainfall" of these gems onto his guests at banquets, then to have thrown the pearls into his wine, watched them dissolve,

Temple of Romulus

Basilica of Maxentius and Constantine

and drunk the liquid without any fear of indigestion or heartburn.

51 Chiesa di Santa Francesca Romana/Santa Maria Nova This church is one of Rome's great examples of layering; it was built in the 10th century incorporating an 8th-century oratorio that had been built using part of the ancient **Temple of Venus and Rome** (see page 79). The bell tower is 12th century, and the facade was added in 1615. Santa Francesca—a Roman woman who founded the Oblate religious order in 1421 and whose body is preserved under the main altar—is, among other things, the patron saint of automobile drivers. On her feast day (9 March), taxi drivers and anyone else worried about staying alive in Rome's traffic come to the piazza below this church to receive her much-needed blessing.The interior of this church is also a palimpsest of almost every century. The painting over the main altar was discovered when the restoration of a 19th-century painting uncovered a 12th-century work beneath it, and underneath that fresco, yet another painting, probably from the 5th century.

For magic fanciers, this church also contains paving stones that are said to bear the imprints of the kneecaps of Sts. Peter and Paul, who were challenged by the ancient magician, Simon Magus, to a test of levitation. Simon won the contest but crashed to earth and was killed, while the two saints, unable to get off the ground, left only dents in the pavement.

The letters "SPQR" that are stamped on Roman manhole covers and public offices stand for *senatus populusque Romanus*, or The Senate and the Roman People. A different reading, however, is provided by the Milanese, who have always felt their city should be the capital of Italy. According to their interpretation, the letters stand for *sono porci questi romani*—"What pigs these Romans are!"

52 Arch of Titus Domitian erected this arch to record Vespasian's victory over the pharaoh as well as to honor Vespasian's son Titus's (AD 79-81) destruction of Jerusalem. A panel on the inner right side of the arch shows a procession carrying off the spoils of the Temple of Jerusalem, including the great seven-branch candelabra. The figure lying by the river represents the defeated Jerusalem.

53 Temple of Jupiter Stator Romulus, the legendary founder of Rome, is said to have built this temple in 700 BC after he conquered the Sabines, in honor of the patron god of Rome. All Roman consuls were draped in white when they took office in deference to the color Jupiter wore. A general facing battle always prayed at this temple—it was Jupiter who determined the course of human events and knew the future, which his priests predicted from the flight patterns of birds and the entrails of chickens.

54 Private Baths Most Romans, rich and poor, went daily to the monumental public baths with their hot-, tepid-, and cold-water tubs. The baths were more than places to have a quick dip and maybe a rubdown. They were a total experience, equivalent to a modern club, where men could spend an entire day exercising in the gym, browsing in the library, listening to poetry readings and, most important, socializing. To ensure their popularity, the emperors built more than one public bath and adorned them with statuary, reflecting pools, marble floors, and frescoes. By 33 BC there were no fewer than 170 baths in Rome, most of which were public and free. The private baths were not expensive, although women paid more than men and could bathe only during the early morning hours, as the afternoons were reserved for men.

55 Temple of Venus and Rome Built by Antoninus Pius in AD 121-36 on the Velia Ridge—and partly destroyed by Mussolini in 1932 to create his military boulevard—this was the largest temple of ancient Rome, measuring 361 by 174 feet. It was a late temple, which is why it is at the far end of Via Sacra. Emperor **Hadrian** himself came up with its daring design, which is actually two temples set back to back: One faced the **Forum** and was dedicated to Rome, the other was devoted to Venus and fronted the **Colosseum.** The temple was built over the site of the vestibule of Nero's **Golden House,** which was so large that it stretched up the adjoining Esquiline Hill beyond the **Colosseum.** To raise it, the colossal statue of Nero that stood at the entrance had to be moved, a feat that required 24 elephants. The temple was dedicated in AD 135 and was an especially propitious temple for newlyweds to visit to offer a sacrifice. Some of the 50 columns of the portico were set upright again in 1935.

Palatine

Excavations of the first of Rome's seven hills to be permanently inhabited uncovered postholes dug into the Palatine's soft stone as early as 800 BC. The hill's relatively secure and healthy high ground (it rises steeply to 164 feet above sea level and 131 feet above the marshy lowland valley) made it the ideal place for early inhabitants to build their small wood-framed houses. A village developed a century later, and as its population continued to defend its territory, walls and cisterns were built.

Augustus was born in a simple house on the Palatine. When he became Rome's first emperor, he wanted to remain in his family home, but pressure—perhaps from his wife, Livia—eventually forced him to build the first imperial palace on the hill. Every emperor after Augustus lived here, and most of them, if they lived long enough, added their own new royal palaces, sometimes demolishing the upper parts of older palaces to do so. By late Republican times, the hill was so crowded that the nouveaux riches had to wait for a property owner to die or fall from grace in order to move onto the Palatine.

When the popes began to acquire more temporal power, they lived here in the remodeled imperial palaces, and in medieval times, the hill and its ruins were partly taken over by monasteries. During the Renaissance, two wealthy families—the Barberini and the Farnese—built summer houses on the hill, and in the 16th century, the Farnese went so far as to fill Tiberius's palace with rubble in order to plant the world's first botanical garden.

Though only suggestions remain of its former grandeur, the Palatine is an inspiring place to stroll. The rambling antique roses, the clusters of acanthus (the plant that inspired the capital of the Corinthian column), the umbrella pines, and especially the views of the **Circus Maximus** and the distant Alban Hills make it one of the world's most memorable places.
♦ Admission. M-Sa (no midday closing); Su morning. Two entrances: Via della Salaria Vecchia (just southwest of Via dei Fori Imperiali), and Piazza del Colosseo and Via Sacra. 6990110

56 **Library and Temple of Augustus** Today only foundations remain, but the structure that once stood here—housing Augustus's Greek and Latin libraries—was considered one of the three most beautiful buildings in ancient Rome (along with the **Temple of Peace** and the **Basilica Aemilia**). From here a ramp wound up to the Palatine Hill.

57 **Romolo's Cabin** This is the oldest inhabited part of the Palatine (ca. 800 BC) and one of several excavated early houses in Rome. A rivulet to keep out rainwater and foundation holes for wood beams were dug into the soft tufa on which the rectangular house was built. Archaeologists date this hut as close to the legendary founding of Rome in 753 BC.

58 **Temple of Magna Mater** In the second century BC, one of the sibyls, Cybele, delivered her prophecies here, one of which enabled the Romans to win a decisive battle in the Punic Wars. The rostrum belongs to a reconstruction of her temple dating from 111 BC; another nearby podium is from a third-century BC Temple to Victory.

59 **Casa di Livia (Livia's House)** This house was built between 75 and 50 BC and modernized in AD 30. It's conventionally named for the wife of the Emperor Augustus because of the lead drain pipes inside stamped *Julia Aug*(usta). The three small rooms with faded wall paintings are below ground level, off a courtyard that was used as a kitchen; they are covered by corrugated metal roofing and can be seen only from a landing above. Beneath the house are tombs from the 10th century BC.

60 **Cryptoportico** A 425-foot subterranean tunnel was built by Nero before he moved to Celio Hill. Located near **Livia's House,** it burrowed under Tiberius's palace and served as an underpass to other buildings. Caligula was supposedly stabbed in this tunnel. At the far end are reconstructed examples of the lavish stuccowork decoration that once covered the entire ceiling.

61 **Temple of Apollo** Completed in 28 BC to celebrate the Roman victory at Anzio six years previously, this temple was surrounded by a portico adorned with 100 statues and richly decorated with precious marble. Nearby are the excavated ruins of Augustus's imperial palace (36 BC) with a great hall and private study and some wall paintings that are considered the finest extant from imperial times. Unfortunately, the imperial palace cannot be visited.

62 **Domus Flavia** Designed by **Rabirius,** this grandiose building complex was the last and most lavish imperial residence built on the Palatine. Diocletian commissioned it; Septimius Severus completed the structure in AD 92 and added the adjacent monumental private baths.

Arch of Constantine

Within Domus Flavia:

Basilica Augustana The emperor's cabinet presumably met in this arched basilica with three naves. It is adjacent to the **Aula Reggia,** a throne room north of the hexagonal fountain and a guardhouse. The (lost) decor of marble and paintings was so lavish it has been termed Flavian Baroque. A century ago, an eccentric Scot, Charles Mills, built a farmhouse in the middle of the ruins to the southeast, thus becoming the last plebeian to live on the Palatine.

63 Domus Augustana Midway between the stadium and the fountain was the official public residence of the emperor, used as a home and working area. Remnants of its central porticoed garden and surrounding offices can still be seen.

64 Augustana Stadium Once ringed by a 2-story portico, this 443-foot stadium was built for private games, footraces, and aristocratic strolling. In the fifth century AD, the Gothic king Theodoric moved in and used the stadium for horse shows. Today it's impossible to read the faded explanations on the signpost of this neglected treasure.

65 Belvedere At this vantage point you are standing on the **Severian Arches,** first begun in the second century AD by Domitian, who artificially expanded the Palatine to make room for his palace. Septimius Severus later built the arches higher for his residence's foundations and gave the building a 295-foot facade facing the **Circus Maximus** so that he could watch the horse and chariot races. The stadium was ringed by a portico and held up to 150,000 spectators; here, too, was a great imperial box from which the royal family watched races without mingling with the mob. The last horse or chariot race was run in the fifth century AD. Today it is popular with strolling couples and neighborhood soccer teams, who join the lizards lazing in the sun.

Colosseum and Environs

In the eighth century the English theologian known as the Venerable Bede prophesied that as long as the **Colosseum** stood, Rome would stand, but when the Colosseum fell, Rome would fall, and when Rome fell, the world would end. In 1992 archaeologists determined that the amphitheater—best known for its gladiator spectacles—rested on pieces built on a landfill site. Apparently, Emperor Nero's architects had stopped up a stream to create a lake for his house on the adjacent hill. The stadium's architects then daringly filled the dried riverbed with rubble, and on this rest the foundations of one of the largest single surviving structures from antiquity.

66 Arch of Constantine Although this arch (illustrated above)—the largest and best-preserved of the Roman arches—has passed into history under the name of the first Christian emperor, its foundations date from the time of Hadrian (AD 117-138), and most of its decoration celebrates several other emperors. Excavations at the base revealed that in AD 315 Constantine redecorated an earlier arch and dedicated it to his victory over his political rival Maxentius after a decisive river battle near Rome's still-extant Ponte Milvio. It survived the various sacks of Rome because it had been incorporated into a noble medieval family's fortress. The medieval additions were stripped away in 1804.

Most of the decoration was recycled from buildings in **Trajan's Forum** and other vanished monuments. The best are the eight *tondi* (circle scenes) of the hunt and sacrifices that show Hadrian and, in profile, his favorite, Antinous, who drowned in the Nile in the year

AD 130 and was made a god by the grief-stricken emperor. Constantine wasn't baptized until just before his death in 337, but when the arch was dedicated, he declared that the new belief in Christ could coexist with the official faith in Jupiter as long as it did not interfere with the politics of the empire.

The arch is an icon of ancient Roman history. Not only does it commemorate the christianization of Rome, while at the same time glorifying its imperial past, but it also anticipates its decline, since it was Constantine who started its dissolution by moving the capital to Constantinople. ♦ Piazza del Colosseo (between Via di San Gregorio and Via Sacra)

67 Meta Sudans Ongoing excavations are returning to light this imperial-era fountain, which was torn down in 1936 by Mussolini's architects during construction of Via dei Fori Imperiali. Its odd name, which means "sweating goal post," comes from its reported resemblance to the *meta* (cone-shaped marker) of racetracks, down which water trickled or "sweated" *(sudans)*. ♦ Piazza del Colosseo and Via Sacra

68 Colosseo (Colosseum) For some, this former stadium is the greatest of all ruins, the monarch of European monuments, but for others, it is the sad reminder of one of humanity's less noble ideas of entertainment. For Byron and the other Romantics it evoked the enchantment of a "magic circle" (an oval, actually), but to Mark Twain it looked more like "a looped and windowed bandbox with one of its sides bitten out."

Toward the end of his reign (AD 54-68), Emperor Nero had 12 pairs of elephants hoist

a 120-foot gilded bronze statue of himself near the site where this arena would be built several years later. The statue, which Nero insisted had to be taller than the Colossus of Rhodes, was called the *Colossus*. This also became the nickname of the giant sports stadium—its true title is **Flavian Amphitheater,** so named because it was begun under the Flavian emperor, Vespasian, and completed eight years later (AD 72) under his son Titus. It was the world's first freestanding structure of its type at the time— all earlier arenas had either been carved out of the rock or built at least partially against embankments.

The arena's oval shape features four stories: three tiers of arches, each with a different type of column—Doric, Ionic, and Corinthian— and a flat fourth story. The stadium is 150 feet high, and if unwound and laid flat, the whole exterior surface would cover about 2,000 feet. The 80 entrances, wide and unencumbered, allowed 50,000 spectators to take their seats quickly—within 10 minutes of the starting trumpet. They also served as the exits, or *vomitoria* (speedy egresses). There were three special gates: one for the emperor and his family, the **Gate of Life** for victorious gladiators, and the **Gate of Death** for the vanquished. An underground corridor led to the gladiators' locker room, the ruins of which are at the beginning of the nearby Via di San Giovanni in Laterano.

Wild animals were caged beneath the arena's now vanished sand-covered wooden floor (the Latin word for sand is *arena*), which measured 287 by 180 feet. They were brought to the stadium level on rope-pulled elevators, thus

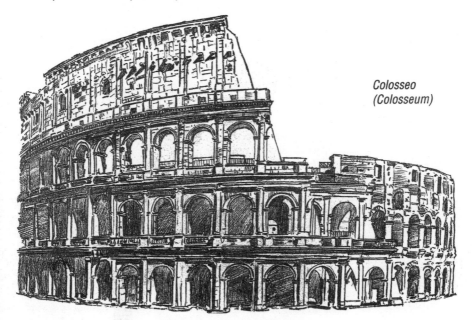

*Colosseo
(Colosseum)*

Colosseum interior

appearing as if out of nowhere. When it rained, a special crew went into action to draw the huge *velarium,* a canvas awning that protected spectators.

Ancient records tell of the **Colosseum**'s inauguration, which lasted 100 days. It attracted Roman citizens from every part of the empire and involved the slaying of 5,000 beasts, most imported from Africa. In AD 249, the 1,000th anniversary of the city's founding was celebrated here in a weeklong spectacle during which 2,000 gladiators fought and slaughtered 32 elephants, 10 tigers, 60 lions, 10 giraffes, 40 wild horses, and 6 hippopotamuses.

No historic proof supports the tales that Christians were martyred in the **Colosseum,** although it does for other arenas; however, anyone sentenced to death in ancient Rome (thieves, murderers, and assassins) could be fed to the lions.

Besides resisting attempts to turn it into a fullers' factory, dung heap, medieval fortress, and marble quarry, the **Colosseum** has withstood fire, two major earthquakes, pillage by nouveaux-riches Renaissance families building town houses, and today's exhaust fumes and air pollution. Until the late 18th century, shops, stables, and dilapidated dwellings filled most of the ground-level arches. The huge pockmarks in the soft limestone facade were caused by sulfur used in the Middle Ages to blast the metal clamps securing the giant travertine blocks so that the metal could be recycled. The large wooden cross inside was erected for the 1950 Holy Year; each year on Good Friday the pope leads a procession carrying a wooden cross here. ◆ Admission. Daily 9AM-6PM Feb-Oct; daily 9AM-3PM Nov-Jan. Piazza del Colosseo

69 Ludus Magnus The principal training ground for gladiators was located here, only steps away from the **Colosseum.** Excavated in 1960-61, it was used for centuries to prepare athletes for sports events on horseback, on foot, and in chariots, often armed with deadly weapons. Gladiators date back to an Etruscan funeral rite that involved to-the-death battles with wild beasts in order to provide deceased nobles with proven heroes to escort them to the next world. The Roman version began with a ceremony involving 3 groups of combatants, but the idea quickly gained popularity so that by 44 BC—the time of Julius Caesar's funeral—3 had become 300. Under Emperor Titus (AD 79-81), exhibitions sometimes lasted 100 days, and in AD 107 during Trajan's reign, as many as 5,000 pairs of gladiators battled. These bouts were immensely popular, as were various famous gladiators who were known by name, had their own fan clubs, and enjoyed particular privileges. Their eventual deaths went unprotested; however, one account from AD 404 tells of a monk who threw himself into the arena in protest against this sport. He was killed by the crowd, and it wasn't until 30 years later during the reign of Honorius that this form of spectator sport was banned throughout the empire. ◆ Piazza del Colosseo and Via di San Giovanni in Laterano

70 Domus Aurea After being closed to the public for more than a decade, Nero's **Golden House** was reopened in 1999. The emperor had this palace built following the devastating fire of 64 AD, but it lay unfinished four years later when the Senate condemned him and he committed suicide. Trajan later built over Nero's home, confiscating the marble for his nearby baths and inadvertently preserving the rooms until they were rediscovered during the Renaissance. The original structure housed a vestibule, located where the **Arch of Titus** now stands, a 120-foot-high statue of Nero, and a circular main dining room that continually turned on its axis, like the world. The **Colosseum** was erected where Nero once had gardens, vineyards, and a lake. Today, frescoed walls are visible in 33 rooms, out of an original 150. The "room of the gilded vault" is a masterpiece by Fabullus (the most fashionable painter of the time), who gilded, stuccoed, and painted the ceiling with mythological scenes from the *Iliad*. The octagonal hall, which is lit by an open dome, is said by some to be the inspiration for the **Pantheon.** Another room's ceiling features a grand mosaic depicting the *Myth of Polyphemus.* The **Vatican Museums** now hold several items from here, including the large porphyry basin where Nero's second wife, Poppaea, took her bath, and the *Laocoön* sculptures, which were found in a room adjacent to the octagonal hall in 1506. ♦ Daily. Parco di Traiano, Piazza del Colosseo and Viale della Domus Aurea. 4872432

71 Osteria da Nerone ★★$$ This restaurant is one of the few near the **Colosseum** that has maintained its quality in spite of heavy tourist traffic. Try *pasta e ceci* (a thick soup with pasta and chickpeas, flavored with rosemary), homemade ravioli filled with ricotta and chopped spinach and garnished with melted butter and tiny sage leaves, or the house specialty, *fettuccine al Nerone* (with peas, mushrooms, eggs, and salami). Dine alfresco in nice weather. ♦ M-Sa lunch and dinner. Via delle Terme di Tito 96 (between Via del Monte Oppio and Largo della Polveriera). 4745207

72 Pizza Forum $ Sixteen varieties of thick, bready Neapolitan pizzas and bruschetta with various toppings such as chopped tomatoes and basil or prosciutto and melted cheese are served here. Unlike thin Roman pizzas, Neapolitan pizzas are a full meal. The place is pleasantly air-conditioned. ♦ M-F lunch and dinner; Sa-Su dinner. No credit cards accepted. Via di San Giovanni in Laterano 34 (between Via Ostilia and Piazza del Colosseo). 7002515

73 Arte Colosseo In addition to a small but carefully chosen selection of prints, this shop also has antique and pseudoantique rings and other jewelry. ♦ Tu-Sa. Via di San Giovanni in Laterano 58 (between Via Celimontana and Via Ostilia). 7096404

74 Hotel Celio $$ The best of the hostelries in an area where there are few, this quiet hotel offers 16 rooms, including one suite with a terrace and view of the Colosseum, and two junior suites. Each of the guest rooms is named for a famous Italian artist, and the ones facing away from the street are quite tranquil. All boast high ceilings, and walls and headboards frescoed with copies of famous Renaissance paintings. Air-conditioning, cable TV, a VCR, safe, and an excellent in-room breakfast (included) are some of the other highlights. Don't be put off by the poker-faced brothers who run it; they can be quickly won over, and the service is generally good. There's a private parking garage in the building. ♦ Via dei Santissimi Quattro 35 (between Via Celimontana and Via Ostilia). 70495333; fax 7096377

75 Pasqualino ★★★$ Large portions of pasta are the norm in this homey, working-class trattoria where the waiters joke with patrons, in true Roman style. Try the fettuccine with fresh *funghi porcini* (porcini mushrooms), *pappardelle* (broad ribbon pasta) in a hare-and-tomato sauce, and the house *spaghetti al pasqualino* (meat-and-cream sauce). Outdoor tables boast a view of the **Colosseum.** With its location, tasty food, hearty servings, and excellent prices, this place is a real find. ♦ Tu-Su lunch and dinner; closed in August. Via dei Santissimi Quattro 66 (between Via Ostilia and Piazza del Colosseo). 7004576

76 Enfant Prodige The English-speaking staff at this children's shop will help you choose gifts for new arrivals and their older siblings. There are hand-crafted wooden toys, mobiles, and music boxes of all types, as well as a selection of shoes and sundresses. ♦ Tu-Sa. Via Marco Aurelio 27 (at Via Ostilia). 7004630

One of Rome's most notable survivors is the gray-striped tabby cat, which in ancient times was worshiped in the temples of the imported (from Egypt) cults of Isis and Osiris that were common in Rome before the advent of Christianity. The *gatti* (cats) still have a dedicated following, mostly retired army officers and elderly ladies, known as *gattari*. These gentlefolk operate first-aid stations out of their homes and distribute leftovers to the city's hundreds of stray cats, who can be seen sunning themselves along the arches of the Colosseum or lying under the umbrella pines in Largo Argentina. The cats still bear their kittens amid the centuries-old ruins of the Teatro Marcello, in the Celian park, where Pope Gregory the Great once strolled, or in the alleys off Via del Corso, under the balcony where Napoleon's mother once sat and fanned herself.

Roma di Notte

Although Rome doesn't offer as much in the way of nightlife as other European capitals, such as Paris or London, there is still an abundance of after-work amusement to be found, with plenty of wine bars, discos, and jazz clubs.

Romans who wish to make a night of it dress up and meet their friends in the **Centro Storico,** usually at a wine bar or outdoor cafe, then move on to a meal or pizza, ending up at a disco or piano bar. Activity in cafes and bars starts after dinner at around 10PM. Piano bars and discos begin to get going at midnight, but even in the liveliest neighborhoods, like **Trastevere,** most places start closing around 2AM (some, however, stay open until 4AM). Most clubs charge a cover, and some require a membership fee.

For music, the young and the restless have discos (many in the **Via Veneto** area). Those inclined to lower-key activities can gravitate to the area around the **Pantheon,** and the more adventurous might want to check out the **Testaccio** neighborhood across the river from Trastevere, which has a number of spots.

Bars and Cafes

Aldebaran, in the increasingly trendy Testaccio neighborhood, serves drinks and ice cream. From Thursday through Sunday, the mixed-age crowd fills two grottolike rooms to listen to the latest world music. ◆ M-Sa 10PM-2:30AM. Via Galvani 54 (at Via Marmorata). 5746013

Antico Caffè della Pace is the reigning "in" spot for young professionals. Near **Piazza Navona,** this is a lively outdoor cafe in summer with an international clientele that often includes movie stars and media people. ◆ Daily 10AM-3AM. Via della Pace 4 (between Vicolo di Montevecchio and Piazza Santa Maria della Pace). 6861216

Caffè Latino features one space with live jazz, blues, or rock performances; another offers videos and dancing; and a third is a restaurant. ◆ Tu-Th, Su 10:30PM-2AM; F-Sa until 4AM; closed July through September. Via di Monte Testaccio 46 (at Via Nicola Zabaglia). 57288384

Il Fico, a popular cocktail bar near **Piazza Navona,** is *the* place to people watch—that is, if you can get in the door. It's even more difficult in summer, when eager throngs spill back to **Piazza del Fico** waiting to get in. A thriving fig tree shades the outdoor tables and gives the cafe and piazza their name. Lunch offerings include a salad bar, vegetable pies, and several desserts. ◆ Daily 8AM-2AM. Piazza del Fico 26/28 (at Via della Fossa). 6865205

Selarum features live music and ice cream (among other things) in a refreshing outdoor bar-in-a-garden in Trastevere. ◆ Daily 9PM-2AM Apr-Sept. Via dei Fienaroli 12 (between Via delle Fratte di Trastevere and Via dell'Arco di San Calisto). 5806587

Discos and Nightclubs

L'Alibi, a gay disco in Testaccio, is like Carnival every night. This was the first gay disco in Rome, and its popularity—especially in summer when the dancing moves to the roof terrace—has never been rivaled. ◆ Tu-Su 11PM-2:30AM. Via di Monte Testaccio 44 (between Via Nicola Zabaglia and Viale Campo Boario). 5743448

Alien is reliable, witty, amusing—and LOUD. Sporting an interior modeled after the eponymous film series, this trendy dance club east of the **Villa Borghese** draws a young crowd. ◆ Tu-Su 11PM-4AM. Via Velletri 13/19 (between Via Nizza and Via Savoia). 8412212

Fantasie di Trastevere is a dinner-theater club that offers folk singers and musicians—dressed in regional costumes—performing a 2.5-hour show of traditional Roman and Neapolitan songs and dances. ◆ Shows: Nightly at 9:30PM. Reservations recommended. Via di Santa Dorotea 6 (at Piazza San Giovanni di Malva). 5881671

Follia, a multi-theme disco just north of **Castel Sant'Angelo,** offers a bit of *follia* (madness) for everyone. A long bar snakes down the side of the first room, where live music plays most nights. Another room is devoted to the latest dance hits, while a third tones it down as a romantic piano bar. ◆ Daily 10:30PM-4AM. Via Ovidio 17 (between Via Crescenzio and Via Cola di Rienzo). 68308435

Gilda, in the **Piazza di Spagna** neighborhood, is a nightclub with swank. It's *the* after-hours watering hole for today's conservative political crowd. There's also a restaurant and nightclub that features big-name performers and glitzy revues. ◆ Tu-Su 11:30-4AM; closed July and August, when it moves to the beach at Fregene. Jacket and tie required. Via Mario de' Fiori 97 (at Via delle Mercede). 6784838

Jackie O', near Via Veneto, is the grand dame of Rome nightclubs—going strong since the 1970s—and full of people who remember or want to remember those days. There's also a restaurant and piano bar. ◆ M-Sa 9PM-2AM. Via Boncompagni 11 (between Via Toscana and Via Marche). 42885457

Piper hosted the Beatles in the 1960s and has been going strong ever since. Large and bustling, it still packs in the disco revival crowd and has live performances on weekends. Sunday afternoon is reserved for teens, and Wednesday is roller disco day. ◆ Tu-Su 10PM-4AM. Via Tagliamento 9 (between Via Clitunno and Piazza Buenos Aires). 8555398

West Side Saloon's style is distinctly North American. Attracting a young crowd, this new disco near Via Veneto even serves burgers, fries, and Tex-Mex food. ◆ Tu-Su. Via Sardegna 27 (at Via Vittorio Veneto). 4821838

Jazz Clubs

Alexanderplatz, a few blocks north of **Vatican City,** features traditional jazz, with a different band every night. ◆ M-Sa 9PM-1AM; closed July through August. Via Ostia 9 (between Via Leone IV and Via Santamaura). 39742171

L'Alpheus, a converted dairy factory just south of Testaccio, has three separate dance-and-music areas. A variety of music—from jazz to salsa—is on tap here. There's also a pizzeria. ♦ Tu-Su 10PM-3AM. Via del Commercio 36 (at Piazza del Gazometro). 5747826

Big Mama is true to its name. The doyen of Rome jazz clubs, this Trastevere spot also features rock, blues, and folk music. ♦ M-Sa 10PM-1:30AM; closed July through September. No credit cards accepted. Vicolo di San Francesco a Ripa 18 (between Via di San Francesco a Ripa and Via Carlo Tavolacci). 5812551

Saint Louis Music City, a modern club in the old **Gladiators' Quarter,** offers a menu of music ranging from traditional to salsa. Both big-name entertainers and young, talented new groups perform here. There's also a restaurant, video bar, and billiards room. ♦ Tu-Su; closed July through September. Via del Cardello 13/1 (at Via Cavour). 4745076

Piano Bars

RiverSide is a good place to stop for a listen and a cocktail when you're near **Piazza del Popolo.** ♦ Tu-Su 9PM-2AM. Via del Fiume 4 (at Via di Ripetta). 3612389

Tartarughino, near Piazza Navona, requires that men wear jacket and tie—Roman high society and finance come here to relax, hence the dress code. Downstairs is live piano music; upstairs is a small restaurant. It's popular with the after-dinner drink crowd. ♦ M-Sa 9PM-3AM. Via della Scrofa 1 (at Via d'Ascanio). 6864131

77 La Taverna dei Quaranta ★$ Run by 40 aspiring actors and artists who take turns staffing it, this cooperative eatery offers such hearty Roman standards as polenta and roast veal, as well as nontraditional fare like risotto with radicchio. The service is sometimes chaotic and slow. ♦ Daily lunch and dinner. Via Claudia 24 (at Via Annia). 7000550

78 Basilica di San Clemente In his history of illustrious men written in 385, St. Jerome mentions this church, named for the fourth pope (AD 88-97), who converted from Judaism. This is where he lived and built a chapel. Between the fourth and tenth centuries three different churches were built over Clement's house, which itself abutted a pre-existing temple to the Persian god Mithras. In the 11th century the church was sacked and abandoned; it was rebuilt on the same site in 1108.

In the nave is a marble choir enclosure assembled during the sixth century that utilizes columns from **Trajan's Forum.** Above the apse is a glittering late Byzantine mosaic. The anchor design of the canopy over the high altar refers to the martyrdom of Clement, who was banished by Trajan to the Crimea and thrown into the Black Sea weighted down by an anchor around his neck. When the water miraculously receded, his body was recovered and brought back to Rome. A side chapel features delicately drawn frescoes of the life of St. Catherine of Alexandria (c. 1430) by Masolino, who was the teacher of Masaccio.

From the sacristy, proceed down a flight of steps built in 1857 when excavations on the fourth-century church began. Like the rest of the basilica, the first impression is somewhat confusing—some of the walls in the early church were actually added to support the newer church when it was constructed 700 years later, and part of the old church was filled in with rubble for additional support. Glimpses of the older church's frescoes can be seen at every turn; they have faded badly since the 19th-century excavations, but copies were made at the time and can be seen at the entrance to the stairs. The 12th-century fresco on the left wall recounts an incident in St. Clement's life and bears the first inscription known to be written in Italian rather than Latin.

Near the bust of Cardinal O'Connell of Boston—who in 1912 collected funds to drain the flooded lower level—is the entrance for the descent to the ancient **Temple of Mithras,** built for worshipers of a Persian sun god. Roman armies in the Middle East brought the religion back with them, and it became so popular among Roman aristocrats that it was Christianity's chief rival until outlawed in AD 395. Two emperors became converts, and Roman legionnaires built Mithraic temples throughout the empire, including one in London and another on the Danube. Like Jesus, Mithras was a savior god who came to earth to fight evil, died, and was later resurrected. His followers were baptized in bull's blood.

In 1989 archaeologists uncovered more layers of history in the bowels of the basilica. A dozen feet below the present sacristy they found the floor of a sixth-century room where Pope Gregory I prepared himself for Mass until his death in 604 (Gregory mentions it in his writings). The floor is a handsome mosaic of colored marble paving blocks; next door was a sixth-century bathroom. ♦ Admission to lower church and Temple of Mithras. Via di San Giovanni in Laterano and Via dei Querceti

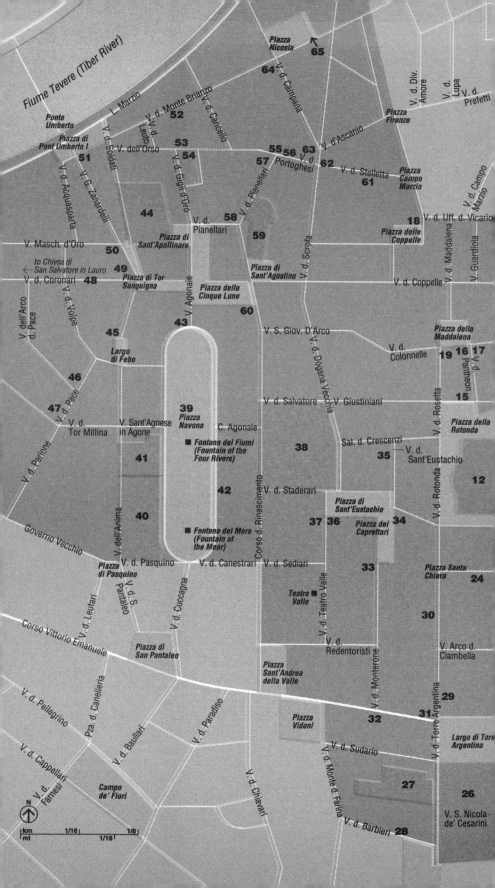

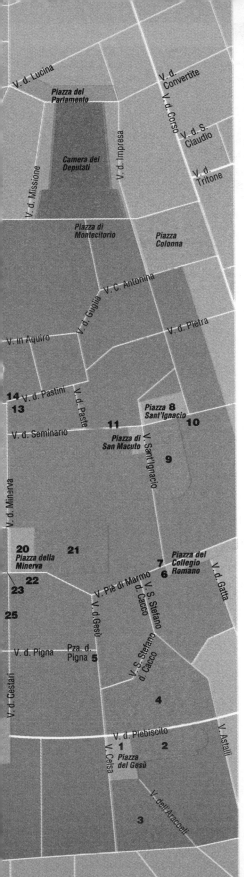

Piazza Navona

In earliest Rome, this neighborhood was an open plain, full of meadows, farms, and later, military parade grounds. By the height of the Roman Empire it had been transformed into an urban center rich in magnificent public buildings, circuses, theaters, temples, libraries, and baths. With notable exceptions (the largely intact **Pantheon** and the ruined temples at **Largo Argentina**), most of these structures were destroyed. In place of the great oval-shaped Domitian stadium stands **Piazza Navona**, which many consider Rome's most beautiful piazza.

Unlike the other ancient Roman buildings in this area, the **Pantheon** escaped destruction because it was under the popes' protection. In 608, Byzantine Emperor Phocas gave the magnificent edifice to Pope Boniface IV, who consecrated it a year later as a church—thus preserving it from further plunder.

Having languished for centuries under a hill of dirt, the ruins of the temples at **Largo Argentina** were rediscovered in 1928. They were put under government protection by Mussolini's Imperial Act, thereby safeguarding the newly excavated sites and forbidding any new construction over them.

No such nostalgia prevailed during the Middle Ages, when the rubble of the ancients was summarily smoothed over to make foundations for new buildings. Houses from the 13th century, no wider than a room, are jumbled together with the occasional medieval tower, particularly in the older area west of **Piazza Navona**, between **Corso Vittorio Emanuele** and the **Tiber**. A walk along these narrow alleys, cobblestoned and without sidewalks, gives a sense of what medieval Rome must have been like.

Centuries later, this area became the site of many of the finest Renaissance (and later, Baroque) churches, palaces, fountains, and city squares. The Counter-Reformation was the occasion of still more construction, most notably the **Chiesa del Gesù.** As the main church of the Jesuits, it was designed in response to the Lutheran revolt, to reaffirm the power and glory of the Catholic Church. Other nearby Jesuit venues include the **Chiesa di Sant'Ignazio** (on the piazza of that name); the **Collegio Romano** (Piazza del Collegio Romano), seat of the first Jesuit seminary in Rome (now a public high school); and **Palazzo Pamphili**, built as the private palace of the Jesuit pontiff Innocent X.

At the neighborhood's heart is **Corso Vittorio Emanuele** (not to be confused with Via del Corso, which runs between **Piazza del Popolo** and **Piazza Venezia**), a broad avenue with heavy bus traffic that was punched through the maze of tiny streets in 1870, after Rome became the capital of united Italy. The blocks nearest the **Piazza del Gesù** are lined with inexpensive clothing shops, tradition left from the time when silk, wool, and cotton were manufactured in the nearby quarter. Farther down, at the intersection of **Via dei Cestari** where shops specializing in ecclesiastical supplies are clustered, shoppers can pick up a pair of crimson cardinal's socks. Gourmets will find these streets full of tantalizing treats: from the best cappuccino in Rome to diabolically designed chocolate confections.

1 Piazza del Gesù There's a story about this piazza, one of the windiest spots in Rome. According to a 19th-century legend, the Devil, out walking with the Wind one day, excused himself and stepped into the nearby Jesuit church, saying he had something to discuss with the Jesuits. The Wind has been waiting for him to return ever since.

2 Chiesa del Gesù This church of the Jesuits in Rome (illustrated below) was built by **Giacomo da Vignola** in 1575. The ponderous scrolls on either side of the facade—designed by **Giacomo della Porta**—hold together Greek-style columns, in what has come to be described as Jesuit-style church architecture. The exuberant High Baroque decoration inside was meant to rebut the austerity of the Protestant Reformation with overpowering visual effects. In the opulent **Chapel of Saint Ignatius,** the ex-soldier and founder of the Jesuit Order lies buried under an altar where his statue, originally cast in 600 pounds of pure silver, has been replaced with one of silver alloy. Do not be deceived by what seems to be the largest chunk of lapis lazuli crowning the altar; it is actually only the largest shell of lapis lazuli covering a wood frame in the world. A tiny museum devoted to St. Ignatius is located nearby. Check with the sacristan to visit it.
◆ Piazza del Gesù and Via del Plebiscito

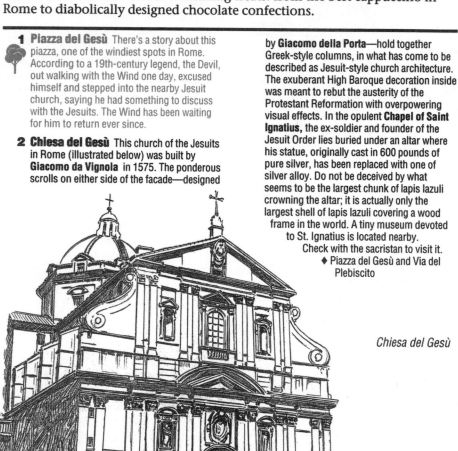

Chiesa del Gesù

Chiesa di Sant'Ignazio

3 Palazzo Cenci-Bolognetti The Christian Democrats, the political party that dominated Italy from World War II until 1994, was headquartered in this palazzo, notable for the Baroque facade added in 1737 by **Ferdinando Fuga.** Because of its proximity to the main church of the Jesuits, some considered the location very appropriate. The building is not open to the public. ♦ Piazza del Gesù (between Via dell'Aracoeli and Via Celsa)

4 Palazzo Altieri This huge palazzo, which occupies the whole block, was built in 1670 for the Altieri pope Clement X. While it was going up, its size provoked this comment from Rome's sharp-tongued talking statues: "Rome is becoming a single house!" Anna Magnani, one of Italy's most famous actresses and one of Rome's most beloved citizens, lived in a penthouse. Also known in the US, she won an Oscar in 1955 for her performance in *The Rose Tattoo.* To Romans she was known as *Mamma Roma,* and when she died in 1973, nearly the whole city turned out for her funeral. ♦ Via del Plebiscito 46 (at Via del Gesù)

5 Enoteca Corsi ★$ Originally a wine bar, this nondescript place now serves food as well. The lentils with sausage and *pasta e fagioli* (a thick bean soup with different kinds of short pasta) have a longstanding tradition of excellence. One of the best items on the menu is the *insalata completa,* which includes several kinds of greens, mozzárella balls, black olives, tuna, tomatoes, white beans, and wedges of hard-boiled egg. Finish the meal with *panna cotta* (whipped cream and gelatin) topped with chocolate syrup, or pine-nut cake. Be prepared for slow service. ♦ M-Sa lunch. Via del Gesù 87 (at Piazza della Pigna). 6790821

6 Confetteria Moriondo & Gariglio Rome's finest chocolatier has been making mouth-watering temptations since 1886. Fill a box or basket with an assortment of hand-dipped chocolates, creams, and nougats. The truffles are almost as expensive as the fungus of the same name, and the after-dinner mints are often found on the tables of Rome's nobility and heads of state. Nonchocoholics can try the plump, golden brown marrons glacés. ♦ M-Sa; closed in August. Via del Piè di Marmo 21 (at Piazza del Collegio Romano). 6990856

7 Lillo al Piedone ★$$ This tiny trattoria with two rooms on an upper floor is named after the gigantic fourth-century marble foot on the corner outside. It was probably part of a colossal statue of Constantine; the other pieces are dispersed throughout the city. (The gigantic head and hand are in the courtyard of the **Palazzo dei Conservatori Museum** on Capitoline Hill.) *Orecchiette con broccoletti* (small earlobe-shaped pasta with broccoli and red pepper) is a spicy specialty, and don't miss the roasted veal stuffed with prunes and almonds if it's on the menu. ♦ M-Sa lunch and dinner. Via del Piè di Marmo 28 (at Piazza del Collegio Romano). 6798628

8 Piazza Sant'Ignazio Designed by **Filippo Raguzzini** in 1727, this Baroque square feels more like a stage set than a piazza—especially at night when the buildings are illuminated by the soft lights from lamps that look like tiny candelabra.

9 Chiesa di Sant'Ignazio Named after St. Ignatius, the founder of the Jesuit order, this church (pictured on page 89) was built in 1626-50 by **Fra Orazio Grassi.** Severe on the outside, the interior is richly decorated and full of surprises. The vaulted ceiling has a famous trompe l'oeil fresco depicting St. Ignatius entering paradise in a whirl of angels and saints. Its painter, Fra Andrea Pozzo, used a skillfully drawn architectural setting to make the ceiling seem far higher than it actually is. In fact, the pillars and arches seem to soar straight up to heaven. Even more amazing is the false dome, which is a painting and actually as flat as the floor below. A disc set into the floor halfway up the nave offers the best view, and a few coins in a nearby box will light it. ♦ Piazza Sant'Ignazio (between Via della Caravita and Piazza di San Macuto)

10 Le Cave di Sant'Ignazio ★$$ Tourists and politicians frequent this restaurant, especially in summer when tables are spread out in the opera-setlike piazza. The fish on display is best on Tuesday and Friday, when the markets are open. Cooked vegetables from the antipasti table inside are a good bet, as are the pasta dishes and the pizza. ♦ M-Sa lunch and dinner; closed 10 days in August. Reservations recommended. Piazza Sant'Ignazio 169 (at Via della Caravita). 6797821; fax 6791012

11 Due Colonne ★★★$$ A short walk from the **Pantheon** is this simple, elegant osteria with terra-cotta tiles underfoot and white-clothed tables circled by bentwood chairs. Brother-sister owners Pino and Gina Lanzola hail from Puglia, which inspires their signature pasta, *orechiette,* served al dente with a sauce of tiny sweet tomatoes, fresh arugula, and hot pepper. You'd have to travel to the Amalfi Coast to get better *tagliolini* (thin bands of pasta tossed with fresh cream and lemon) or such delicious grilled calamari. The house white, Romanella, is a refreshing, slightly bubbly offering from **Castelli Romani.** ♦ M-Sa lunch and dinner; Su dinner. Via del Seminario 122 (between Piazza di San Macuto and Via delle Paste). 6781449

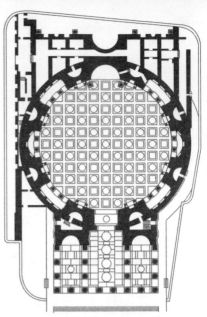

Pantheon (floor plan)

12 Pantheon Built by **Emperor Hadrian** in AD 125, this is one of the most perfectly preserved ancient buildings in Rome. Although each brick of this edifice bears **Hadrian**'s imperial stamp, the inscription on the outside, by his fiat, pays homage to Augustus's son-in-law, Consul Marcus Agrippa, whose smaller square temple (27 BC) **Hadrian** incorporated into the pillared front porch. The design—an enormous Roman dome set on top of a Greek temple—is an unequaled architectural and aesthetic feat. It is called "Pantheon" because it was dedicated to "All the Gods."

Patches of the original marble facing on the sides make it easier to imagine how impressive this building was when its brick exterior was entirely covered in marble. The great bronze doors are original, as are 13 of the 16 immense granite columns holding up the front porch. The bronze tiles that once covered the roof were taken by Constantius II to adorn his capital of Constantinople. Hijacked, they ended up in Alexandria, Egypt. In 735, Pope Gregory III, worried about the tileless dome, protected it with a sheathing of lead—which is how it appears today. Originally, there were beams under the porch roof wrapped in bronze, but they were taken by the Barberini Pope, Urban VIII, to construct the canopy over the main altar in **St. Peter's.** This gave rise to a famous accusation: "What the barbarians didn't do (to the Pantheon), the Barberinis did!"

The mystery was how the Romans built this enormous dome, 143 feet in diameter, wider

Pantheon (interior)

than **St. Peter's,** without supporting columns or outside buttresses. The answer is that it was constructed underground, or at least under a hill of dirt, and then the earth around it was removed. The dome rests on a concrete drum 20 feet thick, while a network of brick arches, visible from the outside, carries the weight. The dome itself becomes increasingly thinner and lighter as it nears the top. At the base, heavy travertine is mixed in the concrete; tufa, a light volcanic stone, is used in the middle; finally, feather-light pumice takes over at the top. The interior (pictured above) is a symphony of harmony and simplicity played out in perfect proportions. The theme is euclidean, and the first place to notice this is in the flooring where the geometric circle-in-a-square design is repeated in the precious marble pavement. Mathematical harmony also dictates the symmetry of the interior space: The diameter of the dome is equal to its height so that a giant sphere could fit snugly inside the rotunda. Finally, high above in the center of the dome, is the most perfect of all the circles—the 30-foot wide oculus, or eye of the dome, which is the only source of light.

When the sun shines through the oculus, it produces a shaft of light, ending in another brilliant circle that moves slowly around the walls and floor. To handle rain, the flooring is sloped so that water would run off.

The niches in the walls (see floor plan on page 90) are **Hadrian**'s original designs and have inspired generations of architects. The elegant fluted Corinthian columns and pilasters are of a rare marble called *antico giallo,* a venerable yellow hue that was already becoming rare in **Hadrian**'s time. After the temple became the church of **Santa Maria ad Martyres** in AD 609, most of **Hadrian**'s original decoration in the attic zone around the base of the drum was changed, but enough of it remains to show how superior it was. ♦ Tu-Sa; Su morning; closed 15 August, 25-26 December. Piazza della Rotonda (between Via della Minerva and Via della Rotonda)

13 Hotel del Senato $$ The postmodern lobby of this 51-room hotel leads to recently renovated, attractive rooms done in soft shades of green, yellow, and beige. Each room has new walnut furnishings, a marble-and-chrome bathroom, and a mini-bar, safe, and TV. The tiny elevator is an appropriate prelude to the size of the rooms, but when you open your window and look down upon the **Pantheon**, you'll probably forget about square feet. There's air-conditioning, no restaurant—but breakfast is included. ◆ Piazza della Rotonda 73 (at Via dei Pastini). 6793231; fax 69940297

14 Tazza D'Oro ★★$ This bar serves its own brand of "espresso," which many claim is superior. Buy as many beans as you can carry, but don't overlook the specialty: *granità di caffè*, coffee which has been frozen and crushed into a smooth slushlike ice, then put into a glass (or plastic cup to go) between layers of whipped cream. Eat it, or slurp it, with a spoon, and guaranteed you'll be back for more. ◆ M-Sa 7AM-8PM. No credit cards accepted. Via degli Orfani 84 (at Via dei Pastini). 6789792

15 Albergo del Sole al Pantheon $$$ Built in 1467, this hotel claims to be one of Rome's oldest inns. All 25 rooms have private baths, a few have whirlpool tubs, and some offer fabulous views of the **Pantheon**. The piazza is a pedestrian island, and strollers carouse late into the night. Ask for a room in the back if quiet is a prerequisite for staying here. But what this hotel lacks in tranquillity, it makes up for in historical charm. For 500 years, the hotel has catered to theater people, pilgrims, and tourists. The composer Pietro Mascagni celebrated the triumphant opening of his opera *Cavalleria Rusticana* here in 1890, and the poet/playwright Ludovico Ariosto stayed here in 1513 on the eve of a papal audience. The five rooms in the nearby annex, facing the **Pantheon**, are more spacious, and one has a terrace. There's no restaurant. ◆ Via del Pantheon 63 (at Piazza della Rotonda). 6780441; fax 69940689

16 Fiocco di Neve The mecca for serious gelato eaters begins on the winding Via del Pantheon that leads out of **Piazza della Rotonda**. With many of the best gelaterias in Rome, the street has been nicknamed "ice cream alley." But the first—and best—place is this shop, which makes a limited number of fresh homemade flavors. Try *riso alle fragole,* a kind of rice pudding made with strawberry ice cream. ◆ Daily 7AM-midnight; closed two weeks in January. Via del Pantheon 51 (between Piazza della Rotonda and Piazza della Maddalena). 6786025

17 Da Fortunato al Pantheon ★★$$$ Politicians from the nearby Parliament

buildings come to this classy dining spot not only to indulge in the perfect risotto but to meet and greet. The best dishes are seasonal, such as *puntarelle* (raw curly chicory dressed with garlic, olive oil, and mashed anchovies), polenta with country sausages, salmon carpaccio, and at the end, an orange deftly peeled in one long ribbon and cut into wedges by your waiter. The homemade tiramisù comes without a floor show. ◆ M-Sa lunch and dinner; closed second half of August. Reservations required. Via del Pantheon 55 (at Piazza della Maddalena). 6792788

18 Maccheroni ★★$$ The glassed-in kitchen at this bright and airy modern eatery turns out such well-prepared dishes as spaghetti tossed with a simple sweet *pachino* tomato sauce (best eaten as Italians do: without grated cheese, to let the tomatoes take the spotlight) and *maccheroni all'amatriciana* (in olive oil and garlic with diced bacon, tomato, red peppers, and onion). Since you've skipped cheese on your pasta, why not indulge in *Scamorza alla piastra* (a small head of local cheese, soft on the inside, grilled to crisp perfection on the outside) or a lighter-than-the-French chocolate mousse. ◆ M-Sa lunch and dinner. Piazza delle Coppelle and Vicolo delle Coppelle. 68307895

la Rosetta

19 La Rosetta ★★★$$$$ Rome is not a mecca for seafood, but this upscale restaurant earns high points for freshness. The menu depends on what the boat brings in at dawn, but try the fish soup—it's more refined than bouillabaisse but just as generous. Wash it down with a fruity Gaja Chardonnay from Piemonte. ◆ M-F lunch and dinner; Sa dinner; closed in August. Reservations required. Via della Rosetta 9 (at Piazza della Maddalena). 68308841; fax 6872852

20 Piazza della Minerva In the center of this square is an obelisk mounted on an elephant's back, designed in 1667 by **Bernini** for Pope Alexander VII of the Chigi family. As Pope Alexander wrote on the inscription, the elephant symbolizes the massive intelligence needed as a base for wisdom. This is one of the smallest of the 13 obelisks that the ancient Romans brought back as war trophies after their conquest of Egypt. It was placed in front of a Roman temple—no longer there— dedicated to the goddess Minerva. Now it stands in a piazza in front of a Christian church, both named for that temple. The piazza spent some time under water over the centuries. The plaque to the right of the entrance to the church shows the high-water level of the Tiber floodings.

Obelisk, Piazza della Minerva

21 Chiesa di Santa Maria Sopra Minerva

This is the only Gothic church (1280) in Rome, and it houses some important art pieces. Notables include Michelangelo's nude statue of the *Risen Christ*—the gilded bronze loincloth was not in his original plan—and Filippino Lippi's superb frescoes (1489) in the **Carafa Chapel** at the south transept (take along coins for the lighting). Lippi's realistic paintings are dedicated to St. Thomas Aquinas, whose life is depicted on the right-hand wall—along with portraits of two young Medici who became popes Clement VII and Leo X and who are entombed behind the high altar.

The church's Gothic character was compromised somewhat in the 19th century when gray marble was wrapped around the six pairs of piers in the central nave. This was particularly unfortunate for Bernini, whose contribution to this church was the High Baroque tomb (1653) of the venerable Sister Maria Raggi on the second pier from the altar on the north side. The great 15th-century painter Fra Angelico is buried under the floor of the first chapel to the left of the altar.

Accessible from the nearby sacristy is the **Capella di Santa Caterina da Siena**, named after the woman who arranged the popes' return from their long exile at Avignon in the 14th century. Catherine died in 1380, and her room in the nearby Dominican convent was moved here in 1637. She is buried under the main altar.

This church is also famous because it was in this complex that Galileo was tried by the Inquisition and convicted of heresy for claiming that the earth moves around the sun, which he deduced using his new invention, the telescope. During his interrogation Galileo recanted. But legend has it that as he was being taken away, he added in an aside: *Eppur, si muove* (And yet it *does* move). In 1993 the Catholic Church formally agreed with him.
◆ Piazza della Minerva (between Via di Santa Caterina da Siena and Via della Minerva)

22 Crowne Plaza Minerva $$$$

This hostelry (formerly the **Holiday Inn Minerva**) rests partly on the site of Rome's oldest baths, the **Terme di Agrippa**. Built in the 16th century, it became a hotel in the early 1800s and counted Stendhal among its guests. Famed Roman architect **Paolo Portoghesi** remodeled it in 1989, keeping the historic flavor while providing 20th-century comforts. The sumptuously adorned lobby boasts a large Roman statue of Minerva, and some of the common rooms have retained their ancient frescoes. All 117 rooms have private baths, and the 16 suites also feature Empire furnishings. The downstairs restaurant is equally lovely. The rooftop terrace and restaurant (summer only) have spectacular views of the Centro Storico. For luxury and location, this place is tops. ◆ Piazza della Minerva 69 (at Via di Santa Caterina da Siena). 69941888; fax 6794165; minerva@pronet.it

23 Ditta Annibale Gammarelli This tiny shop has served cardinals and popes since 1798 and is still the pope's tailor (note the white skullcap in the window worn only by popes). It's also the place to buy socks for a cardinal (red scarlet) or a bishop (purple). ◆ M-F. Via Santa Chiara 34 (at Piazza della Minerva). 68801314

24 Albergo Santa Chiara $$ Clean, comfortable—if somewhat small—rooms, and friendly, efficient service are the draws at this reliable hotel without a restaurant (breakfast is included). Some of the 96 rooms have facilities for people with disabilities. The windows are double-paned, and there is air-conditioning plus an interior courtyard. ◆ Via Santa Chiara 21 (between Via dei Cestari and Piazza Santa Chiara). 6872979; fax 6873144

25 Via dei Cestari Harking back to the Middle Ages and the streets of the different occupations, this narrow street of the "basket makers" still has some shops selling wickerwork. Today it is also the street par excellence for ecclesiastical shopping: golden embroidered cassocks, burnished miters, and pure linen soutanes—crimson cardinal's socks. Chalices, crèche figures, or such secular necessities as underwear and simple black shoes are for sale, too. The first part of this street was formerly called Via del Calcalari (Street of the Lime Kilns) because during the Middle Ages the marble stripped from Rome's ancient edifices was boiled in cauldrons and reduced to lime here.

26 Area Sacra del Largo Argentina These ruins (illustrated below) of four Roman temples (600-200 BC) are rare examples of Republican architecture, the earliest built 500 years prior to the imperial period. They were constructed on what was then the ground level, but today is three or four yards below. This is generally true of most of ancient Rome's ruins, because accumulated dirt caused the street level to rise about one yard every 500 years. Little is known about the four temples—not even to whom they were dedicated; in fact, they are referred to by letters, reading from right to left (or north to south). **Temple A** is the best preserved, having been restored under the first emperors. Don't be misled by the indications of round construction; they are left over from two churches subsequently built here, one above the other and not part of the original temple. **Temple B,** in the center, was consecrated in 101 BC by Catulo. It is the only originally round structure and has a black-and-white mosaic floor. Between these two temples is an addition from the imperial era of which only three broken walls remain. **Temple C,** the last fully visible podium on the left, dates from 400-300 BC. **Temple D** is half covered by Via Florida, but the visible part dates back to 200 BC. From the opposite side of the excavations, on Via di Torre Argentina, across from the **Teatro Argentina,** look over the edge to the right behind **Temple A,** to see the remains of one of ancient Rome's public toilets—a row of marble seats unpartitioned so that citizens could visit while doing their business. The ruins are closed, but guided

Area Sacra del Largo Argentina

tours are often given by one of the historical societies. Check *Roma C'è* for schedules. ◆ Via San Nicola de' Cesarini (between Piazza dei Calcarari and Largo di Torre Argentina)

27 Teatro Argentina At the disastrous opening of Rossini's opera *Barber of Seville* in this theater in 1816, the audience booed and hissed, apparently on orders of Napoleon's sister, Pauline Borghese. Verdi's opera *Rigoletto* fared better at its first performance here in 1851 and was a huge success. Today the theater is noted more for prose productions than opera. Works by Italian playwrights Goldoni and Pirandello are often part of the season, along with visiting international theater groups who sometimes perform in English. See *Roma C'è* for schedules. ◆ Largo di Torre Argentina 52(at Via di Torre Argentina). 68804601

28 Spazio Sette For the best of contemporary hi-tech Italian design in furniture, kitchenware, lamps, and flower vases, this amazing shop, once a nobleman's palazzo, can't be beat. The frescoed ceiling on the top floor is worth the climb. ◆ M afternoon; Tu-Sa. Via dei Barbieri 7 (at Largo Arenula). 6869708; fax 68307139

29 Pascucci ★$ This bar is a milkshake mecca for many. The *frullati* are whipped in blenders with the fresh fruit and/or ice cream of your choice. ◆ M-Sa. Via di Torre Argentina 20 (between Largo di Torre Argentina and Via Arco della Ciambella). 6864816

29 Antica Erboristeria Romana Founded in 1783, this herb-and-potions shop is the oldest continuous shop of its kind in Rome. Inside are floor-to-ceiling drawers full of spices and herbs. Stop by just to catch a glimpse of the coffered ceiling in painted stucco and to sniff the rich aroma of cinnamon, clove, and other spices. A framed etching on the wall shows how little the store has changed over the centuries. Depending on what ails you, the herbalist will prescribe essence of mint, chamomile, or belladonna. ◆ M-Sa. Via di Torre Argentina 15 (between Largo di Torre Argentina and Via Arco della Ciambella). 6879493

29 Furla This is the place for high-quality handbags, wallets, and glass cases without somebody's initials or an animal on them. ◆ M-Sa. Via di Torre Argentina 7 (between Largo di Torre Argentina and Via Arco della Ciambella). 6865098

30 Borra This hardware store—one of the oldest in Rome (1891)—has a frescoed ceiling and walls made up of countless tiny drawers. On the outside of each drawer is a clue to what lies inside. ◆ M-Sa. Via di Torre Argentina 78 (between Corso Vittorio Emanuele and Piazza Santa Chiara). 68308577

31 Passamanerie Ribbons, cords, and elaborate silver-and-gold tassels in a variety of sizes are the featured merchandise at this small buttons-and-bows shop. ◆ M-Sa. Via di Torre Argentina 14 (at Corso Vittorio Emanuele). 6893365

32 Hotel della Torre Argentina $$ Old-fashioned and reliable, this 53-room, air-conditioned hostelry is very well located. All rooms have TVs and baths or showers. The windows have double glazing, but light sleepers should ask for rooms off the noisy Corso Vittorio Emanuele. A buffet breakfast is included. Check for weekend package specials and discounts during August. ◆ Corso Vittorio Emanuele 102 (between Largo di Torre Argentina and Piazza Vidoni). 6833886; fax 68801641

"L'Eau-Vive" de Rome

33 L'Eau-Vive de Rome ★$$ The servers at this unique restaurant, whose name means "The Living Water," are members of the Order of Christian Virgins of Catholic Missionary Action Through Work, so don't be surprised if they break into a hymn at any point. These young women from the French-speaking developing world wear colorful native dress rather than nuns' habits. The service is gracious, and the food abundant, but—save for the daily special from a faraway place—there are fewer exotic dishes than one might hope to find. The 16th-century dining rooms are handsome, and there's an inexpensive, fixed-price menu at lunch. ◆ M-Sa lunch and dinner; closed in August. Reservations recommended for dinner. Via di Monterone 85/A (at Piazza dei Caprettari). 68801095

34 Archimede ★★$$ The tiny square where this cozy restaurant is located includes a miniature Renaissance palace frescoed on the outside by Zuccari and the handsome hunters' church, **Sant'Eustachio,** next door. This place serves the best *fritto misto* (battered and deep-fried vegetables) in Rome, but be prepared for slow service. Also try the carpaccio with *rughetta* (wild arugula) on top. ♦ M-Sa lunch and dinner; closed half of August. Reservations recommended. Piazza dei Caprettari 63 (between Via di Monterone and Piazza di Sant'Eustachio). 6861616, 6785216

35 Spiriti ★★$ At this tiny wine bar with outdoor tables, the specialty is bruschetta topped with anything from tuna to gorgonzola cheese to the standard tomato version. What's not standard is the size: Made from huge specially baked loaves of bread, they fill a whole plate. Also worth a try are the pasta dishes, such as lasagna with radicchio and béchamel or rigatoni with tomatoes and eggplant. ♦ M-Sa lunch and dinner. No credit cards accepted. Via di Sant'Eustachio 5 (between Piazza di Sant'Eustachio and Salita dei Crescenzi). No phone

36 Sant'Eustachio Cafe ★$ Many claim that this cafe serves the best cappuccino in Rome, and now that it's no longer presweetened (better keep an eye on the barman just to be safe), the

number of devotees has increased a hundredfold. Romans stop here late at night after the theater or a movie and pack the little square outside even in winter. ♦ Tu-Su 8:30AM-1AM. Piazza di Sant'Eustachio 82 (at Via del Teatro Valle). 6861309

37 Chiesa di Sant'Ivo alla Sapienza The epitome of the Roman Baroque style and the culmination of **Francesco Borromini**'s work, this extraordinary church (illustrated below) built in 1660 is nonetheless difficult to get to see from the inside—it is officially open only on Sunday morning for Mass. At other times, try to track down the *portiere* (custodian) and implore him with whatever means to open the doors. It's a masterpiece.

Limitations only inspired **Borromini** to invent new constructs for his demanding clients. The proposed site was a square box hemmed in by two arched courtyards that were part of **La Sapienza,** the **University of Rome,** which is now located in the **University City** complex. Since his patron was Pope Urban VIII of the Barberini family, **Borromini** planned the church in the form of a bee—the Barberini family symbol. He later

Chiesa di Sant'Ivo alla Sapienza

changed it to an even more daring design based on two intersecting triangles that form a six-pointed star of David, a token of *la sapienza* (wisdom). These two symbols—the bee and star—are repeated in the design and surface decoration of both the exterior and interior, culminating in **Borromini**'s fantastic spiraling zigguratlike dome that recalls a bee's stinger. Stand at the center of this pristine white church and notice how much movement there is even though there is hardly any decoration and very little color. From alternating curved and straight-line bases, the six arms of a star soar to form the dome. The idea was total design, and the better part of an hour could be spent noting how ingeniously **Borromini** has worked the small details into his overall theme. The floor, for example, is the only instance of color, the alternating blue-and-grey marble slabs adding an opposing wavelike rhythm to the otherwise strong vertical movement. Even after a short visit, you will know why art historians say that the eye never comes to rest in a **Borromini** church. ♦ Su morning. Palazzo della Sapienza, Via del Teatro Valle and Piazza Sant'Eustachio

38 Palazzo Madama The facade of this Baroque palace was completed in 1610 by **Ludovico Cardi** and **Paolo Marucelli.** Guarded by two carabinieri sentinels, the building has housed the Italian Senate since 1871. Before that it was the Crescenzi family palazzo and then passed, as part of a dowry, to the Medici. Catherine de' Medici lived here before she moved to Paris, but the building derives its name from the woman who inherited it from her, Margaret of Parma, the wife of Alessandro de' Medici. As Margaret was the out-of-wedlock daughter of Charles V of Austria, her title was simply "madame." Be sure to see the beautiful 16th-century granite fountain behind the palazzo. It was discovered in 1986 when an underground passage was being built to connect this palazzo with an adjoining office building. ♦ Guided tours (in Italian) the first Saturday of every month 10AM-6PM. Corso del Rinascimento and Via del Salvatore

39 Piazza Navona *Navona* is a corruption of the Latin *circus agonalis* (an arena for athletic games), which was rendered in medieval Latin first as *in agone* then corrupted to *n'agona* and finally became *navona*. The current piazza (see illustration below) retains the elliptical shape of the original circus built by Emperor Domitian on this spot in AD 86. Shops and buildings now occupy the spaces where tiers of stone bleachers once stood. Those seats were still in use during the mid-15th

Piazza Navona

century, when Romans came here to watch armored knights joust. (Remnants of the first-century stadium are preserved behind glass in **Piazza di Tor Sanguigna**—under the buildings outside the square's north end.)

In the 17th century **Piazza Navona** became a Baroque spectacle when Pope Innocent X went on a construction spree and expanded a small building that his family, the Pamphili, owned here. Like most, this binge was motivated by his desire to keep up with the Joneses—or in this case, the rival Barberini family, whose favorite son, Urban VIII, had just left the papacy. Fortunately, Innocent's drive to outshine his predecessor came at the height of a new and exciting style. Although the addition of these Baroque buildings transformed the space forever, an element of continuity between the **Navona** of the emperors and that of the popes remained because the piazza continued to be a public place. Just as the ancient Romans flooded their circuses and staged mock sea battles in them, the new owners—the cardinals and princes of the 17th and 18th centuries—had their gilded carriages driven around the water-filled piazza during the stifling heat of August.The tradition of public spectacle continues today. Every December an Epiphany fair takes place here when the piazza is taken over by vendors' stands selling crèche figures and *Befana* dolls. *La Befana,* or the Christmas witch, is the Italian counterpart of Santa Claus. She rides on a broomstick and delivers presents or *carbone* (sugar coal) to good and bad children respectively.

On Piazza Navona:

Fontana dei Fiumi (Fountain of the Four Rivers) Located in the middle of **Piazza Navona,** the Egyptian obelisk that crowns this fountain—completed in 1651—and carries the Pamphili coat-of-arms was brought from Emperor Maxentius's great circus on the **Appian Way** by Pope Innocent X. Below it are four figures (illustrated below) which represent the great rivers of four continents: the Danube, Ganges, Nile, and Plate. Around the grotto holding the obelisk are various animals associated with these continents.

The rivalry between **Bernini** and **Borromini** was legendary (see "Baroque Adversaries" on page 102). In this instance, **Bernini** allegedly stole the commission for this fountain away from **Borromini** by presenting the pope with a solid silver model of his design for the fountain. To finance it, the pope raised a vast sum in gold coins by taxing bread. This action of course did not sit well with the Roman populace. Both the pope and his sister-in-law and confidante, Olympia Maidalchini, were publicly reviled. Olympia's name was henceforth written in two words— *olim pia,* meaning "once virtuous" in Latin.

Fontana del Moro (Fountain of the Moor) At Pope Innocent X's request, **Bernini** added the Moor pinching a dolphin's tail to an earlier fountain of four tritons blowing into seashells. (The four tritons can now be seen at the **Villa Borghese.**)

40 Palazzo Pamphili Pope Innocent X built this palazzo in 1650 for Olympia Maidalchini. Architecturally speaking, it is too big, too flat, but lighter in feeling than the **Palazzo Barberini** (which it was intended to outshine) because **Borromini** was able to reduce some of the heaviness of **Rainaldi**'s original design. Inside, visible through the windows on the second floor, is the great salon, with a ceiling painting by Pietro da Cortona. The building is now the residence of the Brazilian ambassador and is not open to the public.

MARJORIE J. VOGEL/RHODE ISLAND ORIGINALS

Fontana dei Fiumi
(Fountain of the Four Rivers)

♦ Piazza Navona (between Via di Pasquino and Via Sant'Agnese in Agone)

41 Chiesa di Sant'Agnese in Agone
Adjoining the **Palazzo Pamphili** is Pope Innocent X's family church, which incorporates a shrine built on the spot where the 13-year-old St. Agnes was martyred in AD 304. The site had originally been a bordello where the child was forced to strip in front of clients, but apparently, her piety was so great that her hair suddenly grew sufficiently to cover her embarrassment. In much the same way, **Borromini**'s original and daring 1657 facade covers the conventional and uninteresting church that had been started by **Girolamo** and **Carlo Rainaldi** in 1652. Rather than having the central pediment come forward, as it does on most churches, **Borromini** pushed it in back of the flanking belfries so that the whole facade ripples with movement.
♦ Piazza Navona (between Via di Pasquino and Via Sant'Agnese in Agone)

42 Bar Tre Scalini ★★$$$
The "three little steps" that made this bar famous are gone, but the *tartufo*—over 800 are sold daily in summer—is still available and known from Tokyo to Rio. A *tartufo* is a ball of dark chocolate that resembles the rare mushroom of the same name. But what an exquisite ball of chocolate! Outside are chips of dark chocolate; inside is milk chocolate ice cream studded with chunks of more chocolate and at the center—if you're lucky—a cherry. Sit at one of the outside tables and enjoy your *tartufo* while taking in the sights and sounds of the piazza or stand at the bar—and pay less—while watching the barmen slap the *tartufi* onto paper doilies, flatten them into discs, and then bless them with a dollop of whipped cream. Drinks, sandwiches, and other flavors of gelato are also available. ♦ M-Tu, Th-Su 8AM-1AM. Piazza Navona 28-32 (between Via dei Canestrari and Circo Agonale). 68801996

Al Sogno

43 Al Sogno
The window displays of dolls and teddy bears at this toy shop could turn the meanest old Scrooge into a kid again. Inside is a Noah's Ark of stuffed animals, wooden Pinocchios of all sizes, and models of the latest Ferrari. ♦ Daily (no midday closing). Piazza Navona 53 (at Via Agonale). 6864198

44 Palazzo Altemps
During the 16th century, Marco Sittico Cardinal Altemps amassed an impressive collection of antique sculptures, which were dispersed after his death to a number of museums and private collectors—including Cardinal Ludovico Ludovisi. More than three centuries later, when the Ludovisi property near **Villa Borghese** was displaced by the current **Via Veneto**, the Italian government acquired the artworks. Then, in 1982, they also took possession of the **Palazzo Altemps**. A subsequent restoration project uncovered the structural elements and frescoed details of the palace and returned the sculptures to their original home. The quiet elegance and simplicity of the two-story palace, with a central courtyard and 35 airy rooms, carries visitors back to a world governed by gods and goddesses. Apollos, Athenas, and Aphrodites share these rooms with more than 150 other sculptures—the most famous of which is perhaps the fifth-century BC *Ludovisi Throne,* a three-sided bas-relief showing the goddess Venus being raised from the sea by two kneeling maidens. **Palazzo Altemps** along with **Palazzo Massimo** (see page 52) and the **Aula Ottagona** make up the **National Museum of Rome.** ♦ Admission. Tu-Su. Piazza di Sant'Apollinare 44 (at Via di Sant'Apollinare). 67102733

45 Hotel Raphaël $$$$
The ivy-draped facade and a long-standing reputation for service have convinced many that this is the perfect small hotel in the Centro Storico, and the location is second to none. Although the lighting in the lobby might be considered gloomy and uninviting, the hotel boasts antiques and a collection of Picasso ceramics. Some of the 71 rooms are small (there are also 5 suites), but all feature air-conditioning, minibars, marble baths, and pink terry-cloth robes. There's a small fitness center and sauna. The **Cafe Picasso** serves better-than-average fare that can also be enjoyed on the **Bramante** rooftop garden. ♦ Largo di Febo 2 (at Via di Tor Sanguigna). 682831; fax 6878993

46 Chiesa di Santa Maria della Pace
The semicircular portico of this 1656 church (illustrated on page 100) makes it one of Rome's most picturesque and theatrical. **Bramante** designed the charming cloisters (see below). **Pietro da Cortona** had to jiggle things a bit (and remove a few structures) to make the church fit into the surrounding buildings, which is exactly what it does. The curves and chiaroscuro effect of its facade have made it a favorite with artists and movie directors. Some say it, not Jill Clayburgh, was

Chiesa di Santa Maria della Pace

the star of Bertolucci's film *Luna*. Inside is Raphael's famous fresco of the *Sibyls* above the first altar on the right and next to it the fine chapel of the Cesi family decorated by Sangallo in the mid-16th century. At press time, the church was undergoing a major restoration scheduled to be finished by 2000. ♦ Tu-Sa; Su 9-11AM. Piazza Santa Maria della Pace and Vicolo della Pace

Next to Chiesa di Santa Maria della Pace:

Bramante Cloister Go through the arch to the left of the church, and on the right is the entrance to what many consider one of **Bramante**'s best works. Stand in the middle of this elegantly designed double-loggia courtyard completed in 1504, and notice how harmoniously the arches march around the square with reassuring repetitions. Classical music concerts are held here in summer. ♦ Tu-Sa; Su 9-11AM. Vicolo dell'Arco della Pace 5

47 Antico Caffè della Pace ★$$ Young professionals have adopted this antique coffee bar and tearoom, in which a 2,000-year-old

Roman column stands. It's a good place to sit and admire **Santa Maria della Pace.** Prices at the bar are standard, but expect to pay triple to sit at one of the in- or outdoor tables. Be sure to try the superb fresh fruit tortes. ♦ Tu-Su. Via della Pace 4 (between Vicolo di Montevecchio and Piazza Santa Maria della Pace). 6861216

48 Via dei Coronari Antiques dealers line this street, whose name came from the rosaries once sold in shops here to medieval pilgrims en route to **St. Peter's.** (*Corona* means a string of beads and was another word for a rosary.) Today the shops sell more mundane items—Baroque bookcases, Roman columns, marble busts, Art Deco lamps, and Neapolitan ex-votos. Halfway down the street, take a moment to duck into the lovely Renaissance cloister of the **Chiesa di San Salvatore in Lauro** (enter to the left of the church at **Piazza San Salvatore in Lauro**). According to tradition, this church is named for a forest of laurel trees that stood here in ancient times. Built in the 12th century and rebuilt in the 1400s, this church burned down in 1591 and was restored several times, the last being in 1734. The handsome **Palazzo Taverna** (up a ramp on your left) stands on **Monte Giordano,** an artificial hill made of rubble from the ruins of an ancient river port. Also on this site once stood a medieval fortress whose 12th-century tower is mentioned in Dante's *Inferno.* This palatial stronghold passed through several families, including the Giordano and the Orsini. Two marble bears from the latter's family crest (*orso* means bear) are enthroned amid the bushes on either side of the fountain.

49 Hotel Genio $$ This serious, no-nonsense, staid hotel is just a stone's throw from the northern curve of **Piazza Navona.** The 60 rooms are furnished in a functional and efficient way with the business traveler in mind. It also offers convenience and good service. There's no restaurant, but breakfast is included. ♦ Via Giuseppe Zanardelli 28 (at Piazza di Tor Sanguigna). 6833781; fax 68307246

50 La Fiammetta ★★$$ If you want to participate in the cappuccino-drinking/newspaper-reading rite that takes place Sunday mornings in **Piazza Navona,** this is the place to come afterward for lunch—it's just five minutes from the piazza. The restaurant—which serves the best eggplant parmigiana in Rome—and **Piazza Fiammetta** are named for Cesare Borgia's Florentine mistress whose beauty was legendary and whose little 15th-century house stands in the piazza. Get here early (it opens at 12:30) or reserve one of the outdoor tables under the Virginia Creeper arbor. ♦ M, W-Su lunch and dinner. Piazza Fiammetta 8 (at Piazza di Tor Sanguigna). 6875777

51 Museo Napoleonico In 1809 the French kidnapped Pope Pius VII and declared Rome their second capital; two years later Napoleon conferred the title King of Rome on his newborn son. This museum houses memorabilia from that era. The 16th-century palazzo, which belonged to Napoleon's grandson, Count Giuseppe Primoli, consists

of 15 rooms dedicated to members of the Bonaparte family. Napoleon's sister Pauline married an Italian prince and lived in the **Borghese Palace;** his mother had apartments overlooking **Piazza Venezia.** The collection includes some spectacular pieces of Empire furniture, elaborate state robes and jewelry, and a death mask of Napoleon. ♦ Admission. Tu-Sa; Su morning; closed in August. Via Giuseppe Zanardelli 1 (entrance on Piazza di Ponte Umberto I). 68806286

52 Antiques Shop You could easily miss this small shop, as nothing outside indicates its name or its specialty. But a tiny window with a few fine pieces might catch a sharp eye. Inside is a fine collection of silver, ivory, and bronze, all dating from between 1700 and 1860 (Louis XIV, Louis XVI, Napoleon I, and Napoleon III). There are superb Empire candlesticks, and proprietor Sergio Scarapazzi has a predilection for porcelain with a history behind it. Look for cups, jugs, and plates with exquisite painted views. ♦ M-F, Sa morning; closed in August. Via di Monte Brianzo 73 (between Via del Cancello and Via del Leuto). No phone

53 L'Orso 80 ★★$$ Start with a selection from the excellent antipasto table at this modest restaurant, but leave room for the main course, as the menu is varied and the portions generous—although sometimes salty. For the discerning *stracciatelle* (broth with egg and cheese) lover, the search ends here. ♦ Tu-Su lunch and dinner; closed in August. Via dell'Orso 33 (between Via del Cancello and Via del Leuto). 6864904

54 Opificio Romano Intricate mosaics inspired by ancient Greek and Roman designs are made and sold here for less than you might think. See artisans at work on tables, wall decorations, and floor tiles. ♦ M afternoon; Tu-F; Sa morning. Vicolo della Palomba 1A (at Via dell'Orso). 68802762

55 Massimo Maria Melis Ancient Roman

coins, semiprecious stones, and bits of antique Roman glass are hand-crafted by this very talented goldsmith into unique 21-karat gold rings, brooches, bracelets, and earrings. It's worth a stop here just to browse the windows and display cases and see the pieces inspired by the Romans and Etruscans. ♦ M afternoon; Tu-Sa. Via dell'Orso 57 (at Via dei Portoghesi). 6869188

Restaurants/Clubs: Red   **Hotels:** Blue
Shops/ ♀ Outdoors: Green   **Sights/Culture:** Black

Baroque Adversaries

The contrast between the two Baroque archrivals—**Gian Lorenzo Bernini** and **Francesco Borromini**—couldn't have been more pronounced. Bernini came from a good family, moved in all the right circles, and enjoyed the patronage of popes. In contrast, Borromini had nothing but his genius; a renegade and a depressive, his paranoia eventually led him to take his own life. Bernini strove to include all the arts in his designs, whereas Borromini emphasized architectural form above all else.

Their competition became so heated that when Borromini was granted the commission to design Pope Innocent's family church **(Sant'Agnese)**, the enraged Bernini used all his influence to gain the contract for the monumental fountain that would stand in front of Borromini's church. Bernini's gift to the Pope of a solid silver model of his design finally won him the commission. His revenge took the form of four gigantic male statues, representing four river gods, around the fountain's central obelisk in such a way that each seems to be commenting on the church behind.

Two of the river gods are turning their backs contemptuously to the church. One of them faces it directly, but cringes, raising his arm and spreading his fingers in a pleading gesture that exhorts the church not to collapse on him. The fourth statue, representing the Nile, is desperately trying to cover his head with a cloth so that he won't have to look at the construction errors in the church.

When the fountain was unveiled on 12 June 1651—six years before the church was finished—**Borromini** met this affront to his skills by immediately ordering a statue of the church's patron, St. Agnes, to be made, and placed high on the right side of the facade. Naturally, the statue's head is turned away from the offending fountain, and her hand rests on her breast as if to say, "Fall? This beautiful work of art? You must be joking."

55 Hotel dei Portoghesi $$ Many people swear by the no-fuss attitude and convenient location of this nearly 160-year-old hotel. All 28 rooms have air-conditioning and private baths. There's no restaurant, but breakfast (included) is served on a rooftop terrace watched over by enormous trumpeting angels from the church next door. ♦ Via dei Portoghesi 1 (at Via dell'Orso). 6864231; fax 6876976

56 Chiesa di Sant'Antonio dei Portoghesi This small, beautifully ornate Baroque church took almost 50 years to complete (1695). Built by **Martino Longhi** and **Carlo Rainaldi** to minister to Portuguese pilgrims, the shield and arms of the royal Portuguese house of Bragança adorn the facade. Inside is a sculpture by Canova (1806-8). ♦ Via dei Portoghesi (between Via della Scrofa and Via dell'Orso)

57 Palazzo Frangipani The tower that rises from the front of this 16th-century fortress is known as the **Torre della Scimmia** (The Tower of the Monkey), as well as "Hilda's Tower" because it figures prominently in Nathaniel Hawthorne's Roman novel *The Marble Faun*. According to an old legend, the owner's pet monkey fled with his baby to the top of the tower and remained there until the family prayed to the Virgin. As a thank-you offering, the father placed a picture of the Madonna on top of the tower and vowed that a lamp would always be kept burning in front of it. Electricity has abetted his efforts. The building is not open to the public. ♦ Via dei Portoghesi 18 (at Via dei Pianellari)

58 Da Pietro ★★$$$ The very Roman proprietor of this small restaurant likes to create new and original dishes. He doesn't always come up with winners, but those that are include *risotto alla fragola* (strawberry risotto) and *manzo al barolo* (tender beef fillets in a Barolo wine sauce). Strawberry risotto was supposedly invented by mine workers in Milan who, at a loss for something to mix with the rice, tossed in a handful of wild strawberries they found growing in the fields. ♦ M-Sa dinner; closed in August. Reservations required. Via dei Pianellari 19 (between Via dei Portoghesi and Via dei Gigli d'Oro). 6868565

59 Chiesa di Sant'Agostino An early (1479) example of Renaissance architecture in Rome by **Giacomo Pietrasanta** and **Sebastiano Fiorentino**, this church was built from travertine plundered from the **Colosseum**.

The interior was modified in the 18th century by **Vanvitelli.** Just inside the entrance is the much venerated statue of the *Madonna del Parto,* an interesting example of how a pagan statue was recycled (by Jacopo Sansovino in 1521) into an image of the Virgin. The foot of the Madonna has been worn smooth. On the third pillar on the left side of the nave is Raphael's painting of the prophet *Isaiah,* but the showpiece of the church is one of Caravaggio's last works, *Madonna of the Pilgrims* (1605), in the first chapel on the left. The painting caused a sensation when it was unveiled because of Caravaggio's insistence on realistic elements, including the dirty feet of the Madonna's devotees. ◆ Piazza di Sant'Agostino (between Via di Sant'Agostino and Via dei Pianellari)

60 Ai Monasteri Monasteries and convents from all over Italy supply this shop with liqueurs, herbal teas, and other elixirs, honeys, and toiletries. A bottle of olive oil, a jar of quince marmalade, or a bar of chocolate made by Cistercian monks makes an unusual gift. ◆ M afternoon; Tu-W, F-Sa; Th morning; closed in August. Piazza delle Cinque Lune 76 (at Corso del Rinasciamento). 68802783

61 Scatole Custom-made boxes in all sizes and shapes using beautiful decorative paper are the specialty of this artisan shop. The paper trays, pencil holders, and diaries also make unique gifts. ◆ Daily. Via della Stelletta 27 (between Piazza Campo Marzio and Via della Scrofa). 68802053

62 Volpetti There's no better place in Rome to sample *mozzarella di bufalo* (made from buffalo milk), prosciutto salami (two hams together), or *torta di mela* (apple cake) than this celebrated gourmet take-out shop. Don't miss the bottles in the window with tiny artichoke hearts, mushroom caps, baby onions, and other vegetables, packed in olive oil. ◆ M-Sa (no midday closing). Via della Scrofa 31-32 (at Via della Stelletta). 6861940

63 Alfredo alla Scrofa ★$$$ On the walls hang autographed photos of movie stars, statespeople, and other famous clients who have visited this touristy restaurant in the days before cholesterol. Mary Pickford and Douglas Fairbanks started it all off by presenting the owner with a gold fork and spoon in appreciation for his triple-butter, heavy cream, and parmesan cheese concoction—*fettuccine al Alfredo.* Don't worry about whether or not this Alfredo is the original—at least two others lay claim to the gold. Regardless of pedigree, the fettuccine is served with a flourish—and a song or two—by waiters who make the most out of whipping the butter and tossing the cheese; unfortunately, almost everything else on the menu isn't worth a song. However, that didn't keep Audrey Hepburn, Liz Taylor, or Gregory Peck from coming back for more. Another original **Alfredo's** is at Piazza Augusto Imperatore 30 (6878615). ◆ M, W-Su lunch and dinner. Via della Scrofa 104 (at Vicolo della Campana). 68806163

64 La Campana ★★★$$$ Rome's oldest (1450) continual in-service restaurant has been serving high-quality Roman cuisine at modest prices for over a hundred years. (For 300 years before that, it was an inn.) The nonpareil *vignarola,* a thick vegetable soup (medley of fava beans, onions, artichokes, and peas, etc.) is a meal in itself. But it's the pasta and artichoke cream sauce and homemade ricotta cheese torte that have won this place a loyal clientele. ◆ Tu-Su lunch and dinner; closed last three weeks in August. Vicolo della Campana 18 (at Via di Monte Brianzo). 6867820

65 Due Ladroni ★★★$$$ The name implies that the owners are expert thieves, but you'll be running away with the goods at this excellent rustic restaurant serving such satisfying dishes as linguine with shrimp and cherry tomatoes, spaghetti and octopus, risotto in saffron and butter, *tagliolini* with porcini mushrooms (in season), and roasted veal and sweet potatoes. During the week this dining spot stays open for late-night supper. ◆ M-F lunch and dinner; Sa dinner; closed in August. Reservations required. Piazza Nicosia 24 (just east of Via dei Somaschi). 6861013

65 Due Pi Stylish glass, china, and other household items at modest prices make this store a standout. Italians excel in this type of casual but smart design. Look for Swiss and Italian cookware, square drinking glasses, colorful tableware, plastic trays in floral patterns, or large juice pitchers with silver covers and handles. ◆ Tu-Sa (no midday closing). No credit cards accepted. Piazza Nicosia 30 (just east of Via dei Somaschi). 68307384; fax 6875851

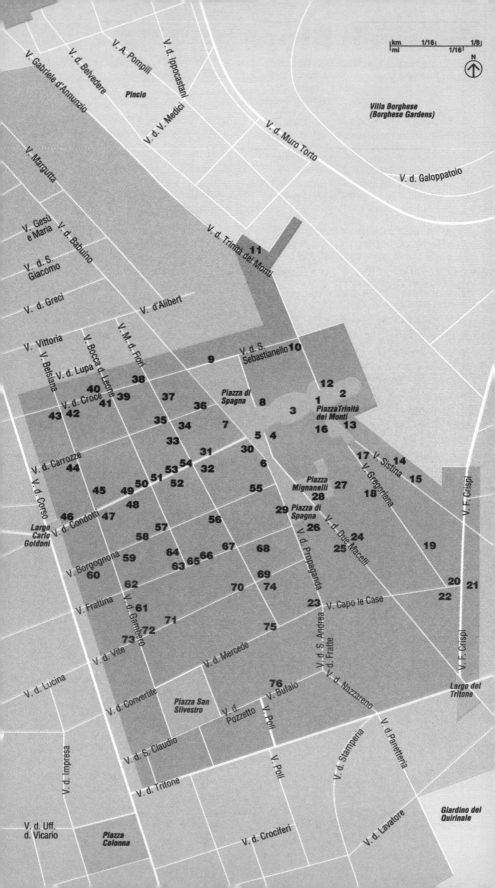

Spanish Steps

During the 18th century tens of thousands of Spanish, including soldiers, were quartered near this piazza named for the **Palazzo di Spagna**, home of the Spanish Embassy, still situated here. And for at least three centuries this area also has been the unofficial headquarters for the many foreign colonies in the city. Although the large tourist hotels are now a short distance away (around Via Veneto), for the nostalgic and those drawn to Rome's shopping mecca, this remains Rome's premier international corner.

Leading up from **Piazza di Spagna** to the **Chiesa di Trinità dei Monti** are the broad, graceful Spanish Steps, better known to Italians as "La Scalinata della Trinità dei Monti." The steps are famous for having attracted Rome's first wave of secular tourists in the 18th century—the German artists and poets and English gentlemen who congregated here during the Roman leg of their grand tours of Europe. Enhancing its reputation at the time was the ever-present population of pretty women dressed in feast-day costumes, lured to the city from outlying towns by the prospect of posing for foreign artists working nearby on **Via Margutta**. In response to the increase in tourism, inns and cafes, such as the **Caffè Inglese** and the **Villa di Londra Hotel**, sprang up all over the neighborhood.

The long **Via dei Condotti**, which leads into the **Piazza di Spagna**, is named for the pipeline that conducts the aqueduct still beneath it. These days, the street has become better known for "conducting" the international crowd, especially Japanese, along one of the world's most glamorous shopping streets. Rome's oldest cafe, the 18th-century **Caffè Greco**, provides a tony breakfast for those considering a buying spree early in the day, and the culinary choices in this neighborhood will satisfy even those on a tight budget, as restaurants—from fast-food spots to gala gourmet grandeur—abound.

Piazza di Spagna

Chiesa di Trinità dei Monti
(Church of the Holy Trinity on the Hill)

1 Obelisk At the summit of the **Spanish Steps** stands a 46-foot pink granite column—an ancient replica of an equally ancient Egyptian obelisk—built in the first century BC. Between 200 BC and AD 200, Romans carried off about 50 obelisks from Egypt on specially built boats powered by four stories of rowers. Toward the end of that period, Roman emperors even had obelisks made to order, adding their own, sometimes meaningless, hieroglyphs after the monuments arrived at the Ostia port and before shipment up the Tiber to Rome. This copy was found in the Gardens of Sallust and placed here in 1787.
♦ Piazza Trinità dei Monti

2 Chiesa di Trinità dei Monti (Church of the Holy Trinity on the Hill) Charles VIII of France founded this twin-towered church of golden stone in 1495 to commemorate his stay In Rome. Inside are several chapels, including one endowed by Monsieur Gouffier, the French ambassador who financed the **Spanish Steps.** Also within are frescoes by the brothers Taddeo and Federico Zuccari, illustrating the life of the Virgin, as well as works by Giulio Romano and other students of Raphael and Michelangelo. ♦ Piazza Trinità dei Monti

Scalinata della Trinità dei Monti (Spanish Steps)

3 Scalinata della Trinità dei Monti (Spanish Steps) Although they could have been called the "French Steps," in recognition of 17th-century benefactor and neighbor, French ambassador Gouffier, these 137 travertine steps have always been associated with the Spanish piazza below. Completed in 1726 by **Alessandro Specchi** and **Francesco de Santis,** the world-famous staircase is valued as a work of art. Its form alludes to the holy trinity, with three sets of flights and three main landings leading to the church above. Seen from a distance, the grand steps are also stirringly musical, seeming to use space the way a baroque concerto uses time. The first three flights flow outward in convex waves, while the fourth reverses in a concave turn, sweeping climbers to and fro before the final coda at the top; balustrades mark intervals and separate the movements with pauses.

Over the years, people have come to appreciate this staircase for a more practical function: a place to sit and relax, thus earning it the nickname, "Il Salotto di Roma" (the Living Room of Rome). The crowds are worth enduring for the breathtaking view from the top. The vista from Via dei Condotti is equally lovely—especially at Easter time, when the steps are covered with pink and white azaleas. No drinking or eating is allowed. ♦ Open from dawn to midnight

4 Casina di Keats (Keats House) Under doctor's orders to leave damp London for sunny Rome, English Romantic poet John Keats lived his last few months in a pensione overlooking the **Spanish Steps** (he died of tuberculosis in 1821, at age 27). Purchased in 1903 by the Keats-Shelley Memorial Association, the small museum includes the room where Keats died, his death mask, portraits of him and members of his social circle, and a fine 10,000-volume library, featuring manuscripts, letters, and documents on the lives of Keats, Percy Bysshe Shelley, Lord Byron, and Leigh Hunt. ♦ Admission. M-F; closed in August. Piazza di Spagna 26 (at Scalinata della Trinità dei Monti). 6784235

5 Fontana della Barcaccia (The Old Barge, or Leaking Boat Fountain) This Baroque fountain was designed by **Pietro Bernini** but probably completed, in 1629, by his more famous son **Gian Lorenzo.** Some say the inspiration for its unusual shape was a boat that washed up here when the Tiber flooded in 1598. The stone bees are part of the coat-of-arms of the fountain's patron, Pope Urban VIII, of the Barberini family. Because of the low water pressure in the **Acqua Vergine** aqueduct that feeds it, this fountain actually lies below street level. ♦ Piazza di Spagna

6 Balloon For pants, skirts, Chinese silk blouses, and even cotton underwear, at competitive prices, this is the most central of the shop's 12 locations in Rome. Enter through the courtyard. ♦ M-Sa (no midday closing). Piazza di Spagna 35 (between Via Borgognona and Via dei Condotti). 6780110

7 Missoni The famous high-fashion, high-colored knitwear has spread beyond sweaters to jackets, dresses, towels, and even rugs. ♦ M afternoon; Tu-F; Sa morning. Piazza di Spagna 78 (between Via dei Condotti and Via delle Carrozze). 6792555

8 Babington's ★$$$ Traveling artists, poets, and English "milords" lodged here during their grand tours of Europe, hiring carriages on the nearby Via delle Carrozze to take them around town. Today's traveler can still get a proper English breakfast, a light luncheon, and an authentic afternoon tea here. Service sometimes takes on a 19th-century rhythm, and the prices remain leveled at the carriage class, but nothing—not even the uncomfortable chairs—seems to deter customers. The walnut cake and open fire in winter are two good reasons. ♦ Daily (no midday closing). Piazza di Spagna 23 (between Scalinata della Trinità dei Monti and Via di San Sebastianello). 6786027

FRETTE, Inc.

9 Frette Superb custom-made linens, embroidered and monogrammed towels, and everything else for bedroom and bath is available at this long-established shop. ♦ M afternoon; Tu-Sa. Piazza di Spagna 11 (between Via di San Sebastianello and Via del Babuino). 6790673. Also at: Via Nazionale 84 (at Via dei Serpenti). 4882641; Via del Corso 381 (between Piazza Colonna and Via del Parlamento). 6786862

9 Antichità Alberto Di Castro Antiques shops with the Di Castro name abound on nearby Via del Babuino, but this one stands out. Alberto started his business after World War II, and today his grandchildren, Allessandra and Alberto, mind the store. They pride themselves on carrying museum-quality antiques, each of which has a special peculiarity: a glass tabletop engraved in gold with images of famous ancient sculptures, a late-Renaissance, 12-foot mahogany table from Siena (a similar piece stands in New York's Metropolitan Museum of Art). They also have quite a collection of 17th- and 18th-century Roman antiques, including inlaid wooden tables, commodes, and chairs. ♦ M-Sa. Piazza di Spagna 5 (between Via di San Sebastianello and Via del Babuino). 6792269; fax 6787410

10 Bottega Veneta This Venetian craftsman makes such classic and distinguished leather goods that they are immediately recognized by aficionados, even without a designer logo. They are not for the faint of wallet. ♦ M afternoon; Tu-F; Sa morning. Via di San Sebastianello 18 (east of Piazza di Spagna). 6782535

11 Villa Medici Around 1590, **Annibale Lippi** converted Cardinal Giovanni Ricci's once-modest country house into this magnificent villa (illustrated below). The facade is discretely spare of ornamentation, while walls on the private garden side are covered by a solid tracery of sculpted decoration.

Pope Leo XI from the Medici family lived in this palazzo in the 17th century and gave it his name. Since 1804, when Napoleon purchased

Villa Medici

the villa, it has been home to the **French Academy,** where talented and lucky *Prix de Rome* scholars stay and study art, history, architecture, or archaeology. The villa is open only for guided tours on Sunday mornings and for periodic art shows. ♦ Admission. Su 9AM-12:30PM. Viale della Trinità dei Monti (between Piazza Trinità dei Monti and Viale Gabriele d'Annunzio). 67611

12 Ciampini ★$$ At the summit of the **Spanish Steps,** this trilevel gelateria offers some of the more enchanting views of Rome from a lush garden setting. Indulge in homemade gelato or the house specialty, *tartufo* (chocolate ice cream with chocolate chunks). ♦ M-Tu, Th-Su 9AM-2AM. Viale della Trinità dei Monti 1 (just north of Piazza Trinità dei Monti). 6785678

Hôtel Hassler

13 Hôtel Hassler $$$$ Royalty, presidents, and movie stars—including Sharon Stone and Richard Gere—consider this 101-room property their favorite. The nicest apartments abut the church belfry at the top of the **Spanish Steps,** offering wonderful views; some even have balconies. If you aren't a celebrity, however, you may be consigned to one of the small rooms in the back. In summer the courtyard restaurant offers open-air dining. Breakfast is not included in the rate, but parking is available. ♦ Piazza Trinità dei Monti 6 (between Via Sistina and Viale della Trinità dei Monti). 699340; fax 6789991

14 De la Ville Intercontinental $$$ With Oriental rugs, crystal chandeliers, and marbletop tables, this member of the upscale hotel chain superbly blends Old World charm with modern comfort. Each of the 189 rooms has a TV, air-conditioning, and private bath. Within the hotel is a bar and a small restaurant, **La Piazzetta,** whose fresh fish offerings highlight a Mediterranean menu. The upper floors and roof garden terrace—where a Sunday brunch is served in summer—have spectacular views, while rooms on the lower floors overlook a central courtyard. Special weekend rates are available. Breakfast is included in the price; garage parking is available. ♦ Via Sistina 67 (between Via Francesco Crispi and Piazza Trinità dei Monti). 67331; fax 6784213

15 Femme Sistina This high-fashion boutique/beauty salon is a Roman institution. The store's own line of classic daywear is perfect for businesswomen. Hats, scarves, jewelry, perfume, and a wide array of hair accessories complete the look. Hair, skin, and nails receive lavish attention in the adjoining salon. Fashion shows are held here occasionally. ♦ Boutique: daily. Salon: Tu-Sa. Via Sistina 75/A (between Via Francesco Crispi and Piazza Trinità dei Monti). 6780260; fax 6798481

15 Albergo Internazionale $$ Set among deluxe properties at the top of the **Spanish Steps,** this unassuming place has a long-standing reputation as one of the best-run moderately priced hotels in the city. Dating back to the 17th century, this 42-room hostelry features ornately carved furnishings and frescoed ceilings. All guest rooms have satellite TV and those on the top floor boast terraces. Free parking is available. There's no restaurant, but breakfast is included. ♦ Via Sistina 79 (between Via Francesco Crispi and Piazza Trinità dei Monti). 6793047; fax 6784764

16 Hotel Scalinata di Spagna $$$ Once a bargain, this small family-run hotel has upgraded its amenities and raised its rates. Now all 18 charming—but small—rooms have satellite TV, air-conditioning, and private baths. A hit with honeymooners, the top-floor guest room has a small private terrace, where intimate breakfasts and memorable city views can be enjoyed. A complimentary breakfast buffet is served daily, but there's no restaurant. Reserve well in advance. ♦ Piazza Trinità dei Monti 17 (between Via Gregoriana and Scalinata della Trinità dei Monti). 69940896; fax 69940598

17 Palazzetto Zuccari This building's whimsical Rococo facade forms a monster's face: The portal is the mouth, with the door as its tongue, and the windows its eyes. Designed in 1591 as a school for artists by **Federico Zuccari,** Rome's outstanding painter (some of his work hangs in the **Chiesa di Trinità dei Monti**), today the palazzetto houses the **Biblioteca Hertziana** (Hertzian Library for the Study of Art History), a private library for the study of art and architecture (call 699931 for membership information). ♦ Via Gregoriana 30 (between Via Capo le Case and Piazza Trinità dei Monti)

18 Hotel Gregoriana $$ Surrounded by many of Italy's high-fashion ateliers, this small, stylish ex-convent was decorated by Erté hence each room's door bears one of his anthropomorphic letters instead of a number.

Rooms F, M, and R have small balconies overlooking an inner courtyard, and **Room C** preserves elements of the former chapel. Hallways are lined with leopard-skin wallpaper (added after the nuns departed). There's no restaurant or bar, but all 19 rooms have private baths. The courteous, efficient service is legendary. Reserve well in advance. ◆ No credit cards accepted. Via Gregoriana 18 (between Via Capo le Case and Piazza Trinità dei Monti). 6794269, 6797988; fax 6784258

19 **Carla Panicali Gallery** After losing its former large space, this gallery opened a small office to represent its impressive roster of prominent international painters and sculptors. Works by such modern Italian artists as Jo and Arnaldo Pomodoro, Giorgio Capogrossi, Manzù, Burri, Lucio Fontana, and the younger Roberto Almagno and Maria Dompè are featured. Three exhibitions are installed each year. ◆ M-F (no midday closing); closed in August. No credit cards accepted. Via Gregoriana 44A (between Via Capo le Case and Piazza Trinità dei Monti). 6784678, 6790029

20 **Suisse** $ As the name implies, this reasonably priced hotel is Swiss-owned, which may explain why service is so efficient. Add a rooftop terrace and 13 large guest rooms furnished with a blend of antique and modern decor, and the result is a very popular hostelry. Reserve well in advance. There's no restaurant, but breakfast is included. ◆ Via Gregoriana 54 (at Via Capo le Case). 6783649; fax 6781258

21 **Galleria Comunale d'Arte Moderna e Contemporanea di Roma (Municipal Gallery of Modern and Contemporary Art)** A notable collection of works by 19th- and 20th-century artists (De Chirico, Carrà, Guttuso) is exhibited in a former convent. Free guided tours are given on Sunday morning. ◆ Admission. Tu-Sa; Su morning. Via Francesco Crispi 24 (between Largo del Tritone and Via Sistina). 4742848

22 **Palazzo Toni** The facade of this 17th-century *palazzetto* (now a private residence) is decorated with bizarre, twisted caryatids. It is one of the rare examples of Rococo art in Rome. ◆ Via Capo le Case 3 (between Via Francesco Crispi and Via Due Macelli)

23 **Poltrona Frau** The motto of this celebrated furniture store is "One of a Kind," and when you see the wide array of leather sofas, *poltrone* (armchairs), and beds—all rigorously and colorfully Memphis School of the 1950s—you'll understand the reason why. ◆ M afternoon; Tu-Sa. Via di Propaganda 8 (at Via delle Mercede). 6792271

24 **Pineider** Italy's famed stationer has been stamping out classic calling cards and elegant gray-green boxed stationery since 1774. If you're hiring them to design a family crest or some such lucrative project, you'll be treated courteously; otherwise, try not to take their attitude toward you personally. ◆ M-F June-Aug; M afternoon, Tu-Sa Sept-May. Via Due Macelli 68 (between Via Capo le Case and Piazza di Spagna). 6789013. Also at: Via Fontanella di Borghese 22 (between Largo Carlo Goldoni and Largo Fontanella di Borghese). 6878369

25 **Mettimi Giù** "Put me down" is a constant refrain from kids, and not a bad name for this cozy shop carrying trendy clothes for children aged 3 months to 14 years. Tiny hand-knit sweaters, wool skirts, and coats from the Dutch firm Oilily will put your kid in the running for best dressed in town. ◆ M-Sa (no midday closing). Via Due Macelli 59 (between Via Capo le Case and Piazza di Spagna). 6789761; fax 69940702

26 **Palazzo di Propaganda Fide** In 1622, shortly after founding the Holy Congregation of the Propagation of the Faith, Pope Gregory XV donated this building to the order. A decade later Cardinal Barberini—later Pope Urban VIII—commissioned its enlargement to **Gian Lorenzo Bernini,** who added some soft Baroque curves to the austere facade and crowned it with the Barberini bee; he also added a new wing along Via Due Macelli and an oratory. But in 1644, when Urban VIII died, **Bernini**'s commission was transferred to his rival, **Francesco Borromini,** who rebuilt the oratory and redid the side on Via di Propaganda as a wave of undulating convex windows and concave doorways. Today the palace is the property of the Holy See and is not open to the public. ◆ Piazza di Spagna (between Via Due Macelli and Via di Propaganda)

27 **La Rampa** ★★$$ This popular trattoria reportedly has the widest selection of antipasti in the city, and the main courses include such tasty offerings as osso buco and lasagna. If you opt for the traditional three-course extravaganza, you may want to skip the antipasto. Inside, the decor calls to mind a medieval Roman street; in summer, the restaurant spills out into the piazza. Come early to beat the crowds. ◆ M dinner; Tu-Sa lunch and dinner. No credit cards accepted. Piazza Mignanelli 18 (just east of Piazza di Spagna). 6782621

27 **Valentino Haute Couture** The long-reigning king of Italian fashion designers has his own idea of classic elegance, which often includes his signature color, Valentino red. For nearly 50 years his designs have appealed to film stars (Elizabeth Taylor), American first ladies (Nancy Reagan), and half the aristocrats of Europe. His haute couture salon is by appointment only, while the following ready-to-wear boutiques are more accessible: **Miss V** (for women), Via Bocca di Leone 15/18, at Via Frattina, 6795862; **Valentino** (for men and women), Via dei Condotti 12-13, at Via Mario de' Fiori, 6739285; and **Oliver** (for young adults and children), Via del Babuino 61, between Via d'Alibert and Via dell'Orto di Napoli, 36001906. ♦ M afternoon; Tu-F; Sa morning. Piazza Mignanelli 22 (just east of Piazza di Spagna). 67391

28 **Monumento della Immacolata Concezione (Monument of the Immaculate Conception)** This antique Roman column used to be part of the **Basilica di Massenzio** in the **Roman Forum** and in the 17th century stood before the **Basilica di Santa Maria Maggiore**. On 8 December 1856 it was moved here and crowned with a bronze statue of the Virgin Mary to commemorate Pope Pius IX's promulgation of the doctrine of the Immaculate Conception, proclaiming the Virgin Mary the only person to have been born "without the stain of original sin." Every 8 December the mayor and the pope host a ceremony at which a wreath is placed atop the statue. ♦ Piazza di Spagna and Piazza Mignanelli

29 **Palazzo di Spagna (Spanish Embassy to the Holy See)** This building, which gave its name to the whole neighborhood, dates back to 1624 when Rome was capital of the Papal States. After it passed into Spanish possession in 1647, **Borromini** remodeled it and was knighted by the Spanish king for his work. However, only his stairs and vestibule were ever built, and these were modified in the 19th century by **Antonio del Grande**. Some well-preserved Roman sarcophagi stand in the vestibule and a verdant, ivy-covered courtyard lies beyond. ♦ Not open to the public. Piazza di Spagna 57 (between Via Frattina and Via Borgognona)

29 **Di Cori** Boxes of gloves line the walls from floor to ceiling in one of Rome's oldest glove boutiques. Luxurious yet fair-priced apparel for the hands include cashmere-lined, woolen, pigskin, chamois, suede, and more. Gift wrapping is available. ♦ M-Sa. Piazza di Spagna 53 (between Via Frattina and Via Borgognona). 6784439

A legend surrounds the historic Caffè Greco: Any cardinal who enters the cafe will eventually become pope. The most recent proof of this occurred in 1878, when Cardinal Gioacchino Pecci had coffee there with friends; three months later he was elected Pope Leo XIII.

Via dei Condotti and Environs

30 **Gucci** Recognizable the world over, these handsome leather goods, ties, scarves, and ready-to-wear clothes still look good, despite their having become somewhat kitschy and widely counterfeited. ♦ M-Sa Sept-May; M-Sa, several Sundays June-Aug. Via dei Condotti 8 (between Piazza di Spagna and Via Mario de' Fiori). 6789340

31 **Caffè Greco** ★★★$$$ Rome's oldest *caffè* vaunts more than three centuries of illustrious guests: Goethe, Dickens, Franz Liszt, Mark Twain, Oscar Wilde, and even Buffalo Bill. The frescoed back room is worth admiring. Sandwiches are tiny but delicious, and the waiters, in frock coats and black ties, are as brusque as they come. Nevertheless, Italian surrealist painter Giorgio De Chirico may have been right when he proclaimed **Caffè Greco** the only place in the world to sit and wait out the end. Cups and tea sets with the distinctive gilt-edged orange band make nice, albeit expensive, gift items. ♦ M-Sa. Via dei Condotti 86 (between Piazza di Spagna and Via Mario de' Fiori). 6791700

BVLGARI

32 **Bulgari** Striking settings, rare gemstones, and an assortment of jewelry from antiquity lie beyond the beveled glass entrance to this celebrated jeweler. Check out the pendants with micromosaic, gold-framed views of old Rome, and the gold or platinum evening bags. Less intimidating are the elegant fountain pens and finely chiseled key chains. ♦ M-Sa; closed one week in mid-August. Via dei Condotti 10 (at Via Mario de' Fiori). 6793876

33 **Ristorante G. Ranieri** ★$$$ This is where the **Fendi** crowd sups between fittings. Expect a long, elegant, old-fashioned meal in a plush setting. Gourmets may be disappointed and nonregulars left to fend for themselves— but it's a landmark. ♦ M-Sa lunch and dinner. Via Mario de' Fiori 26 (between Via dei Condotti and Via delle Carrozze). 6786505

SIRAGUSA

34 **Siragusa** At this shop carved stones, ancient beads, and coins from the third and fourth century BC are set in handmade chains, rings, and earrings. The staff speaks English. ♦ M-F. Via delle Carrozze 64 (at Via Mario de' Fiori). 6797085

35 **Hotel Carriage** $$ Turn-of-the-century gilded furniture graces the lobby of this charming hotel, named for the street where touring carriages awaiting repair once parked.

The 24 air-conditioned rooms (all with private baths) are small but adequate. The two rooms on the top floor open onto the terrace; **No. 501** is especially nice, and **No. 601** has a large bathroom. There's no restaurant, but breakfast is included. ◆ Via delle Carrozze 36 (at Via Mario de' Fiori). 6990124; fax 6788279

36 De Clercq & De Clercq Two sisters design the distinctive hand-knit sweaters, scarves, and bags sold here. Framed miniatures of their best designs hang on the walls. ◆ Via delle Carrozze 50 (between Piazza di Spagna and Via Mario de' Fiori). 6790988

37 Hotel Piazza di Spagna $$ This air-conditioned hostelry, with an impressive grand staircase, has 17 small but comfortable rooms (all with private baths). ◆ Via Mario de' Fiori 61 (between Via delle Carrozze and Via della Croce). 6793061; fax 6790654

38 Ristorante Otello ★★$$ This family-run restaurant's longstanding popularity is built on solid renditions of traditional Italian cuisine, featuring specialties that reflect the season. The cannelloni is always fresh and delicate; their famous *melone e lampone* (fresh melon with raspberries tucked inside a half moon)—available in early June—is a delicious treat. The glass-enclosed courtyard abutting a vine-covered pergola allows "garden" dining, even in inclement weather. ◆ M-Sa lunch and dinner. Via della Croce 81 (at Via Mario de' Fiori). 6781454

39 F.lli Fabbi The king of delicatessens and a good place to get *gocce di tartufo* (olive oil flavored with truffles); just a few drops transform any pasta sauce. ◆ M-Sa. Via della Croce 27 (between Via Mario de' Fiori and Via Bocca di Leone). 6790612

39 Pasticceria D'Angelo ★$ Here since 1890, this bar/bakery/gelateria is noted for its strips of orange rind dipped in bittersweet chocolate. ◆ Daily. Via della Croce 30 (at Via Bocca di Leone). 6782556

40 L'Enoteca Antica di Via della Croce ★★$ Sample Italian vintages at the long wooden bar of this former tavern, now a wine shop/bar/*caffè*. You also can enjoy a meal of hearty soup, pâté, or a cheese platter at a table in the back. ◆ Daily; closed one week in August. Via della Croce 76/B (at Via Bocca di Leone). 6790896

40 Vertecchi Lovers of stationery can peruse aisles of handsome pens, unusual gift wrap, daily planners, and stylish notebooks. A wide selection of art supplies is also on hand. ◆ Via della Croce 70 (between Via Bocca di Leone and Via Belsiana). 6790100

41 Ristorante Re Degli Amici ★★$$ Classic Roman cuisine is supplemented here by such steak dishes as *filetto di pepe verde* (filet with green peppercorns). The waiters can be cheeky, but ignore them and go right to the antipasto table, featuring a choice of 20 dishes. Many patrons say the pizzas (served only at night) are the best in the area. ◆ Tu-Su lunch and dinner. Via della Croce 33/B (between Via Bocca di Leone and Via Belsiana). 6795380

42 Fiaschetteria Beltramme ★$ This small, no-frills eatery hints at what neighborhood restaurants used to be like. The drab decor and sometimes long-faced waiters are part of the larger picture, which includes such hearty, wholesome dishes as tortellini in fresh chicken-beef broth and boiled meat in green sauce. ◆ M-Sa lunch and dinner; closed two weeks in August. No reservations accepted. No credit cards accepted. Via della Croce 39 (between Via Bocca di Leone and Via Belsiana). No phone

42 Pantofole Slippers, as the name of this tiny shop implies, are what you'll find in nearly every size, shape, and material. ◆ Via della Croce 40 (at Via Belsiana). No phone

43 Prenatal For Mom, chic maternity clothes are made in comfortable cotton, wool, or denim. There's also everything for newborns from infantwear to toys and nursery furniture. ◆ M afternoon; Tu-Sa. Via della Croce 48 (between Via Belsiana and Via del Corso). 6793932

44 Lilia Leoni Antichità Step into this decorator's shop, if only to see the beautiful mosaics and floor, laid with antique tiles. ◆ Tu-Sa. Via Belsiana 86 (at Via delle Carrozze). 6790514

45 I Numeri ★$$ Roast beef, *spaghetti al limone* (in lemon sauce), salads, and 42 different kinds of crepes are all unpretentious and quickly prepared at this breezy eatery. ◆ M-Sa lunch and dinner; Su lunch. Via Belsiana 30 (between Via dei Condotti and Via delle Carrozze). 6794969

Steps of Rome

Because of the famous seven (and then some) hills, Rome is by necessity a city of steps. In addition to the **Spanish Steps,** other elegant staircases of marble and travertine curve, swirl, and rise majestically. Here are some worth noting:

- The two flights of stairs on **Capitoline Hill.** One is a steep, arduous incline that medieval penitents scaled on their knees to reach **Chiesa di Santa Maria in Aracoeli.** The other, **Michelangelo**'s *cordonata,* is a stately gradual rise to a world of Renaissance palazzi built for the reception of Holy Roman Emperor Charles V.

- **Borromini**'s brilliant corkscrew staircase winds around itself inside **Palazzo Barberini.**

- Behind **Santa Maria Maggiore,** the steps flair out like a skirt.

- Hundreds of *scale* decorate the exterior of the monument to Vittorio Emanuele in **Piazza Venezia,** with more inside. Unfortunately, like sculpture under glass, these great steps can't be touched, only stared at from behind tall iron gates.

- At the north end of the porch of **St. Peter's Basilica, Bernini**'s **Scala Regia** can be viewed through a doorway. These stairs were meant to impress—and they do—with skillful use of perspective in the arrangement of barrel vaults and columns.

- The **Salita dei Borgia (Via San Francesco di Paola),** off Via Cavour leading to the church of **San Pietro in Vincoli,** bear a sinister reputation. They lead through a tunnel where Cesare Borgia did away with one of Lucrezia Borgia's husbands.

- The **Scala Santa,** or Holy Steps, next to the **Basilica di San Giovanni in Laterano,** have been worn down over the centuries by the knees of millions of pilgrims.

Stairs of Capitoline Hill

46 Trussardi Boutique Superior leather goods as well as scarves and foulards bear the designer's logo. The shirts, pants, and blouses are cut from soft-as-silk leather. ♦ M afternoon; Tu-Sa. Via dei Condotti 49 (between Via Belsiana and Largo Carlo Goldoni). 6780280

47 Buccellati Those who value top-of-the-line craftsmanship shop at this eminent Milanese jeweler. The house's trademark is an inimitable, brushed-gold Florentine finish. The silversmith works with a microscope to chisel fine, understated works of art. ♦ M afternoon; Tu-F; Sa morning. Via dei Condotti 31 (at Via Belsiana). 6790329

48 Bijoux de Paris, Burma Those who can't afford the jewelry at **Bulgari** can try this shop, where Italian *contesse* buy less risky versions of their favorite designs to wear on the street. (They keep the good stuff in bank vaults for special occasions.) ♦ M afternoon; Tu-F; Sa morning. Via dei Condotti 27 (between Via Bocca di Leone and Via Belsiana). 6798285

49 Battistoni Stop here for men's shirts in colorful cotton cambric, piqué, and Egyptian gossamer-weight silk, plus shoes, suits, and more. Genial shirt king Gianni Battistoni also sells his own men's cologne called *Marte* (Mars, the god of war). The women's store is at **No. 57** (6795527). ♦ M afternoon; Tu-Sa. Via dei Condotti 61/A (between Via Bocca di Leone and Via Belsiana), Inner courtyard. 6786241

50 Palazzo Torlonia Architect **G.A. de Rossi** designed this splendid private residence in 1660. Peek inside the large inner courtyard and admire the moss-covered fountain and classical Roman statue. In spring, it's ablaze with wisteria. ♦ Via Bocca di Leone 78 (at Via del Condotti)

51 Headquarters of the Sovereign Military Order of Malta You'll recognize this palazzo by the Maltese cross over the doorway. This—not the Vatican—is the seat of the smallest sovereign state in the world, with its own license plates, postage stamps, and ambassadors. In the 16th century, Charles V granted the Knights of St. John the island of Malta, which they held until Napoleon occupied it in 1798. They then settled in this palace, bequeathed to them by the Italian archaeologist, Antonio Bosio. ♦ Not open to the public. Via dei Condotti 68 (at Via Bocca di Leone)

52 MaxMara Another Mad Max clone has invaded Via dei Condotti. His canny off-the-rack jackets and well-cut pants are popular with career women. ♦ M afternoon; Tu-F; Sa morning. Via dei Condotti 19 (between Via Mario de' Fiori and Via Bocca di Leone). 69922104 Also at: Via Frattina 28 (at Via Mario de' Fiori). 6793638

52 Louis Vuitton In addition to the signature bags and luggage, you'll find great steamer trunks and overnight cases in all sizes and shapes at this famous-name leather goods shop. ♦ M afternoon; Tu-F; Sa morning. Via dei Condotti 15 (between Via Mario de' Fiori and Via Bocca di Leone). 6990000, 6990177

Salvatore Ferragamo

53 Ferragamo Everything created by this Florentine shoe-and-bag dynasty is well made and elegant. Vests, bathrobes, and other kinds of menswear are available, along with an array of uniquely patterned silk ties. Lines for the annual mid-January sale stretch down the block. ♦ M afternoon; Tu-F; Sa morning. Via dei Condotti 66 (between Via Mario de' Fiori and Via Bocca di Leone). 6781130. Women's store: Via dei Condotti 72-73 (between Via Mario de' Fiori and Via Bocca di Leone). 6791565

54 Giorgio Armani If Valentino is the bold and colorful Michelangelo of Italian fashion design, then Armani is its more refined Leonardo da Vinci. His simple, elegant designs for men and women are almost as much an attraction as any work of art in the city. The more affordable **Emporio Armani** is at Via del Babuino 140 (between Via Vittoria and Via dei Greci, 6788454). ♦ M afternoon; Tu-F; Sa morning. Via dei Condotti 77 (at Via Mario de' Fiori). 6991460

55 Nino ★★$$$ Many consider this the finest Tuscan restaurant in Rome. The *zuppa di fagioli* (white-bean soup) prepared *al fiasco* (steamed in bottles) is a favorite of regulars, especially in winter, as is the *bistecca alla fiorentina*, a grilled T-bone drizzled with olive oil and lemon and accompanied by the excellent house Chianti *a consumo* (pay for only what you drink). The strawberry tiramisù is a delicious finale. ♦ M-Sa lunch and dinner; closed in August. Reservations recommended. Via Borgognona 11 (between Piazza di Spagna and Via Mario de' Fiori). 6795676

56 Gianni Versace Uomo The son of a Calabrian tailor, Gianni Versace grew a small business in Milan into an internationally acclaimed designer label; his design genius now lives on under the guidance of his sister Donatella. Frescoed walls and Neo-Classical furnishings provide the backdrop for luxurious goods, including suits and printed ties in rich Como silks. ♦ M afternoon; Tu-F; Sa morning. Via Borgognona 24 (at Via Mario de' Fiori). 6795292. Women's store: Via Bocca di Leone 26 (at Via dei Condotti). 6780521; fax 677911631

57 Hotel d'Inghilterra $$$$ A perennial favorite of travelers, this refurbished, 102-room hotel has been a home away from home to such famous writers as Mark Twain, Henry James, and Ernest Hemingway. Each of the four top-floor suites has a different decor; the **Roman Garden** suite features walls decorated with trompe l'oeil paintings of a garden. Its lobby namesake, the **Roman Garden** restaurant—serving lunch and dinner—is perfect for a business luncheon. Some rooms are small, breakfast is not included, and the street noise could drive a writer mad, but the bar is legendary and by all accounts has the best bartender in Rome. High-season rates are considerably more than rates the rest of the year, so check in advance. ♦ Via Bocca di Leone 14 (at Via Borgognona). 69981; fax 69922243

58 FMR This tiny shop with its elegant black-and-white decor is the Roman base of the noted Florentine publicist and Marquis di Parma, Franco Maria Ricci. It carries distinctive notecards, art books, and English copies of his fine arts magazine, *FMR*. ♦ M afternoon; Tu-F; Sa morning. Via Borgognona 4/D (between Via Bocca di Leone and Via Belsiana). 6793466

59 Fendi This stretch of Via Borgognona (between Via Bocca di Leone and Via Belsiana) might have to be renamed Via Fendi: It holds as many **Fendi** shops as there are Fendi sisters (six in both cases). ♦ Fur Atelier: M afternoon; Tu-Sa. Other shops: M afternoon, Tu-Sa (no midday closing). Ready-to-wear boutique: Via Borgognona 40; Furs: Via Borgognona 39; Menswear: Via Borgognona 38/A; Institutional fabrics and accessories: Via Borgognona 38/B; Bags, shoes, and leather articles: Via Borgognona

36/B; Fendissime, for the young: Via Fontanella di Borghese 56/A (at Largo Carlo Goldoni). 6797641 (for all stores)

60 Laura Biagiotti Sophisticated, chic designs in knitwear and pastel-colored cashmere separates are available in both *alta moda* and ready-to-wear lines. Biagiotti may find inspiration in her medieval castle on the edge of town, but her sizzling silks and colorful cashmeres look great in a modern urban setting. ♦ M afternoon; Tu-F; Sa morning. Via Borgognona 43-44 (between Via Belsiana and Via del Corso). 6791205

60 Diego della Valle Patent leather creations are the draw here, including shoes for both women and men and belts with bold silver buckles. ♦ M afternoon; Tu-F; Sa morning. Via Borgognona 45-46 (between Via Belsiana and Via del Corso). 6786828

61 Anticoli Sweaters, and more sweaters, are all nicely designed, Italian made, and very reasonably priced. ♦ M afternoon; Tu-F; Sa morning. Via del Gambero 36 (between Via della Vite and Via Frattina). 6784496

62 Vanni $ Perhaps the most popular snack bar in this area serves light meals and sandwiches, as well as gelato and pastry. But the real draw are the *vanini*, ice-cream bon-bons the size of golf balls on a stick, dipped in different kinds of chocolate. ♦ Daily (no midday closing). Via Frattina 94 (at Via Belsiana). 6791835

63 Versace Jeans Couture Versace's line of jeanswear includes belts and other leather goods, umbrellas, and hats. For the little fashion hound, baby clothing is on the top floor. ♦ M afternoon; Tu-Sa. Via Frattina 116 (at Via Bocca di Leone). 6787680

64 Bozart Here you'll find top-of-the-line original Italian costume jewelry, including a peddler's pack of trendsetting gypsy chains, glitzy rhinestone earrings, frosted pearl necklaces, and feather pins. ♦ M afternoon; Tu-F; Sa morning. Via Bocca di Leone 4 (between Via Frattina and Via Borgognona). 6781026

65 Santini Trendy shoes for both sexes are available here; women's shoes are mostly flat or low-heeled. ♦ M afternoon; Tu-F; Sa morning. Via Frattina 120 (at Via Bocca di Leone). 6784114

66 Cartotecnica Romana Handsome writing paper, expensive pens, and fun gifts are the attractions at this emporium. ♦ M afternoon; Tu-Sa. Via Frattina 124 (between Via Mario de' Fiori and Via Bocca di Leone). 6789830

67 Mancini This jeweler specializes in the rarer (and more valued, by some) white gold jewelry. ♦ Via Mario de' Fiori 6 (at Via Frattina). 6797332

68 Intimità Lingerie for young women or those who want to feel young. ♦ M afternoon; Tu-F; Sa morning. Via Frattina 16 (between Via di Propaganda and Via Mario de' Fiori). 6780577

69 Onelli Pamper tired feet and worn-out shoes at this purveyor of fine foot creams, shoe liners, wood stretchers, slippers, and more. ♦ M afternoon; Tu-F; Sa morning. Via della Vite 78 (at Via Mario de' Fiori). 6792971

70 Peppino Italian barbers are still the best in the world. At this new location, you'll find a survivor of the old school, one who has served statesmen and stars but keeps his shop the way he thinks a barber shop should look—complete with old-fashioned swivel chairs. ♦ M-F, Su. Via della Vite 62 (between Via Mario de' Fiori and Via del Gambero). No phone

71 Da Mario ★★$$$ At this popular Tuscan restaurant, game (duck, wild boar, rabbit) is served in season. Try *pappardelle alle lepre* (wide noodles in a rich and hearty hare sauce), but save room for the homemade *torta di ricotta* (ricotta cheesecake). Though the 20 tables make for a slightly tight fit, the atmosphere in this old-fashioned dining spot can be heartwarming, especially on a chilly day. ♦ M dinner, Tu-Sa lunch and dinner Jan-May, 15 Sept-Dec; M dinner, Tu-F lunch and dinner June-July, 1-15 Sept; closed in August. Reservations recommended. Via della Vite 55 (between Via Mario de' Fiori and Via del Gambero). 6783818

72 Al Gambero ★★$ Unlike some eateries nearby, this family-run neighborhood coffee bar treats even tourists like old friends. Whether you want a quick coffee, a *tramezzino* (three-decker) sandwich, a plate of pasta, or a dish of their homemade ice cream, you'll find an amazing choice for such a small place. There are tables inside and out. ♦ M-Sa 7AM-8PM. Via del Gambero 40 (at Via della Vite). 6784294. Also at: Via della Croce 70 (between Via Bocca di Leone and Via Belsiana). 6782696

73 Vanina Women shop here for reasonably priced, quality clothing. ♦ M afternoon; Tu-F; Sa morning. Via della Vite 4A (at Via del Gambero). 6793650

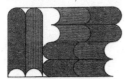

74 Anglo-American Bookstore Books on travel and the classical world predominate, but CD-ROMs and cookbooks in English also are available. ♦ M afternoon; Tu-F; Sa morning. Via della Vite 102 (at Via Mario de' Fiori). 6795222; fax 6783890

75 BabyGilda Not far from the **Spanish Steps,** this place is a fun outlet for the 5-to-11 set. Besides prizes for the best dancers, there are clowns and magicians, a pool, and games led by trained instructors. From mid-June to early September **BabyGilda** moves waterside and becomes **Gilda on the Beach,** adding fun-in-the-sun to the roster. ♦ Admission. Daily. BabyGilda: Via Mario de' Fiori 97 (at Via delle Mercede). 8558046. Gilda on the Beach: Lungomare di Ponente 11, Fregene. 66560649

76 Hotel dei Borgognoni $$$$ This elegant little gem sits on a tiny, narrow street where inhabitants of Burgundy settled in the 17th century. The 50 smallish rooms are richly decorated with antiques, and some overlook a glass-enclosed, plant-filled inner courtyard. All the usual amenities are offered—air-conditioning, satellite TV, mini-bars, room safes, a private garage—but one novelty—free baby-sitting service—stands out. There's a snack bar, but no restaurant. ♦ Via del Bufalo 126 (between Via di San Andrea delle Fratte and Via del Pozzetto). 69941505; fax 69941501

Bests

Gene Baldini
Artist/Painter

That which I love most about Rome is the importance of the sky in relation to the architecture. The presence of soft sea light predominates the city in any season or weather. The narrow streets of the medieval quarters of **Trastevere** and the zone behind **Lungotevere dei Sangallo** are special. One can enjoy the magical way in which the light and architecture interact. Often the streets and piazzas seem like incredible stage sets where everything is lighted in the most illogical way.

Two of my favorite churches are **San Clemente** and **Santa Maria in Cosmedin.** They are both splendid examples of the way in which architecture can express intimacy and humility while simultaneously being rich in decorative detail and historical layering.

More than 20 million Italians drink at least two cups of coffee a day in one of Italy's 250,000 bars. But they rank only thirteenth in worldwide per capita consumption.

Via del Corso and the Trevi Fountain

Via del Corso's name comes from a Carnival *corso* (race), run here annually during the 18th century. The starting point was **Piazza del Popolo**, where the *barberi* (jockeyless horses) lined up. At the signal they were released and ran down the **Via Lata** (later renamed "Via del Corso," in their honor) to **Piazza Venezia**. Along the street, people in colorful Carnival costumes urged them on, while the aristocracy watched from the windows and balconies of their *palazzi*. In 1775 the prize was a bolt of damask sewn with gold thread.

Today the Corso is still the most popular and populous street in Rome. During the evening *passeggiata* (stroll), usually around 6 to 8PM, it is so packed with people that if you didn't know about this daily practice, you might think you'd chanced on some extraordinary event. At the turn of the last century the Corso was lined with elegant shops. A few of these *negozi d'epoca* still sell gloves or woolens, but, alas, most of the shops today trade in jeans, leather jackets, or sportswear. Reminders of the street's grand past include the **Hotel Plaza**, with its atmospheric Belle Epoque palm court, and **La Rinascente** department store, which was one of the first wrought-iron and glass buildings in Rome.

Day or night, the most congested area of the city is around the queen of Roman monuments, the **Trevi Fountain**. Originally built to decorate the back of a nobleman's home, the **Trevi** became one of the most enduring icons of Western civilization—thanks to a Hollywood song and a Fellini film. The area around the **Trevi** thrives on the tourist trade, and restaurants and trattorie here have to be given a wide berth. But Romans, too, are enamored with this massive fountain, which was restored in the early 1990s.

Via del Corso and Environs

La Capricciosa

1 Pizzeria La Capricciosa ★★$$ This is the birthplace of the *capricciosa* pizza— topped with everything. Pizzas are only served at night, but pasta and meat dishes round out the lunch menu. ♦ M, W-Su. Largo dei Lombardi 8 (between Via del Corso and Piazza Augusto Imperatore). 6878480, 6878636

2 Mausoleo di Augusto (Mausoleum of Augustus) Built in 28 BC, this massive drum-shaped tomb of Rome's first emperor is the most important ancient building in the **Campus Martius,** the area between Quirinal Hill and the Tiber River and Capitoline Hill and **Porta Flaminia.** Named after and consecrated to Mars (the god of war), it was once a marshy plain where Roman soldiers practiced military exercises. The mausoleum originally stood alone in what was then a *campo,* or vast grassy field, and was faced with gleaming marble and topped with two tiers of columns that held up a conical hillock planted with cypress trees. At the summit was a 50-foot bronze statue of Caesar Augustus (the adopted son of Julius Caesar), whose reign came to be known as the Augustan Age—a golden era of peace and prosperity.

In the 10th century, the Colonna family turned the tomb into a fortress, which became a public park in the 16th century, and then a bull ring in the 18th century. Finally, in the 19th century, a roof was added, and it became one of the most unusual concert halls in the world. By the 1930s the tomb had become overrun with earth and grass, and Mussolini, wishing to associate himself with the six emperors buried within, restored it and made known his intention to be buried there. History saw otherwise, and the only reminder of Mussolini is the stark fascist architecture of the surrounding square. ♦ Open only for guided tours. See *Roma C'è* for schedule. Piazza Augusto Imperatore

3 Ara Pacis Augustae (Altar of Augustus's Peace) The story of the excavation of this altar, built in 9 BC, is as interesting as the monument itself. It begins in 1525, when some superb ancient reliefs of unknown origin entered the collection of Cardinal Andrea della Valle, a 16th-century art connoisseur. Twenty years later, when the foundations of a palace were being dug in Via in Lucina, similar panels were uncovered, and those not bought by Cardinal Ricci of Montepulciano ended up in the Louvre, Vienna, and the **Vatican Museums.** When the same palace on Via in Lucina was renovated in the 18th century, more slabs were found. By then, experts realized that these giant marbles might well be part of the **Ara Pacis Augustae,** the legendary **Altar of Peace,** and in 1898 the new Italian government began reacquiring the panels from all over the world. Finally, in the 1930s, they were reassembled and housed in this glass pavilion near the tomb of Augustus.

The altar's two front reliefs represent the world of legend: On the right, an austere-looking Aeneas sacrifices on a country altar; on the left (unfortunately destroyed) was a depiction of **Lupercal,** the cave where Romulus and Remus were suckled by the she-wolf. The highlight of this monument is the two exterior sides where high reliefs in stone show a triumphal procession held in 43 BC to celebrate Augustus's return from long wars in Spain and Gaul. (In fact, the **Ara Pacis** was constructed by order of

Ara Pacis Augustae (Altar of Augustus's Peace)

the Senate to commemorate Augustus's success in pacifying these fringes of the empire.) Depiction of the parade begins—in the badly broken left section of the side panel facing the **Mausoleum of Augustus**—with a few lictors (bearers of ceremonial fasces, or bundles of sticks) marching just ahead of the emperor. Augustus himself, taller than the others, appears as the last one in this broken section. Unfortunately, the whole front of his body cannot be seen, and the image breaks across his young and handsome face. Tiberius—who succeeded Augustus as emperor—is next to him in the foreground, almost touching his left arm. After the flamens (lighters of the ceremonial fires) and the man bearing the imperial ax on his shoulder comes a tall figure with his right fist clenched. That is Agrippa, Augustus's best friend and son-in-law, who is followed by the emperor's wife, Livia; his daughter, Julia; and his friends. Notice the child tugging at Agrippa's toga for attention, and another, with a very serious face, holding his own offering.

On the side facing the Tiber River are priests, magistrates, and some of the senators who voted in favor of the monument and ceremony. The *pontifex maximus* (high priest) is recognizable by the toga lightly covering his laurel-wreathed head. On one of the altar's outer walls (almost wholly destroyed) is a depiction of Rome; on the other, Tellus (Italy) is pictured as a serene mother figure watching lovingly over her two children. On either side are the deities of Air, sailing on a swan, and Water, on a sea monster. Inside the inner sanctum, on either side of where the altar would have been, are scroll-shaped carvings with exquisite high reliefs of a sacrificial procession—the ill-fated animals being led by priests. Note the stylized flower-and-leaf scrolls, both inside and outside the enclosure. These sculptures represent some of the most delicate and exquisitely wrought carving in all of Roman art. ◆ Admission. Tu-Sa; Su morning. Via di Ripetta (between Piazza del Porto di Ripetta and Piazza del Ferro di Cavallo). 68896848

4 Old Map and Photograph Shop Here is a treasure trove of fascinating photographs of bygone Rome, in which horse-drawn carriages fill the whole of **St. Peter's Square** and aerial views reveal the old turn-of-the-century streets (which Mussolini demolished) leading up to **St. Peter's**. ◆ M afternoon; Tu-F; Sa morning. Lungotevere dei Mellini 2 (at Via Vittoria Colonna). No phone

5 Hotel dei Mellini $$$ This small yet luxurious new hotel is fast gaining a reputation for efficient, friendly, and personal service. The 80 richly elegant guest rooms, done in warm earth tones, boast solid mahogany furnishings and Italian marble bathrooms. All have the usual amenities—air-conditioning, satellite TV, mini-bars, safes—plus the 11 suites feature 2 baths. Whether lounging in the **American Bar** or taking in a sunset on the roof terrace, guests can enjoy such light meals as *insalata caprese* (sliced fresh mozzarella, tomatoes, and basil) or *bresaola* (cured sliced beef) with arugula and parmigiano shavings. The buffet breakfast (included) offers a selection of cheeses, croissants and cakes, yogurt, cereals, and fresh-brewed espresso. ◆ Via Muzio Clementi 81 (between Via Cossa and Via Belli) 324771; fax 32477801; htl.dei.mellini@flashnet.it; htl.dei.mellini@flashnet.it; www.venere.it/roma/dei_mellini

6 Il Mercato di Piazza Borghese (Open-air Book Market) Old books and prints, reproductions, maps, and some contemporary paintings can be found at this permanent outdoor book fair. ◆ M-Sa morning. Piazza Borghese

® **TOULA'**

7 El Toulà ★★★★$$$$ This prestigious restaurant is one of several spinoffs of the original in Treviso, northern Italy. Rome's version has the warm, welcoming atmosphere of a 19th-century Venetian country house, with white walls, antique furniture, heavy silver serving dishes, and spectacular arrangements of fresh fruit and flowers. The bar off the entrance is a cozy spot to sip Prosecco (sparkling wine) or a Bellini (Prosecco and peach nectar). Among the best dishes are the fresh oysters, breast of roasted goose, and their specialty: *radicchio alla griglia* (grilled radicchio—the long, feathery variety that is grown in Treviso). ◆ M-F lunch and dinner; Sa dinner; closed in August and 24-26 December. Reservations required. Via della Lupa 29 (at Largo Fontanella di Borghese). 6873498; fax 6871115

8 Palazzo Borghese This grand 16th-century Renaissance palace is nicknamed *il cembalo* for its harpsichordlike shape. After passing through several noble families, the palazzo was bought by Cardinal Borghese in 1604, the year before he became Pope Paul V. During the early 19th century, Napoleon's favorite sister, Pauline, resided here as the young bride of Prince Camillo Borghese. She later scandalized the family with her extramarital affairs and by posing nude for Canova (*Pauline Borghese as Venus Victrix* now stands in the **Galleria Borghese**).

Inside is a magnificent double-porticoed courtyard ornamented with colossal antique statues, including the *Bath of Venus,* and fountains. Borghese family descendants still live here, although part of the *piano nobile* (noble floor, one flight up) is rented to the exclusive Circolo Romano della Caccia (The Hunting Club of Rome), a retreat for the ultraconservative "black nobility" who, like the Borghese, got their titles not by birth but by papal fiat. The building on the opposite side of the piazza once housed the legion of domestics that serviced the palazzo. ◆ Largo Fontanella di Borghese 19 (at Via di Monte d'Oro)

9 La Fontanella ★$$$ This eatery takes pride in its selection of homemade pastas prepared with fresh ingredients. Try *maltagliati* (short, diagonally cut pasta) tossed with shrimp, fresh tomatoes, and arugula. For dessert, the vanilla *soufflé* is worth the wait. In summer, dine alfresco. ◆ Tu-Su lunch and dinner; closed two weeks in August. Largo Fontanella di Borghese 86 (at Via Fontanella di Borghese). 6871582; fax 6871092

10 Vini Birra Buffet ★★$ Great soups, inventive cheese platters, and polenta (with sausages, four cheeses, or just gorgonzola) are some of the offerings presented with care and courtesy at this excellent wine/beer bar. Good food and friendly service have made it very popular, so arrive early or expect to wait for a table. ◆ M-Sa lunch and dinner. Piazza della Torretta 60 (between Via di Campo Marzio and Vicolo della Torretta). 6871445

11 Slamp The clean lines and playful images of this shop's modern lamps have gained them entry into the Museum of Modern Art's design collection. The concept is simple: Two sleeves of molded opaque plastic encase a light bulb for floor, desk, or wall-mounted models. Each design is created by such renowned international designers as Alessandro Mendini and Anna Gili, and limited production runs make them worthy of collecting. ◆ M-Sa (no midday closing). Piazza del Parlamento 7 (between Via Giardino Theodoli and Via in Lucina). 68892901; fax 3235405

12 Suzuki Flower Shop The fakes here are so expertly wrought that only a smell or a touch will give them away. Peonies and zinnias are amazingly lifelike, and a whole Renaissance bouquet would slip right into a suitcase. ◆ M afternoon; Tu-F; Sa morning. No credit cards accepted. Via del Leone 2 (at Via del Leoncino). 6876454

All the coins in the Trevi Fountain are collected by an underwater vacuum cleaner once a month and separated into Italian lire (20-30 million, or $12-$18,000 at press time) and foreign currency. The former are used to maintain the fountain, and the latter is donated to the International Red Cross.

Restaurants/Clubs: Red   **Hotels:** Blue
Shops/ ⚘ Outdoors: Green   **Sights/Culture:** Black

13 L'Europeo Pasticceria ★★$$ One of the best in Rome, this *caffè* serves tables inside and out in a traffic-free piazza. Hot and cold sandwiches are available, but the specialty is Sicilian pastries like cassata cream cakes and ricotta-filled cannoli. Chocolates and other candies—even balls of "string" made of chestnut paste—are sold by the gram. ◆ M-Tu, Th-Su. Piazza di San Lorenzo in Lucina 33 (between Via del Corso and Via del Leoncino). 6876300

14 Pizzeria al Leoncino ★$ Favored by the young and those on a tight budget, the menu here offers only one thing—pizza, the thin, crunchy variety that Romans prefer. The wood-burning oven is a relic from some remote era when marble was used even for ovens. ◆ M-Tu, Th-Su dinner. No credit cards accepted. Via del Leoncino 28 (at Via Fontanella di Borghese). 6876306

15 Trattoria da Settimio all'Arancio ★★ $$ Brightly lit and perpetually full, this neighborhood trattoria attracts a varied crowd of diners. Here Roman princes have been known to mingle with trade-union leaders amid crowds of partying teenagers. Every Friday, the menu features fresh fish dishes at reasonable prices. Otherwise, the braised porcini mushrooms and *fusilli all melanzana* (corkscrew pasta in a tomato-and-eggplant sauce), followed by an excellent Bavarian cream pie, make a memorable meal. ◆ M-Sa lunch and dinner. Via dell'Arancio 50 (between Via del Leoncino and Piazza di Monte d'Oro). 6876119

16 Arancio d'Oro ★★$$ Second in the small family chain of Arancio restaurants, this spot is known for its excellent price-to-quality ratio (little money for lots of food). In addition to such out-of-the-ordinary pasta dishes as tagliatelle with baby squid, there's also delicious grilled steak and (nights only) pizza. Montepulciano d'Abruzzo wine is available by the liter. The lemon mousse is a tasty finale. ◆ Tu-Su lunch and dinner. Via di Monte d'Oro 17 (at Via dell'Arancio). 6865026

17 Rammendi Not only can Signora Durastante mend tears in both natural and synthetic fabrics, she also repairs lace and spangled net—just don't expect the repairs to be done right away. ◆ M-F. No credit cards accepted. Via Fontanella di Borghese 70 (at Largo Carlo Goldoni). 6876548

Child's Play

Italians love children, and the younger members of your entourage will garner plenty of attention, especially if they are not sufficiently swaddled against drafts or look like they could use a few pounds. Italian mothers dispense with all language barriers, affectionately giving advice to young and old alike.

Here are a few special touring suggestions for *bambini*:

1 Spend a morning scouting for cannonballs at **Castel Sant'Angelo.** It has dungeons, parapets, turrets, and a catapult that was actually used in battle. To see a six-foot-tall lockbox that once was filled with solid gold coins, hunt out the castle's **Sala del Tesoro** (Treasure Room).

2 Walk along the ancient walls Roman sentries once patrolled. Enter through the **Museo delle Mure** (Museum of the Walls) at **Porta San Sebastiano,** and follow a passageway cut with long narrow windows for crossbow archers.

3 Take a truth test. In the foyer of **Santa Maria in Cosmedìn** lies a huge stone slab with a face carved on it. Stick your hand in the **Bocca della Verità** (Mouth of Truth), a hole in the middle. It is said that anyone who doesn't tell the truth might not get their hands back.

4 Climb to the top of the dome of **St. Peter's.** Count the steps and see if the figure matches the one on page 21.

5 See how many bees, the symbol of the Barberini family, you can find around the city. Hint: Start around **Piazza Barberini,** in **Palazzo Barberini,** or St. Peter's Basilica. A dozen bees earns a gelato.

6 To assure your return to Rome, toss a coin over your back—right hand over left shoulder—into **Trevi Fountain.** Then count the horses leaping about in the water.

7 Conduct your own taste test to discover the best gelato in the city. Start along Rome's ice-cream alley, **Via della Maddalena,** the little street just north of the **Pantheon.**

8 Play in the sandboxes at the **Orto Botanico's** (Botanical Gardens) scent garden, where there are also plants you can touch and a carp pool.

9 **BabyGilda,** a disco for the 5-to-11 set near the **Spanish Steps,** offers prizes for the best dancers as well as clowns and magicians, and all kinds of games.

10 Hike up the **Aventine Hill** to see St. Peter's dome scaled down to dollhouse size: Peer through the keyhole on the main door of the **Knights of Malta Headquarters** in **Piazza dei Cavalieri di Malta.**

---

17 Palazzo Ruspoli This large palace was built in 1586 by **Bartolomeo Ammannati** for the Ruccellai family and was subsequently bought by the Ruspolis in 1776. Note the elegant windows of the second floor. After the fall of Napoleon in France, his sister Hortense—the former queen of Holland—lived here with her family. One of her sons left the palazzo to go back to Paris, where he became Napoleon III. The building is closed to the public. ♦ Largo Carlo Goldoni 56 (at Via del Corso)

18 Hotel Plaza $$$ This air-conditioned hotel with a knowledgeable, helpful staff caters to a sophisticated clientele. The Old World grandeur is visible in the renovated great hall, where time has not diminished the spectacular Belle Epoque stained-glass ceiling. The best rooms (**No. 257,** for example) are set around a cool, quiet inner courtyard and have large, comfortable old-fashioned bathrooms. The palm court bar has deep-padded chairs to flop into after a harrowing morning doing what the Romans do. The new **Mascagni** cafe serves lunch and dinner (until midnight), and a full-service restaurant is in the works. ♦ Via del Corso 126 (between Largo Carlo Goldoni and Via delle Carrozze). 69921111; fax 69941575; plaza@italyhotel.com; www.venere.it/roma/plaza

19 Bruscoli Down the street from the **Hotel Plaza,** this lingerie shop stocks a wide range of weaves, colors, and fabrics (including pure silk) as well as a selection of hosiery, bathing suits, and gloves. ♦ M afternoon; Tu-F; Sa morning. Via del Corso 113 (between Via delle Carrozze and Via della Croce). 6795715

20 Naka This ceramics and pottery shop carries treasures from kilns in Puglia and Sicily as well as all the Alessi products and colorful, Picassoesque DeSimone ceramics from Palermo. The friendly staff speaks English and can pack and ship your purchases (although postal costs may double your bill).

♦ M afternoon; Tu-Sa. Via del Corso 149 (at Via Frattina). 6791996; fax 6991143

21 Schostal Originally part of an Austrian chain, this traditional millinery shop has been carrying high-quality sweaters, underwear, and other knitwear since 1870. No fancy cuts or colors are in stock, but if a classic navy sweater or a good pair of black socks is on your list, this is the place to find them. ♦ M afternoon; Tu-Sa. Via del Corso 160 (between Via della Vite and Via Frattina). 6791240

21 Grilli Shoes Not just shoes, this shop also sells its own line of classic, casual handbags and sandals at reasonable prices. ♦ M afternoon; Tu-F; Sa morning. Via del Corso 166 (at Via della Vite). 6793650

HOTEL
★ ★ PENSIONE
PARLAMENTO

22 Hotel Pensione Parlamento $ As the name suggests, this place offers some typical hotel amenities (private baths, TVs, telephones), but the 22-room operation is kept small and attractively priced like a pensione. The refurbished fourth-floor guest rooms offer lovely panoramic views. ♦ Via delle Convertite 5 (at Via del Corso). 6792082

23 Frette Luxurious embroidered towels, linen, bathrobes, and pajamas are available at this long-established shop. ♦ Daily (no midday closing). Via del Corso 381 (between Piazza Colonna and Via del Parlamento). 6786862. Also at: Via Nazionale 84 (at Via dei Serpenti). 4882641; Piazza di Spagna 11 (between Via di San Sebastianello and Via del Babuino). 6790673

24 La Rinascente Rome's idea of a department store may make Fifth Avenue window designers laugh, but most Romans prefer a neighborhood boutique where they know the salespeople and the merchandise. **LAR,** as it is known, has ready-to-wear clothes, including some designer names, for men, women, and children. Nonclothing items (mostly housewares) are available at the **Piazza Fiume** location (8841231). English-speaking hostesses and money-exchange facilities are on the premises. ♦ M-Sa 9:30AM-9PM; Su 10:30AM-8PM. Via del Corso 189 (at Largo Chigi). 6797691

25 Rizzoli Bookshop Motherhouse to the noted New York City store, Rome's largest general bookseller stocks a decent selection of English-language books and an interesting collection of illustrated fine-arts volumes. ♦ M afternoon; Tu-F; Sa morning. Largo Chigi 15 (at Via del Corso). 6796641

26 Piazza Colonna This busy square near the convergence of two major shopping streets, Via del Corso and Via del Tritone, is the center of Rome's principal industry: government. The **Palazzo Chigi,** on the corner of Via del Corso closest to **La Rinascente,** is the office of the prime minister; it was designed by **Maderno** in the 16th century.

On Piazza Colonna:

Colonna di Marco Aurelio (Column of Marcus Aurelius) In the center of the square stands a marble column 30 meters high dedicated to Emperor Marcus Aurelius in AD 193. Sculpted bas-relief strips wind up to the top, recounting in 116 scenes the not-always-peace-loving philosopher's military adventures. He favored the arts and letters during his reign, and his statue crowned the column until 1589, when Pope Sixtus V, Rome's city planner, replaced it with the present effigy of St. Paul.

27 Galleria Colonna Although this enclosed shopping arcade, built in 1923, may remind you of a mall, it was around long before that idea took off. Like similar ones in Milan and Naples, it was designed at the turn of the century with an immense glass dome to let in light and keep out rain. On the upper walls are colorful Art Nouveau paintings. ♦ Piazza Colonna and Via del Corso

At least one of the obelisks carried off by Romans may yet go home. The Obelisk of Axum—almost 79 feet high—is now located near the Circus Maximus in Piazza di Porta Capena. Mussolini had it brought to Rome from Ethiopia in 1937 along with numerous other archaeological artifacts. After the peace treaty between Italy and Ethiopia was signed in 1947, most of the treasures were returned. Although the obelisk was mentioned in the treaty, it has yet to return to its homeland (politics rears its ugly head).

Fontana di Trevi and Environs

28 Al Moro ★★$$$ The legendary Moro—whose son, Franco Romagnoli, runs this small air-conditioned restaurant—was famous for his sharp tongue and bad manners, even before he was typecast as a crotchety Roman in *Fellini Satyricon*. That didn't stop Fellini and a host of other public figures from becoming regulars; perhaps the braised porcini mushrooms helped. Nowadays Franco oversees the production of such Roman standbys as *abbacchio scottadito* (tiny grilled lamb ribs), *carciofi alla romana* (artichokes cooked in garlic and fresh mint), and, for dessert, chestnut mousse. The noise is unbearable and the smoke inches thick—but the delicious porcini are still worth it. ♦ M-Sa lunch and dinner; closed in August. Reservations required. No credit cards accepted. Vicolo delle Bollette 13 (at Via dei Crociferi). 6783495

29 Fontana di Trevi (Trevi Fountain) In 1762, architect **Nicola Salvi** had surrounding houses torn down to make room for this internationally recognized icon that decorates the back of **Palazzo Poli** (illustrated below). The fountain is so vast and the High Baroque sculpture so vivid that the prancing horses seem to be splashing their way out of the fountain and about to gallop... minute. **Trevi** is a shortening of... streets, which converge on the sm... containing Rome's most popular touris... attraction. The fountain marks the spot wh... the **Acqua Vergine** aqueduct, only 14 miles long and dating back to 19 BC, brings water into Rome. Like ancient Rome's other external water sources, it was cut off during the barbarian invasions. Then, 800 years later, the popes repaired the aqueducts and reinstated the emperors' custom of decorating the water's arrival point in the city with a great fountain. When Pope Nicholas V restored the **Acqua Vergine** aqueduct in 1453, he commissioned a modest monument to himself, the basin of which was built by **Leon Battista Alberti.** About two centuries later Pope Urban VIII commissioned **Bernini** to build him a major fountain on the same spot, but another century passed before the plan was approved by Pope Clement XII. The fountain was completed two popes later, under Clement XIII; his architect, **Nicola Salvi,** died before it was finished. The rite of drinking the fountain's sweet water to assure one's return to Rome gradually transmuted into the custom of tossing a coin in the water with your back to the fountain, right hand over left shoulder—as in the movie *Three Coins in a Fountain.* A night stroll is the most spectacular

Fontana di Trevi (Trevi Fountain)

...stored Neptune,
...ng from the
... Anita Ekberg took
...s *La Dolce Vita*), the
...real-life plunges.
...revi (between Via
...oli)

...enzo ed Anastasio
This many-co... ...urch was built in 1650
by **Martino Longhi the Younger.** A strange
collection is preserved in the crypt—the
hearts and lungs of almost all the popes from
1590 to 1903. ♦ Piazza della Fontana di Trevi
and Vicolo dei Modelli

31 Il Chianti Vineria ★★$$ Ignore the
young waiters imploring you to sit in their
lackluster cafes around the **Trevi Fountain**
and head over to this Tuscan trattoria. Warm
and welcoming with a paneled ceiling and
bottles of *vino* adorning the walls, this spot
offers a tender scallopini al Vin Santo and a
can't-miss tagliatelle with tomatoes and
porcini mushrooms. But it might be more
adventurous to sample the tastes of Tuscany
with a selection of antipasti: wild-boar
pancetta, fennel-scented salami, and a
selection of cheeses with thin, fresh-baked
focaccia. To go with it, try a refreshing white
like Vernaccia di San Gimignano or one of the
dozen or so Chiantis. ♦ M-Sa lunch and
dinner; closed in August. Via del Lavatore 81
(between Via della Panetteria and Piazza della
Fontana di Trevi). 6787550

32 Palazzo Carpegna Around 1500, Cardinal
Carpegna bought the houses on this site with
the intention of incorporating them into
Borromini's plans for a palace. There was to
be an extraordinary circular courtyard with a
bridge linking the palace's two halves, but
since the cardinal was unable to get
permission to close the intervening public
thoroughfare, the only parts of **Borromini**'s
plans that were executed were the magnificent
oval ramp and the entranceway's Baroque
stucco curlicues, out of whose center
emerges a face that some say bears a
Carpegna family resemblance. ♦ Via della
Stamperia (between Piazza della Fontana di
Trevi and Piazza dell'Accademia di San Luca)

Within the Palazzo Carpegna:

**Galleria Nazionale dell'Accademia di
San Luca (Academy of St. Luke
National Gallery)** The confraternity of
artists and art appreciators took its name in
the 15th century from the apostle Luke, who
legend says was a painter. There's an annual
open house at 5PM on St. Luke's feast day, 18
October. Specializing in art from the 16th to
19th centuries, the gallery contains works by
Bernini, Cortona, Raphael, Guercino, Titian,
and Rubens. ♦ Free. M, W, F morning, and
last Sunday morning of each month; closed in
July and August. 6798850

RISTORANTE
Sora Lucia

33 Sora Lucia ★★★$$ Good home-
cooking and friendly family-style service
have made this a neighborhood favorite
over the years. The cozy one-room spot
accommodates at most eight tables and
a mélange of wall-hangings depicting
18th-century Roman street scenes and
monuments. The fresh fettuccine with ham,
peas, mushrooms, and cream is incredibly
satisfying, as are Roman favorites like *coda
alla vacinara* (pieces of young-calf tail in
garlic, onion, carrot, celery, tomatoes, and
white wine) and scallopini al Marsala.
♦ Daily lunch and dinner. Via della
Panetteria 41 (between Via in Arcione
and Piazza dell'Accademia di San Luca).
6794078

**34 Trattoria Scanderberg al Piccolo
Arancio** ★★$$ This little sister of the
popular **Arancio d'Oro** and **Trattoria da
Settimio all' Arancio** (see page 120 for both)
offers dependably good Roman cuisine and
English-speaking servers. On Tuesday and
Friday there is a selection of fresh fish appe-
tizers and entrées (15 of each). Otherwise,
start with fried zucchini, artichokes, tomatoes,
and ricotta, or house-style ravioli (made with
ricotta, orange juice, and cream sauce), and
then move on to baby lamb, osso bucco, or
rolled beef with stuffed tomatoes—all served
in a glistening setting. ♦ Tu-Su lunch and
dinner. Vicolo dei Scanderberg 112 (at Via del
Lavatore). 6786139; fax 6780766

**35 Museo Nazionale delle Paste
Alimentari (National Pasta Museum)** A
whole museum celebrates the national dish
but sadly, it has no restaurant; after viewing
the origins and development of pasta, you're
sure to want a sample. The Agnesi family of
pasta producers put together the interesting

collection of pasta-making machines that ranges from early industrial models to the latest streamlined home versions. Audio tapes in English are available. ◆ Admission. Daily (no midday closing). Piazza dei Scanderberg 117 (at Vicolo dei Scanderberg). 6991119; fax 6991109

Fratelli Viganò

36 Capelleria Fratelli Viganò Since 1873, this classic haberdashery has carried the right hat for every occasion. The furniture, walnut shelves, and hat boxes are original, and the shop's history is illustrated in photos, framed letters, and copies of hats sold to the famous—including a fez for Mussolini. ◆ Via Marco Minghetti 7-9 (between La Galleria Sciarra and Via del Corso). 6991709

37 La Galleria Sciarra In 1883, **Giulio De Angelis** built this atrium, with a rare example of Art Nouveau design in the center, as an elegant passageway. Giuseppe Cellini painted the fresco cycle of floral designs and maidens, representing his ideal of feminine virtue in women of good breeding. The Art Nouveau Movement—dubbed "Liberty" by Italians—did not have as much influence here as it did in Paris or Prague, but the buildings in this area reflect its effect, especially in the use of glass and wrought iron.

38 Palazzo Doria Pamphili This immense complex, boasting five courtyards and more than a thousand rooms, rests on 15th-century foundations built over ancient ruins. Several families owned it before it was bought by the seafaring Doria family (a relative gave his name to the ill-fated liner *Andrea Doria*) in the mid-17th century, when one of them married into the Roman Pamphili nobility. In the 18th century, the splendid Rococo facade was added, with the most imaginative fenestration in Rome. Family members still live in the palace, which is not open to the public (except for the **Galleria,** see below); you can peek at the lovely porticoed courtyard from a gate on the Corso. ◆ Via del Corso 304 (between Piazza Venezia and Via Lata)

Within the Palazzo Doria Pamphili:

Galleria Doria Pamphili The art collection and some salons of the Doria Pamphili family are exhibited in this gallery, featuring important works by Velazquez, Bernini, Titian, and Caravaggio. Guided tours of the apartments offer a rare opportunity to see the mirrored halls, private chapels, and canopied beds of the Roman aristocracy. ◆ Admission. M-W, F-Su 10AM-5PM; closed 15 August. Piazza del Collegio Romano (between Via Lata and Via della Gatta). 6797323

Coronet

Pensione Coronet $ This pensione has 13 simple and very clean rooms, some with antique furnishings. Ask for a room with partial (but lovely) views of the **Palazzo Doria Pamphili** gardens. ◆ Piazza Grazioli 5 (at Via della Gatta). 6792341; fax 69922705

Bests

Ann Barak Stutch
Musician (Violinist and Violist)

The Pantheon—Just being there! Oldest intact building in Rome. Awesome.

Chiesa di Santa Maria della Concezione—In the basement is the **Cimitero dei Cappuccini:** Five chapels decorated in flamboyant High Baroque style all made of human bones, the remains of 4,000 monks. Weird and quite beautiful.

Sant'Eustachio Cafe—The best coffee. They blend and roast their own beans, which you can buy and take home.

Find the obelisks of Rome—13 of them—this pursuit makes several splendid walking tours.

Look for the fountains of Rome—big and small, they're all wonderful.

Coppedè Quarter—Apartments and villas in Art Nouveau at the extreme: wild, outrageous, beautiful architecture. Really unique.

Piazza Navona—No traffic, three marvelous **Bernini** fountains, a **Borromini** church, sidewalk artists, ice cream at **Bar Tre Scalini,** the passing parade of people. At night it's illuminated and looks like a fabulous stage set, a great place to sit and think and look and just relax.

Ara Pacis Augustae—Altar of Augustus's Peace on the bank of the **Tiber.** One of the greatest masterpieces of Imperial Rome. Simply magnificent.

Favorite walk—From the **Ara Pacis Augustae** along the Tiber to **Ponte Sant'Angelo.** Cross the bridge lined with ten Bernini angel statues. Great view of **St. Peter's** from here. Visit **Castel Sant'Angelo,** then walk the short distance to **St. Peter's.**

Tour the **Vatican Gardens**—Tickets available in **St. Peter's Square.**

Bargains—Scarves sold along **Viale Vaticano, Porta Portese Market** every Sunday: best kitchen gadgets, many demonstrated before your eyes with real veggies. Everything imaginable sold in this market. Come early and allow lots of time. Be prepared to bargain.

Savor the cool breezes, gardens, and wonderful views from **Capitoline Hill.**

Piazza del Popolo

Nowadays the trendy heart of Rome has shifted from Via Veneto of "La Dolce Vita" days (from the late 1950s to the early 1960s), when movie stars drove up and down that street in foreign automobiles, to the no-car zones in and around Piazza del Popolo of the 1990s. (Still to be dodged, though, are taxis, buses, and an occasional motor scooter or Alfa Romeo). The neighborhood boasts some excellent small restaurants and good booksellers. Not to be missed, either, are the many shops with racks of ready-to-wear designer clothes, as well as a seemingly infinite number of smaller boutiques. Walk along the quiet **Via Margutta** (where film director Federico Fellini lived) and poke into one of the artists' studios or galleries that line that street. In May the street hosts an annual fair during which the artists display their work outside. The handsome Renaissance **Via del Babuino**, which extends from **Piazza del Popolo** to **Piazza di Spagna**, is a center for antiques dealers, many of international renown. **Piazza del Popolo** and the twin roads winding up to the **Villa Borghese** were designed by **Giuseppe Valadier** in 1816. The wide-open, oval space, which has three main arteries leading into it, is the most Parisian of the Roman piazzas. Even so, it has the requisite obelisk, fountain, and church (in this case, three churches) found in most Roman squares.

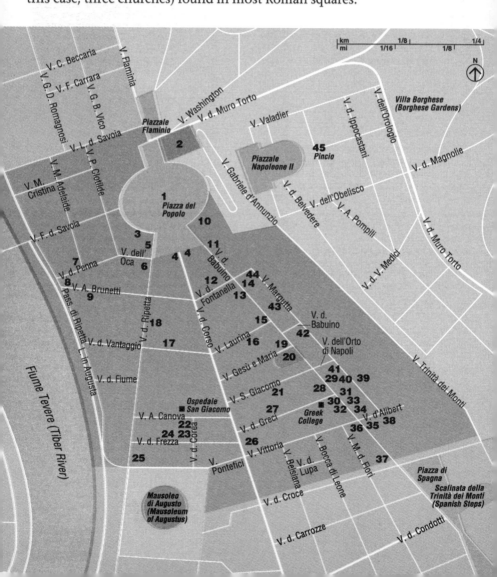

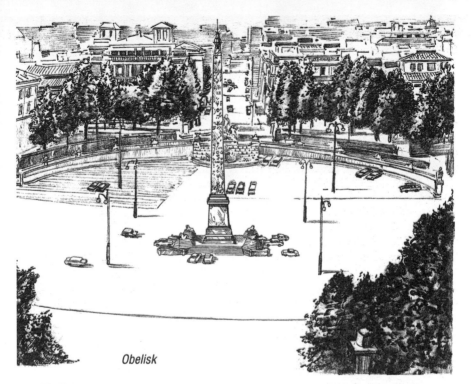

Obelisk

1 Obelisk The city's tallest (almost 80 feet), this obelisk was shipped to Rome from Heliopolis after Augustus Caesar, the first emperor of Rome, conquered Egypt. Its hieroglyphics celebrate the achievements of Pharaohs Ramses II and Merenptha (13-12 BC). First located in the **Circus Maximus,** it was moved here in 1589 as part of Pope Sixtus V's revival of urban planning. Using a 16th-century design by **Domenico Fontana,** in 1823 **Valadier** added four Egyptian lions who spray fanning arcs of water to the base. ♦ Piazza del Popolo

2 Chiesa di Santa Maria del Popolo On the north side of the piazza, tucked into the ancient walls near the **Porta del Popolo,** this church (illustrated on page 128) was constructed in 1099 over the presumed tomb of Nero to chase away his ghost, which was said to be haunting the area. The church was rebuilt in 1477 during the reign of Pope Sixtus IV. The remains of the Duke of Gandia and of his mother, Vanozza Cattanei, mistress of Alexander VI, the Borgia pope, lie here, as do those of one of Rome's most important Renaissance patrons of the arts, Agostino Chigi. The church contains a treasure trove of paintings by Raphael, Pinturicchio, and Caravaggio. ♦ Piazza del Popolo and Viale del Muro Torto

3 Rosati ★★$$$ The Rosati family has been serving Romans and visitors for three generations in one of Rome's few remaining grand caffès. What's left of the "La Dolce Vita" crowd of artists and actors is often in attendance here, showing off their fashions, expensive cars, and exotic pets. Late at night during summer the scene gets positively Felliniesque, even though the "maestro" is said to have preferred the rival bar across the street. Upstairs is a tearoom and restaurant with a limited menu. ♦ Daily 7:30AM-1AM. Piazza del Popolo 5/A (between Via dell'Oca and Via Ferdinando di Savoia). 3225859

4 Chiesa di Santa Maria dei Miracoli and Chiesa di Santa Maria di Montesanto The uncompromising sense of symmetry often seen in Rome is exemplified in the design of these twin Baroque churches with lovely tiled domes (illustrated on page 129). Designed by **Carlo Rainaldi,** with help from **Gian Lorenzo Bernini** and **Carlo Fontana,** the churches were completed in 1679. Even though the plots of land on which the churches stand are quite different, **Rainaldi** struggled to make the buildings themselves appear the same. Actually, their shapes are disparate—look carefully. ♦ Piazza del Popolo and Via del Corso

In the diary notations of his travels in Italy Stendhal described the panic that overwhelmed him in the face of so much art and history. When he visited Santa Croce in Florence and saw the Giotto frescoes for the first time, he was taken by a violent emotion: "Everything spoke so vividly to my soul. I had heart palpitations; the life began to drain from me, and I feared falling."

Chiesa di Santa Maria del Popolo

5 Dal Bolognese ★★$$$ A favorite for more than 50 years, this nicely located restaurant has an outdoor terrace and specializes in the cuisine of Bologna—which many say is Italy's finest. Start with any of the homemade pastas served *al ragù* in a meat and (very little) tomato sauce or *tortellini in brodo* (in broth), another bolognese classic. Though *cotoletta alla bolognese* (breaded veal cutlet covered with a slice of prosciutto and melted cheese) is a standard, the more adventurous should try *bollito misto,* a sampling of boiled meats and poultry served from a domed steam cart, accompanied by a green sauce of parsley, capers, and onions. Unfortunately, service is not always what it should be, and quality tends to break down at the height of tourist season. ◆ Tu-F lunch and dinner. Reservations required. Piazza del Popolo 1 (at Via dell'Oca). 3611426

6 Ristorante Porto di Ripetta ★★$$$ This popular restaurant advertises that it receives fresh fish daily from ports in The Marches region. Of the two fixed-price menus, one has lots of little courses, and the other is more modest, but both travel the route from antipasto to dessert. ◆ M-Sa lunch and dinner; closed in August. Via di Ripetta 250 (between Via Angelo Brunetti and Via dell'Oca). 3612376

7 Hotel Locarno $$ Art Nouveau sprinklings in the lobby—Tiffany-style lamps and beveled glass doors—add charming touches to this 48-room hotel. The good-sized guest rooms are decorated in a more contemporary fashion. There's no restaurant, but sit by the open fire in the cozy parlor in the winter and have a drink; in nice weather, breakfast (included) is served in the wisteria-draped garden or (for a nominal fee) on the rooftop terrace. This small hotel is the favorite of many people; book well in advance. Free bicycles are provided to guests. ◆ Via della Penna 22 (at Via Maria Adelaide). 3610841; fax 3215249; locarno@venere.it; www.venere.it/roma/locarno

8 Osteria St. Ana ★★$$ Now a hangout for the business community's movers and shakers (it used to be the international film crowd's haunt), this eatery offers alfresco dining in summer and is open late year-round. The rough, whitewashed walls are loaded with paintings and pictures, making this cozy cellar feel like somebody's basement art gallery. The filet mignon is excellent, as is the antipasto richly laid out on the tables, but be fore-warned: Anything you taste from the selection will show up on your bill. ◆ M-F lunch and dinner; Sa dinner. Via della Penna 68 (at Passeggiata di Ripetta). 3610291

9 Al Ristorante 59 ★★$$$ Located on a side street leading toward the Tiber, this clublike restaurant is usually packed with journalists and businesspeople, who find it just right for interviews or power lunches. The most powerful item on the excellent bolognese menu is *tortelli di ravioli,* filled with pumpkin squash, parmesan cheese, and nutmeg, and garnished with butter and sage leaves. This is one of the few places in Rome that serves this dish. ◆ M-Sa lunch and dinner; closed Saturday in June and August. Reservations recommended. No credit cards accepted. Via Angelo Brunetti 59 (between Via di Ripetta and Passeggiata di Ripetta). 3219019

10 Canova ★★$$$ A rival alternative to **Rosati**'s (see page 127), this cafe gets more sun and is packed at lunch time both outdoors and at the counter inside. It's named after the early–19th-century Venetian sculptor, Antonio Canova, whose studio was nearby. He is famed for, among other works, his full frontal statue of Napoleon's sister *Pauline* in the **Villa Borghese Gallery.** ♦ Daily 24 hours. Piazza del Popolo 16 (between Via del Babuino and Viale Gabriele d'Annunzio). 3612231

10 Borsalino Such diverse personalities as Mikhail Gorbachev, Alain Delon, and Ben Gazzara, as well as former President of Italy Francesco Cossiga, sport the famous Borsalino felt hat sold here. Other styles are available, as is women's headgear. ♦ M-Sa (no midday closing). Piazza del Popolo 20 (between Via del Babuino and Viale Gabriele d'Annunzio). 32650838; fax 3233353

11 Via del Babuino Not a single new addition breaks the elegant parade of 16th- and 17th-century buildings that line this street for over half a mile. It is one of the few thoroughfares in Rome that offer such an uninterrupted glimpse into the past.

11 Cesari Fabrics This elegant store entices with its curving staircase and candle lamps on the facade. Inside are the finest upholstery fabrics, including cut velvet from Venice. Across the street is its sister store (No. 195, 3207854), which blends chic outdoor furniture with matchless interior furnishings. ♦ M afternoon; Tu-F; Sa morning. Via del Babuino 16 (at Piazza del Popolo). 3611441

12 Hotel Valadier $$$ This charming, well-located hotel has 40 spacious air-conditioned rooms (including 6 suites), 1 with a terrace. Unusually large bathrooms (it was once a bordello), a restaurant, and a parking garage round out the amenities. Breakfast is included, but winter rates are 30 percent lower than in summer. ♦ Via della Fontanella 15 (between Via del Babuino and Via del Corso). 3611998; fax 3201558

13 Favà This antiques dealer has a quality collection of old silver and small "objects of virtue"—snuffboxes, porcelains, and miniatures. He also has a passion for 18th- and 19th-century pictures of Mount Vesuvius erupting. These "disaster postcards" were churned out by Neapolitans—preferably showing the event by moonlight—as souvenirs for English milords doing their "grand tour" of the continent. ♦ M afternoon; Tu-F; Sa morning. Via del Babuino 180 (at Via della Fontanella). 3610807

14 L'Artistica Roma Students at the nearby art institute on Via di Ripetta and the artists in their studios on Via Margutta don't run out of watercolors and brushes with this well-stocked shop in the neighborhood. ♦ M afternoon; Tu-F; Sa morning. Via del Babuino 24 (at Via Margutta). 36000963; fax 36000998

Chiesa di Santa Maria dei Miracoli and Chiesa di Santa Maria di Montesanto

The Coffee Rite

Italians have a passion for coffee and coffee making, so it comes as no surprise that the espresso machine was invented by an Italian, Luigi Bezzera, in 1901. The geyserlike pressure cookers used in bars (as cafes are called in Italy) produce in less than 10 seconds a tiny cup of infused liquid that is never bitter and has minimal effect on cardiac fibrillation.

In general, Italians remain on their feet throughout the coffee ritual and knock it back without sipping. Moreover, they drink coffee in the morning with the conviction that it will wake them up and in the evening with equal certainty that it will put them right to sleep. You might want to follow suit. Alternatively, you can sit at a table and be served while you sip and savor; you'll never be rushed, but the price will double.

Coffee is offered in a variety of ways—here are a few options:

un caffè—a simple, single (one-inch) serving of espresso

un caffè corretto—espresso with a shot of brandy or other whiskey

un caffè doppio—a double serving (two inches) of espresso

un caffè Hag (pronounced "ahg") or *decaffinato*—a decaffeinated espresso

un caffè latte—espresso and steamed milk

un caffè lungo—espresso with more hot water than a regular serving

un caffè macchiato (mah-kee-*ah*-tow)— espresso with a drop (literally a "stain") of milk

un caffè ristretto—very concentrated (strong) espresso

un caffè americano—watery coffee and milk in a large cup

cappuccino—one-half espresso, one-half steamed milk, with a sprinkling of bitter cocoa on top, but only if you ask for it.

These choices may seem like enough, but devotees of the coffee ritual also must decide whether they want their coffee in a *tazza* (cup) or a *vetro* (glass), and their cappuccino frothy or *senza schiuma* (without foam), *tiepido* (lukewarm) or *bollente* (scalding). The bartenders take it all in stride, and don't be surprised if they give you a glass of water with your coffee; it's meant to clear the palate. Drinking cappuccino after 11AM is a mortal sin for purists, who also are split over whether the *cappuccio* (hood) of a cappuccino refers to the frothy foam or to the cocoa sprinkling.

15 Café Notegen ★$ Roman bars rarely have places to sit, but this one has lots of tables and chairs, and sometimes it's the venue for lectures and theatrical productions. ♦ M-Sa 7AM-midnight. Via del Babuino 159 (at Via Laurina). 3200855

16 Hotel Margutta $ Decked out in the bold colors of an artist's studio, in the spirit of the neighborhood, this small, inexpensive hotel is sparsely furnished but clean. Three of its 21 rooms are on the roof with a terrace that overlooks tile rooftops and the distant **Pincio** gardens. Breakfast is included. ♦ Via Laurina 34 (between Via del Babuino and Via del Corso). 3223674; fax 3200395

17 Hosteria Pizzeria Al Vantaggio ★$$ Romans traditionally eat gnocchi on Thursday. At this simple trattoria, the homemade variety is lighter than elsewhere, and the tomato sauce they are served in is rich and delicious. ♦ M-Sa lunch and dinner. Via del Vantaggio 35 (between Via del Corso and Via di Ripetta). 3236848

18 La Buca di Ripetta ★★★$$ This excellent, cheery family-run trattoria serves simple, delicious food. The wonderful vegetable selections include pencil-thin, succulent *asparagi* (asparagus) served *alla Bismark* (with a fried egg on top). There are traditional Roman pasta dishes as well as such grilled-meat specialties as *lombata di vitello* (veal chop drizzled with lemon). The place is air-conditioned and open on Sunday, but go early—it's always crowded. ♦ Tu-Sa lunch and dinner; Su lunch; closed in August. Reservations recommended. Via di Ripetta 36 (between Via del Vantaggio and Via Angelo Brunetti). 3219391

19 Armeria Antiquaria This little curiosity shop is crammed with ancient guns, sabers, old military uniforms, helmets, and an army of lead soldiers. ♦ M afternoon; Tu-F; Sa morning. Via del Babuino 161 (at Via Gesù e Maria). 3614158

20 All Saints Anglican Church Designed by **George E. Street** in 1879, this Gothic Revival structure holds Communion services in English. ♦ Su 8:30AM, 10:30AM; evensong 6:30PM. Via del Babuino 153/B (entrance on Via Gesù e Maria). 6794357

21 Livio de Simone The chic bags and suitcases of all sizes displayed here may be expensive, but the hand-painted canvas they're made from is exquisite, and they have luxuriously soft leather corners. ♦ M afternoon; Tu-F; Sa morning. Via San Giacomo 23 (between Via del Babuino and Via del Corso). 6783906

22 Canova's Studio Now an art gallery, this was once the studio where the sculptor Antonio Canova (1757-1822) created his masterpieces of realism in marble, so polished and smooth they seem alive. ♦ M afternoon; Tu-F; Sa morning. Via del Corea and Via Antonio Canova. No phone

23 Galleria Gabbiano One of Rome's premier contemporary art galleries (with New York connections), this space often mounts eye-catching works by new international artists. ♦ Tu-Sa. Via della Frezza 51 (at Via del Corea). 3227049

24 Antonio & Raffaele It's getting increasingly difficult to find an old-time barbershop in Rome, making the jovial Franno brothers a rare (and popular) breed. Their traditional shop, in the neighborhood since 1959, overlooks a tiny courtyard with a garden. ♦ Tu-Sa by appointment. Via della Frezza 56 (between Via del Corea and Via di Ripetta). 3227001

25 Gusto ★★★$$ In Italian, *gusto* means taste, and there's certainly no lack of it here. The crowd is well-heeled, the decor industrial-chic, and the menu progressive for provincial Rome. Four main areas on two levels include a 500-bottle wine bar, with 20 by the glass; a pizzeria offering authentic Neapolitan-style pizza; a restaurant serving everything from spaghetti with vegetables and ginger sautéed in a wok to the more traditional fillet of swordfish with roasted red pepper and zucchini; and a store stocked with an amazing collection of kitchenware, cookbooks, food products, and wines. A series of wine-tasting seminars and cooking courses are in the works, as are plans for a cigar-smoking corner. There's live music two nights a week. ♦ Daily lunch and dinner. Piazza Augusto Imperatore 9 (at Via di Ripetta). 3226273

26 Bar Maneschi ★$ Real fruit sherbets in at least 15 flavors are among the selections in this popular ice-cream parlor. In the heat of summer, nothing quenches thirst faster and better than a *granita di limone,* crushed ice with freshly squeezed lemons. Just keep adding water to it or drink it straight. ♦ M-Sa 7AM-10PM. Via del Corso 66 (between Via Vittoria and Via dei Greci). 36001733

Hotel Mozart

27 Hotel Mozart $$ The rooms are not vast, but the high ceilings go on forever in this 56-room hotel, which has a reputation for personalized service. Each room is spanking clean and has its own bath and satellite TV. Ask for one of the 14 new rooms with elegant terra-cotta floor tiles and, in some, a bathtub. There's no restaurant, but breakfast is included. ♦ Via dei Greci 23/B (between Via del Babulno and Via del Corso). 36001915; fax 36001735

Within the Hotel Mozart:

La Luna d'Oro This American-style bar is worth seeking when you want a real martini, or you want to linger over a cup of coffee. ♦ M-Sa. 36001716

28 Chiesa di San Atanasio Giacomo della Porta designed this home of the Greek Orthodox Church of Rome in about 1580. Services are conducted here in Greek. Every 2 May, St. Athanasius's Day is observed with the Byzantine rite. Inside, a wooden iconostasis divides the triple apse from the rest of the short nave. Adjacent is the **Greek College** founded by Pope Gregory XIII in 1576 to educate young Greek priests whose seminaries were lost in 1453 when Byzantium fell to the Turks. The facade was rebuilt in 1769 and is connected to the church by an overhead bridge. ♦ Via del Babuino (between Via dei Greci and Via San Giacomo

28 Fontana da Babuino (Babuino Fountain) This is one of the famous "talking statues" of Rome, so-named because they were decked with satirical, witty placards criticizing the city's rich and powerful. The fountain's basin is from a classical Roman bath. The reclining figure behind the waterspout was meant to be Silenus, the mythological figure with a horse's ears and tail, but the local wits quickly dubbed it a baboon; the street soon followed suit and was changed to Via del Babuino. One of the first privately financed public fountains, it was placed here by Alessandro Grandi, whose vast holdings stretched up to Pincio Hill behind **Piazza del Popolo.** Behind the fountain is the oldest artist's studio in the area, belonging to four generations of sculptors from the Tadolini family. ♦ Via del Babuino and Via dei Greci

29 Oliver Headlining here is high-fashion designer Valentino's off-the-rack line for young men and women. But you don't have to be young to enjoy the interior of this well-designed store named after Valentino's pet pug. ♦ M-Sa (no midday closing). Via del Babuino 60 (between Via d'Alibert and Via dell'Orto di Napoli). 36001906

29 Amedeo Di Castro Now under the direction of Amedeo's son Richard, this traditional and reliable antiques dealer specializes in period paintings and such art objects as bas-relief sculptures and large terra-cotta statues. ♦ M afternoon; Tu-F; Sa morning. Via del Babuino 77 (between Via d'Alibert and Via dell'Orto di Napoli). 3207650

30 Il Cortile Art Gallery Inside the courtyard of a palazzo is a contemporary art gallery emphasizing the avant-garde. When an opening is staged here, the cream of Roman society fills the courtyard. ♦ M afternoon; Tu-F; Sa morning. Via del Babuino 51 (between Via Vittoria and Via dei Greci). 6785724

30 Zoffoli Antique silver, tiny Fabergé eggs, and old hat pins are among the charming objects featured in this little shop. ♦ M-F (no midday closing); Sa morning. Via del Babuino 137 (between Via Vittoria and Via dei Greci). 6790628

30 W. Apolloni Red velvet swags, white marble busts, big paintings, and glistening fountains adorn this commercial temple of period pieces and antiques. The highly lacquered 17th-century convivial genre scenes complete the precious ensemble. ♦ M afternoon; Tu-F; Sa morning. Via del Babuino 133 (between Via Vittoria and Via dei Greci). 36002216

30 Artimport Sheffield silver pieces and Victorian silver teething rings and ivory rattles are featured here along with nutcrackers of all sizes and shapes. ♦ M afternoon; Tu-F; Sa morning. Via del Babuino 150 (between Via Vittoria and Via dei Greci). 36002189; fax 3222529

The population of the city under the Roman Empire reached three million; during the Middle Ages it shrank to tens of thousands.

---

31 Gente Extremely popular among young Roman women, this boutique has four siblings sprinkled throughout the city. The merchandise is not cheap, but well-cut, well-made original styles are the norm. ♦ M afternoon; Tu-F; Sa morning. Via del Babuino 81 (between Via d'Alibert and Via dell'Orto di Napoli). 3207671. Also at: Via Frattina G9 (between Via Mario de' Fiori and Via Belsiana). 6789132

32 Emporio Armani It's the hallmark of elegant simplicity: beige-on-beige for summer; gray-on-gray for winter. Designer Giorgio Armani showcases his ready-to-wear line at this eye-catching store, which is worth seeing even if you can't afford to buy anything. The men's and women's haute couture boutique is at Via Condotti 77 (6991460). ♦ M afternoon; Tu-Sa. Via del Babuino 140 (between Via Vittoria and Via dei Greci). 3221581

33 Flos This light store features lamps in simple linear designs that create their own space. ♦ M-W, F-Sa; Th morning. Via del Babuino 84 (between Via d'Alibert and Via dell'Orto di Napoli). 3207690

34 Arturo Ferrante Antiques Run by one of the most reputable dealers in Rome, featured here are classic still lifes, 18th-century bas-reliefs in pale pink clay, a selection of micromosaics, and such Neo-Classical furnishings as armchairs, sofas, and consoles. ♦ M afternoon; Tu-F; Sa morning. Via del Babuino 42 (at Via d'Alibert). 36001723

35 Missoni Sport Missoni applies super-colorful, super-busy designs to sportswear, ties, umbrellas, and shoes. ♦ M afternoon; Tu-Sa (no midday closing). Via del Babuino 96/B (at Via d'Alibert). 6797971. Also at: Piazza di Spagna 78 (between Via dei Condotti and Via delle Carrozze). 6792555

36 Pinci There's a good assortment of all forms of brass paraphernalia here—drawer pulls, soap dishes, ornaments, fixtures, clothes hooks, even small statues. Objects in such unusual finishes as dull brass or permanently treated silvery-gray pewter are also featured. ♦ M afternoon; Tu-F; Sa morning. Via del Babuino 128 (at Via Vittoria). 6795154

37 C.U.C.I.N.A. This is no bargain-basement kitchen outlet, but even the turkey basters look great in this shop that stocks everything you need to create perfect pasta dishes and anything else in the *cucina* (kitchen). ♦ M-Sa (no midday closing). Via del Babuino 118/A (between Via della Croce and Via Vittoria). 6791275

ARCHIVI ALINARI

38 Alinari Photographs by the three 19th-century Florentine brothers—Giuseppe, Romualdo, and Leopoldo Alinari—are almost as treasured as Botticelli paintings. This store carries their vintage photos, as well as ones by other great camera-wielding chroniclers of Italy's past. The staff will help you locate turn-of-the-century shots of **Piazza Venezia**, for example, in their archives, and order prints from the Florence headquarters. Selected photography books are also available. ♦ M afternoon; Tu-F; Sa morning. Via d'Alibert 16/A (just east of Via del Babuino). 6792923; fax 69941998

39 Via Margutta 110 Renowned film director Federico Fellini and his actress wife Giulietta Masina *(La Strada, Nights of Cabiria)* lived at this address until their deaths in 1994. ♦ Between Via d'Alibert and Via dell'Orto di Napoli

40 Mario Oasi In this antiques shop a highly ornate 18th-century mirror with almost life-sized cherubs and Venuses looks as if it came from one of Rome's many princely palaces. Go through the store to check out the two stunning 17th-century terra-cotta Turks that guard the Via del Babuino entrance. ♦ M afternoon; Tu-F; Sa morning. Via Margutta 66 (between Via d'Alibert and Via dell'Orto di Napoli); alternate entrance at Via del Babuino 83. 3207585

40 Osteria Margutta ★$$$ An attractive restaurant reflecting the bohemian atmosphere of this studio-lined street offers largely traditional fare like *bucatini all'amatriciana* (thick spaghetti in a sauce of bacon, onion, tomato, and hot pepper) and roast lamb. ♦ M-Sa lunch and dinner until late. Via Margutta 82 (between Via d'Alibert and Via dell'Orto di Napoli). 3231025

41 Via Margutta 53/A Step into this courtyard and you will find two beautiful black-and-white mosaics draped on the right-hand wall. These are excellent examples of the antique Roman manner. ♦ At Via dell'Orto di Napoli

ROBERTO DELLA VALLE
WORKS OF ART &
INTERIOR DECORATION

42 Roberto della Valle The mosaic floors, marble busts, and heavy red silk curtains (really trompe l'oeil wallpaper) make this antiques shop seem like a Roman villa. ♦ M afternoon; Tu-F; Sa morning. Via Margutta 85 (between Via dell'Orto di Napoli and Vicolo del Babuino). 3207693

42 Turchi Bodies and limbs of ancient marble statuary greet customers at this antiques shop. Valerio Turchi has also collected superb Carthaginian-style mosaics from the third century AD, some showing antelopes in polychrome marble. ♦ M afternoon; Tu-F; Sa morning. Via Margutta 91/A (between Via Orti di Napoli and Vicolo del Babuino). 3235047; fax 3233209

43 Avignonese Attilio Amato always has some new line of beautiful objects for the home: wonderful terra-cotta boxes, bowls, lamps; burnished wooden pots and columns; marble obelisks and spheres; and great misty glass jars wired as lamps. ♦ M afternoon; Tu-F; Sa morning. Via Margutta 16 (between Vicolo del Babuino and Via del Babuino). 3614004

44 Margutta Vegeteriano ★★$$ A warm, inviting ambience and such unusual pasta dishes as tagliatelle with avocado and mushrooms are the draws at this small vegetarian restaurant. The prix-fixe buffet at lunch includes an assortment of salads, cooked vegetables, and cold pastas. ♦ Daily lunch and dinner. Via Margutta 118 (between Vicolo del Babuino and Via del Babuino). 32650577

45 Pincio This attractive public park connects directly with the gardens of the **Villa Borghese** (see page 145). The view of the city looking down to **Piazza del Popolo** from the terrace is without parallel, especially at sunset, with the dome of **St. Peter's** silhouetted across the Tiber. The garden is known for the busts of famous Italians that edge its lanes and for an unusual 18th-century water clock in the center. ♦ Bounded by Viale dell'Orologio, Viale Gabriele d'Annunzio, Piazzale Napoleone I, Viale di Villa Medici, and Viale Valadier

"The blessing of Rome is not that this or that or the other isolated object is so very unsurpassable, but that the general air so contributes to impressions that are not as any other impressions anywhere else in the world."
Henry James, *Italian Hours*

Parla Italiano?

Italians have one of the healthiest attitudes toward their language: They don't expect you to speak Italian nor are they wildly ecstatic if you do. Rarely do they waste time giving grammar lessons—when they do correct your attempts, it usually is a reaction to what they hear rather than an admonition. Here are some basics to get you started. *Buona fortuna!* (Good luck!)

Hello, Good-Bye, and Other Essentials

Good morning	*Buongiorno*
Good afternoon/evening	*Buona sera*
Good night	*Buona notte*
How are you?	*Come sta?*
Good-bye	*Arrivederci*
Yes	*Sì*
No	*No*
Please	*Per favore/Per piacere*
Thank you	*Grazie*
You're welcome	*Prego*
Excuse me	*Permesso* (in crowds)/ *Mi scusi*
I'm sorry	*Mi dispiace*
I don't speak Italian	*Non parlo italiano*
Do you speak English?	*Parla inglese?*
I don't understand	*Non capisco*
Do you understand?	*Capisce?*
More slowly, please	*Più lentamente per favore*
I don't know	*Non lo so*
My name is . . .	*Mi chiamo . . .*
What is your name?	*Come si chiama?*
miss	*signorina*
madame, ma'am	*signora*
mister	*signor/e*
good	*buono/a*
bad	*cattivo/a*
open	*aperto/a*
closed	*chiuso/a*
entrance	*entrata*
exit	*uscita*
push	*spingere*
pull	*tirare*
What time does it open/close?	*A che ora apre/ chiude?*
today	*oggi*
tomorrow	*domani*
yesterday	*ieri*
week	*settimana*
month	*mese*
year	*anno*

Hotel Talk

I have a reservation	*Ho una prenotazione*
I would like. . .	*Vorrei. . .*
a double room	*una camera doppia*
a quiet room	*una camera tranquilla*
with (private) bath	*con bagno (privato)*
with air-conditioning	*con aria condizionata*
Does that price include . . . breakfast? taxes?	*Il prezzo comprende . . . prima colazione? tasse?*
Do you accept traveler's checks?	*Accettate i traveler's checks?*
Do you accept credit cards?	*Accettate le carte di credito?*

Restaurant Repartee

Waiter!	*Cameriere!*
menu	*lista*
I would like . . .	*Vorrei . . .*
a glass of . . .	*un bicchiere di . . .*
a bottle of . . .	*una bottiglia di . . .*
a liter of . . .	*un litro di . . .*
The check, please	*Il conto, per favore*
Is the service charge included?	*Il servizio è incluso?*
I think there is a mistake in the bill	*Credo che ci sia uno sbaglio nel mio conto*
lunch	*pranzo*
dinner	*cena*
tip	*mancia*
bread	*pane*
butter	*burro*
pepper	*pepe*
salt	*sale*
sugar	*zucchero*
soup	*zuppa*
salad	*insalata*
vegetables	*verdure*
cheese	*formaggio*
egg	*uova*
bacon	*pancetta*
omelette	*frittata*
meat	*carne*
chicken	*pollo*
veal	*vitello*
fish	*pesce*
seafood, shellfish	*frutta di mare*
pork	*maiale*
ham	*prosciutto*
chops	*costoletta, braciola* (pork)
dessert	*dolce*

As You Like It

cold	*freddo/a*
hot	*caldo/a*
sweet	*dolce*
(very) dry	*(molto) secco*
broiled	*alla griglia*

baked	al forno	one-way ticket	biglietto di solo andata
boiled	bollito/a	round-trip ticket	biglietto di andata e ritorno
fried	fritto/a	first class	prima classe
raw	crudo/a	second class	seconda classe
rare	poco cotto/a	smoking	fumare
well done	ben cotto/a	no smoking	non fumare
spicy	piccante	Does this train go to . . . ?	Questo treno va a . . . ?

Thirsty No More

		Does this bus go to . . . ?	Quest'autobus va a . . . ?
hot chocolate (cocoa)	cioccolata calda	Where is/are . . . ?	Dov'è/Dove sono . . . ?
black coffee	un caffè	How far is it from here to . . . ?	Quanti chilometri sono da qui a . . . ?
coffee with hot milk	cappuccino, caffè latte		
milk	latte		

The Bare Necessities

tea	tè	aspirin	aspirina
fruit juice	succo di frutta	Band-Aids	cerotti
water	acqua	barbershop, beauty shop	barbiere, estetista
mineral water	acqua minerale	condom	profilattico
carbonated	gassata	dry cleaner	tintoria
non-carbonated	non gassata	laundromat/laundry	lavanderia automatica/ lavanderia
ice	ghiaccio		
beer	birra	letter	lettera
red wine	vino rosso	post office	ufficio postale
white wine	vino bianco	postage stamp	francobollo

Sizing It Up

		postcard	carta postale
How much does this cost?	Quanto costa?	sanitary napkins	assorbenti igienici
inexpensive	a buon mercato	shampoo	shampoo
expensive	caro/a	shaving cream	schiuma da barba
large	grande	soap	sapone
small	piccolo/a	tampons	assorbenti interni
long	lungo/a	tissues	fazzoletti di carta
short	corto/a	toilet paper	carta igienica
old	vecchio/a	toothpaste	dentifricio
new	nuovo/a	Where is the bathroom/toilet?	Dov'è il bagno/ la toiletta?
used	usato/a		
this one	questo/a	men's room	signori, uomini
a little	un poco	women's room	signore, donne
a lot	molto		

On the Move

Days of the Week (lowercased in Italian)

north	nord	Monday	lunedì
south	sud	Tuesday	martedì
east	est	Wednesday	mercoledì
west	ovest	Thursday	giovedì
right	destra	Friday	venerdì
left	sinistra	Saturday	sabato
highway	autostrada	Sunday	la domenica
street	strada		

Numbers

gas station	stazione di benzina	zero	zero
straight ahead	sempre diritto	one	uno
here	qui	two	due
there	là, lì	three	tre
bus stop	fermata dell'autobus	four	quattro
bus station	stazione degli autobus	five	cinque
train station	stazione ferroviaria	six	sei
subway	metropolitana	seven	sette
airport	aeroporto	eight	otto
tourist information	informazione turistica	nine	nove
city map	pianta	ten	dieci

Piazza Barberini and Via Veneto

In the last decades before Christ, when this side of **Quirinale Hill** was rolling countryside, the area was populated by rural estates belonging to wealthy Roman politicians like Sallust and successful generals, including Lucullus. The latter held sumptuous banquets in the gardens of his villa and has been immortalized by the word "Lucullan," used to describe lavish feasts. During the Renaissance the powerful Barberini family carried on the Lucullian tradition in **Palazzo Barberini**, which today houses the **Galleria Nazionale d'Arte Antica** (National Gallery of Ancient Art). Topping the Quirinale is the largest of these private villas, the **Villa Borghese**, a 17th-century estate turned public park that includes three museums and a lake.

In the middle of the 19th century, the **Termini** railroad station was built nearby, radically changing the destiny of the entire **Piazza Barberini** district—sleepy rural roads soon became bustling thoroughfares carrying travelers to and from the new station. The surrounding neighborhood developed into a dense area filled with hotels, restaurants, and cafes for tourists.

Halfway through the 20th century, one of these thoroughfares, Via Vittorio Veneto, attracted world attention as the epitome of a heady era known as "La Dolce Vita" from the movie of the same name. The great director Federico Fellini intended the title of his film, "the sweet life," as an ironic indictment of the depersonalization and emptiness of postwar materialism and centered it on this area of posh hotels and expensive cafes frequented by the famous and would-be famous. The 1950s and 1960s were also the heyday of filming at Cinecittà— Rome's Hollywood-on-the-Tiber, as it was nicknamed. When they weren't on

...e set, stars like Elizabeth Taylor, Richard Burton, Ingrid Bergman, Gina Lollabrigida, Sophia Loren, Orson Welles, the battling Frank Sinatra and Ava Gardner, and Anthony Quinn held court in Via Veneto's sidewalk cafes, surrounded by a coterie of fans and flashbulb-popping paparazzi. Today what is left of that beautiful life seems to prefer more enclosed hangouts like the discos around the **Pantheon** or the cafes in **Piazza del Popolo**. But luxury remains the keynote on Via Veneto, where the restaurants, cafes, and hotels still try to live up to the lavish standards set by Lucullus more than 2,000 years ago.

1 Bernini's Fountains Bernini's cleverly designed fountains in **Piazza Barberini** illustrate the importance of water, rocks, and sea animals in Baroque sculpture. For example, the **Fontana del Tritone** (Triton Fountain; 1637), in the center of the square shows a triton (a mermale) blowing a jet of water out of a conch shell while kneeling on an opened scallop shell held aloft by four dolphins. At the corner of Via Veneto, three giant bees crawl along another scallop shell to drink in the big basin of the **Fontana delle Api** (Fountain of the Bees; 1644). This fountain was dedicated to one of Bernini's patrons, Pope Urban VIII, of the Barberini family, whose emblem—the bee—appears frequently in this square and in the adjacent palazzo. In the early 17th century, about the time the Barberini name became important in Rome, the city was invaded by swarms of bees—an event that, by some accounts, contributed to the origin of this ubiquitous family symbol. ♦ Piazza Barberini

Behind the Fontana delle Api:

Palazzo Coppedè There are several examples of Art Nouveau and Art Deco elements on Via Veneto. This palazzo was designed in 1927 by the Art Nouveau architect **Gino Coppedè,** who also shaped an entire quarter—Quartiere Coppedè—of the city around **Piazza Quadrato** (also known as **Piazza Coppedè**). Notice the carved wood monkey over the main doorway, and above it the gruesome stylized Medusa. ♦ Via Vittorio Veneto 7

2 CIR Hand-embroidered baby linens, christening gowns, and other items for the well-dressed baby are made in Florence by this outstanding traditional firm. Household linens include place mats and appliquéd or cutwork banquet cloths. Embroidered and mono-grammed handkerchiefs are also featured items. ♦ M afternoon; Tu-F; Sa morning. Piazza Barberini 11 (between Via Vittorio Veneto and Via della Purificazione). 4883433, 4885470

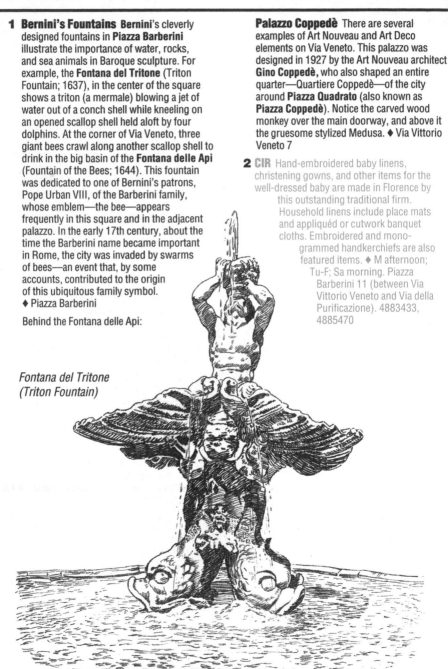

Fontana del Tritone
(Triton Fountain)

3 Moriconi Buy presents here for the folks back home—silver frames, Venetian glass, and ceramic bells. ◆ M-Sa (no midday closing). Piazza Barberini 7 (between Via della Purificazione and Via Sistina). 4881949

4 Il Giardino ★$$ The *giardino* (garden) at this establishment, originally an Inn opened in 1909, was at one time a boccie court. Now it's a courtyard dining area that offers alfresco meals in summer and is converted into an indoor conservatory in winter. Roman dishes, including *penne all'arrabbiata* (pasta with spicy tomato sauce, sausage, and bacon) and *saltimbocca alla romana* (veal cutlets fried with sage, ham, and white wine) are featured, although numerous other pasta and meat dishes are served; *chateaubriand al Giardino* is also a specialty. The house wine is Morello di Scanzano and other Italian wines are available. Smiling service and reasonable prices make this restaurant worth a stop. ◆ Tu-Su lunch and dinner. Via Zucchelli 29 (between Via del Tritone and Via Sistina). 4885202

5 Le Colline Emiliane ★★★$$ An unprepossessing entry leads into a quiet, country-style trattoria that serves unforgettable, hearty specialties from the Emilia-Romagna region. The ingredients are always fresh, and the Parma ham and homemade pasta choices (often being rolled out before you) approach perfection. For a main course, try the veal cutlet Bologna-style (breaded, with prosciutto, melted cheese, and a dab of tomato sauce on top). Truffles are offered in season. Be sure to leave room for the homemade apple cake. The house white wine is an agreeable Sangiovese, but there is an excellent selection of Lambruscos and other Emilian wines. ◆ M-Th, Sa-Su lunch and dinner; closed in August. Reservations required. No credit cards accepted. Via degli Avignonesi 22 (at Via del Boccaccio). 4817538

6 Palazzo Barberini The Barberini family's pontiff, Urban VIII, commissioned the best architects of the time—**Gian Lorenzo Bernini, Francesco Borromini,** and **Carlo Maderno**— to work on this palace from 1625 to 1633. The imposing, harmonious facade was designed to impress, and although it lacks both lightness of touch and architectural variety, the last windows on the ends of the top floor are ingenious. They were designed by the fanciful young **Borromini** while he was apprenticed first to **Maderno,** whom he worshiped, and then to **Bernini,** whom he hated. These two windows reveal **Borromini**'s ability to transform flat classical forms into imaginative, new sculptural motifs. Another good example is just inside the entrance on the right—**Borromini**'s whimsical corkscrew oval staircase, with its gently rising steps. Compare it to **Bernini**'s heavy square stairwell to the left. ◆ Admission (includes entrance to Galleria Nazionale d'Arte Antica, see below). Tu-Su morning. Via delle Quattro Fontane 13 (between Via XX Settembre and Piazza Barberini). 4814591

Within the Palazzo Barberini:

Galleria Nazionale d'Arte Antica (National Gallery of Ancient Art) One flight up **Bernini**'s square staircase, a collection of 13th- to 16th-century paintings hangs in the ornate former reception rooms of the palace. Most famous is Raphael's early–16th-century portrait **(Room 6)** of his mistress and favorite model, *La Fornarina,* actually painted by Raphael's favorite apprentice, Giulio Romano. Don't miss the portraits of *Erasmus* (1517) by Quentin Massys **(Room 11)** and *Henry VIII* (1540) by Hans Holbein the Younger **(Room 11).** The pièce de résistance is the ceiling in the former ballroom by Pietro da Cortona (1633-39), in which the Barberini family symbols burst through the confines of a fresco and find their way into an allegory of Divine Providence. ◆ Admission (includes entrance to Palazzo Barberini, see above). Tu-Sa (no midday closing); Su morning. 4814591

7 Quattro Fontane (Four Fountains) Pope Sixtus V, Rome's great Baroque city planner, had these fountains built in 1589 and placed to mark the junction of two key streets: Via del Quirinale, which led from **Palazzo del Quirinale** to **Porta Pia,** and Via delle Quattro Fontane (the extension of Via Sistina), which stretches from the **Chiesa di Trinità dei Monti** at the top of the **Spanish Steps** to the important **Basilica di Santa Maria Maggiore.** (It was typical of the era to carve straight streets through the medieval jumble of hovels and alleyways to connect major places of pilgrimage.) At three of the four ends of this symbolic cross—except in front of **Porta Pia**—loom monumental obelisks that act like exclamation points, emphasizing the significance of this nexus. Clockwise, starting at **Chiesa di San Carlo alle Quattro Fontane,** the four fountains have reclining statues representing the Tiber River, the goddess Juno, the goddess Diana (by Pietro da Cortona), and the Nile. ◆ Via delle Quattro Fontane and Via del Quirinale

8 Chiesa di San Carlo alle Quattro Fontane Borromini's most complete architectural work was this monastery church built 1665-68 for the Spanish Discalced Trinitarians, an obscure and poor religious order that had only a tiny, irregularly shaped piece of hilly land on which to construct a church and living quarters. The facade—usually referred to by the diminutive "San Carlino"—is a sweeping double S-curve on two floors, wedged between other buildings on Via del Quirinale. The church's interior intensifies the alternating concave and convex treatment with a profusion of columns and niches that carries the eye down the relentless rippling sides of the nave to the main altar. Above is an oval-shaped dome with fanciful coffering, bathed in light from semihidden windows. This dome is not visible from outside and so comes as a complete surprise. Ahead of his time, **Borromini** was akin to contemporary architects in his passion for abstract geometric forms.Don't miss the adjoining, eight-sided cloister, a cramped and limited space in which **Borromini** produced the impossible: a space that is simultaneously monumental and light and airy. The walls of the cream-colored double loggia are incised with the simple geometric forms that are the basis of the floor plans for the church, dome, and bell tower. Note how the bays along the upper tier swell inward and outward and how the spokes of the balustrade alternate inverted

shapes so that the eye is never permitted to rest for long or become aware of the limited space. Finally, instead of the traditional fountain in the center of most cloisters, here there is a well, with its suggestion of depth.
♦ Via del Quirinale (between Via delle Quattro Fontane and Via Ferrara)

9 Chiesa di San Andrea al Quirinale In sharp contrast to **Borromini**'s church (see above) is this sanctuary (1658-70) designed by **Bernini** for the Jesuits. The interior is a burst of Baroque splendor—precious marbles, gilded sunbeams, stuccoed clouds, and a school of cherubs descending from the dome. The side altars are lit from hidden windows high in the walls. The facade has a projected porch held up by only two columns and emphasized by a sweeping staircase.
♦ Via del Quirinale (between Via delle Quattro Fontane and Via Ferrara)

10 Palazzo del Quirinale (Quirinal Palace) When this part of Rome was still countryside, this villa served as the summer home of the papacy until 1870, when Garibaldi conquered all of Rome except **Vatican City.** Today it is the residence of the President of Italy. Sprawling over an ancient hill named for the Sabine god of war, Quirino, this huge Baroque complex (illustrated below) was built upon the ruined foundations of the Baths of Constantine. Inside it has splendid varicolored marble floors that were once in the **Baths of Caracalla.** A half-dozen architects, including

*Palazzo del Quirinale
(Quirinal Palace)*

Ferdinando Fuga and **Domenico Fontana,** worked on the building after its first stone was turned in 1574. When Napoleon conquered Rome in 1809, he ousted the pope, seized the palace, and brought in French architects to redesign it. ♦ Free. Guided tours: Su morning. Changing of the guard every day at 4PM. Passport required for admission. Piazza del Quirinale and Via del Quirinale. 46991

11 Fontana dei Dioscuri (Fountain of the Dioscuri) In the middle of the square on a high pedestal flanking an obelisk are two giant third-century AD statues of the "Dioscuri," the other twins, besides Romulus and Remus, who are an important part of Roman lore. The figures are Roman copies of Greek originals and were found in the **Baths of Constantine** that once stood here. They show Castor and Pollux reining in their enormous horses. Between them is an Egyptian obelisk that stood in front of the tomb of Augustus and a large, dark gray granite basin (largely ornamental, as the water is rarely turned on) that was once a cattle trough in the **Roman Forum.** ♦ Piazza del Quirinale

12 Hotel Bernini Bristol $$$$ Hands-down winner of the ugliest hotel in the Centro Storico, this 127-room establishment makes up for what it lacks in the architectural inspiration and glamour of its competitors on Via Veneto with efficient, no-nonsense service and beautiful views of the piazza and Bernini's fountain. The bar, just beyond the front hall, is a good meeting place, and the restaurant serves a full breakfast (not included in the rate). ♦ Piazza Barberini 23 (between Via Barberini and Via di San Nicolò da Tolentino). 4883051; fax 4824266

13 Da Tullio ★★$$ Savvy visitors to this genuine Tuscan trattoria start with *pappardelle alla lepre* (very wide ribbon pasta in a thick rabbit sauce) or, in season (late winter into spring), *carciofi* (artichokes cooked in fresh mint and olive oil). The *bistecca alla fiorentina* (T-bone steak) is priced by the kilo or fraction thereof; one is enough for two. ♦ M-Sa lunch and dinner Sept-June; M-F lunch and dinner in July; closed in August. Reservations recommended. Via di San Nicolò da Tolentino 26 (between Vicolo di San Nicolò da Tolentino and Piazza Barberini). 4818564; fax 4874125

14 Hotel Alexandra $$ High ceilings, full-length mirrors, and gleaming polished wood lend Old World charm to this 19th-century mansion that has been managed by the same family for four generations. This is not a luxury hotel (although all 45 rooms have TVs, private baths, and double-paned glass in the windows facing Via Veneto), but it is very well located. Breakfast (included) is served in an antiques-filled salon where black-and-white photos of turn-of-the-century Rome hang on the walls. Free parking is available. ♦ Via Vittorio Veneto 18 (at Via dei Cappuccini). 4881943; fax 4871804

15 Chiesa di Santa Maria della Concezione (Church of the Immaculate Conception) A macabre reminder of death stands in the basement of this otherwise unimpressive 1625 church on the street once world renowned for its uninhibited celebration of *"La Dolce Vita."* To the right of the front steps is the entrance to a cemetery **(Cimitero dei Cappuccini)** entirely decorated with the bones and skulls of over 4,000 Capuchin monks who lived and died here between 1528 and 1870. Tibiae, vertebrae, and skulls of the former friars adorn the walls and ceilings of six rooms, forming bizarre rococo arabesques and curlicues that include a wreath made entirely of skulls and giant flowers made out of femurs. In the last room a skeleton holds a scale in one hand and a sickle in the other in the tradition of the Grim Reaper, while just around the corner are the shops and sidewalk cafes of Via Veneto. This is Rome at its contradictory best. ♦ Donation. Daily. No photographs permitted. Via Vittorio Veneto 27 (between Piazza Barberini and Via Molise)

HOTEL MAJESTIC ROMA

16 Hotel Majestic Roma $$$$ Something is slightly off about this grand 1889 hotel—maybe it's the plastic shower curtains or the recycled and mismatched furniture in some of the 95 rooms and 6 junior suites. Nevertheless over the years it has attracted the Italian-American sector of Hollywood—Frank Sinatra, Liza Minelli, and Madonna. The garden restaurant includes an outdoor tented pavilion in summer. There's no lobby to speak of. The classiest thing in this hotel is the black wrought-iron Art Deco elevators with floors indicated in gold Roman numerals. Breakfast is included. ♦ Via Vittorio Veneto 50 (between Via dei Cappuccini and Via Cadore). 4828014; fax 4880984

17 Caffè delle Nazioni $ Tourists dictate the menu, light by Roman standards, at this cafe. It features pizza (served here at lunch unlike other places), a few pasta dishes, sandwiches, beer on tap, ice cream, and coffee. Tourists sit outdoors; employees from the neighborhood prefer the tables inside. ♦ M-Sa lunch and dinner. Via Vittorio Veneto 97 (between Via Leonida Bissolati and Via Molise). 4884592

Restaurants/Clubs: Red   **Hotels:** Blue

Shops/♥ Outdoors: Green   **Sights/Culture:** Black

18 Grand Hotel Palace $$$$ Designed by **Marcello Piacentini,** this hostelry has long been a favorite with heads of state. The 97 air-conditioned rooms and 5 junior suites are draped in elegance, with Damask-covered walls, canopied beds, and hand-painted 17th-century Venetian furniture. The baths have Jacuzzis and double sinks, and there is double glazing on all the windows. On the ground-floor salon is an Art Deco fresco cycle by Guido Cadorin (1926), showing the smart set of that period attending a party in this area. The men wear tuxedos; the women are in flapper dresses. One is a poker-faced portrait of Mussolini's mistress, Clara Petacci. A cigarette dangling from her mouth, she is staring off in the distance, seemingly bored with the whole show. The furniture is vintage 1920s—gold and red damask sofas and mahogany end tables. In the evening a piano bar is featured. Amenities include a restaurant, beauty salon, and spa. ◆ Via Vittorio Veneto 70 (between Via Cadore and Via Liguria). 47871; fax 47871800

19 Palazzo Margherita This grand 1890 palazzo (illustrated below) is the former residence of Queen Mother Margherita, the widow of King Umberto I of the Royal House of Savoy. Designed by **Gaetano Koch,** today it houses the **US Embassy.** ◆ Via Vittorio Veneto 119 (at Via Leonida Bissolati). 46741

20 La Residenza $$ On a quiet street one block from Via Veneto, this small, attractive villa/hotel with air-conditioning and a garden is favored by US diplomats at the nearby embassy. First it was a private villa, then a convent; today it is a 27-room hotel. Seven of the rooms have terraces; others have small balconies but are larger inside. The public rooms have Louis XVI furniture, fireplaces, and Baroque mirrors. There's no restaurant, but the complimentary breakfast buffet is well recommended. ◆ Via Emilia 22 (between Via Liguria and Via Ludovisi). 4880789; fax 485721

21 Eden Hotel $$$$ This luxurious 100-year-old hotel—considered Rome's best in its class—was renovated by the British Forte chain. Lord Forte has seen to it that all the amenities expected at a deluxe hotel are present in the 101 rooms and 11 suites, including antique oil paintings over the headboards and large baths made from Carrara marble. Guest services include medical assistance, airline reservations, theater and opera reservations, car rental, and a fully equipped gym. Ideally located halfway between Via Veneto and the **Spanish Steps,** it offers striking views from its rooftop and has one of the best-managed bars in the city. It's the perfect place to toast a Roman sunset. Ask about weekend rates. ◆ Via Ludovisi 49 (at Via di Porta Pinciana). 478121; fax 4821584

Within the Eden Hotel:

La Terrazza dell'Eden ★★★★$$$$ Besides being the former personal chef to the Prince and Princess of Wales, Enrico Derflingher—head chef at this lovely rooftop restaurant—has received top ratings by many international food critics. One of his most inspired creations is a vol-au-vent of lobster and fresh asparagus. Equally inventive is a combination of seafood, fennel, and *limoncello* (lemon liqueur). And the climax is a perfect, light-as-air meringue drizzled with fresh raspberry sauce. The service is cordial and impeccable. ◆ M-Sa lunch and dinner. Reservations recommended. 4743551

22 Marcello ★★★$$ Offering the best quality-to-price ratio in the Via Veneto area, this superior, attractive restaurant appeals to both the eye and the palate. Gnocchi, eaten every Thursday all over Rome, come on a large

Palazzo Margherita

plate with roasted veal and a vegetable—three courses in one. The lowly Roman *baccalà* (salt cod) is transformed into a sophisticated antipasto by the addition of raisins, pine nuts, and tomatoes. The house white wine is sparkling but dry, and the summer desserts include scoops of gelato in a snifter smothered with wild berries or peaches. This is one of those rare restaurants where you can put yourself entirely in the care of the hosts. Alfresco dining is available in nice weather. ♦ M-Sa lunch and dinner. Reservations recommended. Via Aurora 37 (between Via Ludovisi and Via Lombardia). 4819467

23 Hotel Savoy Buffet $ This self-service buffet offers a variety of good hot and cold entreés at a fixed price. Wine and other drinks are not included. ♦ M-F lunch. No credit cards accepted. Via Ludovisi 15 (at Via Emilia). 4744141.

24 Regina Hotel Baglioni $$$$ Part of the well-managed northern Italian chain, this century-old property is small enough that the concierge will remember you, yet large enough (132 rooms) to offer such services as faxes and whirlpool tubs in the 7 suites, plus private baths, air-conditioning, rooms for nonsmokers, a garage, bar, and restaurant. ♦ Via Vittorio Veneto 72 (at Via Ludovisi). 421111; fax 42012130

25 Hotel Excelsior $$$$ The preferred hotel of Liz Taylor and other Hollywood luminaries during the *"La Dolce Vita"* era, this architecturally extravagant grande dame (built in 1906) features 321 well-appointed rooms and a minaret towering over the central point of Via Veneto. The marble-and-gold-festooned French Empire–style lobby leads to an attractive and sophisticated bar. The amenities in this member of the Starwood Hotels and Resorts Luxury Collection include a small business center (two computers, a fax machine, and a printer), garage, restaurant, lounge, and health club. ♦ Via Vittorio Veneto 125 (between Via Boncompagni and Via Sicilia). 4708, 800/221.2340; fax 4826205; www.luxurycollection.com

26 Doney's ★$$ During the day there's hardly room for another tourist or businessperson at the outdoor tables in front of this once-trendy bar on Via Veneto, but at night it could use a few more customers. Inside is a tearoom and average restaurant. ♦ Tu-Su 8AM-2AM. Via Vittorio Veneto 145 (between Via Boncompagni and Via Sicilia). 4821790

27 Jackie O' Nostalgia doesn't come cheap in this improbably named, holdover nightclub from the salad days of disco, but it has kept the club ever popular and still swinging. ♦ Cover. M-Sa 9PM-2AM. Via Boncompagni 11 (between Via Toscana and Via Marche). 4885457

28 George's ★★$$$$ This was one of the most famous of the postwar hot spots that catered to the glitterati who lit up this era in Rome. Today you can still sit around a candlelit table on the garden terrace, sipping Dom Perignon, and being served flaming dishes by impeccable waiters in white ties and tails. The specialties, which have a Cordon Bleu touch, include a delicious steak carpaccio, elegant salads, and a creamy, light crème brûlée for dessert. ♦ M-Sa lunch and dinner; closed in August. Reservations recommended. Via Marche 7 (between Via Boncompagni and Via Sicilia). 42084575, 42745204; fax 42010032

29 Zi Umberto ★$ One of the few mamma-and-papa trattorie in an otherwise pretentious area, this place features game during the hunting season and offers flavorful seasonal foods year-round. Follow owners Elena and Franco Paoletti's advice, particularly for any kind of pasta featuring Elena's game sauce. The house white wine is the pale, fragrant, dry Verdicchio from the Lazio vineyards north of Rome. ♦ M-Sa lunch and dinner. No credit cards accepted. Via Sicilia 150 (at Via Piemonte). 4884519

30 Piccolo Abruzzo ★★$$ The chefs from the Abruzzo mountain region are famed the world over, and this restaurant specializes in such famous dishes from that area as *pasta alla chitarra* (square spaghetti), prepared by pressing a sheet of pasta dough through the strings of a cutter that resembles a *chitarra* (guitar). You could go on to roasted baby lamb or rabbit stew, but follow the custom here instead and *assaggiare* (taste) one or two other pasta or risotto dishes. ♦ M-Sa lunch and dinner. Reservations recommended. Via Sicilia 237 (between Via Lucania and Via Puglie). 42820176

31 Girarrosto Fiorentina ★★$$$ The atmosphere Is rustIc In thIs Tuscan restaurant. The fare begins with *crostini* (toasted bread slathered with liver pâté, black olive paste, etc.) Then come tender thin slices of prosciutto and salami, followed by robust bread soups or hearty pasta dishes with game sauces. Be sure to save room for the specialty—*bistecca alla fiorentina* (thick T-bone steak) grilled to perfection with just a bit of olive oil and fresh pepper. This popular spot stays open late for the theater crowd. ♦ M-Sa lunch and dinner. Reservations recommended. Via Sicilia 46 (between Via Toscana and Via Marche). 42880660

32 Giovanni ★★★$$$ Despite its elegant formality and distinguished cuisine, this restaurant is a family affair—Giovanni Sbrega tends to the swarms of serious eaters with the help of his wife, son, daughter, and nephew. The glorious fare of the Marche region is celebrated in such dishes as *castellucci* (soup made from small, tender lentils grown at high altitudes) and *calamaretti* (tiny grilled Adriatic squid). ♦ M-Th, Su lunch and dinner; F lunch. Reservations required for Friday lunch. Via Marche 64 (between Via Sicilia and Via Sardegna). 4821834

33 Murano Glass Examples of the famous glasswork from the island of Murano in the Venetian lagoon, including chandeliers, vases, and lamps, are for sale here. ♦ M-Sa. Via Sicilia 26 (between Via Marche and Via Vittorio Veneto). 4740610; fax 4743623

About 500,000 people get around Rome on *motorini* (mopeds), and about 30 are stolen daily.

In the Rome chapter of *Innocents Abroad* (1869), Mark Twain remarks that when he visited the Capuchin cemetery he was taken by the "weird laugh a full century old" on the face of one of the "dead and dried up monks," and he thought to himself, "surely it must have been a most extraordinary joke that this friar produced with his last breath since he has not got done laughing at it yet."

---

raphael salato

34 Raphael Salato Via Veneto is as much about shoes as *caffès,* and this store is one of the best. The quality of the shoes, bags, and other leather goods is superb. ♦ Daily. Via Vittorio Veneto 149 (between Via Lombardia and Via Lazio). 4821816

35 Andrea ★★★$$$ At first glance, this is just one more tony restaurant, but it really is one of Rome's most respected dining establishments. The cuisine sets the standard to which others aspire, and those seeking modern elegance won't go wrong. The pastas are traditional as opposed to nouvelle (try the homemade ravioli), and the seafood is fresh, not often the case in Rome. Heed the hosts' wine suggestions and book well in advance for an unforgettable lobster bouillabaisse— a meal in itself. ♦ M-F lunch and dinner; Sa dinner; closed three weeks in August. Reservations recommended. Via Sardegna 28 (between Via Toscana and Via Marche). 4740557; fax 4828151

36 Hotel Victoria $$$ Built at the turn of the century, many of the 108 rooms in this Swiss-owned hotel overlook the **Villa Borghese.** Guest rooms are decorated in a Victorian (of course) style and have private baths, satellite TV, and air-conditioning. A roof-garden restaurant, discount rates off-season, and free parking are just some of the other pluses. ♦ Via Campania 41 (at Via Marche). 473931; fax 4871890

37 Girarrosto Toscana ★★$$$ Dining in this bustling cellar of a Tuscan farmhouse is often hectic and less satisfying than a leisurely lunch in a neighborhood trattoria. But the gigantic, Chianti-laced T-bone steaks from the roaring open grill will delight any carnivore, and the dessert trolley will do the same for the sweet-toothed. Bear in mind, however, that the delectables you find on the table or that arrive unbidden—*ovoli* (mozzarella eggs), Tuscan salami, prosciutto, and the like—are not on the house. ♦ M-Tu, Th-Su lunch and dinner. Via Campania 29 (between Via Marche and Via Vittorio Veneto). 4821899

38 Harry's Bar ★★$$$ No relation to the locale of the same name in Venice, this is one of those dark mahogany-paneled places with tables a couple of yards apart, evocative of a London club. It makes for easier conversing than most Roman trattorie, which have yet to discover soundproofing. Start with a Bellini, a glass of Prosecco laced with fruit juice; then order the fresh scampi curry on white rice or the osso buco served with saffron rice. ♦ M-Sa lunch and dinner. Reservations required for dinner. Via Vittorio Veneto 150 (at Via di Porta Pinciana). 484643

Villa Borghese (Borghese Gardens)

39 Eliseo Hotel $$$ Ask for a room overlooking the gardens of the **French Academy** or go up to the rooftop restaurant for one of the most unforgettably romantic views of Rome since Hubert Robert painted the same towers of the **Villa Medici** as seen through the soaring trees. Each of the 50 air-conditioned rooms has a private bath, mini-bar, trouser press, and satellite TV. ♦ Via di Porta Pinciana 30 (between Via Lazio and Via Vittorio Veneto). 4870456; fax 4819629

40 Porta Pinciana This monumental travertine gate dates from the time of Emperor Honorius (AD 403), who built it to breach the **Aurelian Walls** which had surrounded Rome for 17 centuries. When Rome became the capital of a united Italy in 1870, progressive elements wanted to modernize the city, beginning with the old wall. Accordingly, they cut down the century-old trees in the great gardens of the palaces that had become municipal property, pushed through the embankments on either side of the river, and nearly tore down the **Aurelian Wall.** ♦ Piazzale Brasile and Via Vittorio Veneto

41 Villa Borghese (Borghese Gardens) A vast park—four miles in perimeter—was acquired and laid out by Cardinal Scipione Borghese at the beginning of the 17th century, when his uncle became Pope Paul V. It is now Rome's most magnificent public park, attracting joggers, picnickers, bicyclers, and in-line skaters. Don't miss the **Uccelleria** (aviary), the artificial lake, and **Piazza di Siena**

(named after the Borghese hometown), where an international horse show is held every spring. ♦ Entrances at Piazzale Flaminio and Piazzale Brasile

Within the Villa Borghese:

Galleria Borghese Cardinal Scipione Borghese, whose exquisite taste in art places him high among the world's greatest collectors, had this structure—designed by **Giovanni Vasanzio**—built in 1614 on the eastern side of the gardens to show off his collection of ancient statuary. The current sculpture collection occupies the ground-floor "museum"; the upper floor—the **Galleria**—contains the paintings that the cardinal amassed. He is well represented as a bon vivant in two portrait sculptures by Rome's most ubiquitous genius, Gian Lorenzo Bernini, whom Scipione seems to have discovered. Two centuries later, the sculptor of the moment was Antonio Canova (1757-1821), who produced the famous marble statue downstairs. It represents the other leading member of the Borghese clan, Pauline Bonaparte, in a characteristically dissolute pose—as the nude Venus, goddess of love. Other rooms contain more sculptures that Bernini did while still in his twenties. Compare the movement and excitement of his Baroque *David* with the Renaissance calm of Michelangelo's more famous work in Florence. Recently relocated to the ground floor (**Room 8**) are six of Caravaggio's finest paintings, including the alluring *Boy with a Basket of Fruit*

145

MUSEO ETRUSCO DI VILLA GIULIA
(VILLA GIULIA ETRUSCAN MUSEUM)

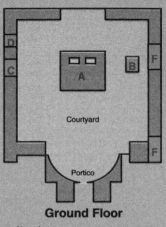

Ground Floor

A Nymphaeum
B Reconstruction of an Etruscan Temple
C Hercules and Apollo
D Sarcophagus of the Married Couple
E Barberini and Bernardini Tombs

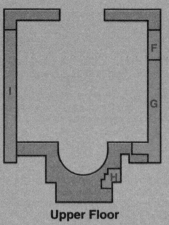

Upper Floor

F Temples of Falerii Veteres
G Tombs from Capena and the Faliscans
H Castellani Collection of Ceramics and Jewelry
I Small Bronze Objects

(1594) and the ominous *Madonna of the Serpent* (1605). Upstairs in the picture gallery are two gorgeous Raphaels: *Deposition* and *Lady with Unicorn*. The central room now houses works by Francesco Albani, di Viola, and Guido Reni. In the last room are Titian's world-famous *Sacred and Profane Love* (1512), a *Madonna and Child* by Giovanni Bellini, and Antonello da Messina's startling *Portrait of a Man*. The latter's self-assured, enlightened look seems to sum up the transition from the 16th to the 17th century—which is what Scipione Borghese's museum is all about. Make reservations by phone or in person for a 2-hour visit; it's best to start in the picture gallery (visitors may spend 30 minutes there) and then head downstairs. ♦ Admission. Tu-Su. Piazzale del Museo Borghese and Viale dell'Uccelleria. 32810

Galleria Nazionale d'Arte Moderna The collection of 19th- and 20th-century art at this museum (illustrated on page 147) spans movements from Neo-Classicism to Impressionism and the so-called Macchiaioli—the Italian Impressionists. It contains works by Balla, Manzù, Carrà, De Chirico, Modigliani, and Morandi plus Cézanne, Degas, Monet, Van Gogh, and Klimt. The Beaux-Arts edifice, designed by **Bazzani** in 1911, built to celebrate the 50th anniversary of the unification of Italy. It was later turned into the world's first museum of modern art. There's an excellent book and gift shop. ♦ Admission. Tu-Sa 9AM-10PM; Su 9AM-8PM. Viale delle Belle Arti 131 (between Via Ulisse Aldrovandi and Piazzale di Villa Giulia). 322981

Museo Etrusco di Villa Giulia (Villa Giulia Etruscan Museum) Pope Julius III (1550-55) consulted the greatest artists of the time on converting his country house on this site into a villa reflecting the new Renaissance style. The conversion was completed in 1553 from a design by **Giacomo da Vignola.** The high point of the current building is the inner courtyard (see floor plan above), with a garden that culminates in a sunken *nymphaeum* that was inspired by ancient Roman architecture. Pope Julius held his outdoor suppers in this grottolike garden pavilion that was half-fountain, half-dining room. The villa now houses the world's greatest collection of Etruscan art. The Etruscans built a center of civilization in the area roughly between present-day Bologna and Rome along the Tyrrhenian Sea from the ninth to the fourth century BC. They were among the first inhabitants and early kings of Rome. The highly civilized Etruscans passed on to the Romans many of their religious and political institutions. The museum's collection includes bronze replicas of the round and oval huts of the early Etruscan period—used as urns to contain the ashes of the dead, who were buried, like the Egyptian pharaohs, surrounded by their most prized possessions—and a very lifelike terra-cotta sarcophagus with statues of a bride and bridegroom lying atop their burial casket and apparently enjoying themselves at their own funeral banquet. Don't miss the sculptures of *Hercules* and *Apollo*, which originally adorned the roof of a sixth-century BC temple in Veii.

Galleria Nazionale d'Arte Moderna

Many of the vases, black and shiny with beautiful modern-looking paintings running around them, were imported by the Etruscans from Greece. The jewelry reveals the true artistry and elegance of this lost culture. Note especially the refined and endlessly inventive examples of fibulae, the pins used to clasp various parts of the toga. A reconstruction of an Etruscan temple in the gardens shows how richly painted their buildings were. There's a snack bar. ♦ Admission. Tu-Sa, Su morning. Piazzale Villa Giulia 9 (at Viale delle Belle Arti). 3201951

42 Auditorium di Roma Architect **Renzo Piano**'s sprawling music center is due to make its debut on the eve of the new millennium, with Christmas concerts planned for late 1999. Previews of the structure's starkly modern design are impressive: On a vast horseshoe-shaped base of brick and travertine, 3 concert halls accommodating more than 4,000 spectators surround an outdoor 3,000-seat amphitheater. The complex will also house restaurants, a multiplex cinema, music museums, and a recording studio large enough for a 150-piece orchestra and 300-person chorus. Remains of a Roman villa, discovered during construction, will be part of a separate museum. ♦ Viale Pietro de Coubertin and Via Giulio Gaudini. 8076255

Bests

Michele Scicolone
Food Writer/Cookbook Author

Cul de Sac—A perfect spot for lunch, though you may have to share your table. Great wine, cheese, salami, prosciutto and bread—inexpensive and informal.

Museo Nazionale delle Paste Alimentari—Heaven on earth for pasta lovers. A visit here finally puts to death the myth about Marco Polo.

Sunday morning in **Campo de' Fiori**—The market stalls are gone and so are the crowds. The little *caffè* spreads its tables out into the square. You can relax over cappuccino and *cornetti* (croissants).

Sunday afternoon in the **Villa Borghese,** especially in May when the chestnut trees are in bloom. Scores of Romans strolling, playing, and listening to the soccer game on their transistors. If you hear a lot of shouting, it probably means the favored team has scored.

Tazza d'Oro—The best *granita di caffè con panna.*

Il Forno di Campo de' Fiori—Great olive bread, sweet cheese tarts, and Roman-style pizza.

Lunch or dinner at **Checchino dal 1887** in the **Testaccio** district, followed by a visit to their amazing wine cellar built into a mountain of broken Roman amphorae. If you order the specialty of the house, you will receive a souvenir plate.

Strolling along **Via dei Coronari.** The antiques-filled shops are lovely to look at, especially in May and October when the street is lit with gas lamps during the twice-a-year antiques market.

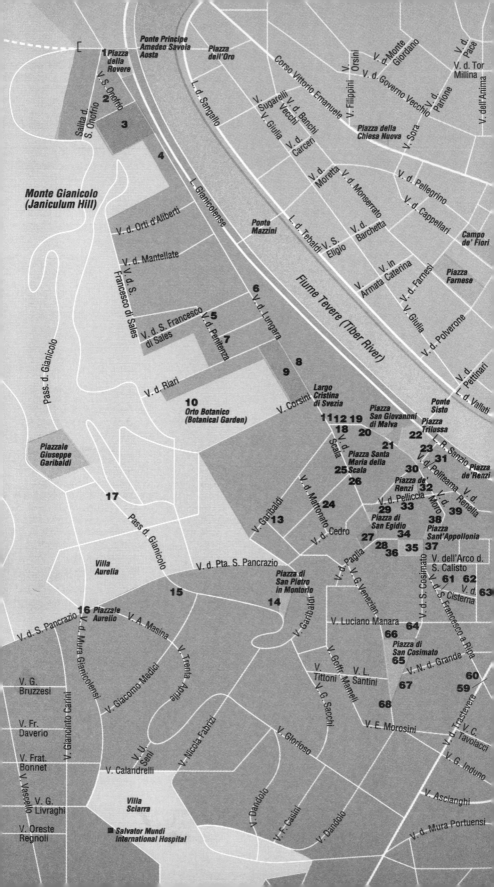

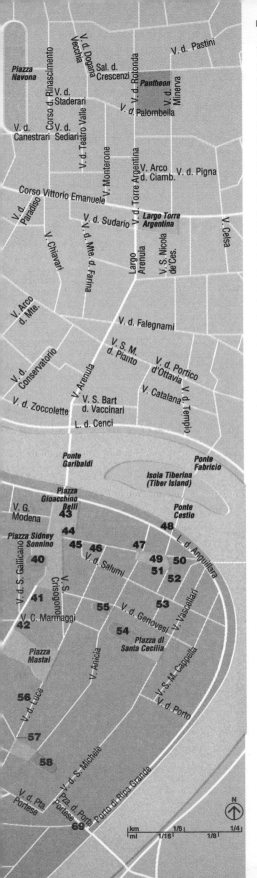

Trastevere

Most people would be hard put to nominate one area of their hometown as more genuine or representative than the rest of it, but in Rome, Trastevere—a small bulge of land in a loop of the Tiber—would fit the bill. This distinction is hard to prove, especially since during the Middle Ages, Trastevere wasn't even considered part of Rome, and the inhabitants of this quarter, the *trasteverini,* had to fight bitterly to have it recognized as an official *rione* or district of the city. Since then, these "ultratiberians" (Trastevere means across the Tiber) have held strongly to their identity, and though they no longer boast of never having crossed the river in their lives, some still insist that only those who can trace their ancestry back to a *trasteverino* or two have the right to be called Roman.

This strong sense of place has given Trastevere its reputation as a bulwark of custom and tradition, although in recent years these have been distorted into false folklore for the benefit of tourists. The authentically quaint has become precious; characteristic has been replaced by kitsch, and tradition manipulated into commercial hype.

But this isn't true everywhere in the neighborhood. Trastevere still has pockets of resistance where the alleys are festooned with laundry, the noise is limited to kids playing soccer in the street, the shop boys deliver bread and wine on bicycles, and the neighborhood women sit in the street and discuss the weather as if it were part of an international crisis. Wandering through its warren of narrow streets, which suddenly open onto sun-washed piazzas, is one of the finest things a tourist can do in Rome. The buildings are mostly small and low, with rooftop gardens and terraces overflowing with the sight and scents of bougainvillea, plumbago, jasmine, and cascading geraniums.

By day Trastevere is quiet, with craftspeople working in their *botteghe* (shops), but at night it turns into a jam-packed street fair with masses of young people hanging out in the piazzas, families out for a pizza, and couples heading to the *caffè* of the moment. The biggest crowds appear on Sunday morning when the **Porta Portese** flea market draws bargain shoppers and antiques hunters by the thousands.

Originally Trastevere was just a stretch of flat river plain that lay outside the city walls. Like the rest of the lowlands, it was unhealthy and malaria-ridden until early in the 20th century. It was, in effect, a no-man's-land of shanties housing prostitutes, rough sailors from all corners of the Roman Empire waiting to sign onto the next ship to Alexandria or the Black Sea, and fugitives from justice, like the thieves who worked the forums. It was first settled by Jews and freed slaves and became the first home of Rome's Jewish community—the oldest continuous community of Jews in Europe. Most of the Trastevere Jews were merchants attracted to the hub of the Roman Empire, but even after it collapsed, the Jews remained, and numerous small places of worship were built, including a medieval synagogue, traces of which can still be seen on **Vicolo dell'Atleta**.

Trastevere also welcomed early Christianity: The first church in Rome dedicated to the Virgin, the **Basilica of Santa Maria in Trastevere**, dominates its principal piazza. Once a tavern, it became a church as early as the third century and is renowned today for its mosaics. Among the other highlights of Trastevere are the **Villa Farnesina**, Rome's finest Renaissance villa, with frescoes by Raphael; the **Palazzo Corsini**, where the scholarly Queen Christina of Sweden lived in the 17th century; and the **Orto Botanico** (Botanical Garden).

The Trastevere *rione* has its own festival (in July): the *Noantri,* a word that underlines its separateness (*Noantri* is Trastevere dialect for *noi altri* meaning "we others"). It used to be a big block party where vendors sold traditional foods, mandolin players strolled, and boats raced on the Tiber. Now it is a cross between a third-rate carnival and a flea market, with the bill of fare being cheap trinkets, plastic household goods, and expensive take-out food.

Don't wait until July to experience Trastevere—on Saturday nights, or any night in summer, the neighborhood pulses with an energy uncommon to the rest of Rome, and the frolicking goes on well past midnight.

1 Sor'Eva ★★$$ *Sor* is Roman dialect for *signora,* but Sor Eva is no longer in the kitchen supervising the mostly Roman cooking served at this quaint, air-conditioned spot. The avuncular *padrone* is around, however, and he will keep you entertained with his memories of the cardinals, popes, and princes who have passed through the doors of this very well-run trattoria. The pastas are the usual but prepared with care, and the pizzas served at night are made in a wood-burning oven. ♦ Tu-Su lunch and dinner. Piazza della Rovere 108 (at Via di Gianicolo). 6875797

Some of Italy's greatest 20th-century writers have been Jewish: Giorgio Bassani, Carlo Levi, Primo Levi, Elsa Morante, Alberto Moravia, and Italo Svevo.

2 Hotel La Rovere $$ Close to Trastevere and the **Vatican,** this 20-room hotel is one of the few in the area. The rooms are small and can be noisy, especially while construction for the Jubilee continues. Ask for an internal room far from the street. All are air-conditioned and have baths with showers. Room **Nos. 301, 302,** and **303** have terraces and views of **St. Peter's.** A small garden completes the picture. There's no restaurant, but a full breakfast is included. ♦ Vicolo di San Onofrio 5 (between Via di San Onofrio and Salita di San Onofrio). 68806739; fax 68807062

3 Palazzo Salviati Today a barracks for *carabinieri* (city law-enforcement officers), in 1943 this edifice served as a detention center for Roman Jews who were being sent north to concentration camps. A plaque on the outside of the building to the left of the main portal commemorates the more than 1,000 Jews who were held here—only 16 of whom returned. The building is not open to the public. ♦ Via della Lungara and Via di San Onofrio

4 Via della Lungara This ancient street paved with *sanpietrini* (square cobblestones so-called because they are the same kind used in **St. Peter's Square**) goes in a straight line from the **Vatican** to Trastevere's main piazza. It is the longest of the streets built by the Renaissance popes and one of the most popular routes for pilgrims traveling to and from **St. Peter's.** Note how much lower this street is than the nearby riverside road and quay, which were built about a hundred years ago as a protection from the Tiber's frequent flooding.

4 Palazzo dei Borgia The Spanish pope, Alexander VI, who reigned between 1492 and 1503, had an out-of-wedlock son, Cesare Borgia, who terrified the good citizens of Rome. He also appropriated land in pursuit of his father's desire to perpetuate his dynasty and keep the papacy permanently in the Borgia family. This simple palace, which was outside the city walls, belonged to Cesare. It had two underground passages, one to the **Vatican** and one to the riverbank, which legend says he used to dispose of the corpses of those who got in his way, including his own brother-in-law. Moreover, if things ever got too hot for him or his equally infamous sister, Lucrezia, they could take flight through the other tunnel, which brought them into the protective arms of **Vatican City.** The palazzo is not open to the public. ♦ Via della Lungara 46 (between Via degli Orti d'Aliberti and Via di San Onofrio)

La Lungara

4 La Lungara Salvatore's old tinker's shop has given way to a handsome antiques store run by one of his apprentices. The largely offbeat collection includes antique curios, toys, icons, clocks, tiles, and odd paintings. The store is also known as "Le Care Vecchie Cose" (Cherished Old Things). ♦ M afternoon; Tu-F;

Sa morning. Via della Lungara 44/A (between Via degli Orti d'Aliberti and Via di San Onofrio). 6893662

4 Da Giovanni ★$ Two or three hearty pasta dishes and an equal number of standard entrées are the bill of fare at this neighborhood trattoria that caters to local workers. The food is inexpensive, good, and filling; the service almost nonexistent. Go early: It fills up quickly, and the kitchen closes at 10:30PM. ♦ M-Sa lunch and dinner; closed in August. No credit cards accepted. Via della Lungara 41/A (between Via degli Orti d'Aliberti and Via di San Onofrio). 6861514

5 Da Benito ★$$ Actually a large shed with a parking lot on the right and a noisy, barnlike dining room on the left, this restaurant serves abundant, typically Roman antipasti, featuring cooked vegetables, prosciutto, and seafood salad. Follow with the tasty *spaghetti alle vongole* (double-horn clams in their shells) or *risotto ai scampi* (with prawns). Efficient service, good house wine, and a rich dessert cart complete the picture. ♦ M-Sa lunch and dinner. Via di San Francesco di Sales 1 (between Via della Lungara and Vicolo della Penitenza). 68308063

6 Chiesa di San Giacomo alla Lungara This 1560 church is all that's left of a shelter for reformed prostitutes founded in the 16th century by Pope Pius IV of the Medicis. It was later donated to the Augustine nuns by Urban VIII (1623-44) of the Barberinis. Look for the bees in their family crest on the facade. ♦ Via della Lungara (between Via della Penitenza and Via di San Francesco di Sales)

L'ARTUSIANA

7 L'Artusiana Restaurant ★★$$$ The Italian equivalent of Escoffier was a 19th-century gourmet named Artusi who wrote *Science in the Kitchen* and *The Art of Eating Well.* The often-changing menu in this upscale restaurant named in his honor tends to be a bit ambitious and heavy on the salt, but the absolute adherence to freshness and avoidance of fats is much appreciated. Pastas include *fusilli provenzale* (with tuna, chopped black olives, sardines, and peppers) and homemade *pesto di rughetta* (with wild arugula sauce). Meat courses include an excellent beef fillet with an apple-and-Grappa sauce. For dessert try the deliciously rich chestnut pudding or the homemade strudel. The bread is baked on the premises. ♦ Tu-Sa lunch and dinner. Reservations required. Via della Penitenza 7 (at Vicolo della Penitenza). 68307053

Restaurants/Clubs: Red   **Hotels:** Blue

Shops/ 🍴 Outdoors: Green   **Sights/Culture:** Black

Villa Farnesina

8 Villa Farnesina This 1511 palace (illustrated above) occupies a section of the site of Julius Caesar's country estate, where he put his consort, Cleopatra, in 44 BC and whence she fled when Caesar was murdered later that same year. At the time the area was covered with Caesar's vineyards and orchards all the way up to Janiculum Hill. Cleopatra was placed here in the countryside because she could not stay within the city walls where Caesar's wife lived. The present small villa at the foot of Janiculum Hill was originally surrounded by a vast garden richly decorated with statuary and rare plants and had a loggia (now gone) overlooking the Tiber. Vasari wrote that the villa didn't look as if it was built but that it grew here. The building was designed by **Baldassare Peruzzi** for Agostino Chigi, an enormously wealthy international banker who controlled most of the commerce with the Orient. Chigi used the waterside loggia to host extravagant dinners for his patron, Pope Leo X (1513-21) and other guests. Legend has it that the extravagant Chigi would impress his guests by ordering the servants to clear the table after each course by throwing the silver dinner plates into the Tiber, never letting on that he had taken the precaution of stringing large nets there so that the plates could be retrieved after the dinner guests had gone. By 1580 the Chigi fortune had been frittered away, and the villa was sold to the Farnese family. In 1870 the beautiful gardens, designed as an extension of the villa, were torn apart and the trees cut down to make way for the Tiber embankment. Today a bit of greenery remains, where you can walk, sit on a bench, and enjoy the gurgling fountain. Raphael, along with his favorite assistant, Giulio Romano, and other apprentices, painted the amazing fresco cycle of *Cupid and Psyche* that appears in the villa's ground-floor loggia, now glassed in but originally open to the garden. The frescoes anticipate the garden, and the ceiling resembles a pergola with gods and goddesses cavorting amid beautifully rendered Renaissance garlands of fruit and flowers. In an adjacent room Raphael created the famous *Galatea* surfing on a seashell drawn by dolphins. The ceiling, by Peruzzi, recreates the pattern of the stars in Chigi's astrological chart, and the half-moon–shaped lunettes below it are by Sebastiano del Piombo and illustrate scenes from Ovid's *Metamorphoses*. An oft-told tale is that Michelangelo painted the colossal monochrome charcoal head on the left wall as a suggestion to Raphael that his work was too small in scale for the size of the room. On the upper floor is the **Hall of Perpectives** with trompe l'oeil paintings of Rome at the time by Peruzzi. Next door is Chigi's bedroom with a fresco by Sodoma that depicts his namesake Alexander the Great's wedding to Roxanne, which is considered one of Sodoma's best works. This floor of the villa also houses the **Gabinetto Nazionale delle Stampe** (National Print Gallery) with its fine collection of drawings and prints. It is closed to the public except during exhibitions. ◆ Admission. M-Sa mornings. Via della Lungara 230 (between Via Corsini and Via dei Riari). 6540565

9 Palazzo Corsini Pope Sixtus IV gave this property to his nephew, Girolamo Riario, in the 15th century. At the time, the whole area was a rambling garden that reached all the way up to the top of the Janiculum Hill and included vineyards, olive groves, and fruit orchards. One of Rome's great historical figures, Queen Christina of Sweden, moved here in 1662 after abdicating her throne and converting to Catholicism. She conducted a lively salon for artists and intellectuals in her home and created the **Accademia Reale** (the queen's academy—later known as **Arcadia**), which became a center for discussion, research, and study. After Queen Christina died in 1689, Pope Clement XII donated her villa to his nephew Cardinal Neri Corsini, who transformed it into the princely palazzo we see today. The facade was designed by **Ferdinando Fuga** in 1736. Today Queen Christina's former home is, appropriately, the seat of the **Accademia dei Lincei,** Italy's most distinguished academic institute (Galileo was among its founders). In the building is the famed **Biblioteca dell'Accademia Nazionale dei Lincei e Corsiniana,** one of the oldest libraries still in situ as originally conceived (in the 18th century by the studious Monsignore Lorenzo Corsini). Its collection, which is accessible to scholars only, includes rare texts and miniatures. ♦ Library: by appointment only. Via della Lungara 10 (between Via Corsini and Via dei Riari). 6838831

Within the Palazzo Corsini:

Galleria Corsini This small collection encompasses fine works from the 14th through the 18th centuries, including paintings by Caravaggio, Murillo, Van Dyck, and Rubens, plus a fascinating, soulful portrait by Guido Reni (1575-1642) of Beatrice Cenci. Tormented and beaten by their father, Beatrice and her brother conspired to kill him. She was beheaded in 1599 after a dramatic, noisy trial that captured the attention of all of Rome for months. ♦ Admission. Tu-F; Sa-Su mornings. 68802323

10 Orto Botanico (Botanical Garden) These gardens once belonged to the **Palazzo Corsini** and are now the property of the Botany Department of the **University of Rome.** In former days the grounds included long avenues of ilexes pruned into a dense canopy, under which Queen Christina strolled past grottoes and gushing fountains—some of which can still be seen. Ignoring the pleas of Italian Queen Margherita, the city fathers sold these ancient trees for firewood in 1878. Today what is left of the gardens covers 30 acres and includes a rock garden, Japanese tea garden, bamboo grove, scents' garden for the blind, rose garden, collection of rare palm trees, and 2 greenhouses—one for cacti, the other for orchids. A romantic Baroque staircase and cascading fountain, lined with azaleas in spring, lead to the upper gardens on Janiculum Hill, which offer an enchanting view of the Roman skyline. The entrance gate is at the end of the short Via Corsini, which is

lined with the gentrified outbuildings of **Palazzo Corsini.** ♦ Admission. M-Sa; closed in August. Via Corsini (just west of Via della Lungara). 6864193

11 Porta Settimiana The entry to Trastevere proper, this magnificent gate, with its crenelated top, was named after Emperor Septimius Severus, to whose country estate it once led. Its incorporation into the **Aurelian Wall** in the third century illustrated the strength of Rome and the expansion of its population. Further modifications were made under Alexander VI (the Borgia pope, who ruled from 1492 to 1503). This remained the city boundary until 1633. On the far side of the wall is a badly damaged Baroque fresco of the *Sermon on the Mount.* ♦ Via di Porta Settimiana (between Via Garibaldi and Via della Lungara)

11 John Cabot University Founded in 1972, this American university abroad is named after the Italian navigator and explorer Giovanni Caboto, whose name was Anglicized when he sailed under the British flag. Independently of Columbus, he envisaged reaching Asia by sailing westward. He laid the groundwork for the British claim to Canada with his voyages to North America in 1497-98. **JCU** has a four-year program offering degrees in business administration, humanities, and social sciences. The school often hosts English-language lectures and entertainment. Check the bulletin board inside the entrance. ♦ Via della Lungara 233 (at Via di Porta Settimiana). 6819121

11 Romolo ★★$$$ It's a shame this restaurant doesn't have a different sense of service, because the backdrop—inside a 400-year-old tavern with a charming wall-enclosed garden strewn with pieces of ancient marble and a wisteria arbor to one side—is one of the most evocative in Rome. Unfortunately the owners know that the setting alone will bring customers flocking in and do nothing to add to your dining experience except to allow you to eat there. The house specialty is a crisp—but juicy—Cornish hen flattened and cooked on the open grill and accompanied by chicory or broccoli reheated in olive oil with garlic and red peppers. Indulge in the tempting *tartufo* (chocolate ice cream loaded with chocolate chunks) for dessert. Legends says that this was the house where "La Fornarina" lived; she was the baker's daughter with whom Raphael was obsessed. He kept coming to **Romolo** to see her, when it was just a simple *osteria* (and a lot friendlier), which annoyed his clients—their visits were holding up his work at the nearby **Palazzo Farnesina.** ♦ Tu-Su lunch and dinner; closed in August. Reservations recommended; required in summer. Via di Porta Settimiana 8 (between Via Garibaldi and Via della Lungara). 5818284

Reel Rome

Federico Fellini was the most famous—and surely the most beloved—Italian filmmaker. His movies include ingenious portrayals of the sights and sounds of Rome's neighborhoods. However, not all of the shots of Rome in his or others' movies are real; some are sets.

Ben-Hur (1926) was the first filming of the story (Lew Wallace's book was published in 1880) of a Jew suffering under Roman rule and the biggest epic of the silent-screen era—the chariot race is its most famous sequence. The 1959 remake stars Charlton Heston in one of his most memorable roles, with the chariot race again taking honors for memorability.

The Bicycle Thief (1948), Vittorio De Sica's stark black-and-white film, paints a sad tale of postwar poverty and disillusionment. Anna Magnani and Gore Vidal make cameo appearances in this granddaddy of Italian Neo-Realism.

Cleopatra (1963) Her entrance into Rome in this blockbuster starring Elizabeth Taylor and Richard Burton is a good image to carry while trying to visualize the grandeur that was Rome.

Fellini Satyricon (1970) is Fellini's garish and very colorful fantasy of life in ancient Rome. The term Felliniesque, referring to bizarre situations and strange-looking people, was never more appropriate.

Fellini's Roma (1972) is the director's Impressionist-style romantic ode to the city of his youth. Fellini also stars in the movie—as himself directing a film in Rome, which is constantly disrupted by the discovery of archaeological artifacts beneath the modern city streets.

A Funny Thing Happened on the Way to the Forum (1966) was based on the Stephen Sondheim Broadway musical that in turn was based on the comedies of the ancient Roman playwright Plautus. It's ancient Rome with a New York Jewish atmosphere, a broad, slapstick musical starring Zero Mostel, Phil Silvers, Jack Gilford, and Buster Keaton.

I, Claudius (1976) is the perfect epic to rent (or read) if you can't tell Marcus Aurelius from Tiberius. Starring Derek Jacobi as the title character, this seven-episode **BBC** miniseries will help you brush up on your history before heading to Rome and the forums. It offers all the deceit, betrayal, plotting, and sex of the best soap operas.

La Dolce Vita (1960) is an episodic, satirical marathon of a film by Federico Fellini that stars Marcello Mastroianni. It depicts the life of the city as seen by a journalist who is both fascinated and discomfited by what he sees, including aristocratic Romans kicking up their heels in restaurants and private homes. The scene in which Anita Ekberg goes wading in the **Trevi Fountain** is one of the icons of cinema history.

Massacre in Rome (1973) features Marcello Mastroianni as a priest battling Richard Burton's German colonel, who must decide whether to execute 330 hostages as retribution for the killing of 33 Nazi soldiers.

Night on Earth (1991) comprises five stories in Jim Jarmusch's film, set in five different taxicabs in five different cities—including Rome—with five different passengers, five different drivers, and five brief encounters. Italian comedian Roberto Benigni has a hilarious turn as a lovesick Roman taxi driver.

Roman Holiday (1953) is a classic fairy tale about a princess (Audrey Hepburn) who leaves her entourage in Rome and falls in love with journalist Gregory Peck. There are many scenes of the city as it was in the 1950s.

Roman Scandals (1933) stars Eddie Cantor as a dreamer transported back to ancient Rome and counts the young Lucille Ball among the dancers in one of its Busby Berkeley production numbers.

The Roman Spring of Mrs. Stone (1961) has a script by Tennessee Williams in which an American widow (Vivien Leigh) on a downward spiral falls in love with an Italian gigolo played by Warren Beatty.

Shoes of the Fisherman (1968), adapted from the book by Morris West, stars Anthony Quinn as a Russian bishop who becomes pope after 20 years as a political prisoner. Some of it was filmed inside **Vatican City.**

Three Coins in the Fountain (1954), a romantic tale about three young American women who fall in love in Rome, won two Academy awards. It's best known, however, for its classic title theme song by Jule Styne and Sammy Cahn.

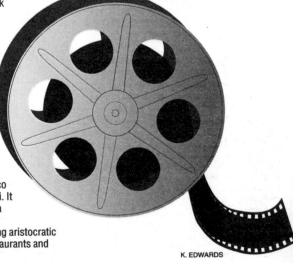

K. EDWARDS

12 **Sarti** Talented master ceramicist Domenico and his daughter Lavinia braid clay into small, medium, or large cachepots, and reproduce the cupolas of San Pietro and Santa Maria del Loreto to form tasteful terra-cotta bells for some of the more distinctive offerings at this shop. Sconces, lamps, bowls, and trays are also available. ♦ M-Sa. Via di Santa Dorotea 21 (at Via di Porta Settimiana). 5882079

13 **Via Garibaldi** This street is named after Giuseppe Garibaldi, the 19th-century patriot of the Risorgimento, the upsurge of patriotism that led to the unification of Italy and the secularization of most of the papal territories. It leads up to the summit of Janiculum Hill, which is crowned by his equestrian statue.

13 **Chiesa di Santa Maria dei Sette Dolori (Church of the Seven Sorrows)** **Borromini,** designer of this church built in 1646, is said to have been influenced in his use here of brickwork and curvilinear forms by the excavations going on at the time at **Hadrian's Villa** in nearby Tivoli. He also designed the much-modified nun's chapel in the adjacent convent entered by a door to

the right of the facade. ♦ Daily mornings. Via Garibaldi 27 (at Via dei Panieri)

14 **Chiesa di San Pietro in Montorio** Farther up the winding Via Garibaldi stands this church, dedicated to St. Peter, which was rebuilt at the end of the 15th century by Ferdinand and Isabella of Spain. Appropriately, next door to it is the entrance to the **Spanish Academy of Rome.** Raphael's *Transfiguration* (now in the **Vatican Pinocateca Gallery**) once stood over the main altar, under which the remains of Beatrice Cenci, who was executed for patricide in 1599, are still buried. In the first chapel on the right is Sebastiano del Piombo's spatially brilliant *Flagellation* (1518), and the fifth chapel on the right features paintings by Vasari.

In the courtyard is **Bramante**'s well-known **Tempietto,** built in 1499 to mark the spot where some say St. Peter was crucified. The perfectly proportioned simplicity of this circular jewel of a temple places it among the best examples of Italian Renaissance architecture. Now it is one of Rome's preferred places for wedding pictures, so don't be surprised to see antique Rolls-Royces or horse-drawn carriages outside. The view from the terrace in front is one of the finest in Rome. The inside of the **Tempietto** is not open to the public. ♦ Piazza di San Pietro in Montorio (off Via Garibaldi)

15 **Fontana Paola (Pauline Fountain)** Pope Paul V, of the Borghese family, pillaged the **Roman Forum** for the marble with which this giant fountain (illustrated below) was built in 1612 by **Giovanni Fontana** and **Ponzio.** The water is supplied by the **Acqua Paola Aqueduct,** an ancient aqueduct built by Emperor Trajan and repaired and renamed by Paul in his own honor. The basin was carved in stone in 1690 by **Carlo Fontana.** Four

Fontana Paola (Pauline Fountain)

of the columns from the facade of the old **St. Peter's Basilica** were used here. The parapet on the other side of the road affords lovely views of the city's monuments and the surrounding Alban Hills in the distance.
♦ Via Garibaldi (between Via Giacomo Medici and Via Angelo Masina)

16 Porta San Pancrazio Pope Urban VIII of the Barberini family, who reigned 1623-44, built this landmark (note the bees of his coat-of-arms). The massive gate (illustrated below) joined the **Aurelian Wall** on either side and was once known as the **Porta Aurelia,** since it marked the start of one of the ancient consular roads, the Via Aurelia. This is where Garibaldi and his valiant "red shirts" withstood the repeated onslaughts of the numerically superior French troops in 1849.
♦ Piazzale Aurelio

17 Passeggiata del Gianicolo (Janiculum Walk) This broad avenue winds along the crest of one of Rome's highest hills, Janiculum Hill, and offers impressive views of the city and the surrounding Alban Hills. A small park area, with a merry-go-round and Shetland pony rides, an open-air puppet show, and a bar makes this a fun place to spend an afternoon. At the summit is the equestrian statue (Gallori, 1895) of the Risorgimento soldier-hero *Giuseppe Garibaldi* (1807-82), who was born in Nice and lived for a while on Staten Island, New York, where he worked at a fireworks factory. On a terrace below the road, a cannon is fired in his honor every day at noon.

18 Da Gildo ★★$$ One of the very few restaurants in Rome with an Umbrian menu, this respectable representative serves commendable samples of those hearty, bread-based Umbrian soups like *zuppa di carciofi,* made with fresh artichokes and cheese. Pasta dishes include *pennette primavera* (short quill pasta with fresh tomatoes, mozzarella, and basil). Pizza is available at both lunch and dinner from an open wood-burning oven situated in one of the dining rooms. Among the unusual choices are *francescana* (with tomato, mozzarella, mushrooms, and sausage) and a calzone filled with mushrooms, mozzarella, and salmon. There's alfresco dining on the sidewalk in pleasant weather. ♦ M-Tu, Th-Su lunch and dinner. Reservations required for outdoor dining. Via della Scala 31/A (at Via di Santa Dorotea). 5800733

19 Cantiniere di San Dorotea ★★$ Lively and pleasant, this rustic-style wine bar has a wide selection of Italian and French wines by the glass or bottle. Food possiblilties include fondue (both the meat and cheese varieties), salads, and fresh oysters on the weekend.
♦ M, W-Su 7PM-2AM. Via di Santa Dorotea 9 (between Piazza San Giovanni di Malva and Via di Porta Settimiana). 5819025

Porta San Pancrazio

20 Fantasie di Trastevere $$$ This theater restaurant in the handsome former **Teatro Tiberino** provides a set dinner of far too many courses, followed by a "folk spectacle" that includes costumed renditions of standard Roman and Neapolitan *canzoni* (folk songs) as well as variety acts and sing-alongs. By midnight the 400-capacity crowd has had enough food and wine and is ready to fly with the final rendition of "Volare." ♦ Shows: Nightly at 9:30PM. Reservations recommended. Via di Santa Dorotea 6 (at Piazza San Giovanni di Malva). 5881671

da CHECCO

21 Checco Er Carrettiere ★★$$$ A large, countrified dining room with garlands of garlic and red peppers dangling from the exposed beams and an outdoor patio with Christmas-tree lights are two sure winners at this touristy trattoria. If strolling musicians in costume, a boisterous, happy crowd, and flowing Chianti are what you like, this is the place to come, despite the overpriced, precooked pasta dishes or frozen fish entrées. The ice cream and other desserts, however, are homemade. ♦ M-Sa lunch and dinner; Su lunch. Reservations required. Via Benedetta 10 (between Piazza Trilussa and Piazza San Giovanni di Malva). 5800985

22 Piazza Trilussa The large fountain in this piazza across from the Ponte Sisto draws its water from a sister fountain up on the Janiculum Hill behind Trastevere. The piazza is named after the sharp-tongued, earthy dialect poet "Trilussa" (Carlo Alberto Salustri), who died in 1950 and whose bust is in a grove of bushes on the right.

23 Il Fontanone ★★$ One of the best of the old-fashioned, friendly trattorie in Trastevere, this place has true Roman style: a combination of good food and convivial spirit. It specializes in fresh fettuccine served in various ways—with a tomato-and-meat sauce, wild mushrooms, or *al Fontanone* (with tuna sauce). In winter *polenta con spuntatura e salsiccie* (with tomato sauce flavored with pork ribs and sausage) is a satisfying meal in itself. Good, thin Roman pizzas—the best is with cheese and chunks of sausage—are served only at night, and there's alfresco dining in summer next to the fountain that gives the restaurant its name. ♦ M, W-Su lunch and dinner. Piazza Trilussa 46 (at Via del Politeama). 5817312

24 Trattoria da Lucia ★★★$$ Located in an ungentrified part of Trastevere, this excellent family-run trattoria is a dinosaur that still serves *la cucina de 'na vorta* (cooking as it was once upon a time). The street outside is permanently festooned with banners praising Rome's two rival soccer teams and testifying to the neighborhood's genuine working-class character. Besides typical Roman vegetables cooked the way Mamma Roma would, the best selections here are *spaghetti alla Griccia*, eaten by shepherds in the hills outside Rome and made with pancetta, pecorino cheese, and freshly ground pepper, and *involtini alla romana* (veal rolls tenderized in tomato sauce). The setting is rustic—dried sausages dangle over the eight tables, not for decoration but because that's where Silvana, the founder's daughter, keeps them until she reaches up with a stick and pitches them down into her son Renato's arms. Dine outside in summer under the soccer banners, but get there early as there are only a few tables, and they do not take reservations. ♦ Tu-Su lunch and dinner. No credit cards accepted. Vicolo del Mattonato 2/B (at Via del Mattonato). 5803601

25 Piazza Santa Maria della Scala The buildings at **Nos. 53-57** will give you an idea of how Trastevere looked earlier in this century—rows of cottages and stalls for the horses and barnyard animals that milled around the unpaved streets. Note especially the window shapes.

On Piazza Santa Maria della Scala:

Chiesa di Santa Maria della Scala and Farmacia Santa Maria della Scala This church was built in 1592 from designs by **Francesco da Volterra** to house a miraculous painting of the Virgin Mary. The canopied altar by **Carlo Rainaldi** was added in 1650. Next to the church is one of the oldest pharmacies in Rome. During a plague that afflicted the city in 1523, the Carmelite monks saved many lives—according to legend—with a ruby-colored potion—*acqua della scala*—believed to cure everything from toothaches to bed-wetting. From 1726 to 1804, the herbal brews of a certain Fra Basilio were in great demand by kings, cardinals, and commoners. One such potion, still sold under the name *Acqua di Melissa,* is a sedative made from daisies and guaranteed to cure "hysterics." Visit the old 17th-century pharmacy upstairs, still faithfully kept as it was, the walls lined with giant wooden cupboards where the elixirs and herbal remedies were stored in vials, urns, and apothecary jars. Basilio's portrait hangs in the corridor. The modern pharmacy on the ground floor sells such banal things as aspirin and cold remedies. ♦ Vecchia Farmacia: M-F 9-11AM. Modern Pharmacy: M-Sa. 5806217

Birreria della Scala $ One of Trastevere's most popular beer halls, this place has both indoor and outdoor tables and serves beer from around the world, including Adelscott, Eku 28, and Guinness on draft. Munch on snacks or indulge in a full meal from antipasto to dessert. ♦ Daily 8PM-2AM. No. 60. 5803763

26 Vini e Olii A hand-painted sign above this hole-in-the-wall shop announces that it is a survivor of a type of shop once found all over Rome that sold only wine and olive oil. Customers brought their own bottles and had them filled from barrels. Note the wide selection of Grappa and their inventive (and expensive) bottles. ♦ M afternoon, Tu-Sa. Via della Scala 64 (at Piazza Santa Maria della Scala)

27 Museo del Folklore e dei Poeti Romaneschi (Museum of Folklore and Roman Poets) This delightful, small museum is devoted to the rich folk history of Rome and includes life-sized realistic tableaux that illustrate scenes from turn-of-the-century Rome. On the second floor is a reconstruction of the studio of the dialect poet Trilussa (Carlo Alberto Salustri), who died in Trastevere in 1950. Don't miss the charming watercolors of Rome by Ettore Franz (1878). ♦ Admission. Tu-Sa; Su morning. Piazza di San Egidio 1/B (at Via della Paglia). 5816563

O   M   B   R   E

R   O   S   S   E

28 Ombre Rosse Caffè ★$ Here is the perfect place to rest—either inside or at an outdoor table—and choose from a vast selection of salads, pastas and sandwiches.

Or simply enjoy a cup of coffee, a glass of beer or wine, or an aperitivo while perusing the *International Herald Tribune* (sold here). The name means "red shadows," the poetic term for a glass of red wine. ♦ Daily 7AM-2AM. Piazza di San Egidio 12 (at Via della Paglia). 5884155

29 Da Otello ★★$$ Specialties from Umbria, the center of Italy's pasta production, predominate here. This cozy, popular tavern, which does duty as a pizzeria at night, offers good food at reasonable prices, and the narrow street becomes its dining room in summer. Standouts on the menu include the grilled eggplant with parmesan cheese and any of the succulent pizzas. Among the homemade desserts are pine-nut–lemon tart and tiramisù. ♦ M-W, F-Su lunch and dinner; Th dinner. Via della Pelliccia 49 (between Piazza de' Renzi and Piazza di San Egidio). 5896848

30 Vicolo del Cinque To get the real flavor of Trastevere, wander into the warren of *vicoli* (tiny alleys) that wind their way through Trastevere's past. This one is still lined with one-room artists' studios, *mamma-e-papa* grocery stores, family-run trattorie, and the dirty, dusty workshops of gilders, framers, and tinsmiths.

On Vicolo del Cinque:

Ciak ★★$$ The owners of this Tuscan restaurant have a passion for cinema, which explains the old movie posters and photos of actors and actresses on the walls. Start with delicious appetizers of *crostini,* circles of bread spread with pâté, olive paste, or mushrooms. Follow with one of the dense Tuscan bread soups like *ribollita,* full of mixed vegetables, or *zuppa di farro* (spelt). A Florentine steak (with olive oil, lemon, and freshly ground pepper) could come next, or perhaps *spiedini* (skewers of grilled meat, sausage, bay leaf, and peppers), which are cooked on the open grill at the entrance. ♦ Tu-Su dinner until 1AM. Reservations recommended. No. 21. 5894774

Cornetti Caldi Here is an all-night bakery where you can get fresh *cornetti,* the ubiquitous horn-shape Roman version of the croissant. This and other pastries are available right out of the oven and before they are delivered to the city's cafes. ♦ Daily 24 hours. No. 40. No phone

The Lively Arts

The music-and-theater season in Rome runs from September through June. Many events are performed in some of the city's most beautiful buildings—historic theaters, churches, cloisters, and palaces. Following are some venues; see *Roma C'è* for specific listings.

Classical Music

The **Accademia Nazionale di Santa Cecilia** arranges performances of Rome's symphony orchestra as well as international soloists at the **Auditorio Pio XII** (Via della Conciliazione 4, at Via Traspontina, 68801044) on Monday, Tuesday, and Sunday from October through June. It moves outdoors to **Villa Giulia** in the **Villa Borghese** in July. The **Istituzione Universitaria dei Concerti** (36001511) holds classical music concerts in the **Aula Magna** (Piazzale Aldo Moro 5, Città Universitaria, 3610051). Special events include summer evening concerts held in parks around the city and a series of Christmas concerts held in city churches. Chamber music concerts and solo performances are given every Thursday evening from November through June in the frescoed **Oratorio del Gonfalone** (Vicolo della Scimia 1B, between Via Giulia and Lungotevere dei Sangallo, 6875952). Call for reservations. Architect **Renzo Piano**'s sprawling new symphony center, **Auditorium di Roma** (Viale Pietro de Coubertin and Via Giulio Gaudini, 8076255, was due to open as we went to press.

Opera and Ballet

Unfortunately, wildcat strikes, tired productions, and inconvenient ticketing often mean that you can see and hear better opera in Houston or Manchester than in Rome. Nevertheless, the situation is changing, and you might get lucky or just enjoy being inside the 20th-century **Teatro dell'Opera di Roma** (Piazza Beniamino Gigli and Via Firenze, 4817003). The opera season runs from late November through April. The traditional summer performances of Verdi's *Aida* may take place at **Piazza di Siena** in **Villa Borghese** or at the **Parco del Celio,** near the resplendent **Baths of Caracalla;** check *Roma C'è* for location.

Italy does not have a national ballet company. As a result, touring companies are in great demand. Likewise, ballets featuring Italian ballerinas—Carla Fracci and Alessandra Ferri—sell out immediately at the **Teatro Olympico** (Piazza Gentile da Fabriano 17, 3234890).

Theater and Cabaret

Legitimate theater in Rome is a mix of contemporary Italian and foreign works (most productions are in Italian) on the one hand, and classic Italian works, leaning heavily toward such old staples as Goldoni and Pirandello, on the other hand. The season runs from October through May, and performances are held in three splendid theaters in various locations around the city: **Teatro Argentina** (Largo di Torre Argentina 52, at Via di Torre Argentina, 68804601); **Teatro Quirino** (Piazza dell'Oratorio and Via dell'Umilta, 6794585); and **Teatro Valle** (Via del Teatro Valle 23, between Via dei Redentoristi and Via dei Sediari, 68803794). Another theater for both classic and avant-garde plays is **Teatro Eliseo** (Via Nazionale 183/E, between Via della Consulta and Via Mazzarino, 48872001). **Teatro Sistina** (Via Sistina 129, between Via dei Cappuccini and Via Francesco Crispi, 4200711) sometimes hosts touring Broadway musicals, and **Salone Margherita** (Via Due Macelli 75, between Largo del Tritone and Piazza di Spagna, 6798269) schedules cabaret performances in a charming, turn-of-the-century theater.

30 Guaytamelli This intriquing little gift shop sells its own line of sundials, including tiny pocket versions, sundial rings, and hourglasses. ♦ M afternoon; Tu-Sa. Via del Moro 59 (at Vicolo del Cinque). 5880704

31 Panificio Arnese All breads, cookies, biscuits, and other baked goods here are baked in a wood-fired oven—ensuring crispy crusts, moist interiors and, most important, a scrumptious homemade flavor. For a walk-with-it light lunch, have a piece of *pizza bianca* with such fillings as buffalo mozzarella and artichoke hearts. Locals swear by their baked goods, so on Sunday mornings be prepared to take a ticket and wait. ♦ Daily (no midday closing). Via del Moro 15 (between Via della Renella and Piazza Trilussa). 5817265

32 Corner Bookshop This is the kind of place that will suggest a good read. The offerings include not only American and British authors, but also Indian, Australian, and other writers who choose to pen their works in English. The small shop is crammed with hardcovers and paperbacks at competitive prices. ♦ M afternoon; Tu-Su. Via del Moro 48 (between Via della Pelliccia and Vicolo del Cinque). 5836942

32 Mario's ★$ This modest family-run restaurant serves standard, Roman meals without any fanfare or flair. The lentil or bean soups with added bits of pasta are filling and delicious. A half-grilled chicken with roasted potatoes and a salad or one of the daily stews will do the trick and cost you very little. ♦ M-Sa lunch and dinner. Via del Moro 53 (at Via della Pelliccia). 5803809

32 Lattoniere Once Trastevere was full of craftsmen like this one-of-a-kind tinsmith. Simple, beautifully designed dispensers for drizzling olive oil on pizzas or salads and portable candle holders with tin windshields for the terrace or patio are just two of the lovely items here. ♦ M-F. Piazza de' Renzi 22 (just north of Via della Pelliccia). 5806737

The vines that you see criss-crossing some streets in Trastevere and sometimes draping whole sides of buildings are called *vite americana*. You may recognize them as Virginia Creeper, which is also known as woodbine or American ivy. It forms dark red berries in summer, and the leaves turn golden and then blood red in early autumn before falling. Sometimes it grows so long the cars can not pass beneath it; the firefighters then come and trim its "bangs."

33 La Galleria Clotilde Sambuco has carefully restored an old carriage house and filled it with hand-painted ceramics, fine woven table linens from Sardinia, dark oak Umbrian farmhouse furniture, and a collection of whimsical painted terra-cotta whistles. From Sicily come jugs representing the knights and damsels of its Norman past, while from Puglia come dinner services in the distinctive *puntini* pattern of blue dots on a cream-colored background. All of Italy's major kilns (Deruta, Vietri, etc.) are represented, and anything can be shipped anywhere in the world. ♦ M afternoon; Tu-Sa. Via della Pelliccia 30 (at Piazza de' Renzi). 5816614

33 Augusto ★★$ When this classic trattoria from the 1960s (formica tables, paper tablecloths) fills up—which is every day and night in summer—the locals take things into their own hands and get their own bread, wine, and silverware instead of waiting for the harried waiters. The food is hearty and heaping, and the *brasato* (braised veal with potatoes) or the *bollito* (boiled beef) are tender and succulent and definitely have a good price-per-quality ratio. But don't go if you're in a hurry. Sit outside in summer. ♦ M-F lunch and dinner; Sa lunch. No credit cards accepted. Piazza de' Renzi 15 (at Via della Pelliccia). 5803798

34 Antica Farmacia Peretti This pharmacy was founded in 1827 by Cavalier Pietro Peretti, a Genoan herbalist and chemistry professor at the **University of Rome,** whose bust is displayed inside. Peretti was an outspoken antipapist and taught his parrot to squawk any time a priest entered the shop. The place still retains many of its 19th-century furnishings, including several carved walnut spice cabinets, brass door handles, and wrought-iron gas lamps. ♦ Daily. Piazza Santa Maria in Trastevere 7 (between Piazza Sant'Appollonia and Via della Paglia)

35 Piazza Santa Maria in Trastevere Most appropriately it was **Carlo Fontana** who designed the fountain in the center of this square—the Roman piazza most like a living room. All day long **Fontana**'s elegant elevated fountain attracts groups of young musicians, teenage lovers, or star-struck tourists who find the perfect armchair or sofa in its stairs. For decades the piazza has been battling to remain a living room—and not a parking lot.

36 Basilica di Santa Maria in Trastevere Legend says that a geyser of oil sprang up on this site on the day Jesus was born. Originally a tavern occupied the site, but Emperor Alexander Severus ceded the land to the Christians in the third century, making this the earliest official Christian place of worship in Rome. The original improvised chapel was built into a church in 337 by Pope Julius I in honor of St. Calixtus (217-22), who was

martyred nearby. Pope Innocent II, who came from a famous Trastevere family, enlarged it into a basilica (illustrated below) in 1140. The beautifully renovated facade has a splendid 12th-century mosaic of a procession of maidens paying homage to the Virgin. Inside, another procession of surprisingly realistic sheep is part of the luminous 12th-century mosaic in the apse, and below it are the sophisticated mosaics by Pietro Cavallini (1250-1330) depicting scenes from the life of the Virgin. Two cardinals' sarcophagi are beautifully sculpted, and five popes are buried beneath the high altar. The gilt ceiling is by Domenichino (1617), and the marble mosaic pavement by the Cosmati family of marble workers (12th-14th centuries), who made intricate geometric designs out of fragments of ancient columns and statues that they pilfered from the **Forum.** Don't miss the tour-de-force Baroque chapel designed by **Antonio Gherardi** (1680) at the end of the left aisle. Its remarkable dome is held up by angels.
♦ Piazza Santa Maria in Trastevere (just south of Via della Paglia)

37 Sabatini ★$$$ There are a lot better restaurants in Trastevere than this often-cited eatery, but a lingering view of the piazza and the church's sun-washed facade from an outdoor table may make up for the lackluster fare. Stick to the basics and avoid the frozen fish, which by law must be specified on the menu as *surgelato.* Here, as at all outdoor restaurants, beware of bag snatchers and do not leave items on chairs. **Sabatini II** is around the corner at Vicolo Santa Maria in Trastevere 18 (5818307); it's open

Monday, and Wednesday through Sunday, for lunch and dinner and is closed for a week in August when the original is open. ♦ M, W-Su lunch and dinner; closed one week in August. Reservations recommended. Piazza Santa Maria in Trastevere 13 (just south of Piazza Sant'Appollonia) 5812026

38 Hosteria Pizzeria Der Belli ★★$$
Named for one of Trastevere's best-loved story tellers, Gioacchino Belli, this rustic, moderately priced eatery is one of the finest in the area. Although the views from the outdoor tables are not nearly as striking as those in **Piazza Santa Maria in Trastevere** around the corner, the food is better and sometimes daring—try the *formaggio arrosto con miele* (grilled cheese steaks with coarse honey)—revealing the Sardinian origins of the owners. ♦ Tu-Su lunch and dinner. Piazza Sant' Appollonia and Via del Moro. 5803782

39 Pasta all'Uovo The sister of the owners of **Der Belli** restaurant (see above) across the street is the proprietor of this shop, which sells fresh egg pasta. Have a look at the tortellini, ravioli, fettuccine, cannelloni, gnocchi, and other delicacies. Several types of "fresh" dry pasta, which don't have to be refrigerated, are also offered here. ♦ M-W, F-Sa; Th morning. Via del Moro 32 (between Piazza Sant'Appollonia and Via della Renella). 5803759

Basilica di Santa Maria in Trastevere

39 **Ferrara** $$ Two sisters run this tiny wine bar and oversee the preparation of soups, cold plates, and savories to accompany the wines. ♦ W-Su 8:30PM-1:30AM. Reservations recommended. No credit cards accepted. Via del Moro 1/A (at Piazza Sant'Appollonia). 5803769

40 **Basilica di San Crisogono** One of the city's oldest Christian worship sites, this church was founded in the fifth century and reconstructed in the 17th by **G.B. Soria.** The interior is a catalogue of marble work that includes a 13th-century marble floor, 22 ancient Roman columns, 2 huge, rare porphyry pillars on either side of the triumphal arch and, holding up the baldachino over the main altar, 4 delicate columns of translucent yellow alabaster. In the apse is a mosaic from the studio of Pietro Cavallini (13th century). Through the sacristy and down a spiral staircase are the remains of some late Roman edifices and the original fifth-century house of worship. ♦ Piazza Sidney Sonnino (between Viale di Trastevere and Via della Lungaretta)

41 **Viale di Trastevere** The main street in Trastevere, this broad avenue goes from Piazza Sidney Sonnino to the Trastevere train station. At the feast of the local patroness, Our Lady of Mt. Carmel, in July, a procession of barefoot devotees carries her statue along this *viale* and places it for a week in the **Basilica di San Crisogono** (see above).

41 **Panattoni** ★★★$ This is the definitive Trastevere pizzeria, full of people, noise, and smoke, and with quick service. One flour-dusted guy does the dough, another spreads the sauces, and a third wielding a wooden paddle puts it into the blisteringly hot wood-burning oven for not more than three minutes. This is all in full view of the cheering crowd. Everybody calls it *l'obitorio* (the morgue), not because the thin Roman pizza is to die for (which it is), but because of the long gray marble counter (best for rolling out the dough) and the marble-top tables you eat on. In summer the show moves outside under floodlights and turns into the kind of Rabelaisian revelry you may recall from the final scenes of *Fellini's Roma,* which were filmed here. ♦ M-Tu, Th-Su 6:30PM-1AM; closed in August. No credit cards accepted. Viale di Trastevere 53 (between Via Cardinale Marmaggi and Piazza Sidney Sonnino). 5800919

42 **La Fonte della Salute** Rome has some of the best gelato in Italy, and the best of the Roman *gelaterie* are those that make it fresh daily on the premises. This place is tops in that category. Besides the usual flavors, there is also a line of yogurt-based taste delights and the Italian version of an ice-cream sandwich made with a sweet roll. The take-out creations in the wall coolers are worth a look, especially *zuccotto*—a Roman standard—that consists of alternating layers of chocolate and zabaglione gelato and sponge cake. ♦ Daily noon-2AM. Via Cardinale Marmaggi 4 (at Viale di Trastevere). 5897471

43 **Statue of Belli** At the entrance to Trastevere is this frock-coated, top-hatted 1913 statue of Gioacchino Belli, the 19th-century dialect poet who has come to symbolize the sharp-tongued, no-nonsense, fun-loving Trastevere. ♦ Piazza Gioacchino Belli

44 **Palazzetto Anguillara** Built in the 13th century, this restored fortified palace once belonged to the powerful Anguillara family, who came from Lake Bracciano, known for its eels. The family coat-of-arms, visible on the side of the building, appropriately bears an eel. Built by this noble family as a symbol of its power and prestige, the palace tower guarded the entrance to Trastevere during the Middle Ages. The palazzo is now the home of the **Casa di Dante** (5812019), where readings from the *Divina commedia* are given in winter (in Italian)—see *Roma C'è* for readings—and a library of the poet's works is maintained. Inside is a lovely courtyard. ♦ M, W, F 5-8PM; Su morning. Piazza Sidney Sonnino 5 (at Via della Lungaretta)

45 **Il Ponentino** ★★$$ The name of this busy, lively restaurant recalls the cool evening breeze that comes into Rome from the Alban Hills late in the afternoon in summer. The outdoor tables fill up fast for lunch, especially on Sunday, and in winter the inside is a cozy place to have a pizza. Try *fettuccine alla boscaiola* with ham, mushrooms, and peas in a cream sauce or *risotto alla pescatore* with clams and mussels. ♦ Daily lunch and dinner. Piazza del Drago 10 (at Via della Lungaretta). 5880688

46 **Latteria** $ In a carefully restored medieval building lies this milk shop, one of the last of its kind in Rome. At the turn of the century, they were very common in Rome and served as meeting places where people gathered not only to buy dairy products, but to drink them, play cards, or chat over homemade ice cream. Owned by the same family for generations, this place preserves that genial atmosphere. Notice the wrought-iron marble-top tables, the long marble counter, and the massive wooden refrigerators. ♦ M-W, F-Su; Th morning. Via della Lungaretta 61 (at Via della Luce). 5816382

47 La Gensola ★★★$$$ Many claim that this rustic Sicilian trattoria has some of the best pasta in Rome. Standouts are rigatoni with broccoli in a spicy tomato sauce, penne with eggplant and tomato, and the exquisite Arab-Sicilian *pasta con le sarde* (with sardines, pine nuts, and raisins topped with a sprinkling of bread crumbs). Entrées are also typical Sicilian dishes—try the grilled swordfish steak or *involtini* (braised veal rolls stuffed with bread crumbs, parsley, and cheese). The fried calamari is light and greaseless. Desserts include such standard Sicilian sweets as cannoli and *cassata* (ricotta cake). Down it all with a Sicilian wine like the heady, white Rapitalà. ♦ M, Sa dinner; Tu-F lunch and dinner. Reservations recommended. No credit cards accepted. Piazza della Gensola 15 (at Piazza in Piscinula). 5816312

48 Sor Mirella Before gelato, Romans fought off the dog days of July and August with *grattachecche,* libations of shaved ice over which they poured syrups or fresh fruit. At one time kiosks like this one were a common sight along the banks of the Tiber, but now only a handful remain. They were part of the Trastevere that included horsedrawn carriages and summer fireworks over Tiber Island. In those days the traditional evening stroll usually ended up at a kiosk like this for a taste treat. The fresh lemon *grattachecca* sweetened with a few sour cherries is guaranteed to lower body temperatures. ♦ Daily noon-2AM May through Sept; closed October through April. Lungotevere degli Anguillara and Ponte Cestio. No phone

49 Piazza in Piscinula At one time this piazza was a fish market, but in the Middle Ages it was the site of several popular inns for pilgrims bound for **St. Peter's.** One of these hostelries is the **Casa dei Mattei** (No. 10), with a 15th-century loggia and 14th-century mullioned windows. The rest of the building has been heavily restored, but it is still one of the few examples of medieval architecture in Rome that survived after Mussolini plowed down the medieval quarter in front of **St. Peter's** to build the modern Via della Conciliazione. Today it's a private apartment building.

50 Taberna Piscinula ★$$ This is a good representative of the new upscale, more expensive pizzerias that offer fanciful, sometimes ridiculous, toppings like corn niblets or chocolate. Here the toppings show more restraint and include spinach and gorgonzola, shrimp and arugula, and zucchini blossom. Dine indoors in a very pleasant air-conditioned setting or outside in Rome's only medieval piazza. ♦ Tu-Su lunch and dinner. Piazza in Piscinula 50 (between Via in Piscinula and Via della Lungarina). 5812525

51 La Cornucopia ★★$$$ Indoors, this small, smart restaurant is air-conditioned; outside, a handful of tables is set in one of Rome's loveliest piazzas. The menu relies heavily on fish, which varies with the season and that morning's market fare. You may find spaghetti with *calamaretti* (baby squid), or *spigola* (grilled sea bass), which the waiter will debone for you and douse with lemon. ♦ Tu-W dinner; Th-Su lunch and dinner; closed part of August. Reservations recommended. Piazza in Piscinula 18 (between Via in Piscinula and Via dell'Arco de' Tolomei). 5800380

51 Chiesa di San Benedetto Rebuilt in the 18th century, this tiny 4th-century church in the far corner of the **Piazza in Piscinula** is said to have been the home of St. Benedict before he left Rome to found the Benedictine order of monks. The 11th-century bell tower is the smallest of its kind in Rome, and the bell in it is Rome's oldest. Inside are a fine early marble mosaic floor and Benedict's room. Ring the bell of the convent door to the right of the facade to enter. ♦ Piazza in Piscinula and Via in Piscinula

52 Perchè No? "Why not?" asks this used clothing-and-collectibles shop. This is where elegant Roman matrons come to turn in their Gucci-Puccis for resale. ♦ Tu-Sa. Via in Piscinula 27 (between Via dei Salumi and Piazza in Piscinula). 5814316

53 Vicolo dell'Atleta One of Trastevere's most picturesque streets, this tiny incline flanked by buildings with fragments of Rome's past stuck into them—bits of columns and friezes found when the houses were built or restored—has a charming medieval synagogue at one end (**No. 14**). It is now a private residence, but some historians believe it housed Nathan Ben Hechiel Anav (1035-1106), author of one of the first compendia of Talmudic rules.

54 Chiesa di Santa Cecilia in Trastevere This fifth-century church with a quiet garden in front was built above the house of two prosperous proselytizing Christian converts—Valerianus, a Roman patrician, and his wife, Cecilia. After the emperor ordered her husband executed, Cecilia was condemned to die by suffocation in her steam-filled bath—a method frequently used to execute noblewomen of the era. But instead of dying quietly, she was heard singing so beautifully that the emperor couldn't bear it and had her beheaded. Under the church are the remains of Cecilia's home, in which the ancient *caldarium,* or steam bath, can be seen through a gate and the catacombs or cemetery that grew up around it. Because of her swan song, Cecilia is remembered as the patron saint of musicians, and many of them have left mementos on the walls. The entrance was built in 1725 by **A. Fuga.** The brick bell tower is one of the earliest (1113) in Rome; the marble statue of the dying *Cecilia* under a side altar is by Stefano Maderno (1618), and the ninth-century mosaic in the apse is by Pasquale. In the convent next door is a spectacular 13th-century fresco of the *Last Judgment* by Pietro Cavallini, found behind some cabinets in the choir during a remodeling some years ago. Cavallini, who is compared to Giotto, is famous for his apocalyptic archangels with technicolor rainbow wings. ♦ Church and excavations: daily 10AM-noon, 4-6PM. Convent: Tu, Th 10-11AM. Piazza di Santa Cecilia (between Via di San Michele and Via di Santa Cecilia)

55 **San Giovanni Battista dei Genovesi (St. John the Baptist of the Genoans)** Don't miss this beautiful 15th-century cloister built by sailors from Genoa to mark their presence in Rome. This part of Trastevere used to be an important port on the Tiber, heavily trafficked by merchants and sailors from Italy's great maritime republics. The cloister attached to the church has a unique portico of octagonal columns that have turned a soft summer orange over the ages and enclose a lush garden of citrus trees, rose bushes, and climbing jasmine. ♦ Tu, Th 3-6PM Apr-Aug; 2-4PM Sept-Mar. Ring the custodian's bell. Via Anicia 12 (at Via dei Genovesi)

56 **Da Albino il Sardo** ★★$$ Dine outdoors at this rustic, Sardinian trattoria, which offers regional specialties grilled on a wood-burning fire. Try *malloredus,* tiny shell-shaped pasta served with tomato or meat sauce, homemade *ravioloni* (jumbo ravioli), and *cinghiale* (wild boar), washed down with Cannonau red wine from the island. ♦ Tu-Su lunch and dinner. Via della Luce 44 (between Via di San Francesco a Ripa and Piazza Mastai). 5800846

57 **Da Paolo** ★★$$ A convivial husband-and-wife team own this Abruzzesi trattoria, which spills out into the piazza in summer. *Spaghetti alle vongole* (with garlic and baby clams in their shells) is the most popular summer dish here. In winter, polenta with a variety of toppings draws the crowds. ♦ M-Sa lunch and dinner. Via di San Francesco a Ripa 93 (at Piazza San Francesco d'Assisi). 5812393

58 **Chiesa di San Francesco a Ripa** This church was built in 1231 (and restored in 1682) to replace the hospice where St. Francis

of Assisi lodged when he came to Rome in 1219 to seek recognition from the pope for his new religious order, the Franciscans. Inside, in the fourth chapel on the left, is Bernini's formidable statue of *Beata Lodovica* (1674), lying on cushions above the altar and lit by a concealed side window. It is another of Bernini's intense emotional works in which the physical and spiritual intensity of mystical ecstasy is reflected in his treatment of the robes, hands, eyes, and feet of Ludovica as she merges with her heavenly spouse. The 20th-century Italian surrealist painter, Giorgio De Chirico, is buried in a room behind the first chapel on the left. ♦ Piazza San Francesco d'Assisi (between Via della Luce and Via Anicia)

59 **Anna** ★★$$ Eat outdoors or inside the air-conditioned dining room at this moderately priced restaurant. The menu features such familiar Roman standards as osso buco and *piccatina di vitello* (veal slices sautéed in lemon or Marsala) prepared with care and attention. Pizzas are also available at night—the best of which is topped with gorgonzola and *rughetta.* ♦ M-Sa dinner; Su lunch and dinner. Via di San Francesco a Ripa 57 (at Viale di Trastevere). 5893992

60 **Pizzeria** The pizza sold here by the slice (actually, by weight) is some of the best in Rome. Try potato and rosemary, eggplant and tomato, or fresh arugula and melted stracchino cheese. Herb-stuffed whole chickens cooked in a giant rotisserie are for non-pizza lovers. ♦ Tu-Sa. Via di San Francesco a Ripa 137 (at Viale di Trastevere). 5897110

61 **Hotel Cisterna** $ This is one of the very few hotels in Trastevere and one of the few bargain hotels in all of Rome. Though most of the 18 rooms are cramped and ugly, all of the basics are present, and there is even a pretty, sunny inner courtyard for breakfast relaxation. Ask for one of the rooms off the courtyard, as the rooms facing the street, and Trastevere's ever-present revelers, are noisy. There's no restaurant. ♦ Via della Cisterna 7 (at Via di San Francesco a Ripa). 5817212; fax 5810091

62 **Camillo a Trastevere** ★$$ Hidden on a side street near **Santa Maria in Trastevere** lies a spacious restaurant with a flaming grill that serves as an open fire in the winter. Camillo and his family get top marks for cutting the prosciutto by hand, thus ensuring its freshness. *Tagliolini* (thin ribbon pasta) is served with a delicate sauce of baby shrimp.

The fish (all fresh) is served at a fixed price (most Roman restaurants charge by the *etto* or a tenth of a kilo, making it hard for you to calculate your bill, but this one doesn't). ♦ Tu-Su lunch and dinner. Via dei Fienaroli 7 (at Via della Cisterna). 5882860

63 Selarum An extraordinarily pleasant place to hear live music (jazz, bossa nova), this club serves drinks (piña coladas), ice cream (peach melba), and light meals (salads and savories) in a hedge and jasmine-vine enclosed garden. ♦ Daily 6PM-2AM Apr–mid-Oct. Via dei Fienaroli 12 (between Via delle Fratte di Trastevere and Via dell'Arco di San Calisto). 5803218

64 Da Vittorio ★$ Home of the heart-shaped pizza, this hole-in-the-wall pizzeria specializes in thick-crusted Neapolitan pizza and is always hard to get into. The appetizers, including grilled eggplant, artichoke hearts, and garlic bread topped with diced tomatoes, are the best part of the meal and lie waiting for you on the table while the pizzas are being cooked. ♦ Tu-Su lunch and dinner. Reservations recommended. No credit cards accepted. Via di San Cosimato 14 (at Via Luciano Manara). 5800353

65 San Cosimato Market This outdoor fruit-and-produce market is a good place to get acquainted with edibles that are particular to Rome, such as *puntarelle* (young spikes of the chicory plant) or *cardi* (cardoons, similar to artichokes)—both of which have to be stripped of their skins. The former becomes a salad dressed with garlic and anchovy paste, and the latter is often baked in the oven *alla parmigiana* with bread crumbs, tomato sauce, and cheese. ♦ M-Sa mornings. Piazza di San Cosimato

66 Alberto Ciarla ★★★$$$$ This fish restaurant boasts a refined, candlelit setting and quality edibles from the sea, everything from Maine lobster to Scottish salmon to Normandy oysters. The olive oil and wine (Bianco di Velletri Vigna Ciarla) come from the owner's farm outside Rome. Fish-stuffed ravioli, sea bass with almonds, and raw seabream with ginger are just a few of the well-prepared dishes. ♦ M-Sa dinner; closed 15 days in August and 15 days at Christmastime. Reservations required. Piazza di San Cosimato 40 (at Via Giacomo Venezian). 5818668; fax 5884377

67 Il Forno Amico Bakery If you want a loaf of perhaps the best brown bread you've ever tasted, come here early and ask for *pane di grano,* made from a mixture of wheat grain and whole-meal flour. Don't neglect the rolls filled with olives, walnuts, and other delicious treats. All baking is done on the premises. ♦ M-W, F-Sa. Piazza di San Cosimato 53 (between Via Roma Libera and Via Natale del Grande). 5810720

68 Il Tulipano Nero ★★$ As rare as a black tulip is a trattoria/pizzeria that serves both good Roman standards, *penne all'arrabbiata* (short quill pasta in a spicy garlic-and-tomato sauce with lots of chopped parsley on top) and thin Roman pizza, and is reasonably priced. This place fits both bills. Go early (7:30PM) for an outdoor table. ♦ M-F, Su lunch and dinner; Sa dinner. Via Roma Libera 15 (at Piazza di San Cosimato). 5818309

69 Porta Portese Flea Market The Romans who shop at this huge outdoor, jam-packed flea market come away with jeans, shoes, T-shirts, missing chandelier crystals, and cheap plastic household goods. Handbags can be a good value and some of the antiques sold by Neapolitan dealers who arrive before dawn are genuine, but plenty of fake Etruscan pots and overpriced jewelry is mixed in. The best buys—and the fewest people—are at dawn. Wear a straw hat at high noon in July and watch your wallet at all times. ♦ Su 6:30AM-1PM. Piazza di Porta Portese and Porto di Ripa Grande

Bests

Clotilde Sambuco
Owner, La Galleria

Passeggiata del Gianicolo: The cannon shot every day at noon (to honor Giuseppe Garibaldi) and the **Teatrino di Pulcinelli** *marionette* (open-air puppet show).

Orto Botanico: Open every day from sunrise to sunset.

Largo Cristina di Svezia: You can take lovely walks and admire the ancient plants.

The Rome Marathon is run every year in March. It is 42 kilometers long (26 miles) and passes some of Rome's most famous monuments. For information, contact Italia Marathon Club, c/o Nuova Tirrena, Via Massimi 158; 30183016.

In the Middle Ages most of the *osterie* (inns) in Rome had signs outside in the form of animals since most of the population could not read, and animal figures were easy to remember. Some examples are: Osteria dell Orso (bear), Osteria del Drago (dragon), Osteria del Gallo (rooster), and Osteria del Falcone (falcon).

Ancient Walls

In ancient times, all the world's roads led—literally—to Rome, so ramparts were needed to keep approaching enemies at bay. Segments of these walls and their great portals remain, primarily in the southeastern part of the city, and nearly all the city's important monuments lie within their enclosure.

In front of the **Stazione Termini** (central train station) is a patch of the ancient **Servian Wall**; south of it and close to the **Porta San Sebastiano** is the **Aurelian Wall,** the single stretch of embankment still intact that best evokes the feeling of Ancient Rome. For a brief distance the **Aurelian** follows the queen of roads—the ancient **Appian Way**, with its tombs, catacombs, and stately cypresses and umbrella pines. Also along the paths of the ancient walls are important churches—including two of the city's four great basilicas (**Santa Maria Maggiore** and **San Paolo Fuori le Mura**)—as well as the remains of the two great ancient Roman baths—**Terme di Diocleziano** and **Terme di Caracalla.**

The **Servian Wall,** which dates from approximately 390 BC, was named for Servius Tullius, an Etruscan who was the sixth King of Rome; it encircled the entire city, stretched 11 kilometers (7 miles), and had 23 gates. While the rampart excluded **Trastevere** and the **Vatican**, it extended in an elongated ring on the left bank of the **Tiber** and embraced all seven Roman hills.

Nearly 700 years later, after bitter battles with the *Allemani* (Germans), Emperor Aurelian (AD 270-75) expanded the defended area with a wall that was 19 kilometers (12 miles) long and had 18 gates and 381 towers; this wall enclosed Trastevere for the first time. Although the new ramparts were insecure and did little more than remind citizens of the danger of invasion, they served as a warning to outsiders. In 403, as the Roman Empire edged toward disaster and sieges threatened, Emperor Honorius (395-423) strengthened the walls, but they fell to barbarians again when the invaders

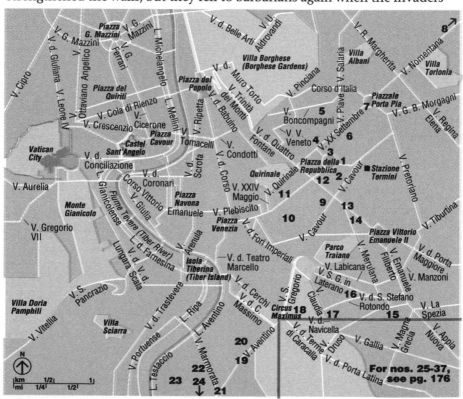

For nos. 25-37, see pg. 176

cut off the aqueducts. At the height of the empire, second-century Romans boasted that their city walls extended—figuratively—to Syria, England, and Spain. Rome's walls, in fact, continued to defend the city until the modern era. When the city became the capital of a united Italy in 1870, there was a movement to modernize Rome—centuries-old trees were cut down in the great gardens of the villas (which became public property), and large sections of the walls were torn down. In the late 1980s, archaeologists discovered a rampart from the eighth century BC composed of blocks of tufa (a volcanic rock) that once guarded the tiny ancient city known as **Roma Quadrata** (Square Rome), which was perched on **Aventine Hill.**

Baths of Diocletian and Santa Maria Maggiore

1 Terme di Diocleziano (Baths of Diocletian) Ancient Romans loved the baths, not only to wash themselves but to enjoy the gardens, gyms, and libraries that were part of the baths. This is one of the last built (AD 305) and largest of the great Roman public baths. More than 3,000 could bathe here at one time. Traditionally, baths had three pools—cold, tepid, and hot. During the more straitlaced years of the Roman Republic, men and women had separate hours; after mores became lax, they bathed together. The price was set by law, but there was no charge on some holidays.

The full rite of the bath included time in the *laconicum* (sauna) as a form of preventive medicine to remove toxins from the body. The baths had doctors on duty; the noted Dr. Celsus prescribed saunas for afflictions of the intestines and the liver, though he warned against them for sufferers of eye maladies, nervous tremors, coughs, or gastric malfunctioning. Bathers also exercised, played ball games, wrestled, had their skin greased and scraped smooth, and relaxed with a professional massage. In the gardens and porticoes of the baths, people strolled and chatted, admired the sculptures, attended lectures or poetry readings, and watched theatrical performances. ◆ Bounded by Via Gaeta, Via Volturno, Viale Luigi Einaudi, Piazza della Repubblica, Piazza dei Cinquecento, Via Cernaia, and Via Parigi

Within the area of the Baths of Diocletian:

Chiesa di Santa Maria degli Angeli
This church was built by **Michelangelo** in 1561 on the site of the *tepidarium* of the baths. Piranesi made etchings of what it looked like before the church was constructed—100-foot-high ceilings, statues everywhere, and sunlight shining through the mica windows. **Michelangelo** respected the ancient building and made minimal changes; later additions included the two stoops, one in Baroque style from the 18th century and the other a modern copy. ◆ Piazza della Repubblica (between Viale Luigi Einaudi and Via Vittorio Emanuele Orlando)

Aula Ottagona Across Via Cernaia from

Santa Maria degli Angeli is a large round building of typically ancient Roman brickwork once known (incorrectly) as the **Observatory** or **Planetarium,** which was a movie theater in the 1970s. Now restored, it houses outstanding ancient statues, including a large bronze of a seated, fatigued gladiator. Notice his cauliflower ears and the tiny cuts his opponent made in his skin. Though a separate building, the Aula is considered part of the **Museo Nazionale Romano.** ◆ Free. Tu-Su mornings. Via Cernaia (between Via Patrengo and Via Vittorio Emanuele Orlando). 4870690

2 Palazzo Massimo Alle Terme/Museo Nazionale Romano (Palazzo Massimo at the Baths/National Roman Museum)
After 14 years of renovations, the archaeological treasures of the **National Roman Museum** finally have been given a proper home—four floors of the climate-controlled **Palazzo Massimo**—where they can be viewed in all their splendor. Eight rooms on the ground floor house a sampling of the statuary and mosaics awaiting on the upper two levels. Don't miss the elegant and haunting marble figure of *Niobid* kneeling to pull an arrow from her back; this fifth-century BC Greek original is thought to have decorated Caesar's garden. Then proceed to the show-stopper second floor, where 11 rooms contain one breathtaking jewel after another: entire walls delicately painted with architectural motifs, landscapes, and mythological figures; 3 rooms of the first-century BC *Villa Farnesina;* delightful garden paintings of *Livia's Villa;* superbly hand-crafted mosaic floors and vibrant, colorful stone-inlay panels. (Tours of this floor are limited to 40 minutes.)

Back down on the first floor is a 14-room treasure trove of ancient statuary. Here lie the second-century bronze statue of *Dionysus,* found on the banks of the Tiber River; the unusually feminine first-century *Apollo,* his locks pulled up into a bunch atop his head; and the famous marble discus thrower, *Discobolus Lancelloti,* a Roman copy of a Greek bronze original. If you have energy left, visit the basement level for an extensive collection of Roman coins and a mummified eight-year-old girl, whose DNA confirms that she is of European descent despite the Egyptian-style burial. ◆ Admission. Tu-Sa 9AM-10PM; Su 9AM-8PM. Piazza dei

Cinquecento and Via d'Azeglio Massimo. 48903500

2 Hotel Diana $$$ Those catching an early train or arriving in the wee hours would do well to stay at this recently renovated Art Deco–style hotel just five minutes from **Stazione Termini.** Though small, the 188 guest rooms are tastefully furnished and dressed in soft stripes and florals. All rooms have air-conditioning, satellite TV, and mini-bars, plus baths with hairdryers and heated towel bars; two junior suites feature Jacuzzis. A breakfast buffet is included and the rooftop **La Brasserie** serves wonderful barbecued steaks and chops. ◆ Via Principe Amedeo 4 (at Via del Viminale). 4827541; fax 486998; diana@venere.it; www.venere.it/roma/diana

3 Le Grand Hotel $$$$ This Old World, quintessentially European hotel is a member of ITT Sheraton's Luxury Collection. Great divas and stars like Maria Callas and Elizabeth Taylor made the suites here their Roman home. Gracious and comfortable, the hostelry boasts 171 large guest rooms, all with ample bathrooms. There are great salons for receptions and fashion shows, a restaurant, and a cozy piano bar. In winter, afternoon tea is served in the lobby. ◆ Via Vittorio Emanuele Orlando 3 (between Via Parigi and Piazza di San Bernardo). 4709; fax 4747307

4 Chiesa di Santa Maria della Vittoria A not-to-be-missed sight at this 1620 church is Bernini's life-sized statue of *St. Theresa of Avila* swooning in ecstasy in the last chapel on the right. Its dramatic immediacy, indirect lighting, and full-power emotion are typical of the Roman Baroque. The saint is portrayed at the moment her heart is being pierced by a flaming arrow held aloft by a grinning angel. Her turned back, her toes, and her sunken eyeballs show how lightly Bernini drew the line between the sacred and the profane. ◆ Via XX Settembre and Largo di Santa Susanna

5 La Lampada da Tonino ★★$$$ The pungent smell of wild mushrooms in season assails you upon entering this rustic restaurant, where Tonino Fereale makes the best mushroom soup in Rome. Roasted—or garlic-flavored and sautéed—porcini sprinkled with fresh chopped parsley can be had as a main course, or else sliced, sautéed, and tossed with pasta. Meat and fresh fish selections are available. A good wine selection and homemade ricotta cheesecake round out a meal. Don't expect quick service or bargains. ◆ M-Sa lunch and dinner; closed in August. Reservations required. Via Quintino Sella 25 (at Via Boncompagni). 4744323, 4815673

6 Trimani Wine Bar ★★★$$ This two-story, wood-paneled wine bar—which also serves such snacks as *torta rustica* (savory pie), cheese platters, soup, and sausages—has one of the most complete selections of Italian wines, aperitifs, Grappas, and *digestivi* in Rome. To help remember it all, pick up a bottle of wine, some stemware, pitchers, or beer mugs around the corner at their **Trimani** store (Via Goito 20, 4469661). ◆ Restaurant: M-Sa lunch and dinner; Store: M-Sa 8:30AM-8PM, Su 10AM-7:30PM; closed in August. Via Cernaia 37/V (between Via Castelfidardo and Via Goito). 4469630

7 Porta Pia After unsuccessful efforts in 1862 and 1867 to liberate Rome from the French, patriot Giuseppe Garibaldi was finally victorious on 7 September 1870. His Red Shirts, having fought their way up from Sicily, entered Rome at this gate in the **Aurelian Wall,** claiming Rome for the newly unified Italy. The decision was ratified by plebescite a month later. The gate was **Michelangelo**'s last architectural work and was commissioned by Pope Pius IV in 1561. ◆ Piazzale di Porta Pia and Via XX Settembre

8 Chiesa di Sant'Agnese Fuori le Mura (Church of St. Agnes Outside the Walls) Emperor Constantine's daughter Constantia had Pope Honorius I construct the original church in the fourth century, but her tomb is housed inside a detached circular chapel behind the church. Its vaulted corridors are decorated with impressive late-Roman mosaics that depict cherubs crushing grapes to make wine. The church stands over the catacombs where St. Agnes was buried, and is one of the few churches that was not redesigned in the Renaissance or Baroque periods. Some of the mosaics show Byzantine influence. The original papal throne is housed here. ◆ Via Nomentana and Via di Sant'Agnese

9 Chiesa di Santa Pudenziana Originally constructed by Pope Siricius as the home of Senator Pudens, whose daughter was baptized by a house guest—a fisherman named Peter—this structure was rebuilt several times. It did duty at one time as a Roman bath and was converted into a Christian place of worship in the late fourth century, making it one of the oldest churches in Rome. Restorations were undertaken by Pope Hadrian (772-95) and by Cardinal Caetani in 1588. ◆ If the church is closed, ring at the door on the left. Via Urbana (between Via Panisperna and Piazza dell'Esquilino)

10 Goffredo ★★$$ Goffredo himself choreographs the whole production of mixing pasta with *vongole veraci* (tiny double-horned clams in their shells, flavored with garlic, parsley, and hot chili pepper) or perfectly peeling an orange at the table. Be forewarned: It's a smokey place. ◆ Tu-Su lunch and dinner; closed in August. Reservations required. Via Panisperna 231 (between Via del Boschetto and Via dei Serpenti). 4740620

11 Palazzo delle Esposizioni This large exhibition hall runs two or three shows simultaneously on topics from architecture and industrial design to fashion and multi-media. Recent events have included *Henri Cartier Bresson: The First Photographs; Valori Plastici: A Retrospective Of Contemporary Italian Artists;* and a Swedish film festival. Even if you're not interested in the exhibits, the **Artesia** book and design store (Via Milano 9A, 4828001) is worth exploring. ◆ Admission. M, W-Su 10AM-9PM. Via Nazionale 194 (at Via Milano). 4885465

12 Hotel Artemide $$$ Popular with business travelers, this modern and efficient hotel is centrally located. Beyond the elegant lobby, lit by an original stained-glass dome, are 85 rooms, including 5 suites with Jacuzzis. All have air-conditioning, satellite TV, hair dryer, safe—and the contents of the mini-bar is free. The **Caffetteria Nazionale** (Via Nazionale 26, 48991716) offers a vast menu and an all-you-can-eat buffet. The generous breakfast is included and a newspaper arrives at your door each morning. ◆ Via Nazionale 22 (between Via Napoli and Via Agostino De Pretis). 489911; fax 48991700; artemide@spacehotels.it; www.spacehotels.it, www.travel.it

13 Basilica di Santa Maria Maggiore (Basilica of St. Mary Major) One of Rome's four major basilicas (**San Pietro, San Giovanni in Laterano,** and **San Paolo Fuori le Mura** are the others), this church (pictured below) crowns Esquiline Hill. On the night of 4 August 352—or so goes a 13th-century tradition—the Virgin Mary appeared here to Pope Liberius and John, a patrician of Rome. In spite of the heat of that night, she told them that they would find a patch of snow on Esquiline Hill in the morning, and it was her wish that they build a church there. After her prediction proved true, **Liberius** himself drew plans while John organized funding for the church that was originally known as **Santa Maria della Neve** (St. Mary of the Snow). To commemorate the event, during Mass on 5 August, unseen hands toss flower petals from the church ceiling, and at night an artificial snowstorm falls on the worshipers in the piazza in front.

Later renamed **Santa Maria del Presepe** (St. Mary of the Crib), this basilica houses what is said to be a relic of the Nativity crib, highly treasured and exhibited annually at Christmas. The church was completed in the 5th century

Basilica di Santa Maria Maggiore (Basilica of St. Mary Major)

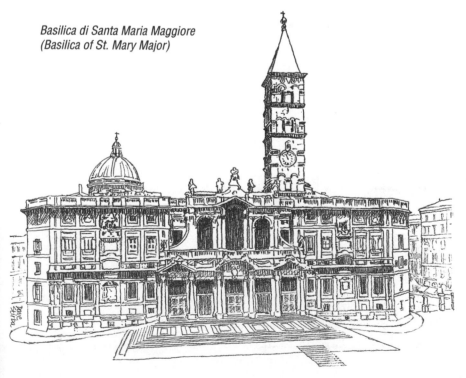

and rebuilt in the 13th century, and its Romanesque bell tower is the tallest in Rome. Most famous are the fifth-century mosaics in the nave depicting Bible scenes. A fine piece in the apse, completed in 1295 by Jacopo Torriti, shows the coronation of the Virgin. The chapel on the right of the nave, built by **Domenico Fontana** (1585-90), houses the tomb of the great urban planner Pope Sixtus V. The **Sforza Chapel,** on the left of the nave, is attributed to **Michelangelo,** and the famed statuary group of the *Nativity* is by Arnalfo da Cambio. ♦ Piazza di Santa Maria Maggiore

14 Agata e Romeo ★★★★$$$ Longtime residents remember this place as a simple osteria with traditional fare and friendly service. It's still family-run, with Agata in the kitchen, husband Romeo greeting guests, and daughter Mariantonietta minding tables. But today's menu is more cultivated, influenced over the years by the family's travels. Especially pleasing are the poached skate salad with raisins, walnuts, pine nuts, and citrus dressing; and the savory breast of duck marinated in Corbezzolo honey and roasted to crisp perfection. A 7-course tasting menu weds selections from the 10,000-bottle wine cellar (the only one in town to carry the flavorful La Tenaglia Chardonnay) to the inspired fare. The two dining rooms are simple and elegant; one showcases a whimsical collection of teapots in wooden cubbyholes. ♦ M-Sa lunch and dinner; closed two weeks in August. Reservations required. Via Carlo Alberto 45 (between Via San Antonio all'Esquilino and Piazza di Santa Maria Maggiore). 4466115; fax 4465842

14 Trattoria Monti ★★★$$ The pasta is always homemade at this upscale trattoria, and you'll taste the difference freshness makes whether it's fettuccine, *tortelli* (large tortellini), or the house specialty, *raviolone al rosso d'uovo con ricotta e spinaci* (jumbo ravioli filled with ricotta cheese, spinach, and a whole egg yolk in each)! The *stinco in vino rosso* (pot roast in red wine) is the perfect follow-up. ♦ M, W-Su lunch and dinner; closed in August. Reservations recommended. Via San Vito 13/A (at Via Merulana). 4466573

San Giovanni in Laterano/Monte Testaccio/San Paolo Fuori le Mura

15 Basilica di San Giovanni in Laterano The first basilica on this site was built by Constantine above the barracks of his private guards. The building suffered from earthquakes, fires, and invading armies through the ages; in 1646 **Borromini** completely redesigned the interior. The facade was added in 1736 by **Alessandro Galilei.** The huge bronze doors are from the **Curia** (Senate House) in the **Forum,** the mosaic of a ship in the foyer is by Giotto, and the glittering marble floor made of ancient scraps arranged in geometric patterns is by the Cosmati family.

Adjoining the basilica to the right is the **Palazzo Apostolico Lateranense** (illustrated on page 171) where the popes lived until the 14th century, and standing in the square behind the palazzo is the oldest obelisk in Rome, dating from the 15th century BC. It was brought from Egypt by Emperor Constantius II in AD 357 and placed in the middle of the **Circus Maximus.** Pope Sixtus V moved the obelisk to its present site in 1587. In front of the basilica is **Porta San Giovanni**—one of the ancient gates in the **Aurelian Wall.** ♦ Piazza di Porta San Giovanni and Via Emanuele Filiberto

Basilica di San Giovanni in Laterano

*Palazzo Apostolico Lateranense
(Apostolic Lateran Palace)*

Within the Basilica di San Giovanni in Laterano complex:

Cloisters These beautiful 1230 arcades were built by the Vassalletto family of marble masons and are a thrilling testament to their superb craftsmanship. Pairs of columns of various designs—some twisted, some fluted—give an uninterrupted sense of movement. The columns are studded with confettilike specks of marble and glass—some of which are gold and glisten in the sun. The harmony of elements together with the open-air garden in the center make this a haven from the noisy bustle of the world outside. ♦ Admission. Enter from the left aisle through a small doorway

Baptistry Built over the private baths of Fausta, Constantine's second wife, this is where Christian baptisms took place in Rome. Because baptisms then required total immersion of the body, the practice of using sunken baths for separate bathing evolved. Constantine's first building was rebuilt during the reign of Pope Sixtus III (432-40). Eight columns surround the font; they are of a rare oxblood marble called porphyry. The bronze doors have been dubbed "musical" because they make a strange plaintive sound when moved. ♦ Piazza di San Giovanni in Laterano and Via dell'Amba Aradam

Palazzo Apostolico Lateranense (Apostolic Lateran Palace) This 1586 palace, built by **Domenico Fontana,** is the administrative office of the Rome diocese. It houses a small museum, the **Museo Storico Vaticano** (Vatican Historical Museum), that

documents the Vatican's role in history as a superpower. The exhibits are located in 10 rooms of the former papal apartments that were frescoed in the 16th century and contain precious French tapestries donated by Napoleon. The displays include clothing, carriages, and furnishings used in pontifical ceremonies and a formidable collection of arms and armor dating as far back as 1500. ♦ Admission. The last Sunday morning of every month. Enter through the foyer of the basilica

Scala Santa (Holy Stairs) When the pope moved to Avignon in 1309, the original papal palace started to crumble, to the extent that the old building was uninhabitable when the papacy returned to Rome in 1377. This is the only remaining part of the original palace and contains an amazing private chapel of the popes—the **Sancta Sanctorum**—full of Giotto-like frescoes and a beautifully executed Byzantine mosaic. The stairs leading to the chapel were built on the site of Empress Fausta's house, probably by **Pope Sylvester** (314-35). Tradition says they came from the palace of Pontius Pilate, and pilgrims go up them on their knees. ♦ Piazza di San Giovanni in Laterano (between Via della Fontana and Via dell'Amba Aradam)

Cannavota ★★★$$ One of the best of the old-fashioned family restaurants in Rome, this cozy place specializes in seafood. But the dish that has kept generations of neighborhood families coming here regularly is *bucatini alla cannavota* (thick spaghetti in a creamy, mildly spicy tomato sauce with bits of seafood). Lots of people have begged for the recipe, but it

171

remains a well-kept secret. ◆ M-Tu, Th-Su lunch and dinner; closed in August. Reservations recommended. Piazza di San Giovanni in Laterano (between Via della Fontana and Via dell'Amba Aradam). 77205007

16 Chiesa di Santi Quattro Coronati (Church of the Four Crowned Saints)

The last remaining fortified abbey of Rome is named for four martyred Roman soldiers: Severus, Severianus, Carpoforus, and Vittorinus. After passing the medieval tower, walk across the courtyard and follow the wall of the ancient convent where various popes lived. The fourth-century church was fortified during the Middle Ages to protect the popes in the nearby **Lateran Palace** and enlarged in the seventh and ninth centuries. Recycled ancient granite columns divide the church into three naves, and a door in the left aisle leads to the enchanting 13th-century cloister, with capitals sculpted into lily leaves and a beautiful brickwork frieze around the inside. In spring the garden is ablaze with camellia trees in bloom. Off the courtyard is the **Oratory of San Silvestro,** which has well-preserved frescoes (1246) of the life of Constantine, who was cured of leprosy by St. Sylvester. ◆ Ring the bell, and one of the nuns will put the key for the oratory on the turntable. Via dei Santi Quattro (between Via di Santo Stefano Rotondo and Via dei Querceti)

17 Celian Hill

This hill takes its name from the Etruscan hero Celio Vibenna, and a walk on it from **Piazza di San Giovanni in Laterano** along Via di Santo Stefano Rotondo (the street name changes to Via della Navicella after it crosses Via Claudia) follows the course of one of the first roads of ancient Rome (then known as Via Celimontana). Traces of the **Neronian Aqueduct,** which bore water to Nero's artifical lake beside the **Colosseum,** can be seen along the way. At the juncture of **Piazza Celimontana,** Via Claudia, and Via San Paolo della Croce, look for the impressive **Arco di Dolabella** (Dolabella Arch) built in 10 BC; the base includes vestiges of a wall that are at least 2,400 years old. On the left is an area where the wall stopped; troops were garrisoned here, hence its ancient name— **Campus Martialis.**

17 Chiesa di Santo Stefano Rotondo (Round Church of St. Stephen)

As its name implies, this not-to-be-missed early (fifth-century) Christian church has a circular floor plan and is one of the largest and oldest of its type in the world. Before adopting the Roman basilica plan of three parallel aisles, many early Christian churches were built in the round with the altar in the middle. This church, inspired by Byzantine models, is actually three concentric circles separated by a double ring of ancient granite columns. A third-century Roman temple to the Persian god Mithras was uncovered under one end of the wooden flooring. In a chapel to the left of the entrance is St. Gregory the Great's throne. The walls were frescoed at the end of the 16th century with realistic Counter-Reformation depictions of the gruesome deaths of martyrs, which include flaying, decapitation, and breast amputation. ◆ Via della Navicella (between Piazza di Porta Metronia and Via di Santo Stefano Rotondo)

18 Basilica Celimontana dei Santi Giovanni e Paolo Martiri

The history of this AD 410 church reads like a gladiator epic: During the reign of Julian the Apostate (AD 361-63), two brothers and officers of the Roman Imperial Army, Giovanni and Paolo, converted to Christianity. They came from a wealthy family that owned a beautiful house overlooking the valley of the **Colosseum** and the adjacent Palatine Hill. After their conversion, they gave their wealth to the poor, an act of political significance because it flagrantly defied their emperor's plan to wipe out Christianity. Late one night, in retaliation, assassins broke into the brothers' house, killed them, and hid their bodies. Fearing the crime might be discovered, the murderers later killed two other Christians, Crispiano and Benedetta, who had learned of the brothers' murders and told others, so the crime—and the burial site—became common knowledge anyway. A century later Roman Senator Pammachius and his senator father—both Christian converts—financed the construction of a basilica above the house in which the brothers had been buried (an exception to the Roman rule that burial had to be outside the city). The church underwent various reconstructions in the 11th and 12th centuries, and its interior was redesigned in 1718 by **A. Garagni.** The lovely medieval bell tower—its base made of large stone blocks taken from a temple to Emperor Claudius— graces a particularly picturesque spot adjacent to a large park. At the top of the lane called Clivo di Scauro is an open square with a Renaissance copy in stone of an ancient Roman votive statue of a small boat, perhaps offered in thanks for a safe voyage. Today this is the titular church of American bishops in Rome and was restored in the 1960s with money raised by Americans. ◆ M-Th, Sa-Su. Piazza dei Santi Giovanni e Paolo (between Via San Paolo della Croce and Clivo di Scauro)

18 Chiesa di San Gregorio Magno al Celio

A flight of imposing steps leads to this church that was originally a Roman temple. A Christian basilica dedicated to St. Andrew was built on its foundations in AD 575 by the future Pope Gregory I. Gregory, who became known as Gregory the Great, was one of the great intellects of the Middle Ages and introduced the liturgical music known as the

Gregorian Chant. Next to the church, and later partly incorporated into it, was Gregory's family home. The church was dedicated to him after he died in 604, and his episcopal throne remains inside, as do 16 Roman temple columns defining the nave. The Baroque facade was added in 1633. Through a gate to the left of the basilica are three Romanesque oratories of **Sts. Andrea, Barbara,** and **Silvia,** the latter containing a famous painting by Guido Reni, *Concert of Angels.* ♦ Piazza San Gregorio and Via di San Gregorio

19 Piazza Albania A first-century BC restructuring of a portion of the old **Servian Wall** is visible at this square. Inside the rampart is a ballistics chamber where catapults—widely used in antiquity as well as in medieval times—were stored.

20 Chiesa di Santa Prisca Built in the fourth century above the house of the virgin Prisca, who was martyred by Claudius the Goth, this venerable church is mentioned in the Epistles of St. Paul. The Normans destroyed the early church, which was rebuilt in 1456 and again in 1660 (the facade was added at this time by **C. Lombardi**). Its badly damaged frescoes were rediscovered in 1940, and Dutch archaeologists painstakingly reassembled the fragments. In the remains of Prisca's house, under the church, is one of Rome's best preserved temples of Mithras, the Persian sun god whose worship parallels Christianity. Note the ritual well in which pigs, roosters, and lambs were sacrificed. ♦ M-F 10AM-noon. Piazza di Santa Prisca and Via di Santa Prisca

21 Porta Ostiense Part of the **Aurelian Wall,** this gate was the main entrance into the city from the road to Ostia Antica, Rome's ancient port. Today—still in near-perfect condition— it's called **Porta San Paolo** because it leads outside the city toward the **Basilica di San Paolo Fuori le Mura.** ♦ Piazza di Porta San Paolo and Piazzale Ostiense

21 Piramide di Caio Cestio (Pyramid of Caius Cestius) After the Roman Empire conquered Egypt, everyone suddenly wanted to live like a pharaoh or at least spend their afterlife like one. Numerous pyramids sprouted all over Rome. This one survived two millennia because it was incorporated into the **Aurelian Wall.** Over 100 feet high, it is flanked by **Porta San Paolo** and the **Cimitero Protestante** (Protestant Cemetery). As the bold inscription carved on its face boasts, it was completed in 330 days to be the tomb of Caius Cestius, a politician with the titles of *praetor* and "tribune." He also had the priestly title *epulo* and was one of seven members of a committee that offered sacrificial meals to the gods. The real sacrifice came from his children, who went bankrupt trying to complete payment on the contracts their father had signed for its building. Inside is a 20-by-15-foot burial room and the remains of frescoed walls. To visit the tomb, apply to the **Sovrintendenza Archeologica di Roma,** Piazza delle Finanze 1, 4824181. ♦ Piazza di Porta San Paolo and Piazzale Ostiense

Piramide di Caio Cestio (Pyramid of Caius Cestius)

21 Taverna Cestia ★$$ Located across the street from the **Piramide di Caio Cestio**, this rustic restaurant has an enticing self-service vegetable antipasto table. At night, order pizza and one of the other variations on the theme—calzone or focaccia. At lunch hour the place is often filled with employees of the FAO (UN Food and Agricultural Organization), whose headquarters are down the block. ♦ Tu-Su lunch and dinner; closed two weeks in August. Viale della Piramide Cestia 67 (at Piazza di Porta San Paolo). 5743754

22 Perilli ★$$ Working-class families come here for Sunday lunch and such very traditional, down-to-earth Roman dishes as *trippa* (tripe), *pajata* (sheep intestines), and *coda alla vaccinara* (oxtail stew). If these seem like culinary areas best left unexplored, the *spaghetti alla carbonara* (with eggs, cheese, and pancetta) is exceptional, although staid by comparison. The setting is cozy; murals depict rustic landscapes and old Roman street scenes. ♦ M-Tu, Th-Su lunch and dinner. Reservations recommended for Saturday dinner and Sunday lunch. Via Marmorata 39 (at Via Galvani). 5742415

22 Mercato di Piazza Testaccio This open-air food market is located in a working-class neighborhood; it's large and lively, and the stalls offer fresh fish, exotic fruits and vegetables, and good buys in men's and women's shoes (no large sizes). ♦ M-Sa mornings. Piazza Testaccio

23 Monte Testaccio Rising almost 150 feet, this hill is the result of the accumulation of an early Roman city dump. It is composed mostly of shards of large terra-cotta amphoras and jars once used for transporting oil, wine, and *garum*—a basic preservative in a lot of ancient Roman cooking that consisted mostly of rotten fish. Eventually, the accumulation of 700 years of shards gave the hill its name and made it ideally cool so that grottoes were dug at its base to serve as wine cellars. Testaccio was excavated only in 1989 under the auspices of Spanish scholars from the University of Madrid, who were interested in the traces of Spanish olive oil found on the pottery (inside each amphora appeared the name of the producer and transporter and city where it was produced, plus an indication of the quality of the oil and the date of production). Requests to visit the site must be in writing and hand-carried to the office of the **Sovrintendenza Archeologica,** Piazza Campitelli 7 (67103819). Follow up with a phone call one week later for the verdict. ♦ Bounded by Via Nicola Zabaglia, Viale Campo Boario, Piazza Orazio Giustiniani, and Via Galvani

At Monte Testaccio:

Checchino dal 1887 ★★$$$ The most chic place to sample the various Roman animal innards is this restaurant run for five generations by the Mariani family. They claim their ancestors invented the Roman standard *coda alla vaccinara,* a stew with more bone than tail in it. (A better choice is pasta garnished with the *vaccinara* sauce.) The menu is very limited and the portions small for the price, but the wine cellar offers the best selection in Rome. A special dessert here is gorgonzola with coarse honey on top (it works), washed down with a glass of Marsala. ♦ Tu-Sa lunch and dinner; Su lunch; closed in August. Reservations recommended. Via di Monte Testaccio 30 (between Via Nicola Zabaglia and Viale Campo Boario). 5746318; fax 5743816

Al Vecchio Mattatoio ★★$$ Right near **Checchino,** this rustic trattoria is named after the old slaughterhouse across the street and serves the same type of food but at more reasonable prices. Try the traditional *frattaglie alla grilla* (grilled sweetbreads) or the slightly less adventurous *carciofi alla romana* (artichokes stuffed with mint and garlic and seasoned with herbs and olive oil). ♦ M lunch; W-Su lunch and dinner. No credit cards accepted. Piazza Orazio Giustiniani 2 (at Viale Campo Boario). 5741382

L'Alibi This is the oldest gay disco in Rome, where the action starts around midnight. In summer it all moves to the rooftop terrace. ♦ Cover. Tu-Su 11PM-2:30AM. Via di Monte Testaccio 44 (between Via Nicola Zabaglia and Viale Campo Boario). 5782343

24 Cimitero Protestante (Protestant Cemetery) Buried in this quiet cemetery are many outstanding non-Catholics, including the Romantic poets John Keats and Percy Shelley, the Italian Communist Party theoretician Antonio Gramsci, and some 4,000 others—mostly English, German, American, Scandinavian, Russian, and Greek.

*Basilica di San Paolo Fuori le Mura
(Basilica of St. Paul's Outside the Walls)*

Keats was buried here on 24 February 1821 by his friend, painter Joseph Severn. In the preface to his *Lament for Keats,* Shelley wrote, "He is buried under. . . an open space among the ruins, covered in winter with violets and daisies. It might make one in love with death, to think that one should be buried in so sweet a place." Shelley died in a boating accident off Livorno in July 1822; the following February his wife, Mary, had his ashes buried here beside their young son William. ♦ M-Tu, Th-Su. Ring the bell, and one of the workers will open the gate. Via Caio Cestio 6 (between Via Marmorata and Via Nicola Zabaglia)

24 **Basilica di San Paolo Fuori le Mura (Basilica of St. Paul's Outside the Walls)** This is Rome's second-largest church (after **St. Peter's**). Begun as a tiny chapel honoring the supposed burial site of the Apostle Paul, the original basilica was erected by the converted Christian emperor Constantine (306-337) and enlarged several times in the following centuries. By the reign of Pope Leo III (795-816) it was the largest church in Rome and was generously covered with glittering mosaics. St. Ignatius of Loyola and the first Jesuits took oaths to establish their religious order here in 1541.

Although a fire in 1823 destroyed most of the ancient basilica, vestiges of its original beauty remain. To the right of the central door are the basilica's original imposing bronze doors, made in Constantinople in 1070 and inlaid with 54 silver panels depicting scenes from the Old and New Testaments. Another outstanding relic is a triumphal arch, richly adorned with mosaics. The canopy is attributed to **Arnalfo di Cambio** (1285). The Corinthian pilasters have been constructed using parts of ancient columns. After the fire, excavations under the church revealed a first-century tomb thought to be that of St. Paul, as well as remains of other Christian and pagan burials. In the **Chapel of St. Benedict** to the right of the apse is a miniature *cella* (inner sanctum); its 23 columns come from the Etruscan city of Veii north of Rome. The cloister (1228), entered from the south side of the transept, has paired columns decorated with mosaics and is the work of the Vassalletti family of marble masons. In the center is a rose garden kept by the monks. ♦ Viale di San Paolo (between Viale Ferdinando Baldelli and Piazzale San Paolo)

Romans consume about four billion liters of mineral water annually even though the water supplied to Rome's more than three million inhabitants comes from uncontaminated springs in the lower Apennines and is among the country's cleanest and healthiest.

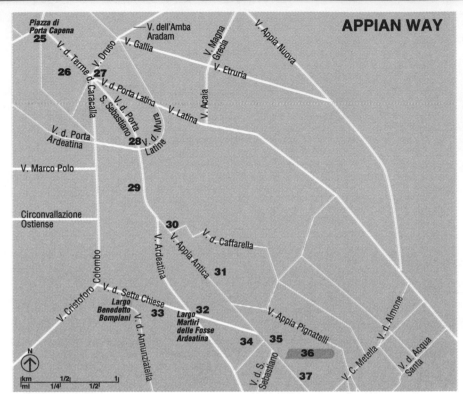

APPIAN WAY

Appian Way

The original **Via Appia Antica** was built in 313 BC by Consul Appius Claudius Caecus; it was 14.6 feet wide—allowing for either two-way cart traffic or 5 Roman soldiers marching abreast—with a posting station and inn every 7 to 10 miles. The road began inside the walls, just beyond **Circus Maximus,** followed the present **Via delle Terme di Caracalla** and **Via di Porta San Sebastiano,** and reached all the way to Brindisi on the Adriatic Sea. As the most important consular road leading south from Rome, the Appian Way was built to last; it is paved with black volcanic stone slabs—some of them over four feet long—laid over a thick, carefully prepared base of layers of sand and pebbles. As a result, it is also the best preserved of the Roman roads; at certain points, where patches have been left with the original paving, it looks as it did 20 centuries ago.

In ancient times burials were not allowed inside the walls, so this road, like most outside the city, was lined with underground cemeteries (catacombs) and funeral monuments. The tradition of elaborate funeral processions and ritual funeral banquets—intended to show family status as do extravagant weddings today—was Etruscan but was incorporated into Roman usage. The first vestiges of tombs begin about 100 yards down Via Appia. On the right is a shiny marble shaft marking one Roman mile (roughly equivalent to a US mile) from the road's starting point.

During the Middle Ages noble Roman families fortified some of the road's positions, including the **Tomb of**

Cecilia Metella, and in the Renaissance, artists Michelangelo and Raphael objected to the sacking of the tombs for construction materials. Until the last century, this part of the Appian Way was the turf of highway bandits, but today it is a posh residential quarter with fabulous walled villas popular with movie stars, wealthy industrialists, and diplomats. Some residents even have their own patches of catacomb in the garden near the swimming pool.

25 Piazza di Porta Capena Unfortunately nothing remains of the gate that was once the main entry from the Appian Way into the city through the **Servian Wall.** Just inside the walls (between today's piazza and the **Circus Maximus**) passed a stretch of aqueduct called **Aqua Appia,** which brought water to the nearby great baths.

26 Terme di Caracalla (Baths of Caracalla)
This was the second-largest spa complex in ancient Rome; it had pools, 2 gymnasiums, libraries, and gardens, and could accommodate more than 1,600 people. Named for Emperor Marcus Aurelius Antoninus (nicknamed Caracalla), who inaugurated them—still unfinished—in AD 216, they were begun by his father, Septimius Severus. As French writer Hippolyte-Adolphe Taine said in 1868, the emperors "provided the Romans with the baths, to which they resorted to gossip, to contemplate statues, to listen to speechmakers, and to keep themselves cool in the heat of the summer."

Visits began in one of the dressing rooms (the mosaic floors are still partly visible); then came a workout in one of the enormous rectangular gymnasiums, followed by a series of baths: The first was hot, in a round pool heated by a wood-burning furnace that sent smoky hot air into a buffer below the tiled floor; the second was an intermediate warm bath, heated the same way; and the final bath was a swim in a cold pool, either indoors or outside. Aqueducts converged here to bring water for the pools and porticoed gardens, which were flanked by two libraries, one for works in Greek and one for those in Latin. Underground, a labyrinth of service rooms extends out beneath the complex.

The structure—whose vaults soar 98.4 feet high—is now a fragile skeleton of bare brick. The building complex was once faced in marble with mosaic decorations, and it held some of the most important sculpture of its time. Among the treasures unearthed was the *Belvedere Torso*, now in the **Vatican Museums,** and several others to the Persian god Mithras. Colored marble flooring from the baths now adorns the floors of **Palazzo del Quirinale,** the state residence of the President of the Italian Republic. ◆ Admission. M morning, Tu-Sa, Su morning Apr-Aug; M morning, Tu-Sa 9AM-3PM, Su morning Sept-Feb (no midday closing). Via delle Terme di Caracalla (between Piazzale Numa Pompilio and Piazza di Porta Capena). 5758626

27 **Orazio** ★$$ Located near the junction of Via di Porta San Sebastiano and the handsome Via di Porta Latina—which leads to the ancient gate opening to Via Latina—is this pleasant tavern that opens onto an outdoor terrace. Antipasto trays rich with the vegetables of the countryside stretch out enticingly, and on early spring days wild asparagus make their appearance. Try *alici sotto aceto* (anchovies marinated in vinegar), bruschetta, and meat grilled on the charcoal fire. ◆ M, W-Su lunch and dinner; closed 10 days in August. Piazzale Numa Pompilio (between Via di Porta Latina and Via Druso). 77207339

28 **Museo delle Mure (Museum of the Walls)** This tiny museum is right inside the **Porta San Sebastiano,** the Appian Way's gateway through the **Aurelian Wall**. This is the most evocative stretch of wall, and it extends for an uninterrupted kilometer (a half-mile) on either side. The museum contains models that illustrate the architectural development of monuments and gates, as well as reproductions of Latin and Greek crosses in marble; from the museum, visitors can walk a short way along the top of the walls, as Roman sentries did in the days of the Caesars. ◆ Admission. Daily. Via di Porta San Sebastiano (just north of Viale di Porta Ardeatina). 70475284

29 **Quo Vadis** ★$ Ever popular, this restaurant serves Roman fare and offers a fine view of green fields from the tables on its outdoor terrace. Specialties include *bucatini all'amatriciana* (thick spaghetti in a pecorino cheese, bacon, and tomato sauce), grilled veal chops, roasted pork with fried potatoes, and market-fresh salad from the countryside. Be sure to save room for gelato. ◆ M, W-Su lunch and dinner. Via Appia Antica 38 (between Via Ardeatina and Viale di Porta Ardeatina). 5136795

Terme di Caracalla (Baths of Caracalla)

Rome by the Book

Much has been written about and taken place in the Eternal City. The following is a sampler of the wealth of literature on Rome.

The Agony and the Ecstasy (Ulverscroft, 1961) by Irving Stone, a fantasized version of Michelangelo's life, will provide a good laugh while waiting in line to get into the **Sistine Chapel.**

The Biography of a City (Norton, 1985) by Christopher Hibbert is a meticulously researched volume on Rome covering everything from the dawn of the Etruscans to the fall of Mussolini.

Cookery and Dining in Imperial Rome (Dover, 1977) edited by J.D. Vehling is a collection of notes of first-century AD gastronome Apicius. Read here to find out what the ancient Romans ate before pasta took over; it offers recipes for such delicacies as rose wine and boiled ostrich.

Daily Life in Ancient Rome (Yale University Press, 1940) by Jerome Carcopino and *The Roman Way* (W.W. Norton & Company, 1932) by Edith Hamilton give the curious some facts about day-to-day existence in the capital of an empire. Included are what traffic was like then (as terrifying as now) and the status of women (better than in Greece).

The Decline and Fall of the Roman Empire by Edward Gibbon (Random House, 1932) is the place to begin reading about Rome. This classic is available in either the six-volume mega-edition or an abridged version.

Italy the Fatal Gift (Dodd, Mead, 1982) by *New Yorker* staff writer William Murray has some interesting things to say about what it was like living in **Campo de' Fiori** in the 1960s.

A Literary Companion to Rome (St. Martin's Press, 1995) by John Varriano is a sampling of this writer's impressions of Rome.

The Marble Faun (1860) by Nathaniel Hawthorne is a haunting tale that will keep you away from the city's catacombs and out of the **Colosseum** at night.

The Memoirs of Hadrian (Farrar, Straus and Giroux, 1957) by Margurite Yourcenar, a monumental invented autobiography of Emperor Hadrian, will succeed like none of the others in getting you past the toga and under the skin of one of the ancient world's most interesting personalities.

Roman Mornings (New Amsterdam, 1956) by James Lees-Milnes is a very personal evaluation, organized around the author's visits to eight famous buildings.

Rome and a Villa (HarperCollins, 1992) by Eleanor Clark is an evocative, illuminating examination of several sights in Rome, plus a long section on **Hadrian's Villa** in **Tivoli.**

Rome, Places and Pleasures (Knopf, 1972) by Kate Simon offers a personal perception of the city.

Rome: The Sweet Tempestuous Life (Congdon & Lattès, 1982) by former *New York Times* Rome Bureau Chief Paul Hoffman offers an appraisal of the city.

A Traveller in Rome (Methuen, 1957) by H.V. Morton is a vivid account of the home of the Caesars and the popes by a great British travel writer.

The Vatican Collections: The Papacy and Art (H.N. Abrams, 1982) by the Metropolitan Museum of Art, a catalog of an exhibition at the museum in New York, will help prepare for the **Vatican Museums.** Highlighted are paintings and sculpture collected by the popes through the centuries.

30 Domine, Quo Vadis Church This 1637 church was built on the spot on the road where, according to legend, St. Peter, fleeing Rome in terror at the persecution of the Christians, saw a vision of Christ walking into the city. Startled, Peter asked, *"Domine, Quo Vadis?"* (Lord, where goest Thou?), and Christ replied, "I go to Rome to be crucified a second time," prompting Peter to return to Rome, where he was martyred. Inside the church is a piece of pavement bearing the supposed imprint of Christ's feet when he chastised St. Peter. ♦ Via Appia Antica (between Via della Caffarella and Viale delle Mura Latine)

31 Hosteria Antica Roma ★★$$ The fresh antipasti are the best part of the menu here and include a wide variety of salami, prosciutto, *bresaola* (cured beef), grilled vegetables, and seafood salad. Follow it with pasta or risotto and a grilled steak or fish. Go at night and dine outdoors in the candlelit *columbarium*. This was part of an ancient cemetery for liberated slaves; the niches in the walls were for their burial urns. Inside is a copy of a Piranesi print depicting the cemetery in the 17th century. ♦ Tu-Su lunch and dinner; closed 10 days in August. Via Appia Antica 87 (between Via Appia Pignatelli and Via della Caffarella). 5132888

32 Catacombe di San Callisto (Catacombs of St. Calixtus) Dating from the third century, this was the first formal Christian cemetery and the most famous of the catacombs. Before then, Christians were buried at private family burial grounds in graves marked with large terra-cotta roofing tiles (if the Christian family was too poor to afford marble). In the catacombs, affluent Christian families were identifiable because they had their own funeral chambers, or *cubicula*, decorated with frescoes. This vast warren of galleries has five layers. ♦ Admission. M-Tu; Th-Su. Largo Martiri delle Fosse Ardeatine (between Vicolo delle Sette Chiese and Via Ardeatina). 51301580

33 Catacombe di Domitilla (Catacombs of Domitilla) These vast galleries were once the private burial ground of Domitilla, niece of Emperor Domitian (AD 81-96) and a member of the rich and powerful Flavian family. Domitilla's husband, Flavius Clemens, was a martyred Christian; it was through him that the area became Christian. The Flavian family tomb is an exception to the generally humble ones of most Christians. ♦ M, W-Su. Via delle Sette Chiese 282 (between Largo Martiri delle Fosse Ardeatine and Largo Benedetto Bompiani). 5110342

34 Catacombe e Chiesa di San Sebastiano (Catacombs and Church of St. Sebastian) Inside this church is a white marble statue of St. Sebastian, smooth except for the many arrow holes, that was sculpted by one of Bernini's students in the 17th century. The catacombs are on various levels and were mostly constructed in the third and fourth centuries. These burial places outside Rome's walls did not originate because of discrimination against Christians (in fact, there are Jewish catacombs not far from here at Via Appia Antica 119/A, and the Appian Way is lined with tombs of non-Christians as well as Romans), but because both Christians and Jews buried the whole body, unlike the Romans who cremated their dead and buried the ashes in an urn. The law was for hygienic reasons and required all Romans—with certain exceptions, such as emperors—to bury bodies outside the city walls. Health hazards were many, in spite of the running water in public lavatories and squadrons of workers assigned specific cleaning tasks, including cleaning out cesspools, carting refuse, sweeping streets, and cleaning food markets. ♦ M-Sa; closed mid-Nov to mid-Dec. Via Appia Antica 110 (at Vicolo delle Sette Chiese). 7850350

35 Ristorante Cecilia Metella ★$$$ Located on a private road behind a fountain of spring water (where Romans still come to fill cases of bottles with free mineral water), this spot is the best-known restaurant in the area. Couples have wedding feasts here on Saturday and Sunday, and Roman families come here to eat after important family events: births, confirmations, marriages, deaths. There is a wood fire for barbecuing meat, a terrace for outdoor dining in summer, and ample parking. ♦ Tu-Su lunch and dinner. Via Appia Antica 125 (between Via Cecilia Metella and Via Appia Pignatelli). 5136743, 5110213

35 Hosteria L'Archeologia ★$$ This old farmhouse-turned-restaurant has an ancient wisteria vine for shade in the courtyard—perfect for alfresco dining—and a cozy fire that burns inside when it's chilly. Antipasto, spaghetti, fettuccine, and grilled meats—like *lombata di vitello* (veal chop)—are straight from the Roman cookbooks and countryside, and the house chocolate cake is a treat. Service tends to break down when there's a crowd. ♦ M-W, F-Su lunch and dinner. Via Appia Antica 139 (between Via Cecilia Metella and Via Appia Pignatelli). 7880494

36 Circus Maxentius Built for chariot racing, this enormous area (about a quarter-mile long) stretches over sloping green fields with only songbirds to interrupt the stillness where 18,000 spectators once shouted their encouragement to the charioteers they were betting on to win the 7-lap races. The **Obelisk of Diocletian**, now in the **Piazza Navona**, used to stand on the dividing island running down the center of the track. Notice that the overarching canopy above the bleachers was made of masonry lightened by the insertion of hollow pots. Adjacent is the huge **Tomb of Romulus** (AD 309), built by Maxentius to honor his son, who died young. The medieval house in the next field stands at the entrance to the tomb's core. Maxentius also built a temple to honor his son on the Via Sacra by the **Roman Forum**. ♦ Admission. Tu-Su. Via Appia Antica 153 (between Via Cecilia Metella and Via Appia Pignatelli). 7801324

37 Tomba di Cecilia Metella (Tomb of Cecilia Metella) Cecilia was the wife of Crassus and the daughter of the conqueror of Crete, Quintus Metellus Creticus. This cylindrical mausoleum has a 60-foot diameter and a square base, similar to **Castel Sant'Angelo**. In 1302 the Caetani family turned the mausoleum into their castle (the towers and battlements are reminders). ♦ Tu-Su. Via Appia Antica (between Via Cecilia Metella and Via Appia Pignatelli)

Day Trips

So much has been written about Rome over the centuries that most visitors feel they have more than enough to see just inside the city walls. But a short distance away is lovely countryside and at least a dozen interesting sites. All you need is a car and some stamina to get out of the city. The effort will be well repaid: The scenery is varied, the ruins fascinating, the food hearty and abundant, and the restaurant prices significantly lower.

Rome is surrounded first by its own ancient walls, and then by a ring road built in the 1970s—the **Grande Raccordo Anulare (GRA)**—which encircles the city approximately 12 kilometers (7 miles) out from **Capitoline Hill.** Other thoroughfares fan out from the GRA; most are the ancient Roman consular roads with a new coating of tar—and plenty of traffic—that still have ancient names: **Via Tiburtina, Via Cassia, Via Aurelia**, and **Via Appia Nuova.**

The region around Rome, known to the ancients as **Latium**, is today called **Lazio**, and its character varies sharply. To the west is the coastline of the **Tyrrhenian Sea**, largely damaged by pollution close to Rome but alluring the farther up and down the coast you go. Northwest of the city is the volcanic landscape of lower **Etruria**—the southernmost outpost of the Etruscans—with several lovely lakes and two significant Etruscan necropolises (burial grounds). Here the art that decorated their tombs provides a glimpse into antiquity. Moving clockwise, to the north are castles and villas from the medieval and Renaissance periods, and to the east is the more mountainous area, originally inhabited by the sheepherding Latins and Sabines, today the site of important churches and abbeys; closer to the city are magnificent villas, including **Emperor Hadrian**'s tour-de-force villa at **Tivoli** and the splendid Renaissance

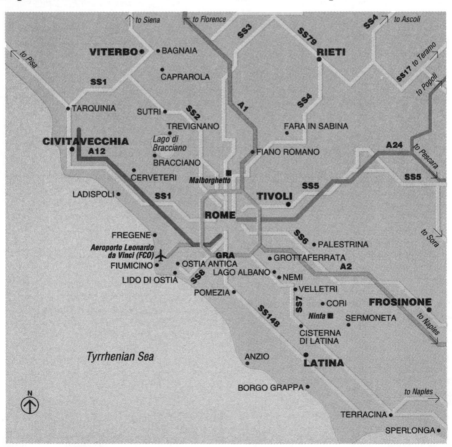

Villa Farnese at **Caprarola.** To the southeast and south of Rome is the agricultural region where the wheat-growing Samnites lived (the Sabines were a related tribe); it is an area of hills, gardens, castles (including the papal summer residence, **Castel Gondolfo**), and churches. Despite the passage of thousands of years—and today's homogenized culture—these areas have maintained their local traditions and characteristics.

Some practical matters: Never take a day trip on a Sunday—the day that Romans flock to the countryside and the beaches—or a Monday, when many museums and ruins are closed. Also, try to get an early start—some attractions are open only in the morning (until 1PM or, in a few cases, 2PM). And from early June through September, take along a bathing suit for a swim; beaches are free and public (although you may have to change under a towel in the back seat of your car). If you opt to take your chances with public transportation, call **COTRAL** (167431784) for bus information or **Stazione Termini** (Piazza dei Cinquecento, between Via Marsala and Via Giovanni Giolitti, 1478/88088) for train schedules.

City code 06 unless otherwise noted.

Cerveteri and Tarquinia

Cerveteri is 51 kilometers (32 miles) or 70 minutes from Rome by the fast toll road— **Autostrada Roma-Civitavecchia (A12)** from the **Grande Raccordo Anulare (GRA);** the old Roman road **Via Aurelia (SS1)** follows the coast north and goes slowly to Cerveteri and—another 45 minutes beyond—to Tarquinia, 90 kilometers (56 miles) from Rome. Blue **COTRAL** intercity buses for Cerveteri and Tarquinia leave every half hour from Rome's **Lepanto Metropolitana** stop on the *A* line. Alternatively, take the train to Cerveteri and then a local bus to Tarquinia.

Located about two kilometers (one mile) outside the town of Cerveteri is the **Necropoli della Banditaccia** (9940001), an archaeological park that is only a portion of a much larger, townlike cemetery that served the ancient Etruscan city of Caere from the eighth to third centuries BC. Grave robbers have been busy here for centuries, plundering the dome-shaped, grass-covered tombs beneath the mounds of turf. The tombs were originally built of local tufa stones, then earth was heaped on top, and finally grass grew over all—what's left today is a landscape of strange hills and dales. Although most excavated tombs are open to visitors (Tuesday through Sunday; admission is charged), the furniture and useful articles the dead had buried with them (pans, candlesticks, oil lamps, perfume bottles, food, ornaments, and precious objects) have either been stolen or moved to museums. The celebrated *Sarcofago degli Sposi* (Sarcophagus of the Married Couple) came from here and is now in Rome's **Museo Etrusco di Villa Giulia** (see page 146). The most fascinating tomb is the *Tomba dei Rilievi* (Tomb of the Bas-reliefs); on its walls are carved pots and other household items.

Near the central square in the town of Cerveteri is the **Museo Nazionale Cerite** (Piazza Santa Maria, 9941354), housed in the refurbished **Castello Ruspoli**, also called "La Rocca." The museum is open Tuesday through Sunday and has a wealth of artifacts from the necropolis.

On the way to Via Aurelia is the family-style restaurant **L'Oasi da Pino** (Via Renato Morelli 2, 9953482), a fine choice for risotto, homemade pasta, and seafood. For an interesting side trip, drive to **Ladispoli,** 8 kilometers (5 miles) from Cerveteri on the coast of the **Tyrrhenian Sea,** where the sand is black, and the beach has a desolate quality. The seafront restaurants here serve fish dishes, including *spaghetti alle vongole* (with clams in their shells), *mazzancolle alla griglia* (grilled prawns), and *spigola* (sea bass).

Along the coast northwest of Cerveteri is Tarquinia, one of the 12 major city-states of the Etruscan league, known then as **Tarquinii.** Although perhaps less important than Cerveteri in Etruscan history, Tarquinia attracts curious visitors from around the world: D.H. Lawrence wrote of it in the 1920s, "to the tombs we must go: or to the museums containing the things that have been rifled from the tombs." More than 6,000 tombs have been discovered a half-mile east of the modern town center, and a small group of them can be visited at the **Necropoli Etrusco** (0776/856308), which is open for guided tours only (there's an admission charge) Tuesday through Sunday (mornings only in winter). Unlike Cerveteri's tombs, which are decorated with bas-reliefs, approximately 150 elaborate underground chambers here are covered with still-bright wall paintings illustrating Etruscan life. There are scenes that depict dancing, hunting, religious ceremonies, and travel. Here you can theorize about this mysterious civilization that dates back thousands of years but left little in writing.

Many of the artifacts found in this necropolis are kept in the town's 17th-century **Palazzo Vitalleschi,** which houses the **Museo Nazionale Etrusco** (Piazza Cavour, 0776/856036). The museum is open Monday through Saturday until 2PM; there's no admission charge. The most valuable of its holdings is a pair of golden winged horses, a late Etruscan masterpiece from the fourth century BC, which was originally part of a decoration for the top of a local temple.

Quality copies of Etruscan works are sold in Tarquinia's shops.

Lago di Bracciano, Caprarola, and Viterbo

To visit Lago di Bracciano, travel 50 minutes or 51 kilometers (32 miles) from Rome via the **SS Cassia Veiientana** (also known as the **Cassia Bis**); take the turnoff marked Bracciano and continue past the town of **Anguillara** to the town of **Bracciano.** Leaving Bracciano, follow the road circling the lake to the turnoff for **Sutri;** from there turn right on the farm road **Sutri-Ronciglione** and continue to **Caprarola.** Caprarola is 68 kilometers (42 miles) or 90 minutes directly from Rome via the SS Cassia Veiientana; Viterbo, 90 kilometers (56 miles) or 2 hours. Buses to Bracciano and Caprarola leave from Rome's **Lepanto Metropolitana** stop on the *A* line (call **COTRAL** for schedules) and to Viterbo from **Saxa Rubra** (take the commuter train at **Piazzale Flaminio** to Saxa Rubra).

The old town of Bracciano nestles around the monumental **Castello di Bracciano** (99804348), which is open Tuesday through Sunday with hourly tours Tuesday through Friday and tours every half hour on Saturday and Sunday; admission is charged. Built after 1470, this castle seems created for a movie about swashbuckling, but it's the real thing and so attractive that castle buff Sir Walter Scott, author of *Ivanhoe,* once described it as nearly perfect. Built by the Orsini nobles, the castle overlooks a volcanic lake and is still inhabited by the Odescalchi, relatives of the Orsini by marriage.

From the parapets of the castle you can see the other villages on the lake: **Anguillara** is to the east (to the right) and **Trevignano,** a gentrified fishing village, is straight across the lake to the north on the site of an ancient Etruscan town. For dining there are small trattorie all along the lakefront serving delicious locally made fresh pastas and such delicate lake fish as trout, salmon trout, and eels. There is fine swimming in the lake—except on Sunday when the beaches are crowded—and Windsurfers can be rented at Trevignano (no powerboating is allowed on the lake).

Caprarola has long been a place of repose for princes and popes. Its best-known site is the **Villa Farnese** (Piazzale Farnese, 0761/646052). Built by Prince Alessandro Farnese, who was elected a cardinal at age 14, this great country mansion surrounded by classical Italian gardens sits amid rolling hills of vineyards and olive and hazelnut orchards. Vignola (1507-73) designed the gardens specifically to fit the palace—with its magnificent pentagonal shape—and divided the gardens into two parts so that two sides of the palazzo would have direct garden views. Bridges connect the palace to the gardens, and between the two gardens is a so-called casino garden, adorned with pruned shrubs, flowers, fountains, and mosaic pavements. It is a delightful surprise, after leaving one of the main gardens via a pretty but plain wooded path, to stumble onto this small, green jewel. The imposing palace itself is beautifully restored, with a grand circular staircase and elaborately frescoed halls. Both the palace and the gardens are open Tuesday through Sunday; there is an admission charge.

Castello di Bracciano

Villa Lante, Bagnaia

Near Viterbo, the Renaissance **Villa Lante** (Via Jacobo Barozzi 71, 0761/288008) at **Bagnaia**—originally built as a hunting preserve—beautifully combines art and nature on a wooded hillside. In the late 1500s Vignola piped in spring water to create an unforgettable series of cascading fountains and shaped acres of woods into formal Italian gardens surrounding small twin houses. Although the villa's name comes from the family Lante della Rovere, who owned the property from 1656 to 1933, its beauty is largely due to Cardinal Giovanni Franceso Gambera, who lived here 1566-87. His family symbol—the name means crayfish—recurs throughout the gardens as a design motif in fountains, sculptures, and even railings.

Although the villa was severely bombed during World War II, it has been carefully restored, and today visitors can wend their way up its five terraces, beginning with formal Italian gardens and four collecting pools. The **Fontana dei Lumini** (Fountain of Small Lights) forms a stairway of leaping streams of water, while just beyond, the same water travels in a trough through the **Tavola del Cardinale** (Cardinal's Table) where bottles of wine were chilled during convivial picnics. The walk up the terraces ends with the **Logge delle Muse** (Muses' Lodge), decorated with frescoes and crayfish, and the **Fontana del Diluvio** (Deluge Fountain), the source of the villa's natural wonders. The villa is open daily (no midday closing); admission is charged.

Tradition says that *spaghetti alla carbonara*, one of the cornerstones of Roman cuisine, was invented as a quick lunch by the *carbonai* or coal miners. But since it combines bacon and eggs, another theory suggests that it was born from the rations distributed by US allies during World War II.

Rieti and Fara in Sabina

To get to Rieti directly, which is 78 kilometers (49 miles) northeast of Rome, take **Via Salaria** or **SS4** 30 kilometers (19 miles) north to **Fiano Romano** and then drive northeast another 48 kilometers (30 miles); total travel time is 80 minutes. Returning to Rome, take Via Salaria (SS4) to the picturesque medieval town of Fara in Sabina (or, if you come directly from Rome, Fara in Sabina is about 70 minutes driving time from the city—50 kilometers/31 miles); follow signs to the abbey, which is 5 kilometers (about 3 miles) beyond the town. There is no train service to Rieti; call **COTRAL** for bus information.

Rieti is a 13th-century walled city that basks beneath a dramatic sweep of the **Apennine Mountains,** dominated by **Monte Terminillo.** In ancient times Rieti was the capital city of the Sabine tribes, which later provided Rome with three emperors of the Flavian dynasty: Vespasian, Titus, and Domitian. In 1208, the medieval village, bordered by the cool Velino River and shady woods, welcomed the youthful St. Francis on his first trip away from Assisi. His greeting upon his arrival in Rieti, "Good day, good people," is remembered every 4 October at a festival in his honor. The saint returned many times to the peaceful Sabine hills to pray and meditate.

Four sanctuaries are located nearby; they and the medieval **Chiesa di San Francesco** in town honor the saint's later visits. The most famous sanctuary is the **Convento di Greccio** (Santuario Francescano del Presepio, 0746/750127) built into the cliffside just northwest of Rieti along the river. It was here, in 1223, that St. Francis inaugurated the first live Nativity scene, still enacted every year at Christmastime. The convent is open daily.

Buon Appetito!

Over the centuries Italian ideas about cooking and the use of fresh, natural ingredients have influenced cooks around the world. Food is an important part of the Italian lifestyle, particularly in Rome, where meals are often lengthy social occasions. Roman cooking, like the people who created it, is straightforward and unpretentious and perfectly suited to a practical people who were better at building roads than creating great works of art. The cuisine doesn't fool around with subtle cream sauces or expensive ingredients like truffles because it didn't come out of the kitchens of the emperors or the popes, but out of the *cucina povera*—the solid home cooking of the common people. This characteristic still survives in the plain and hearty Roman dishes, and accounts for the preponderence of brains, intestines, and other organ meats in Roman cooking, as well as the presence of such natural preservatives as hot peppers and garlic.

A typical Roman starts the day standing up at a *caffè* enjoying an espresso and a croissantlike *cornetto*. Midmorning, school children—and hungry tourists—have a snack of *pizza bianca,* a flat, chewy pizza bread. Lunch is an important, and leisurely, meal in Rome, eaten generally between 1 and 3PM and traditionally followed by a short nap. Dinner is usually served between 8 and 11PM and tends to be the lighter meal of the day.

The classic Italian lunch or dinner begins with antipasti (usually a selection of cold cuts, marinated vegetables, olives, and cheese, and sometimes seafood salad). Next is the *primo piatto* or first course, which is often pasta (although it could be risotto, polenta, or soup). Pasta is the main feature of the midday meal, cooked al dente (chewy; literally "to the teeth" or biteable) and served in a variety of ways. The most common Roman pasta dishes are *spaghetti alla carbonara* (pancetta, egg yolk, parmesan, and black pepper); *bucatini all'amatriciana* (long narrow pasta tubes in a sauce made from salt pork, onions, tomatoes, and grated pecorino cheese); *penne all'arrabbiata* (short pasta with a peppery tomato-and-garlic sauce, topped with fresh parsley); *spaghetti alle vongole veraci* (with double-horn clams in their shells), and potato gnocchi, which are traditionally served every Thursday topped with one of the two standard Roman sauces—*sugo* (tomato and basil) or *ragu* (tomato and meat).

The *secondo piatto* is the meat or fish course. The veal is tender and tasty in Rome, and *saltimbocca alla romana* (literally, "jump-in-your-mouth" veal fillets) topped with prosciutto, mozzarella cheese, and a few sage leaves, and then sautéed in butter and Marsala is a common dish; *coda alla vaccinara* (oxtail stewed in wine, onions, tomatoes, and celery), *peperonata* (chicken stewed in roasted peppers), osso buco (braised veal shank in tomato sauce), and *abbacchio al forno* (roasted baby lamb served with roasted potatoes and rosemary) are other favorites. Look for fish to be featured on menus on Friday—especially fillet of *bacalà* (fried, dried codfish).

The second course is usually accompanied by *contorni,* which can be vegetables or a salad. Two *contorni* particular to Rome and hard to find elsewhere in Italy are *puntarelle,* the crunchy young sprouts of the chicory plant—skinned into spirals and served with a dressing of crushed anchovies, garlic, and olive oil—and *rughetta,* a wilder variety of what is called arugula in other parts of Italy (and rocket in England). Unlike cultivated arugula, it has a stronger peppery flavor.

Finally, fruit, such as *fragole* (strawberries) or *pesche* (peaches), or cheese serves as dessert more often than cakes or sweets.

Many Romans like to end a meal with a *digestivo,* an alcoholic herbal brew that relieves heaviness and settles a full stomach. The most common *digestivo* is an Amaro, which means bitter, and it sure is! (Amari range from the mildly musty herbal flavor of a Montenegro or an Averna to the bracing elixir known as Fernet Branca.) Other after-dinner drinks include the sweet anise-flavored Sambuca, which is served *alla moscha,* with three *mosche*—flies (actually coffee beans)—swimming in it, and a wide variety of Grappas or fruit brandies, which are served frozen in summer with bits of fruit floating in them.

KEELY EDWARDS

Two choices for dining in the area of Rieti are **Da Checco al Calice d'Oro** (Via Marchetti 10, Rieti, 0746/204271), a restaurant that has been in the same family for four generations and offers traditional Italian cuisine, including perfectly prepared *bollito misto* (boiled meat), lamb, and trout;

and **Al Nido del Corvo** (Via del Forno 15, Greccio, 0746/753181), a large, attractive restaurant that fits right in with its woodsy surroundings and serves well-prepared game, polenta, and, of course, wild mushrooms, as well as a tasty risotto with champagne.

At Fara in Sabina, **L'Abbazia di Farfa** (Abbey of Farfa) (0765/277065) sits on a hillside overlooking the Sabine Hills with their olive groves and oak trees. Once one of the great centers of power and influence in Europe, today the abbey is surrounded by vestiges of the medieval village that once clustered around it, with its lanes of shops that the monks rented to merchants as market stalls. The abbey was founded in 680 by Liutprando; it incorporates Roman ruins, and beneath it are traces of walls and frescoes and an inscription related to Emperor Commodus. Farfa became one of the most important Benedictine monasteries, with extensive landholdings—it once owned a huge tract in the Abruzzo—and a great library. Charlemagne, who visited it, praised its scholarship. Thanks to the support of Emperors Henry IV and Henry V, the abbey's reputation once rivaled that of the Vatican, but when Farfa fell under papal jurisdiction in the 12th century, its slow decline began.

Today the abbey proper has been restored, and you can see its original 20,000-volume library and the 15th-century **Chiesa di Santa Maria di Farfa**, with its charming cloister, frescoes by Taddeo Zuccari, and crypt, which has a well-preserved, 3rd-century Roman sarcophagus and 8th-century frescoes. The abbey is open daily, with guided tours on weekends; there's an admission charge. Beside the abbey is the **Convento di Santa Brigida** (0765/277072) where you can have a simple, inexpensive lunch; reservations are required.

Common table salt was not always so common. Before the modern age, salt was regarded as a precious commodity, much like petroleum today. The great consular road, Via Salaria (Salt Road), is so called because it was the main route for bringing *sale* (salt) into the capital from the seaside provinces. The English word "salary" is derived from the Latin *salarium* because part of a Roman soldier's compensation was paid in salt.

Tivoli

Tivoli is 33 kilometers (20 miles) east of Rome (a 45-minute drive) by way of **Via Tiburtina.** There is no train service to Tivoli; buses leave every 20 minutes from the **Rebibbia** stop on the *B line* of the **Metropolitana** and take about a half hour. Buses leave less frequently from the same stop for **Hadrian's Villa.** Alternately, you can take the Tivoli-bound bus and get off and walk a kilometer (half-mile) to **Hadrian's Villa.** There is also bus service between Tivoli and **Hadrian's Villa.**

From earliest times, wealthy Romans built summer palaces in the area of Tivoli; two of the best known are the ancient Roman **Hadrian's Villa** (about 5 kilometers, or 3 miles west of the town of Tivoli) and the Renaissance **Villa d'Este** (in the town of Tivoli), famous for its terraced gardens and fountains.

In AD 120, **Emperor Hadrian**—who was also an architect—designed and built what amounts to a personal resort village for his court's use when summer heat and the risk of malaria made Rome unbearable and dangerous. Having traveled all around the ancient world, **Hadrian** planned this sprawling collection of palaces and buildings to be his version of what he had seen abroad, complete with a network of underground passageways to keep servants out of the way.

As a result, **Hadrian's Villa** (SS5, 0774/530203) contains a fascinating itinerary of small-scale reproductions of great buildings that he admired, plus swimming pools, thermal baths, separate dining rooms and private baths for winter and summer, two libraries where guests could read, a fire station, and a track for footraces. Guests bunked down in the **Hospitaria,** where rooms had their own bathrooms and floors of black-and-white mosaics, worked in a different pattern in each room. The grandeur of the place is staggering. A sunny, unhurried day is ideal for visiting this splendid, still-beautiful country pleasure palace (illustrated above). The villa is open daily, and admission is charged.

Just outside the villa's gates, **Adriano** (Via Adriano, 0774/382235) is a restaurant that has homemade pasta drying in the entrance to the vast kitchen. Grilled baby lamb chops or *lombata di vitello* (grilled veal chop with fresh lemon) are always a good choice, and you can't go wrong with fresh green vegetables, a summer salad with *rughetta* (wild arugula) or *caprese* (sliced tomatoes, mozzarella, and fresh basil leaves). Ice cream and fruit in season are all washed down with a local Castelli wine.

Tivoli is a small town that was founded perhaps even earlier than Rome. Today local handicrafts are on sale in shops and in the stalls lining the walk toward the famous gardens. You'll find beaten copper bowls and pots, cowhide belts, and a variety of objects made of travertine marble from the nearby quarries worked into decorative and inexpensive bookends, tiny obelisks, and paperweights. Looking down from here, the plain below resembles a slab of marble. Four nearby aqueducts from this mountainous area provide Rome with most of its water supply.

The main attraction of the town of Tivoli is the **Villa d'Este** (Piazza Trento, just north of Via Boselli, 0774/312070), built in 1550 by **Pirro Ligorio** for the ambitious Cardinal d'Este, son of Lucrezia Borgia and the Duke of Ferrara, who so irritated the papal court that he was politely punished by being sent far enough out of town to represent no threat. He may have suffered the distance, but he soothed himself with luxuries and created one of the most beautiful gardens in the world.

Tiered down a steep hillside, the gardens have streams from the nearby Aniene River feeding it, providing water for hundreds of fountains of every size and shape—they are literally water sculptures in which the play of water is an integral part. One fountain is called the *organ*—but instead of feet pumping away at pedals, water powers the pipes. Inside the palace are Mannerist frescoes, including several painted by students of Federico Zuccari. The villa is open Tuesday through Saturday, and there's an admission charge.

Dining in Tivoli focuses around the ancient and beautiful **Temple of Sibilla**, a small, round temple that was a favorite of the Romantic painters for its location on a point overlooking a waterfall. The entrance to the temple is in the ancient heart of Tivoli—through the restaurant **Sibilla** (Via della Sibilla 50, 0774/335281), where every famous tourist who has ever visited Rome has dined, or so it would seem. But don't let that stop you; this is a touristy but reliable restaurant. In summer, sit in the superb terraced garden, where hundred-year-old wisteria vines provide shade from the sun, and there is an incomparable close-up of the elegant temple.

For those who abjure anything touristy, circle around the ravine to **Il Ciocco** (Via Ponte Gregoriano 33, 0774/333482), where the locals go. It seems to be everything from a pizzeria to a piano bar, with reasonable prices. Built on different levels—with part of the restaurant actually inside a grotto—this place affords the perfect Piranesian view of the **Temple of Sibilla**, glistening white on a summer's night.

Roma spelled backward is *amor* (love).

Malborghetto

Twenty kilometers (12 miles) north of Rome on **SS3**, or the **Via Flaminia** (one of the ancient consular roads that radiate from the city), is the **Malborghetto,** an unimpressive brick building that looks like an ordinary farmhouse but is filled with history. Archaeologists believe that this structure was almost certainly the place where Constantine the Great slept on the eve of his victorious Battle of Saxa Rubra in AD 312. It was here that his conversion to Christianity began, thus changing the course of history and, according to the great historian Edward Gibbon, speeding the decline and fall of the Roman Empire.

While sleeping here, Constantine had a vision that he must immediately attack the armies of his rival, Maxentius, with his soldiers' shields emblazoned with the sign of Christ. He attacked and defeated Maxentius the next day, thus becoming emperor and, by the Edict of Milan, legitimized the Christian religion. He built the **Malborghetto** (originally a cube-shaped triumphal arch with openings on all four sides) on the spot where he had the dream.

Nemi, Grottaferrata, and Palestrina

Nemi is 35 kilometers (22 miles)—45 minutes—by car from Rome by way of the **Via Appia Nuova (SS7)** past **Ciampino Airport** (turn left immediately toward **Marino**); continue until you reach a large crossroad, take the signposted road to Nemi (don't go toward Marino or **Castel Gandolfo**), skirt around **Lake Albano** (the large volcano rim with **Castel Gandolfo** on the other side), and follow signs to Nemi (after a very woodsy road, there will be a turnoff to the right). Grottaferrata is less than an hour southeast of Rome by way of **Via Tuscolana** and **SS511**; Palestrina lies 37 kilometers (23 miles) east of Rome, via **Via Prenestina**. Blue **COTRAL** intercity buses for Nemi, Grottaferrata, and Palestrina leave from the **Anagnina** terminus of the *A line* of the **Metropolitana**. There is no train service to Nemi, Grottaferrata, or Palestrina.

Lago di Nemi is a dark pool of water at the bottom of an extinct volcano. In ancient times it was called the **Specchio di Diana** (Mirror of the Goddess Diana), and a giant temple was built to this Greek goddess of the hunt in its thickly wooded hills. Emperor Caligula (AD 37-41)—who proclaimed himself the god who would marry Diana—kept two magnificently decorated pleasure barges on this lake for entertaining his court. Engineers in Mussolini's time drained the lake and found the 2 boats, which were over 210 feet long and 60 feet wide, resting in the mud at the bottom (water and mud had preserved them for two millennia). The **Museo delle Navi** (Museum of the Boats; Via del Lago di Nemi, 9368140) was built by the lakeside to house them. On 1 June 1944, German bombs struck the little

Castel Gandolfo

museum, burning the building and the imperial yachts. Reopened in 1989, the museum contains scale models of the boats, one-fifth the original size, as well as other articles recovered from the lake bottom, plus recent finds and a worthwhile photographic exhibition. The museum is open Tuesday through Sunday mornings; admission is charged.

Perched above the lake is a 12th-century town built around the medieval **Palazzo Ruspoli.** While it's not possible to visit the castle, there are charming restaurants and *caffès*, many selling the local specialty: tiny, fragrant woodland strawberries that, although cultivated in hothouses, benefit from the microclimate of the volcano and its rich lava soil. At the height of the season (late May or early June), a *Sagra delle Fragolini* (Festival of Wild Strawberries) is celebrated with processions, brass bands, and culinary delights featuring wild strawberries.

The restaurant **Specchio di Diana** (Via Vittorio Emanuele 13, at Piazza Ruspoli, 9368805), in the town of Nemi, is up a flight of stairs with a moderate view over the road to the lake. In summer dine outside on the terrace on such dishes as *spaghetti alle lepre* (with hare sauce) and chicken with mushrooms; fresh local salads are good, and, of course, the sublime wild strawberries are served in a variety of ways—with white wine, whipped cream, lemon juice, or simply on their own. **Capriccio sul Lago** (Via del Lago di Nemi, 9368120) serves the same sort of fare, but with grilled fresh eels in summer. The mood is pastoral as you lunch among the bulrushes lining the lake's edge.

Located at the next volcano—poised on the rim—is the 18th-century town of **Lago Albano,** site of **Castel Gandolfo** (illustrated above), where the pope spends the hottest months of the summer, blessing the crowd in the tiny town square after Mass on Sunday

around noon. He sometimes also holds a general audience at 11AM on Wednesday in the large auditorium at the **Villa Cyba;** to attend, apply for tickets in advance to the **Prefettura della Casa Vaticano** (Città del Vaticano, 00120 Rome, 6982). Near **Castel Gandolfo, Ristorante Bucci** (Via dei Zecchini 31, 9322244) is a simple family restaurant with a terrace overlooking the dark-emerald lake below. The menu features homemade pastas, lake trout, and fruit tarts.

The fortified **Abbazia di Grottaferrata** (Abbey of Grottaferrata; 9459309) dominates the town of Grottaferrata. More like a castle, with its thick stone walls and buttresses, the abbey devoted to San Nilo was completed in 1064 when it was built on top of the ruins of an ancient Roman summer villa (some of the vaulted construction can be seen). This abbey received support from several popes, including Julius II, who, as a cardinal at the turn of the 15th century, oversaw construction of its defensive structures. Today the monastery is still inhabited by monks who follow the Greek Orthodox rites. It's best to phone ahead, but visitors can ring a bell and make a contribution in return for a tour of the monastery's museum, which includes a large library with precious codices, frescoes removed from the church, and classical and medieval sculptures, among them a splendid fifth-century BC Attic stele showing a young man reading. The monastery museum is open Tuesday through Saturday and Sunday evening; there's an admission charge.

Across a courtyard from the museum is the 11th-century **Chiesa di Santa Maria,** with a delightful medieval baptismal font in the porch. Inside, Greek inscriptions decorate the walls, and off the right aisle of the nave is a chapel to San Nilo with frescoes by Domenichino. A door from the chapel leads into the sacristy and then into two small rooms with iron grille windows. Known as the *crypta ferrata,* these rooms—transformed into a Christian chapel—may have provided the name of the monastery and later of the town.

The local cuisine relies heavily on wild mushrooms; another specialty is *porchetta* (seasoned roast pork sandwiches on crusty country bread). Also worth sampling are some of the region's wines, easily found in any of the town's shops. **Al Fico** (Via Anagnina 134, 9459214), a large, comfortable restaurant, also has summer outdoor dining in the garden; homemade fettuccine with local wild mushrooms, chicory in tomato sauce, juicy lamb chops, and deviled chicken are among the many delicious options.

The medieval hillside town of Palestrina was known in ancient times as **Preneste,** and was the site of the second-century BC **Tempio della Fortuna Primigenia** (Temple to the Goddess Fortune). Primigenia, the goddess of fertility, was Zeus's eldest daughter, who gave birth to and nurtured the gods. (Primigenia is also identified with the Greek Tyche, bearer of good luck, and in antiquity her temple was the greatest shrine in central Italy, as renowned in its day as Lourdes is today.)

Preneste, with its stout walls and citadel, was razed in AD 82 after it unwisely sided against Rome during a civil war (only the shrine was spared). The shattered city then became a flourishing military colony, with its nearby **Ginestro Hills** dotted with sumptuous summer villas built by Augustus Caesar, **Emperor Hadrian,** Horace, and Pliny the Younger. Under Emperor Theodosius, pagan cults were prohibited in the late fourth century, and Preneste's famed Oracle spoke no more. During the Middle Ages Palestrina was built on the temple site. The town was later the home of the composer and creator of polyphony—Pier Luigi da Palestrina (1524-94).

World War II bombings severely damaged Palestrina but brought to light the basic structure of the ancient temple. Today's visitors can still admire the layout of the monumental shrine, built against a hillside on four levels that were connected by stately stairways and decorated with fountains and statues. The lowest level is on Via degli Arconi, just parallel to Via Prenestina; on Via Anicia is the **Duomo;** to the east of it was the **Aula dell'Oracolo** (Oracle's Hall), where the sibyl read the lots cast by supplicants; enter the shrine and museum from the upper level, on **Piazza della Cortina,** reached by Via Eliano and Via del Tempio.

Dominating the top of the complex—where a lost gilded statue of the goddess stood—is the palace built by the princely Barberini family, which wrested control of the town in the 17th century. The palace is the **Museo Nazionale Archeologico Prenestino** (Piazza della Cortina, 9538100), which houses artifacts from the temple—sculptures, bronze mirrors, and vases—plus a model of the shrine and its greatest treasure, a huge and finely wrought mosaic (probably dating from the first century) that shows the Nile in flood stage, with animals, birds,

fish, and people. Both the museum and shrine are open daily; the admission fee is valid for both.

The restaurant of the **Hotel Stella** (Piazzale della Liberazione 3, 9538172) offers pleasant hospitality and has an exceptional antipasto table that includes grilled eggplant slices, marinated zucchini with fresh mint, and cold seafood salad. The specialty is *pasta e fagioli con frutta di mare* (a pasta and bean dish with mussels and clams).

Ninfa and Sermoneta

Ninfa and Sermoneta are about 70 kilometers (43 miles) from Rome and 70 minutes or more by car. There is no efficient public transport, and even when traveling by car, don't set out without a map; Ninfa is hard to get to—but worth the trouble. Take **Via Appia Nuova (SS7)** south to **Cisterna di Latina;** take the next left to **Doganella;** over the crossroads, continue to Ninfa. Or, take Via Appia Nuova and turn left at **Velletri,** taking the road to **Cori;** at Doganella turn left for Ninfa. To reach Sermoneta from Ninfa, travel east on the road between Doganella and the **Abbey of Valvisciolo;** turn south and follow signs for Sermoneta, four kilometers (two miles) further.

English-style gardens in a medieval ghost town create one of Europe's most romantic sites—a stream lazily winds its way past ivy-covered crumbling towers of antiquity in a framework of fragrant rare plants, trees, and flowers. Ninfa and its meticulously groomed gardens are situated a couple of miles from the ancient town of **Norma,** where temple ruins perch precariously on an enormous cliff that was originally part of a volcano, and the **Ninfa River** forms a large, crystal-clear pond where many varieties of fish live and breed.

In ancient Roman times engineers drained the fertile **Pontine Marshes** around Ninfa—a fiefdom of Rome since 320 BC—and 23 farm towns dotted the resulting plain. Three ancient consular roads— Via Appia, Via Setina, and Via Corana—all passed nearby, and as a result, many sacred temples were built here, including one to the Nereidis (water nymphs) and another to the Dryads (wood nymphs). Pliny described Ninfa as having islands in the lakes where people played music and danced.

In the year 1000, Ninfa and nearby Sermoneta were ruled by the powerful Caetani nobles of Rome. Ninfa boasted 10 churches, 2 hospitals, 4 monasteries, 5 principal gates of entry, 4 bridges across the river, a double protective wall to repel invaders, and many water mills, which crushed grain into flour. In 1159 Pope Alexander III was crowned in Ninfa because Holy Roman Emperor Frederick Barbarossa had usurped the Church's power in Rome; Barbarossa then punished Ninfa and the neighboring towns by destroying buildings. Meanwhile, ancient drainage canals, no longer maintained during the Middle Ages, slowly filled with silt and—blocking the water flow— swamped the rich plain; malaria followed. Finally, the two Caetani brothers went to war, and Ninfa fell to rival towns at the end of the 14th century, when the decimated town was entirely abandoned. In 1765 a few repairs were made, but Ninfa remained piteously poor.

The **Giardino Botanico** (Botanical Garden) contains myriad species of birds, fish, and animals in a World Wildlife Fund sanctuary. It is open only the first full weekend of every month, with some additional weekend openings possible. There is an admission charge. For information, call the **Fondazione Caetani** in Rome (68803231).

Premiata Trattoria
GIGGETTO

On the other side of Latina from Ninfa, stop at the famous **Trattoria Giggetto** (Via Mediana, Borgo Grappa, 0773/20007), which is known for its *strozzapreti alla giggetto* (unevenly cut spaghetti in a lamb-based sauce), risotto with mussels, and chicken livers with onions. The local olive oil and wine are excellent, as is the mozzarella (the water buffalo whose milk is used to make this cheese graze in the fields here). Afterward, go for a swim at the nearby beach.

The picturesque medieval castle at Sermoneta offers an annual summer music festival; contact the **EPT** tourist bureau (Sermoneta, Lazio, 0773/30312) for information.

Trattoria Zampi (Via Leopardi 17, Cori, 06/9679688) offers good family fare. Don't be surprised if you come across a wedding or anniversary banquet being held here. Either festive event will give you a unique perspective on rural Italian life. Dishes include lasagna and Zampi's specialty—fettuccine with a ragout sauce.

Rome's finest—the carabinieri—have their own museum. The Museo Storico dei Carabinieri is right outside Vatican City at Piazza del Risorgimento 46 (6896696). It's open Tuesday through Sunday mornings (closed in August).

Terracina and Sperlonga

Sperlonga is 106 kilometers (66 miles) and 90 minutes by car from Rome—approximately 16 kilometers (10 miles) farther along the coast from Terracina. Both are reached by taking **SS148** to Terracina; on the bypass, skirt around Terracina and take **Via Flacca** to Sperlonga. Buses leave from the **EUR-Fermi** stop on the *B line* of the **Metropolitana** for Terracina and Sperlonga; trains depart from **Stazione Termini** for **Fondi-Sperlonga.**

The mighty **Temple of Jupiter Anxur** stands on the high cliffs above Terracina, nestled on a spit of land between the promontory and the sea. It's a tough climb under hot sun (follow the signs from **Porta Romanagate**), but from there you can see a magnificent panorama across the Fondi plains to **Monte Circeo**—even the island of Ischia is visible in good weather. The seacoast here is unpolluted (bring a swimsuit), and there are good restaurants, salt- and freshwater lakes, and ancient sites like this temple guarding Terracina from the wrath of the gods.

The attractive town of Sperlonga—a 20-minute drive east of the temple—was a 12th-century enclave of houses, with a fortress on the cliff's edge facing the sea. The name is from *sperlunca* (cave), and in mythological times this stretch of coast was known for its seductive sirens and dangerous sea monsters, as Homer relates in the *Odyssey*, describing Ulysses's passage during his trip back from the wars. The beach makes a pretty half-moon curve between the grotto and the promontory of Sperlonga and is packed with tourists and swimmers (this is Rome's favorite nearby summer resort). In town are antiques stores, art shops, restaurants, and pizzerias. As its name implies, **Tramonto** (Via Cristoforo Colombo 53, 0771/549597), or sunset, is the perfect place to watch the golden orb descend while enjoying assorted antipasti, pizza, pasta, or grilled fish.

The **Villa of Tiberius,** also known as the "Praetorium Palace," was the imperial villa of Emperor Tiberius (42 BC-AD 37), an adopted son of Augustus, who reigned from AD 14 to 37 but deserted Rome in AD 26 for Capri. In 1954, on a stretch of beach where explosives had been hidden during wartime, archaeologists found foundations of a sprawling villa and various outbuildings, including a fish hatchery and, beside it, a large grotto where the emperor and his courtiers had picnics—the interior ledges of the grotto are wide enough for banquets—and enjoyed concerts. On an artificial islet in the middle of the grotto was a giant sculpture of the *Laocoön* group (see **Museo Archeologico Nazionale di Sperlonga,** below). The seawater swimming pond reflected other marble statues gracing the circumference.

In ancient times, many beautiful country estates were located nearby; Roman pleasure villas like this also incorporated walkways for two-wheeled carriages (like rickshaws) and litters, multiple dining rooms, libraries, gymnasiums, theaters, and parks.

The **Museo Archeologico Nazionale di Sperlonga** (Via Flacca, 0771/54028) houses statues and fragments found on the site of Tiberius's grotto, but it was mainly built to house the large *Laocoön* sculpture, which depicts the death of the Trojan priest who admonished his fellow citizens not to allow the famous hollow wooden horse to enter their gates. As he prepared to sacrifice a bull, two sea serpents coiled themselves around him and his two sons; this sculpture group is often compared to a similar statue in the **Vatican Museums.** The museum is open daily; admission is charged.

Beyond Tiberius's villa on the road southeast is **Il Fortino** (Via Flacca, 0771/54337), a good fish restaurant on the side of the cliff, with a beautiful view toward the sea.

Ostia Antica

Ostia Antica is 45 minutes—37 kilometers (23 miles)—by car from Rome. Take the **Raccordo Autostrada** superhighway to **Aeroporto Leonardo da Vinci** and then follow the signposts to **Fiumicino** and **Ostia.** On the flyover, continue to Ostia Antica. When you reach a turn about 4 kilometers (2.5 miles) down this road, head toward Ostia Antica and Rome. Signposts are scarce, but it's not difficult to find. The fastest way is to take the *B line* of the **Metropolitana** to **Magliana,** then the local tram to Ostia Antica. To get to **Pratica di Mare,** take the **Cristoforo Colombo** road out of Rome until you come to the **Palazzo dello Sport,** then take **Via Pontina (SS148)** toward **Pomezia;** get off at the Pratica di Mare exit.

For 1,700 years the **Tyrrhenian Sea** has receded, so that the ancient seaport of **Ostia** is now inland, but visitors can stop by the **Parco e Museo Archeologico di Ostia Antica** (Via dei Romagnoli 719, 56358099;

museum and excavations open daily except 1 January and 1 May; admission is charged) to get a sense of how the ancient Ostians lived. Abandoned in the fifth century, Ostia was once a prosperous town—the major port of what was the most important city in the world—but its end was not a cataclysm like that of Pompeii, which was covered by lava in two days of agony. Ostia's decline was subtle; the city deteriorated as the empire declined and fell, and Rome lost its role as the hub of the universe. The malaria mosquito—literally *mal aria* (bad air)—spawned in the stagnant water that built up as the canals fell into disuse, and the port itself—now partially under the **Aeroporto Leonardo da Vinci**—silted up.

Stroll down the **Decumanus Maximus** (Main Street) to understand how rigorously every Roman town was laid out (a citizen of Rome could not get lost abroad, because all towns built by the Romans had the same grid pattern). The ancient town was also vast; it included two major public baths, lavatories, many temples, a courthouse, taverns, apartment buildings (five stories high), lovely private houses with gardens, barracks for the soldiers and firefighters, a large town square with mosaics depicting even what each shop traded, and a theater where even today plays are performed in summer. **Isola Sacra** is the site of excavations into early Roman life, including an important necropolis that has been uncovered here; nearby, **Trajan's Port** is a precisely hexagonal basin built in AD 103 by that emperor to provide a well-protected harbor to serve the growing needs of burgeoning Rome. It is closed to the public. The small excellent museum contains a fine collection of ex-votos in terra-cotta; don't miss the superb mosaics in the two baths and the public toilets.

In the adjacent village of Ostia Antica, the restaurant **Il Monumento** (Piazza Umberto Primero 8, 5650021) is tucked into the 15th-century walls of a medieval castle. Small, with a protected outside terrace for lunching from the early spring on, it specializes in

Ostia Antica

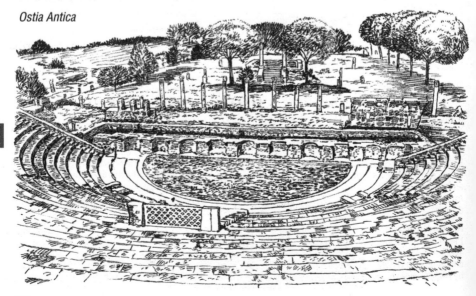

grilled or broiled fish. The spaghetti and seafood salads also are tasty; save room for cake or tart for dessert.

The port town of **Fiumicino** is wall-to-wall with seafood trattorie. **Il Pescatore** (Via Torre Clementina 154, 6505189) is first-class. Try *linguine con astrice* (with Mediterranean lobster) or *mezzancolle alla griglia* (grilled prawns). **Bastianelli al Molo** (Via Torre Clementina 312, 6505118) is the most celebrated fish restaurant in Fiumicino and is open Tuesday through Sunday (reservations

recommended). It is located in a large, whitewashed, Spanish-style building with a view of the sea.

A little farther south and inland is **Al Sabba delle Streghe** (Via Lavinia 1, Pratica di Mare, 9122055)—it's a 45-minute drive from downtown Rome (directions above), but worth it. The restaurant is in a tiny ancient walled city of only 2 streets that was called **Lavinium** 2,000 years ago. There are cow stalls below, and this sumptuous, light, and airy dining spot is above in a 17th-century building. Naturally, the fish is fresh daily.

Architectural Styles and Terms

Rome is known for its architectural treasures and variety of styles. Here are some brief descriptions of the principal kinds of architecture found in Rome and the terms used to explain them:

Architectural Styles

Baroque: Based on elaborate, large-scale forms, complex design, with alternating concave and convex lines

Byzantine: Evolved when Constantinople was the capital of the empire in the fourth century; introduced the domed, square, or Greek cross design

Early Christian: Notable for the development of the basilica (which was based on Roman meeting halls) as a church

Etruscan: Based on Greek styles, but heavier; use of wood and baked clay; only a few walls and underground tombs remain

Gothic: Characterized by pointed arches, ribbed vaults, buttresses, and vertical lines

Mannerist: Evolved from the Renaissance style in the 16th century and characterized by the use of motifs in opposition to their original context

Rationalist: Developed as "Modern" style of the 1920-1930s; associated with Fascism

Renaissance: Represented the 15th- and 16th-century reintroduction, reinterpretation, and refinement of ancient classical standards

Roman: Based on classical Greek architecture with the added use of rounded forms (arches, vaults, domes)

Romanesque: Preceded Gothic in a vaulted style; characterized in Italy by ribbed vaults

Architectural Terms

Architrave: In classical architecture, the part resting on columns' capitals; also the molding around a door

Atrium: The central hall of a Roman house—usually open-air

Campanile: Bell tower

Capitals (tops of columns):

Corinthian: Elaborate floral or leaf designs, especially acanthus leaves

Doric: The earliest and simplest—round tubes

Ionic: Has swirls on either side like a ram's horns

Column Types

Composite: A late-Roman style combining elements of Ionic and Corinthian

Corinthian: Fluted column, tiered base, decorative capital

Greek Doric: Fluted column without a base

Ionic: Fluted column on a tiered base, swirled capital

Roman Doric: Fluted column on a graduated base

Tuscan: Simple, smooth column on a rounded base

Concave: A form that is curved or rounded inward, like a segment of the interior of a hollow sphere

Convex: A form that is curved or rounded outward, like a segment of the exterior of a sphere

Frieze: A decorated band along the upper part of an interior wall

Ogee: A pointed arch having on each side near the apex a reversed curve; also a molding with an S-shaped profile

Pediment: Triangular space forming the gable of a two-pitched roof

Pilaster: A support or flat column projecting only slightly from a wall

Putti: Two or more baby angels; one is a *putto*

History

753 BC The legendary founding of Rome by Romulus. Around this time the primitive huts and small settlements on **Palatine Hill** join into permanent settlements.

715 BC A monarchy is established by King Numa Pompilius, beginning 99 years of Sabine rule.

616 BC The Sabine rulers are overthrown, and 117 years of Etruscan rule begin under King Tarquin the Elder. During the next century, Latin script and the name "Roma" first appear, and Rome becomes an urban center. The **Roman Forum** is laid out, and other permanent stone buildings appear, including the **Mamertine Prison** and the first **Temple of Vesta.**

509 BC The Roman Republic is established with the overthrow of the last Etruscan king, Tarquin the Proud. Rome is governed by the Senate.

500 BC The conflict between the patricians and the plebeians for control of Roman life is resolved and codified in the Twelve Tablets of Roman Law. The construction of the **Temples of Saturn, Apollo, Ceres,** and **Castor** highlights the growth of the new city, while the defeat of the Etruscans and the Latin tribes marks the early expansion of the republic.

400 BC Rome is sacked by the invading Gauls, who are later driven out. The **Servian Wall** is built around Rome to protect the city from future attacks, and the city begins the conquest and colonization of the Italian peninsula. Construction includes the **Appian Way,** the **Aqua Appia**—the first aqueduct—new temples, and the **Circus Flaminius.**

300 BC Rome's expansion by war and conquest continues with the capture of Corsica and Sicily and inroads into Greece.

280-260 BC The earliest Roman coins are minted, and the growing population of Rome is entertained by the first public gladiator contests.

260-241 BC Rome battles Carthage for control of Sicily in the First Punic War.

220 BC The **Flavian Way** is built, extending from Rome to Rimini on the Adriatic Sea. In the early stages of the Second Punic War (219-202 BC) the Roman armies suffer a crushing defeat at the hands of Hannibal before routing the elephant-riding conqueror near Carthage in 203 BC.

197-168 BC Roman armies defeat Philip of Macedonia in the Macedonian Wars and annex Greece as a Roman colony. The influence of Greek art and architecture on Roman life grows.

150-140 BC Rome's conquering armies extend the republic's reach over most of modern-day Europe and Asia Minor. Carthage is destroyed in the Third Punic War (149-146 BC), putting northern Africa, with the exception of Egypt, under Roman rule.

140 BC Rome's thirst for expansion stretches its resources to the limit. Increasingly, the republic and its civilian leaders rely on the army and its generals to protect and expand Roman rule. Closer to home, factional disputes weaken the Senate.

136 BC A revolt in Sicily marks the first of many uprisings by enslaved peoples against their Roman conquerors.

102-101 BC The popular Roman general Gaius Marius defeats Germanic tribes attacking Rome's northern borders.

86 BC Civil war breaks out. Sulla, a general supported by the nobility, defeats Marius and is declared dictator for life.

73-71 BC Spartacus leads a revolt of 70,000 gladiator-slaves and is defeated by Crassus. Six thousand survivors are crucified.

68 BC Roman expansion to the east continues as Pompey conquers Palestine and Syria.

60-10 BC The **Theater of Pompey,** the **Arch of Augustus,** the **Baths of Agrippa,** and the **Curia**—the Senate building—are built.

49 BC Caesar crosses the Rubicon and marches on Rome after his victory in the Gallic Wars.

45 BC Caesar defeats his former allies Crassus and Pompey in the second Civil War and is deified by the crippled Senate. For posterity he mints money with his portrait and introduces the Julian calendar in which he names the month of his birth July.

44 BC On the Ides of March, Caesar is assassinated in the **Theater of Pompey** by a group of republican supporters, including Brutus.

43 BC The Senate is forced to hand over power to Caesar's supporters—Marc Antony, Octavian (Caesar's nephew), and Lepidus—who rule briefly as the Second Triumvirate. This alliance kills Caesar's opponents before disintegrating into a bitter rivalry between Marc Antony (allied with his new wife, Cleopatra) and Octavian.

30 BC Facing defeat, Marc Antony and Cleopatra commit suicide. Octavian absorbs Marc Antony's forces into his own army and subjects Egypt to his personal rule, beyond Roman jurisdiction.

27 BC The Senate grants Octavian the title *Augustus,* meaning "the Revered." Octavian Augustus becomes the first Emperor of Rome.

AD 27-14 Roman arts, letters, and architecture flourish during the golden years of the Augustan Age. Virgil, Ovid, and Horace produce lasting works. The first **Pantheon,** the **Theater of Marcellus,** the **Ara Pacis,** the **Palace of the Emperor,** and the **Mausoleum of Augustus** are erected. Dozen of temples are rebuilt.

14-68 A succession of despots rule Rome. Tiberius (14-37) had Jesus condemned. Caligula (37-41) appointed his favorite horse to the Senate. Nero (54-68) began the first major persecution of Christians, including Sts. Peter and Paul, after a fire destroyed much of Rome in 64.

69-81 Roman leadership stabilizes somewhat during the short rule of Vespasian (69-79) and his son Titus (79-81).

70 Rome crushes a Jewish revolt and sacks Jerusalem.

79 The **Colosseum** is inaugurated with a hundred-daylong festival.

81-96 Despotism returns with Domitian, Vespasian's other son.

98-117 The reign of Trajan sees the Roman Empire at its peak. He begins a massive program of public works, which includes the **Baths of Trajan** and **Trajan's Market.** Rome's population nears one million.

117-138 Hadrian rebuilds the **Pantheon,** constructs a huge villa at **Tivoli,** and erects **Hadrian's Tomb** (now **Castel Sant'Angelo**).

138-192 The reigns of Antoninus Pius (138-161), Marcus Aurelius (161-180), and Commodus (180-192) are overshadowed by the spread of smallpox throughout much of the Roman Empire. The deadly epidemic took a particularly great toll in the year 165.

193-211 Emperor Septimius Severus forbids conversion to Christianity in an effort to stem the growth of the new religion. The **Marcus Aurelius Column** in **Piazza Colonna** and the **Arch of Septimius Severus** are erected.

211-217 Caracalla commits fratricide and is later murdered.

212-222 In an effort to appease the restive colonies, Roman citizenship is granted to all free inhabitants of the provinces. The **Baths of Caracalla** and the **Temple to the Sun** are built.

222 The original **Basilica di Santa Maria** in **Trastevere** is built to honor St. Calisto.

222-235 The murder of Severus Alexander plunges Rome into 50 years of anarchy when emperors are proclaimed and assassinated in quick succession by competing factions of the army.

235-280 Rome's frontiers to the east and north are now extremely vulnerable to attack. The empire declines. Games and spectacles at the **Colosseum** are used to entertain the population of the city of Rome.

280-305 The decline of the empire is temporarily stayed by Diocletian, who restores stability at the price of unity. The empire is divided into four administrative areas. Rome is unseated as the sole capital of the empire.

303-305 The persecution of Christians continues in a great purge. The death of Diocletian triggers another round of anarchy.

312-337 Constantine becomes emperor of the western part of the Roman Empire, where he restores freedom of worship in 313, allowing Christianity to flourish. The empire is reunified in 324, but the seat of power remains in the east, in Constantinople, later called Byzantium. In an attack on paganism, Constantine expropriates the properties of the pagan temples and begins construction of Christian churches, including **St. Peter's Basilica** and **Santa Maria Maggiore.**

361 Idol worship makes a short-lived comeback when Julian the Apostate attempts to restore the privileges of paganism.

380 Christianity is declared the state religion of Rome.

394 Emperor Theodosius I, under pressure from the Bishop of Milan, forces the Senate to abolish paganism.

395 Following the death of Theodosius, the empire splits permanently into east and west.

403 The **Porta Pinciana** is constructed.

411 Visigoths, under Alaric, conquer Italy and sack Rome.

438 The **Basilica di Santa Maria Maggiore** is completed.

440 Leo the Great becomes pope.

455 Rome is pillaged by Geseric, king of the Vandals.

476 Emperor Romulus Augustulus is deposed by the invading Heruli. The western empire collapses, an event commonly called the "Fall of the Roman Empire." More invasions follow.

488 Theodoric is proclaimed ruler of the Gothic Kingdom of Italy.

540 Emperor Justinian, ruler of Byzantium, reconquers Italy and reincorporates it into a truncated Roman Empire.

570 Lombard tribes gain control of Rome.

590 Gregory the Great becomes the first pope to intervene successfully in politics and greatly strengthens the papacy.

610 The western empire is officially dissolved. In the east, the Byzantine Empire continues for another 800 years.

756 The Papal States are established with the pope as ruler.

800 Charlemagne is crowned Emperor of Rome by Pope Leo III in **St. Peter's.**

852 Walls are built around the **Vatican** by Pope Leo IV after Saracen raids.

962 At the behest of Pope John XII, Otto I of Saxony founds the Holy Roman Empire, whose leader names high church appointees.

1057 Pope Steven IX is elected without the emperor's approval.

1073 With the election of Pope Gregory VII, the struggle for supremacy between the papacy and the Holy Roman Empire threatens to break out into war.

1084 Emperor Henry IV invades Rome, followed by Robert Guiscard from Normandy.

1099 The **Chiesa di Santa Maria del Popolo** is built.

1100 Rome is in ruins. Its population shrinks to 30,000.

1143 Popular uprisings against papal rule in Rome lead to the further division and disintegration of the once-great city.

1309 Following centuries of decay and anarchy in Rome, the papacy is moved to Avignon, France.

1334 The Black Death—the Plague—spreads throughout Europe, leaving many millions dead in its wake.

1377 Through the intervention of St. Catherine of Siena, Pope Gregory XI returns the papacy to the **Vatican.**

1455 Construction begins on **Palazzo Venezia.**

1471 The **Musei Capitolini** are founded by Pope Sixtus IV.

1475 The **Ponte Sisto** is named after Pope Sixtus IV.

1485 The **Palazzo della Cancelleria** and **Chiesa di Sant'Agostino** are built.

1492-1503 The papacy is at war against the Italian states. Louis XII of France manages to meddle on both sides.

1495 The **Chiesa di Trinità dei Monti** is founded by Charles VIII of France.

1500 While the rest of Italy flourishes under the Renaissance, Rome for the most part languishes. Some brilliant exceptions are Michelangelo's *Pietà* and Bramante's *Tempietto.*

1506 Pope Julius II starts to rebuild **St. Peter's Basilica.** He commissions **Bramante** as architect, Raphael to decorate the papal apartments—the stanze—and Michelangelo to paint the ceiling of the **Sistine Chapel.**

1510 The **Palazzo dei Convertendi** is designed by **Bramante.**

1514 Construction begins on the **Palazzo Farnese,** to be completed by **Michelangelo,** who is just finishing the statue of *Moses* in **San Pietro in Vincoli.**

1520 Martin Luther publishes his *Great Reforming Theses,* the basis of the Protestant Reformation and a challenge to papal authority.

1527 On 5 May, Rome is sacked by Charles V, the Holy Roman Emperor, backed by Lutheran troops.

1545 In a response to Luther's challenge, the Council of Trent establishes the Counter-Reformation and the Office of the Inquisition.

1546 **Michelangelo** is asked to complete the rebuilding of **St. Peter's Basilica.**

1551 Pope Julius III commissions **Vignola** to design the **Villa Giulia.** Seventeen years later **Vignola** builds the **Chiesa del Gesù.**

1585 Pope Sixtus V begins a campaign to rebuild Rome. He raises monuments and obelisks, restores aqueducts, builds fountains (among them, the **Quattro Fontane**), and oversees the completion of **Michelangelo**'s dome of **St. Peter's.**

1595 The Baroque Age arrives. Over the next century, the city is transformed with the construction of ornate churches and monuments, including the **Chiesa di Santa Maria della Scala,** the fountain of **La Barcaccia** at the bottom of what is now the **Spanish Steps,** and the **Paola Fountain.** The work of artists like the Carraci, Caravaggio, Guidi Reni, and Pietro da Cortona sits alongside the architecture of **Bernini** and **Borromini.**

1625 Pope Urban VIII commissions Rome's top Baroque artists to work on the **Palazzo Barberini. St. Peter's** is completed.

1650 Two of Rome's masterpieces of Baroque art, **Borromini**'s **Chiesa di Sant'Ivo alla Sapienza** and **Bernini**'s **Fountain of the Four Rivers,** are completed.

1655 **Borromini** finishes **Sant'Agnese in Agone** in **Piazza Navona.**

1667 **St. Peter's Square** is completed by **Bernini.**

1735 The **Spanish Steps** are laid out and the **Palazzo Corsini** built.

1762 The **Trevi Fountain** goes up.

1797 Napoleon captures Rome and proclaims a new republic. Pope Pius VI is expelled from the city.

1806 Emperor Francis II abdicates, marking the end of the Holy Roman Empire.

1808 Rome is occupied by French troops again; Pope Pius VII is imprisoned in the **Palazzo Quirinale.**

1809 France annexes the Papal States.

1814 Pius VII returns and is reinstated as the ruler of Rome.

1820 Il Risorgimento, the movement to unify the Italian city-states, is in its early stages, later to be led by nationalists Garibaldi, Mazzini, and Cavour. In 1861, Italy is proclaimed a kingdom with Vittorio Emanuele of Piedmont as king and Turin as its capital.

1870 Italian nationalists, led by Garibaldi, storm Rome and declare it the capital of unified Italy. The Papal States are reduced to an area on the outskirts of Rome.

1904 The main Jewish synagogue is built.

1920 Rome's population grows to 500,000.

1922 Mussolini's fascist Black Shirts march on Rome.

1924 Socialist leader Giacomo Matteotti is murdered. Mussolini accepts responsibility. The incident is a turning point signaling the Fascist party's drive for power at any cost.

1926 Mussolini, with a minority in Parliament, seizes power.

1929 Mussolini and Pope Pius IX sign the Lateran Treaty, formalizing relations between the pope and Italy and establishing a separate Vatican state.

1930 Rome's population reaches one million.

1940 Italy allies itself with the Axis powers in World War II. Mussolini is later captured and shot by partisans. His body and that of his mistress are later hung by their heels in public.

1946 The Republic of Italy is declared in the war-weary country. The immense task of rebuilding begins. Governments come and go, but the republic proves resilient.

1957 The European Economic Community (Common Market) is proclaimed in Rome.

1960 Rome hosts the **Summer Olympic Games.**

1962 The Second Vatican Council under Pope John XXIII redefines church doctrine for the 20th century.

1978 A wave of leftist terrorism sweeps through Europe. In Rome, Premier Aldo Moro is kidnapped and murdered by the Red Brigade.

1979 Karol Wojtyla, a Polish cardinal, is elected Pope John Paul II, the first non-Italian pope since 1523. Two years later, an attempt is made on his life.

1984 The restoration of the **Sistine Chapel** begins, funded by the Nippon Television Network.

1990 Italy hosts the **World Cup** soccer championship.

1992 Anti-Mafia judge Giovanni Falcone leads a crackdown on the Cosa Nostra and is murdered on a Sicilian highway.

1994 A decade of restoration work on the **Sistine Chapel** ends with spectacular results. The filmmaker Federico Fellini and his wife, Giulietta Masina, die. Half the members of Parliament are implicated in *Tangentopolis,* a huge corruption scandal that topples the dominant Christian Democratic Party.

1995 Construction begins near the **Olympic Stadium** on an auditorium for Rome's philharmonic orchestra—part of a complex of three theaters designed by famed Genovese architect **Renzo Piano.**

Milan magistrate Antonio Di Pietro carries on a series of investigations—dubbed *Mani puliti* (clean hands)—against kickbacks in politics and corruption in big business.

1996 The Olive Tree Coalition, a center-left political alliance, wins national elections in April. It is the first leftist- and communist-dominated government in the history of the republic. The restored bronze equestrian statue of *Marcus Aurelius* is returned to the center of **Michelangelo**'s **Piazza del Campidoglio** after an absence of 16 years; this is a copy—the original is on view inside the **Palazzo dei Conservatori.**

1998 The city embarks on a $1.5-billion improvement project for the Jubilee of 2000, totally refurbishing such major museums as the **Galleria Borghese** and **Palazzo Barberini** and opening two new museums: **Palazzo Massimo** and **Palazzo Altemps.**

Pantheon

Index

Index

Restaurants

Only restaurants with star ratings are listed below. All restaurants are listed alphabetically in the main (preceding) index. Always call in advance to ensure a restaurant has not closed, changed its hours, or booked its tables for a private party. The restaurant price ratings are based on the average cost of an entrée for one person, excluding tax and tip.
★★★★ An Extraordinary Experience
★★★ Excellent
★★ Very Good
★ Good
$$$$ Big Bucks ($90 and up)
$$$ Expensive ($65-$90)
$$ Reasonable ($40-$65)
$ The Price Is Right (less than $40)

★★★★

★★★

★★

★

Credits

Writer and Researcher
Diana Willensky

Writers and Researchers
(Previous Editions)
Louis Inturrisi   Judith Harris
Catherine Smith   Frederick Vreeland

ACCESS®PRESS

Editorial Director
Lois Spritzer

Managing Editor
Susan Hoffner

Senior Editors
Mary Callahan
Beth Schlau

Associate Editor
Beatrice Aranow

Map Coordinator
Jonathan Goodnough

Editorial Assistant
Susan Cutter Snyder

Contributing Editor
Elizabeth Russell
 Connelly

Senior Art Director
Robin Artz

Design Supervisor
Joy O'Meara

Designer
Alex Lindquist

Map Designer
Patricia Keelin

Associate Director
 of Production
Dianne Pinkowitz

Special Thanks
Roberto Farino and
 the City of Rome
 press office
Italian Ministry of
 Cultural Heritage
 press office
Cary Appenzeller

Vatican City

MARJORIE J. VOGEL/RHODE ISLAND DESIGNS

ACCESS® Guides

Order by phone, toll-free: 1-800-331-3761

Name _____ Phone _____

Address _____

City _____ State _____ Zip _____

Please send me the following ACCESS® Guides:

☐ **ATLANTA** ACCESS® $18.50
0-06-277156-6

☐ **BOSTON** ACCESS® $19.00
0-06-277197-3

☐ **CAPE COD, MARTHA'S VINEYARD, & NANTUCKET** ACCESS® $19.00
0-06-277220-1

☐ **CARIBBEAN** ACCESS® $20.00
0-06-277252-X

☐ **CHICAGO** ACCESS® $19.00
0-06-277196-5

☐ **CRUISE** ACCESS® $20.00
0-06-277190-6

☐ **FLORENCE & VENICE** ACCESS® $19.00
0-06-277222-8

☐ **GAY USA** ACCESS® $19.95
0-06-277212-0

☐ **HAWAII** ACCESS® $19.00
0-06-277223-6

☐ **LAS VEGAS** ACCESS® $19.00
0-06-277224-4

☐ **LONDON** ACCESS® $19.00
0-06-277225-2

☐ **LOS ANGELES** ACCESS® $19.00
0-06-277259-7

☐ **MEXICO** ACCESS® $19.00
0-06-277251-1

☐ **MIAMI & SOUTH FLORIDA** ACCESS® $19.00
0-06-277226-0

☐ **MINNEAPOLIS/ST. PAUL** ACCESS® $19.00
0-06-277234-1

☐ **MONTREAL & QUEBEC CITY** ACCESS® $19.00
0-06-277160-4

☐ **NEW ORLEANS** ACCESS® $19.00
0-06-277227-9

☐ **NEW YORK CITY** ACCESS® $19.00
0-06-277235-X

☐ **NEW YORK RESTAURANTS** ACCESS®
$13.00 0-06-277218-X

☐ **ORLANDO & CENTRAL FLORIDA** ACCESS®
$19.00
0-06-277228-7

☐ **PARIS** ACCESS® $19.00
0-06-277229-5

☐ **PHILADELPHIA** ACCESS® $19.00
0-06-277230-9

☐ **ROME** ACCESS® $19.00
0-06-277195-7

☐ **SAN DIEGO** ACCESS® $19.00
0-06-277185-X

☐ **SAN FRANCISCO** ACCESS® $19.00
0-06-277169-8

☐ **SAN FRANCISCO RESTAURANTS** ACCESS®
$13.00
0-06-277219-8

☐ **SANTA FE/TAOS/ALBUQUERQUE** ACCESS®
$19.00
0-06-277194-9

☐ **SEATTLE** ACCESS® $19.00
0-06-277198-1

☐ **SKI COUNTRY** ACCESS®
Eastern United States $18.50
0-06-277189-2

☐ **SKI COUNTRY** ACCESS®
Western United States $19.00
0-06-277174-4

☐ **WASHINGTON DC** ACCESS® $19.00
0-06-277232-5

☐ **WINE COUNTRY** ACCESS® France $19.00
0-06-277193-0

☐ **WINE COUNTRY** ACCESS® California $19.00
0-06-277258-9

Prices subject to change without notice.

Total for **ACCESS®** Guides:	$
Please add applicable sales tax:	
Add $4.00 for first book S&H, $1.00 per additional book:	
Total payment:	$

☐ Check or Money Order enclosed. Offer valid in the United States only. Please make payable to HarperCollins*Publishers*.

☐ Charge my credit card ☐ American Express ☐ Visa ☐ MasterCard

Card no. _____ Exp. date _____

Signature _____

Send orders to: HarperCollins*Publishers*
P.O. Box 588
Dunmore, PA 18512-0588

ACCESS®
Makes the World Your Neighborhood

Access Destinations

- Atlanta
- Boston
- Cape Cod, Martha's Vineyard, & Nantucket
- Caribbean
- Chicago
- Cruise
- Florence & Venice
- Gay USA
- Hawaii
- Las Vegas
- London
- Los Angeles
- Mexico
- Miami & South Florida
- Minneapolis/St. Paul
- Montreal & Quebec City

- New Orleans
- New York City
- New York Restaurants
- Orlando & Central Florida
- Paris
- Philadelphia
- Rome
- San Diego
- San Francisco
- San Francisco Restaurants
- Santa Fe/Taos/Albuquerque
- Seattle
- Ski Country Eastern US
- Ski Country Western US
- Washington DC
- Wine Country France
- Wine Country California

Pack lightly and carry the best travel guides going: ACCESS. Arranged by neighborhood and featuring color-coded entries keyed to easy-to-read maps, ACCESS guides are designed to help you explore a neighborhood or an entire city in depth. You'll never get lost with an ACCESS guide in hand, but you may well be lost without one. So whether you are visiting Las Vegas or London, you'll need a sturdy pair of walking shoes and plenty of ACCESS.

HarperResource
A Division of HarperCollins*Publishers*
http://www.harpercollins.com